Marxism-Leninism and theory of international relations

Marxism-Leninism and theory of international relations

V. Kubálková
Department of Government,
University of Queensland

and

A. A. Cruickshank
Professor of Political Studies,
University of New England,
Armidale

Routledge & Kegan Paul
London, Boston and Henley

115358

First published in 1980
by Routledge & Kegan Paul Ltd
39 Store Street, London WC1E 7DD,
Broadway House, Newtown Road,
Henley-on-Thames, Oxon RG9 1EN and
9 Park Street, Boston, Mass. 02108, USA
Set in 10 on 12 point Plantin by Oxprint, Oxford
and printed in Great Britain by
Lowe & Brydone Ltd
Thetford, Norfolk

British Library Cataloguing in Publication Data

Kubálková, V

Marxism-Leninism and theory of international relations.
1. International relations and socialism
2. International relations – Study and teaching – Russia
3. Marx, Karl
I. Title   II. Cruickshank, A A
327'.01   HX550.I5   79-42746

ISBN 0 7100 0361 7

Contents

Contents

Figures and tables

Theories in International Relations are like planes, flying at different altitudes and in different directions.

Stanley Hoffman

Preface

This book is about another 'grand debate' within the theory of international relations,[1] a debate that never was and may never be, because of international relations.

International theory, as it is known here in the West,[2] an infant among the other social sciences, has been so busy putting itself on the map, sorting out its methodological tools, defining concepts and repudiating them shortly afterwards, that underneath the debris of rejected ideas some rather important issues may have escaped attention.

Thus it has remained, however youthfully enterprising, an intra-ideological exercise. Naturally enough it has been, *inter alia*, very much about East-West relations inasmuch as its subject-matter is by no means exclusive but by definition world-wide. In international politics states of different ideologies are able without *de facto – de jure* recognitions to make decisions, enter alliances, wage wars, etc., alongside and against each other regardless of what anyone else's theory may be.

Should a rationally minded creature from another planet be able to visit this world (since it is safer not to postulate an 'omniscient observer' whose mind might be ideology and value biased), it would be confronted with a somewhat confused scene: a planet divided into a multiplicity of units of various sizes and descriptions, all caught up in endless interactions, within a tangled web of relations, heavily involved in a continuously unfolding drama in which they are all at one and the same time both actors and audience. Not the least strange part of this scene are the busy occurrences in the wings and 'green-rooms' where the 'play' is being analysed, the plot discussed, the casting and props criticised, and the content of the next act foretold with everybody only too keen to assist with the prompting. The dressing-room strangely enough is more exclusive than is the stage itself and the opinions voiced in the former are more contentiously argued than is the rigmarole of the latter. There exist 'clubs' whose members would not discuss the play with anyone outside their charmed circle, since they claim not only to be able to follow the action sufficiently from their seats, but indeed so confidently excel at the task that the views of other circles are discounted almost before they are voiced.

And that is precisely the nub. International theory has so far been an almost exclusively West European, American and Australasian enterprise, where not even all the West European countries have decided to join in. Furthermore, in the countries where international theory has become institutionally established, i.e. in the shape of new university departments or specialised institutes, it has none the less been looked at from without and within the social sciences (of which it claims to be a part) with mixed feelings and sometimes disrespect.[3] Partisans of international relations theory maintain for their part that traditional disciplines that used to theorise about international affairs can no longer cope, and an interdisciplinary enterprise is called for where the intellectual tools of many disciplines could be most beneficially developed in a combined effort. In this way, they aver, lies the only hope of keeping in touch with the complexities and – for that matter – the increasing precariousness of international affairs.

The need for perspective such as an entirely new discipline might provide is recognised at present both in the West and in the East although the 'theory of international relations' may mean very different things to each of these ideological hemispheres. Even within the 'omnipotent' Marxist-Leninist ideology a considerable amount of thought appears to be devoted to the problem of how to explain that 'scientific communism' and 'historical materialism'[4] are too general in their reference to have meaningful application to this matter, and the need for the foundation of a new discipline is recognised and called for.

While some theorists in the West deny outright that there is such a thing as a communist theory of international relations, still others argue that if it does exist it can easily be ignored since all that it offers is an *a posteriori* justification of political expediency. It is further argued that in the merger of theory and practice in the communist world there is very little space left for theory. Theory, they would continue, is tantamount to the resolutions of Communist Party Congresses, drafted by the party ideologues on behalf of the ruthless, power-thirsty (sometimes semi-literate and certainly semi-educated) politicians. Not only is such 'theory' to be elaborated upon by the academic community, but deviations from the official creed are neither permitted nor are they advisable since heresy merges with *crimen laesae maiestatis*. The objectors would point out that in order to enhance the authority of such theories ample reference is made to the incoherent century-old set of antiquated ideas of Marx and Engels and of their 'legitimate' successor, Lenin. This Asiatic astute political leader, who claimed to have translated the ideas of his intellectual progenitors into reality, founded a promised land in accordance with their dictates which they might not even recognise.

While admitting the validity of many of these objections it still seems incredible that marxist thinking on international relations (or any other explicitly ideological paradigms of international theory) has not yet really been accorded the status of a theory and listed alongside the numerous theories mushrooming in the West. However brilliant and enlightening Western theories may have been, most would find it difficult or impossible to substantiate a claim to have permeated the minds and become, in one way or another, part of the day to day thinking of a sizeable part of humanity (including that of the policy-maker and of his ideologue alike). But this is part of the Marxist-Leninist achievement. Not only is it an ideology embraced by governments representative of one-third of mankind but, thus ideologically armed, it is they who in some fashion have been involved in almost all international conflicts since the Second World War. Popularity of a theory is of course no guarantee of its validity, and the same may be said of its expansion.

It all comes down to the question of whether ideologies and ideological theories play any part in international politics.[5] But does not the fact of trying so hard to ignore ideologies in the name of science itself reveal a carefully hidden ideological bias?

The tendency in the West has been to view ideology as something irrational, and yet it has been Soviet communist ideology that has contributed to the transformation of international politics from a 'game' into a profoundly intense conflict. In the realm of theory the existence of communist ideology created the necessity to base international conduct less and less on legal and diplomatic devices and more and more on political sociological insights which cut across state frontiers.[6]

Our contention will be that we are divided by ideologies

irrespective of whether or not we choose to recognise them. The great privilege of Western ideology, however, is that unlike its intolerant communist counterpart, it allows imaginary debates where real ones cannot take place.

To be more specific, it can be said that there have been two 'monologues' going on: the first one being in the East European countries regarding their own theories of international relations (and also hints dropped concerning 'bourgeois' international theory). In this context a unique opportunity presents itself for comparing the 'elements' of a theory of international relations contained in Marx's original vision with the contemporary version, and of positing therefrom certain conclusions. This we hope will further facilitate the understanding of theory of the East, which would in any case be easier to give account of since it indeed cannot (and will not *rebus sic stantibus*) be possible to theoretically indulge itself so freely as it can here in the West. In this context also, it might be noted, there is no multiplicity of concepts, or if they occur, they will flourish less exuberantly within the tight confines of Marxist-Leninist ideology. The other 'monologue' – the presentation of international theory in the West – will in this respect offer more difficulty. There is here not one theory but rather a plurality of concepts which are largely unrelated to one another (and indeed look somewhat 'unrelatable'). In this respect, therefore, Western and Eastern theories could hardly be more different. Whereas the East is filled with a fear of deviating from the word of the official creed, Western international theory is on the contrary 'iconoclastic'.[7] Although this latter is indisputably a much healthier state of affairs in a discipline's infant years, it neither makes it easier for the neophyte nor does it facilitate such a task as ours – a prerequisite of which is an over-all, easily comprehensible picture of the field. The discipline (in the West) is still very much in a state of 'conceptual disarray'[8] wherein some of its protagonists do not even believe that it will last. Alger in 1968 prophesied that 'borrowed' conceptual materials will be humbly put back into the fields whence they came and that the various aspects of international relations would be reincorporated into the concerns of each of the social sciences.[9] The majority of international theorists, however, seem to believe that it would be a great mistake to give up the perspective that only an interdisciplinary international theory can provide. One of the great figures in the field, Quincy Wright, believed as early as 1955 that theory building would be a task of synthetically weaving together the diverse abstract materials of a number of fields into an integrated theory.[10] It should be added that attempts along these lines were to prove insufficient and were abandoned quite recently.[11]

Some theorists, as a result of the nature of the field, doubt the feasibility of theory building in general, while others think international theory has just about reached the stage astronomy was in after the end of the geocentric theory of Ptolemy.[12] Some more hopeful voices express the opinion that in as little as ten to fifteen years someone 'will rediscover the fascinating problem of relating theories to each other' which will be (dialectically?) followed by a new interest in the conceptual unification of 'whatever the field, discipline or emphasis is then called'.[13]

But what is to happen in the meantime? Can we afford another decade of 'publication explosion'[14] which in so many cases means inundation with 'new' partial concepts, very often duplicating or setting at naught the efforts of their respective authors? Platig's call for pausing a little and concentrating more on serious attempts to review and assess the field's various strategies is just as relevant now as it was in 1967.[15] Or do we really have to wait, and is it true to say that 'to understand what is taking place, we need the advantage of historical perspective over as long a period as possible'?[16] In support of this last position one might argue that international theory here in the West has already too many problems of its own to want to be dragged into yet another 'debate'. But is there not a certain speciousness in the argument? Whether grappled with now or later the theoretical issue will be forever latent or 'in the air'. After all, political activity will continue whether or not we have an adequate theory about it; international relations we might confidently assume will develop at an unprecedented pace and, commensurate with them, the degree of hazard involved. We may also assume that the revolution in weaponry, techniques of warfare and the hydra-headed scientific-technological revolution will continue to increase the inter-dependence of peoples. This process cannot into the indefinite future be complemented by continuous and deepening ideological mis-understanding. The West now already lists as one of the main sources of impetus for its theoretical strife, the growth of communist power.[17] The East now already declares an 'offensive against the far-reaching ideological diversification of imperialism'[18] and goes even further to state that 'Marxist-Leninist theory . . . as a part of the ideology of the working class . . . is bound to be a militant [sic] science . . .'[19] It is difficult for us to determine the point to which ideological warfare can be escalated or what happens when that point is reached and passed. Our guess is that as the acrimony intensifies and the theoretical rift widens so that 'edge' will lie with the side which perceives a main instrument in an understanding of the internal processes of the other. 'He who wants to know the enemy must go into the enemy's territory' ('wer den "Feind" will verstehen, muss im Feindes "lande gehen" ').[20]

In the process of clarification of the present position (and the situation if left can only become more confused as maoists and others join in) we will attempt here to place them in juxtaposition. By engaging in an imaginary debate and thus appraising the positions of the West and the East we will thus hope to find out what dichotomies exist and explore areas of potential meeting or overlap. But why include Marx? Or for that matter Engels, Lenin, or Stalin? If a staging of such a debate is justified it must surely be between contemporary living politicians/theoreticians with no part in it for four dead men. The justification turns on Marx's legacy which, it is claimed, is largely responsible for the present divisions of the world and their multi-faceted relationships – towards which attitudes, neither in the East nor in the West, have been clearly or adequately formulated.

Our contention is that regardless of the increasing interest in international relations theory in the East very little research can be expected from that part of the world into the actual ideas of the 'classics' of marxism, let alone a comparison made or contrast drawn between the ideas of Lenin and those who claim him as ideological forebear. In fact, we find that if the corpus of doctrine is taken as a whole, and the process of selecting at random single concepts in authentication of present directions is resisted, it could well prove in some respects rather embarrassing to contemporary marxist leaders. This will perhaps become clearer when four theories[21] of international relations are presented side by side.

But our purpose in surveying the sweep of marxist thinking on the subject of international relations, or in analysing that of those contemporary Marxist-Leninists who claim to have assumed his mantle, is not to embarrass. Less trivial, more far-reaching conclusions are aimed at as we investigate what some have been pleased to refer to as the intellectual sterility of contemporary marxism, or the 'irrelevant' ideas of Marx, Engels, and Lenin on the subject – ideas that, after all is said and done, constitute at the very least the foundations of Marxist-Leninist ideology. In the first place we hope that such analysis will be made to yield meaningful insights into an understanding of 'marxist' thinking. Second, it is to be noted that marxist thought – or at least ways of thought that are marxisant – have continuously made their contribution to the Western mind. As a matter of fact, marxism is itself a part of that mind and some of its insights have been incorporated into the common stock of the twentieth century's intellectual discourse. Such an idea as, for example, 'the recognition that knowledge is never an abstract act of observation or contemplation but involves man as an active being in a concrete social situation . . . that all institutions and ideas must be understood within the broader framework of human production', or the essentially hegelian critical idea that the world is never to be accepted as it appears phenomenally but is 'to be examined in terms of its rationality'[22] are now commonplace in the Western world. It will be pointed out that marxist analysis is one of the clearest structural-functional models of society and some modern social sciences (sociology, political economy, historical theory, etc.) have absorbed or utilised many of the ideas developed by Marx. And, as we shall see, in terms of international theory many of the ideas of Marx, Engels and Lenin still await – or, more precisely, cry out for – exploration.

Indeed the field of international relations seems to have assumed a very special attitude *vis-à-vis* Marx's legacy: an attitude which is strikingly different from that assumed by the other disciplines of social science.[23] If at the opening session of the symposium on 'The Role of Karl Marx in the Development of Contemporary Scientific Thought' Professor Charles Frankel could state that 'by defining where we stand in relation to Marx . . . most of us in human studies define where we stand in relation to the problems of our discipline and the problems of our time',[24] why is it that Marx has not even become 'a silent partner' in the realm of international theory, nor even allowed to 'participate' in those dialogues which do not engage consciously and explicitly in the study and criticism of him? Is it because Marx's attention to international relations, undeveloped as they were in his time, was so tenuous? Or can it be that what he did say has no relevance today because he was again 'wrong'?

Here we propose to include Marx as a 'silent partner' in this twentieth-century theoretical progression that began with him. He will take part in the unspoken East–West 'dialogue' on the theory of international relations, and in that context we will bear in mind the inescapable fact that it is with the non-silent partners that the last word rests.

The authors acknowledge the kindness of the *British Journal of International Studies* and the *Australian Journal of Politics and History* for granting permission to quote from their own works previously published in these journals, and to Lawrence & Wishart for permission to quote the material in Appendix 2.

CHAPTER 1

Introductory: basic assumptions of theories of international relations

> My hunch is that the quantitative-qualitative data gulf is not so unbridgeable as differences of commitment to various ways of knowing – more particularly opposed notions of what it is possible to know.
>
> Richard C. Snyder

It has become almost a tradition to assume that the East-West divide runs as deep as is the sphere of intellect, and that the thinking of each side follows paths incomprehensible to the other. Because of that and before we begin to talk about their respective theories of international relations we have to pause for a while and consider what can be meant by a theory to both East and West. In other words we shall try to forget the divide and instead speculate in general terms as to what the word theory *can* mean before we proceed in succeeding chapters to the question of what it is by each side *supposed* to mean.

The word 'theory' has been used so vaguely and indiscriminately within the perimeters of social science that it has virtually lost such meaningful content as it once possessed.[1] Indeed it would be possible (and perhaps useful) to come up with a 'theory of theories' that would cover all possible meanings of the term since the time when it meant no more than 'the action of observing'.[2] Although 'theories of theories' may well stand to become the most abstruse of all international theories,[3] they remain nevertheless as important and as essential as any of the others.

If we could speak of such a thing as a 'theorology' applied to the field of international relations, it would have to be placed at the junction of some six disciplines: philosophy, epistemology, sociology, politology, political philosophy, and logic. In other words, the arbitrariness of divisions into these disciplines, notwithstanding any

1

venture in theory building in international relations, has to come to terms with some of the basic questions that are traditionally associated with these disciplines. This is perhaps one of the most fascinating features of international theory; that it no more stops (or should not stop) at the boundaries of states than it is restricted by disciplines – or ideologies. Whether the theorists pay any attention to these questions, consciously or unconsciously, explicitly or implicitly, evading or trying to evade any of them, they cannot help but express their attitudes towards them. Talking about laws regulating international relations – or their absence; choosing a particular aspect for purposes of explaining a certain range of phenomena; delineating the width of this range; using quantitative methods; rejecting values; working for peace, etc., lead into much deeper water than would seem at first to be the case – or than some authors would willingly wish to enter. As regards disclaimers of meddling and of refraining 'from attempting to settle the profound questions of epistemology which have remained unsettled for centuries'[4] one should not confuse two separate things: there is a difference between 'attempting to settle' those questions on the one hand and, on the other, keeping them in mind, where the latter does not necessarily imply the former since, after all, those questions may not be 'resolvable' in the sense that is usually accorded to this word. What could be 'settled' however, even at the highest level of discussion of theory building, is the problem of putting an end to the absence of a clear distinction between and among all these various aspects of a theory, and settling the confusion that results from mixing them or of emphasising some at the expense of others – a process that makes infinitely more perplexing the theories themselves as well as creating problems for their exposition. How can a debate lead to any meaningful conclusions if, for example, one side attacks a theory in epistemological terms and is replied to in terms of its logical virtues?

Since we have set out to juxtapose the international theory of the West and that of the East, a '*theorological*' exercise is absolutely essential. Only by accepting the broadest preliminary assumptions can we hope to find the roots of the basic differences and account for the similarities.

Since a degree of correlation among the attitudes to the above mentioned groups of questions has been admitted or is implied, the attempt (Figure 1) to make this correlation more obvious in a graphical and hence heavily oversimplified manner might be

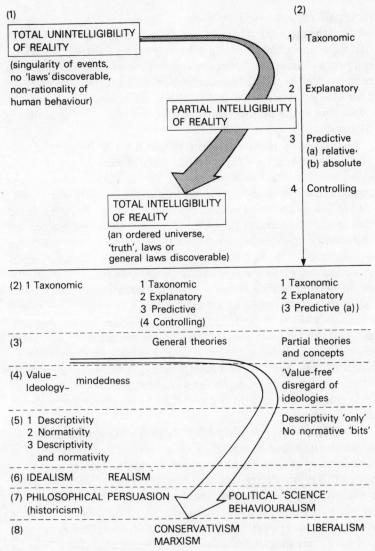

Figure 1 Assumptions of theories of international relations
(a continuum)

considered worthwhile. Figure 1 is to be understood as a continuum with a preponderance of border cases over those that fall within clear-cut extremes of black or white. In the course of this chapter,

3

recurrent reference will be made to Figure 1 as section succeeds section (the numbers in brackets are the respective section numbers in that figure). Furthermore, since we may expect a shared concern on the part of various disciplines in regard to some questions, we shall refer to them where the boundaries are not always clear and no direct comparison between East and West is at issue, as simply 'groups of questions', without the arbitrary superimposition of disciplinary barriers.

To begin with then, let us observe that the definition of the term 'theory' itself – that is to say the establishing of what the term conveys – is an epistemological exercise[5] *par excellence*. And, since contemporary epistemology is no longer the preserve (as was its classical antecedent) of philosophy alone and tends to be found throughout the sciences in the form of discussions on 'basic issues' and reflections on the history of each discipline,[6] international theory must, alongside other branches of social science, take cognisance of this expanded range and application where theoretical first principles are in debate. Suffice it to say that the expanded interdisciplinary application of epistemology referred to ranges from the 'basic issues' of psychology (in so far as questions of fact – that are *ipso facto* the affair of epistemology – inevitably involve questions of perception, associations, psychological formations of ideas and so on) to those issues of logic beyond the basic questions of validity (relationship between subject and object and how knowledge is to be made to relate and come to terms with the real world, etc.) with which that particular discipline deals.

Though we experience no difficulty in finding a preliminary and workable definition of theory in, for example, 'an integrated set of statements about some phenomena under observation', as soon as we begin to try to determine what the function of such a 'set of statements' can be we must expect to become involved in a philosophical debate. Questions that probe the reality of the external world, the nature of mind, the nature of their mutual relationship – and all of these in search of an answer to the basic questions: How far is reality intelligible? How much can we ever hope to know? Questions that are age-old and have been answered in so many different and often conflicting ways by various philosophical schools. Let us however for our purposes content ourselves with the simplification of the argument. Basically the answers given fall into one of three categories, with many shades of attitudes between. These are as follows:

1 The phenomenon of international relations is so complex
that its comprehension is beyond human capacities. Our grasp of
it is erroneous and confused; international relations theory like
other 'social sciences' can never become a science in the sense of
its consisting of knowledge that is verifiable, systematic and
general. The events are singular; therefore no 'laws' are discoverable. All we can ever hope for are 'theories' that are no
more than 'a conglomeration of plausible folklore'[7] (see Figure
1, section 1).

2 Reality is totally intelligible, there is nothing *a priori* incomprehensible, although there are areas not as yet comprehended.
There are discoverable regularities or patterns of behaviour,
hence 'laws', even 'general laws', can be identified.[8]

3 There is only a partial possibility of understanding reality since
only the occurrence of certain regularities may be observed.

Correlated with these attitudes is the perception of the role that a
theory can fulfil (Figure 1, section 2). Thus international relations
theory is variously seen as being able to serve these purposes:[9]

1 *Taxonomic*, consisting of classification of data (i.e. arranging
them into items on the basis of some stipulated quality which
they share) in such a way that similar sets of data may be similarly
arranged, and compared.

2 *Explanatory* (generally based on the above), consisting of
definitions of (a) variables into which data may be organised
(b) relationships between variables with some degree of precision, and, where possible, introducing quantification.

3 *Predictive*, consisting of anticipation with some degree of
probability of the occurrence of certain variables and relationships in the future. To produce:
(a) *relative* predictions: There is a probability of C per cent that
condition A is associated with effect B.
(b) *absolute* predictions: Condition A is always associated
with effect B.

4 *Controlling*, consisting of influencing and/or manipulating the
occurrence of predicted events. It should be noted that it does not
follow that having achieved purposes 1–3, the theory can

5

become *ipso facto* a basis for controlling the phenomena; in this regard Oran Young points out that although we have an excellent theory of the dynamics of the solar system we still have very little ability to manipulate its variables.[10]

The following statements from current Western literature on international relations show that the correlation of philosophical assumptions with the aims of theory as indicated above is acknowledged.

Kaplan, apropos of the objects of international relations theory, states:

to discover laws, recurrent patterns, regularities, high-level generalizations; to make of predictability a test of science; to achieve as soon as possible the ideal of deductive science, including a 'set of primitive terms, definitions and axioms' from which 'systematic theories are derived'.

to which Hoffmann replies:

These objectives are the wrong ones. The search for laws is based on a misunderstanding by social scientists, of the nature of laws in the physical sciences; these laws are seen as far more strict and absolute than they are. The best that we can achieve in our discipline is the statement of trends. . . . Accuracy of prediction should not be a touchstone.[11]

Prediction is often based upon approximately the same elements as explanation but there are sufficiently serious practical differences between the two as to throw some doubt on the validity of claims to their congruency made by those theorists who consider the principal object of theory to be prediction. Those who do not so consider prediction to be a central aim generally distinguish it from explanation. This difference is easier to understand in Hempel's 'pattern of scientific explanation' (see p. 7):[12]

If E is given and a set of statements $C_1, C_2 \ldots C_k$ and $L_1, L_2 \ldots L_k$ is provided afterwards, we speak about explanation. If, on the other hand, the statements $C_1, C_2 \ldots C_k$ are given and E is derived prior to the occurrence of the phenomenon it describes, we speak about prediction. Hempel's thesis that an explanation is not fully

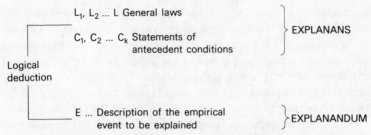

L₁, L₂ ... L General laws

C₁, C₂ ... C_k Statements of antecedent conditions — EXPLANANS

Logical deduction

E ... Description of the empirical event to be explained — EXPLANANDUM

adequate unless its explanans, having been taken into account in time, could have served as a basis for predicting the phenomenon under consideration, is not generally accepted and, in international relations theory in particular, it would 'invalidate' a great number of 'explanations'.

Similarly, we encounter the most varied views concerning the nature of and relationship between prediction and explanation, as well as the place of both of them in social science.

There are many questions arising from Hempel's scheme, the most obvious of which are:

1 What is the nature of 'statements of antecedent conditions' (C_1, C_2, ... C_k). Hempel himself distinguishes between deductive and statistical ones.

(Deductive: All F are G, Statistical: Almost all F are G,
x is F, x is F,
x is G x is almost certainly G)

Thus statistical statements do not guarantee that the event to be explained or predicted is a logical consequence of statements. It is obvious that a great number of statements about international relations will be of this nature, at least for the time being.

2 How many such statements $C_1, C_2, \ldots C_k$ are required; in other words, what is 'k'? Hempel assumes that one should be able to establish laws, indeed general laws, the acceptance of which depends entirely of course on the philosophical assumptions. (It should be noted here that recently, even in the field of natural science – physics in particular – many cases have been observed where the 'laws' failed to work and doubts about the predictive capacities of the natural sciences have been expressed.)

Most international relations theorists in the West agree that international relations theory has managed so far to meet only the requirements of taxonomic and explanatory purposes.[13] Others, including Quincy Wright, and also a no less widely sanctified system than marxism itself (in its generic sense), claim that all (1–4) purposes of a theory are attainable and that the controlling function is not only desirable but imperative.[14] They would refuse to call anything less by the name of theory.

But even in order to satisfy the taxonomic and explanatory functions, the 'set of statements' should still ideally be:[15]

> Comprehensive (taking care of all aspects of the phenomenon).
> Comprehensible (including as few axioms as possible).
> Coherent (every part logically consistent with the remainder; some of the statements – premises, logically implying the others – theorems), self-correcting (susceptible to continual improvement).

These often quoted desiderata summarise the logical requirements of a theory. There is in fact a gross imbalance of attention to and knowledge about the statement of theory in formal terms on the one hand, in contrast to the lack of attention paid to the creative process leading to the statement on the other. There can be two theories perfectly elaborated from the logical point of view but if their protagonists do not acknowledge basic differences in the philosophical assumptions, there can never be any meaningful debate.

The choice of level of generality or, as it is sometimes called, range of theory, may also be correlated to the philosophical assumptions (Figure 1, section 3) as follows:

1 Narrow range and partial theories deal with fairly specific subsets of facts.
2 Middle-range theories explain some more general sets of facts and link wider collections of laws and generalisations.
3 Theories that seek to account for all the range of relevant facts, hypotheses, generalisations, etc., in the given area.
4 General theory which purports to provide an explanatory system capable of accounting for all relevant relationships between the elements of the subjects in areas to which it applies.[16]

There is no consensus as to the suitability (possibility) of any one of these levels for application to international relations theory (note the conjunction here once again of Quincy Wright and marxism in their belief in the possibility of general theories). At present, as attempts to build a general theory of international relations in the West have apparently been abandoned this abandoned direction has coincided, oddly enough, with the shift to behaviouralism. The choice of level of abstraction or generality and the role played by models in the analysis of an historical situation are basically of a sociological nature, but international relations theorists in the West appear at present to lack a global sociological account of the nature of social phenomena in general, comparable to that furnished by Marxism-Leninism. The various theories of protracted conflict for example are developed side by side without being organised in a coherent whole of one single conceptual framework. This, naturally, has a profound influence on the choice of methods that are to be used. [17]

At one extreme, those theoreticians nearest to the tradition of diplomatic history find authenticity only in the surface of the event itself, in its singularity and uniqueness. At the other extreme are to be found those who are more inclined to construct models with numerous variables. The models are compared with historic situations in the framework of a given moment or period of evolution.

The fact that some of the differences in the basic assumptions of international relations theory could be of an ideological nature has not, to our knowledge, been seriously broached in books on international relations. Nor would there appear to have been much call for such an exercise since international relations theory has often been taken to mean Western international relations theory. Where major shifts in basic philosophical assumptions had to be accounted for this would be done in terms other than ideological or, failing that, described as shifts within one ideology; which is perhaps one good reason why international relations theory has so far remained aloof from 'ideological' debates. This would indeed be a comfortable position were it not for the uncomfortable notion that philosophies are at the heart of ideologies and that shifts in the former may find their wider interpretation in terms of the latter. The notion is hard to refute and not only has it found support from some theorists apropos of political science in general but, at a more specific level, it has been suggested that there is also a discernible correlation between the properties of theories about politics and the ideological orientations of their authors. Strauss notes that most political scientists nowadays (which is to say in the West) are classifiable as 'liberals', having as their objective 'empirical endeavour resting on value-free propositions, rejecting the existence of truth and ordered universe that is essentially a conservative feature in at least some of the contemporary meanings of that term'.[18] Golembiewski goes as far as to make an explicit assertion that a debate between 'philosophical and scientific orientation is more than a debate but a revolution and therefore ideological differences are understandable'.[19] This would be a highly contentious issue. However, inasmuch as one might accept the proposition as broadly indicative of a tendency there is added one further correlation to our continuum (Figure 1, section 8).

There have been many attempts made within other social sciences to account for the fact that the perception of what could be described as 'the same reality' by people or groups of people in a particular epoch can be totally different. That the perception should be affected by the different social situation or different 'point of view' shared by a particular social group, whatever sociological nomenclature may be used for these groups, makes for an intriguing social phenomenon. *Weltanschauungen*, ideologies, belief systems, value systems, derivations or myths, these all describe to a great extent the same thing. The claim of non-partisanship made by many philosophies has been vigorously rejected by some thinkers who have proceeded to draw the conclusion that social science is forever condemned to contamination by a subjective factor that will prevent it from becoming a science. The presence of such a factor, they have contended, places the discipline unalterably beyond the reach of science's rigorous control and strict rules of verifiability. A simple untested, and untestable, acceptance of information as 'true' and existing is no substitute for objective knowledge.

It is indeed extremely difficult, if not impossible, to draw the line between knowledge and belief in all cases. We should be able, however, even in social science, to distinguish at least in some measure between the two. Where there are definite, consistent, usable, and generally accepted criteria for testing against reality, it should be possible to distinguish the ideas that pass the test from those that do not. As Mannheim suggests,[20] we should be able to distinguish between studies acceptable for all (logic, mathematics) and others which are at best 'true' for people who look at what they study from the 'same point of view'. But, in regard to those same 'scientific and generally acceptable bits of knowledge', would they not be condemned to uselessness by virtue of the fact that they would indeed consist of self-evident 'truths', and nothing beyond; and there the consensus would stop? At one extreme there are these 'scientific' theories that generalise (or are believed by their authors to do so) about how people individually and collectively do in fact behave, and why; claiming to avoid normative prescriptions about what is good and bad, and why. At the other extreme there are theories consisting of statements of what ought to happen, and explaining values or ideals including the reasons why they are held, the effects they may have on behaviour, and their interrelatedness with other values (Figure 1, sections 4 and 5). And in all of this we must be aware of those theorists who, styling their theories 'scientific' and claiming to take into account only statements of what does exist or happen, offer themselves as objective and value-free as possible and avoid all moral entanglement – and who by explicit rejection of all values often imply an adamant adherence to some.

Whatever maxim will be inscribed on the banner of an international theory, because the nature of its subject-matter shows a correspondence with all social theory it must to some extent be ideology – and value-bound. In this respect, as in so many others, inter- national theory cannot be an exception. Attitudes that confuse facts and values (a position taken by the Soviet version of marxism) discount all value systems for the sake of meeting 'scientific' requirements (many 'behaviouralists'), and are contemptuous of all but their own value systems,[21] are attitudes that will not, especially in the long run, have a lasting impression. Only by keeping ideologies and the different value systems in mind can we hope to set up a meaningful theory of social phenomena which would be able to set forth the problems and frame the questions in such a way as to facilitate the task of research teams in their quest for answers. Such teams could then attack the problem regardless of the ideology and/or value system that they severally espouse.

In the pages that follow we shall be returning to many of the questions adumbrated in this introductory chapter and elaborating upon them. Thus the basic scheme as outlined in Figure 1 will remain with us throughout and we hope convenient reference will be made to it.

CHAPTER 2

Marx and Engels on international relations

> Natural science will one day incorporate the science of man, just
> as the science of man will incorporate natural science; there will
> be a single science.
>
> Karl Marx

To study any one aspect of Marx's work is an exercise full of
frustration: on the one hand one should have a familiarity with almost
every field of human knowledge,[1] with the theories that his polemical
writings repudiate,[2] with the historical circumstances in which he
wrote each of his works, and with the languages he used or in which he
freely quoted.[3] On the other hand, since Marx has dominated the
political horizons of this century 'one cannot help but feel that
everything has been said about him that is possible to say'.[4] Perhaps
this may be one of the reasons why specialists in particular aspects of
social science but who are not experts on Marx feel inhibited if not
debarred from undertaking such research into those fields which
would seem to be identical with their own. The hardships and pitfalls
involved seem not to be worth the possible fruits of their labours
since, as is sometimes contended, even where concepts are similar and
would seem to be direct ancestors of some contemporary version, the
complexity of events – and often terms used to reflect them – has
become immeasurably greater and the analysis of the 'prehistoric'
version must be of diminished relevance.[5]

Thus, we may find it strange that however carefully marxologists
have scrutinised Marx's work, what he had to say on the subject of
international relations has been rather neglected. Whether or not it is
also because international relations constitutes a problem of a possibly
intractable nature for marxism,[6] the fact is that it has been

acknowledged only on the level of empirical politics and ideological controversy and 'it is still too little an appreciated issue in the context of a thoroughgoing theoretical analysis of Marxian thought'.[7]

The main difficulty in studying Marx's ideas on international relations seems to be that he paid such small *explicit* attention to them. It would be a fallacy, however, to assume on this slender basis that he had nothing of importance to say on the subject. We would do well to consider that international relations seems to be what could be described as a contextual concept; and although it would be true to say that Marx's ideas on the subject were never explicitly formulated or brought together in one place, many of his discourses have a direct bearing and it is only through the collation of their implications that his thinking on this subject can be fully appreciated. Thus a clear notion of the context of all of Marx's works becomes a precondition of this appreciation.

This does not of course make the interpretation of Marx's ideas relevant to this particular subject (complex and difficult as it already is) any easier. Pareto's apt simile that Marx's statements are like bats[8] is of course applicable not only to Marx but to interpretation in general. We can see in the bat something of the appearance both of a mouse and of a bird.[9] But perhaps we may point out that the factors contributing to this appearance lie not only with the bat. In addition to those, there is also, for example, the subjective perception of the viewer to be taken into account. And additionally, the angle from which they are viewed – and the quality of the viewer's eyesight.

Indeed how are we to interpret or, in the parlance of the *Oxford Dictionary*, expound the meaning of abstruse expressions – of which unfortunately Marx and Engels supplied more than their share? Or perhaps, rather than abstruse expressions, it would be more correct to refer to clusters of abstruse ideas in abstruse constellations. For, as exemplified by the case of international relations theory, Marx and Engels were inconsiderate enough to fail to provide for their readers a neatly referenced synthesis of their work with the main ideas and theories carefully plotted. As a consequence, these have given rise to an endless variety of interpretations and discussion and the 'true' inheritance – the 'authentic' interpretation – has been, and remains, in endless dispute. Not only did Marx and Engels never coherently spell out their main ideas but they changed their perspective several times in the course of their lifetime, a fact which has further encouraged selectivity in reception – either of a deliberate or of an accidental nature. As a classical example of misunderstanding following upon the interpretative range of which Marx's work is capable, the case of Lenin and Kautsky is often quoted: both of them were lifelong students of Marx and Engels and yet they disagreed radically about the interpretation of many very crucial notions.

In case of a clear meaning no interpretation is necessary, says an old juristic rule. But what should one do in the remaining cases or indeed in those areas of the social sciences where such rules as '*lex posterior derogat priori*' or '*lex specialis derogat generali*' do not exist – and do not make sense?

With difficulty one can imagine a set of ideas in any social science, including law, where 'no interpretation' would be necessary. Yet lawyers have a set of rules specifying who after the actual author is to provide the 'authentic' interpretation and what weight is to be apportioned and account taken of semantic, logical, grammatical, and historical considerations. Although such specific guidance is hardly conceivable in non-juristic fields, it is in the case of Marx perhaps above all others that its absence makes itself felt. Practically all of Marx's work must be subjected to interpretation in the above manner and a careful reader struggling through Marx's writings is haunted by the feeling that he has forgotten or overlooked that one small but crucial manual or 'introduction' where the main notions and concepts would have been expounded. Since, however, no such guide written by Marx himself exists, one is compelled to deduce the 'authentic' interpretation from such fragmentary evidence as is to be found in his voluminous analytical and polemical writings. The post-Marx generations of marxists (starting from Engels) have been attempting to do exactly that. In the East, marxism has been reduced to textbooks to which some illustrations might have been added *ad libitum*, from in particular the *Communist Manifesto*, the preface to the *Critique of Political Economy* and the first volume of *Capital*, together with more extensive references to Engels and Lenin. The interpretations of Marx have almost managed to do away with him.

In addition to the usual problems of interpretation which one expects to encounter in reading any thinker's work, in Marx's case there are some additional ones.[10] Without pretending to offer a definitive solution to any of them the need for some indication of their scope and outline – as well as of the standpoint in regard to them adopted by the present writers – will be appreciated. Although other factors will be seen to operate in this regard we will content ourselves at this stage by reiterating only the fact that these problems have a direct bearing on the interpretations of particular importance in the case of international relations.

In the first place the forty years of Marx's most prolific writing is divided into periods, or stages; namely, the period of 'original marxism' prior to 1845 (including *Theses on Feuerbach* and *German Ideology*) and the period of 'mature marxism' thereafter. Support for this division, it is thought, is to be found in Engels's statement to the effect that the *Poverty of Philosophy* (1847) and the *Communist Manifesto* (1848) contained the first presentation of the doctrine in a coherent manner. And indeed there would probably have been something very wrong with Marx if his ideas had not developed in the course of his life. Similar phases in intellectual development can be found in the case of many other thinkers, but in the case of Marx the notion that there is much more to it than a mere maturation of ideas has been not infrequently expressed. The notion that in fact what we are dealing with here are two periods fundamentally distinct from one another and suggestive of an intellectual dichotomy from each branch of which completely different sets of ideas – and conclusions – flow. And it is indeed beyond doubt that the early works influenced by Marx's hegelian upbringing are youthfully romantic and overwhelmingly humanistic with a strong emphasis on psychological and social aspects – aspects that noticeably fade in his later works.

The difference in attitude taken towards these two phases in the West and in the East is characteristic: some time ago it was fashionable in the West to 'discover' the young Marx and to try to interpret the later works in terms of, and in the light shed by, the early ones. The official Soviet and East European view,[11] shared by some Western marxists,[12] regards the mature works as the more important and sees the earlier product as immaturely expressed and idealistically tinted. If they go to the earlier period at all it is only for the purposes of discovering the origins and constituent elements of his later theory. (Paradoxically this attitude is shared also by some of Marx's most ardent opponents who see in him an antisocial, dehumanised creature, obsessed with economics.)[13] The Soviet attitude has certainly been influenced by Lenin, who is believed not to have read some of Marx's early works, in particular the *Economic and Philosophic Manuscripts* which were published only in 1932.[14]

The points of divergence in the two conflicting approaches are only too obvious. Proponents of the first interpret all of Marx's work in terms of some hegelian categories, alienation in particular. Into these hegelian categories they fit his mature work, and might reach the conclusion that 'the *Capital* is nothing but a theory of fundamental alienation'.[15] On the other hand, those who incline to the second approach argue that Marx himself ceased to use the term 'alienation' and used 'exploitation' and 'oppression' instead.[16] They argue that Marx and Engels themselves indicated a certain measure of disgust towards their own youthful works. As Engels says of some of the early formulations, they were 'absolutely useless and sometimes worse, in practice'.[17]

Even if we disregard such reasons as are adduced for Marx's changing vocabulary, Engels's assessment seems to be eminently justifiable: initially the emancipation of workers was conceived by Marx to involve the overcoming of alienation as well as of wage labour. Later on, as his studies in economics progressed, he emphasised more the role of industrial development and capitalist accumulation by means of surplus value. But to try to discover in this a basic shift of underlying principles, rather than a change in strategy only,[18] seems to be rather contrived. The humanistic theme of the emancipation of labour as an ultimate goal has remained a constant throughout his work, and to deny such examples of organic continuity and development and place the whole of the emphasis on the fact of division into two phases (that in any case is clear for all to see) seems to go beyond interpretation, in the case of the Eastern attitude, to encompass onto-ideologically motivated Marxist-Leninist revision.

We may say here that in the present study the early works are going to be neither dismissed nor depreciated. Indeed, since Soviet marxists see fit to disregard certain of the concepts along with their implications, the early origins of these will be scrutinised. We will hope, among other objects of this exercise, to discover the explanation for this rejection. And in pursuing this 'middle way' we will be travelling for at least part of it in the company of a third school of thought; a most recent one which denies the priority of either period of Marx's life and instead regards as the most important work – indeed the bridge between the two periods – Marx's *Grundrisse* (1857–8). This central work they claim, although in fragmentary form, exceeds in importance by far either *Manuscripts* or *Capital*.[19]

The second major problem to be dealt with is Marx's association with Engels. The association gives rise to many complex, perhaps insoluble, questions that are nevertheless too important to be ignored.

In this regard let us say briefly that the questions we refer to here are contained in any one of three categories: the interpretation and evaluation of Engels's thought as a whole; the comparison of Engels and Marx; and Engels's influence on marxism.[20]

Significantly, the partnership of the two men has been discussed and analysed more in the West than in the East. Early interpreters such as Mehring, Kautsky and Plekhanov, as well as contemporary Soviet marxists, have dismissed this question as unimportant, and there are also no lack of other revisionists and non-marxists who believe that Engels either distorted Marx's ideas or was to be blamed for his ideas becoming an ideology – or indeed believe both to be true.

Engels, who survived Marx by twelve years, is certainly responsible for the posthumous interpretation of marxism; indeed one has to agree with Carlton[21] that it was Engels who 'put the match to the explosive material in Marx's mind'. Engels is responsible for what has sometimes been described as 'orthodox codification' on which Lenin's subsequent translation could have been based. Many authors have treated Marx and Engels between 1844 and 1883 (when Marx died) as the authors of a single system of ideas[22] and in that period it would be rather difficult if not impossible, in the case of the collective works and those that were written by Engels under the name of Marx, to distinguish between the two writers, since their ideas must have been to a great degree convergent (hence the possibility of their partnership). In our opinion, nevertheless, where possible the separate authorship of the individual works is to be borne in mind: Marx was, of the two, much more erudite with a considerably wider, particularly philosophical, background of knowledge. In contrast to Marx's cumbersome writing, Engels's thoughts seem at first sight to be clearer and more concise but on closer analysis turn out to be highly problematical. To summarise the difference between the two of them in terms of Marx being an anthropocentrist and Engels a cosmocentrist may not be quite fair to either, but it does suggest different interests and emphases. These differences will be elaborated as in the course of our study their implications have a bearing.

There is certainly no such thing as 'true' answers to the questions deriving from these two areas (youthful versus mature Marx, Marx versus Engels) and it may well be the case that due to the scantiness of available evidence more conclusive answers will never be found. However, important though the answers may be in other areas, in fields such as ours they are of marginal consequence and we need only bear in mind that certain interpretations are based on certain assumptions and that some of these are only hypothetical. In other words, certain conclusions about international relations depend entirely on whether or not we find acceptable the laying of an equal emphasis on the work of the young and the 'mature' Marx, and whether – aware of the differences between Marx and Engels – our studies of each of their contributions is accorded the same weight. Since Marx and Engels have been treated as equals by Lenin and Marxism-Leninism, and part of our purpose is to follow their argument, it follows that we should do likewise. Thus our approach will differ considerably from the standard marxologue approach which by dismissing Engels does no service to the student interested in relating Marxism-Leninism to Marx.

In the introduction it was suggested that international theories either imply or reveal explicitly strong links with the philosophical systems on which they are based, and that certain groups of shared characteristics are correlatable.[23] Our assumptions in this regard were prompted by Marx, in whose work the correlation is so pronounced as to have made of marxists and marxism generally a tradition that exemplifies the link. Marx's philosophy and hence also his epistemology were too distinct and too much *sui generis* to be neglected or skipped without impairing the understanding of the ABC of theories that proceed to encompass all aspects of society.

Rather than begin with the reconstruction of Marx's international theory, stepping aside occasionally to supplement our partial comprehension with dips into philosophy and epistemology – or leaving such enlightenment to the end – it would seem justifiable to reverse the order and survey at the outset those areas of philosophical and epistemological relevance appropriate to our needs.

A succinct and well-known expression of the epistemological assumptions at the roots of Marx's teaching is the eleventh of the *Theses on Feuerbach* of 1845: 'The philosophers have only *interpreted* the world, in various ways; the point, however, is to *change* it.'[24] This is in our opinion the quintessence of Marx's perception of the role a social theory can play. The implications of the statement are, of course, far-reaching: the background reasoning that led to the conclusions (or rather programme) considerable. But it also heralds something of the nature of the problem that confronts us. If the eleventh thesis were to be taken as a statement of a goal of 'philosophers', we would have to conclude that Engels was in his reasoning less consistent with its premises than was Marx. Indeed the eleventh thesis constitutes something of a problem from the point of view of the traditionally assumed rigorous dictates of marxist economic determinism. It is a fact that both Marx and Engels indicated their firm belief in the existence of 'impelling forces' or 'true final impulses' or 'laws of development', and throughout *Capital*, Marx talks of 'society discovering the natural laws of its movement'; capitalism as subject to 'the immanent laws of capitalist production' which have the character of 'immutable natural laws'; and of the 'economic formation of society as a process of natural history'. But the nature of Marx and Engels's determinism and the room left within it for human activity, the origin of these 'laws of development' and their exact nature, remain an enigma.

The framework of Marx and Engels's theory is without a doubt hegelian, especially in two respects: first, the hegelian identification of the ideal and the actual. This, it has been claimed, was the forerunner of their determinism that may be briefly stated as follows: in the history of mankind, which is basically a single, non-repetitive process obeying discoverable laws, two factors are involved. There exists an objective development which contains within it the formation of a subjective factor which is instrumental in realising the development. Engels sees history much more as an objective, economically determined process running its naturally inevitable course. It takes minute attention to detect a difference in Marx, who, by way of contrast, tends to explain history as a process effected by subjects acting concretely in revolutionary practice.

The second respect is in regard to the concept of dialectic. We, says Engels, speaking also for Marx,[25] have once again comprehended our ideas materialistically as images (*Abbilders*) of real things, copies of this or that stage of the Absolute Idea. Thus, continues Engels, dialectics reduced itself to the science of the general laws of motion both of the external world and human thought. As a result of this, there are two sets of laws: in substance they are identical, but they differ in their expression in so far as the human mind makes conscious use of them; while in nature, and up to the present also in the history of mankind, they become actual in an endless series of apparent contingencies, devoid of consciousness in the form of external necessity. Materialist reading has made conceptual dialectic a conscious reflection of the dialectical motion of the real world. Hegel's dialectic, says Engels, was turned upside down and put on its head, or back on its feet, since it had stood on its head previously.[26]

The fact that Marx in his explicit devotion to dialectic was more cautious is believed to indicate that he understood by dialectic considerably less, at most the transitory impermanent character of form and the presence of internal contradiction between form and content.[27] Nevertheless one difference is quite obvious: Engels elaborated a dialectical philosophy of nature which he thought was basically the same for society. Marx conceives nature only in reference to man as the alienated object of human labour which must be recovered; there is biographical evidence, however, to show that he took some interest in Engels's 'application of dialectic to nature' exercise.

Engels gives somewhat uncritical acceptance to Hegel's account of the history of dialectic but whatever historical mists shroud the origins, this conception, when carried out consistently to its marxist conclusions, entails an end to absolute solutions and 'eternal' truths in scientific explanations: knowledge is of necessity finite, since it is affected by the conditions under which we acquire it. Thus what is considered as truth today has its latent or, overtly to become, false side:[28]

> The world is not to be comprehended as a complex of ready made *things*, but as a complex of *processes*, in which the things apparently stable, no less than their mind images in our heads, the concepts, go through an uninterrupted change of coming into being and passing away, in which, in spite of all seeming accidentally and of all temporary regressions, a progressive development asserts itself in the end – this great fundamental thought has, especially since the time of Hegel, so thoroughly permeated ordinary consciousness that in this generality it is now scarcely ever contradicted. But to acknowledge this fundamental thought in words and to apply it in reality in detail to each domain of investigation are two different things. If, however, investigation always proceeds from this standpoint, the demand for final solutions and eternal truths ceases once for all; one is always conscious of the necessary limitation of all acquired knowledge, of the fact that it is conditioned by the circumstances in which it was acquired. On the other hand, one no longer permits oneself to be imposed upon by the anti-theses, insuperable for the still common old metaphysics, between true and false, good and bad, identical and different, necessary and

accidental. One knows that these antitheses have only a relative validity; that that which is recognised now as true has also its latent false side which will later manifest itself, just as that which is now regarded as false has also a true side by virtue of which it could be previously regarded as true. One knows that what is maintained to be necessary is composed of sheer accidents and that the so-called accidental is the form behind which necessity hides itself – and so on.

According to Marx and Engels's epistemology, a concept is simply a reflection of a brain event but, unlike Hegel, they do not distinguish between two kinds of knowledge: a higher dialectical one and a merely rational one that does not overcome contradictions. Both Marx and Engels reject most vigorously *a priori* knowledge (Engels does not even acknowledge *a priori* forms of sensibility such as time and space, in the specially relevant chapter in *Anti-Dühring*). There is absolutely nothing of idealism or subjectivism in Marx. Hence Marx seems to be wholly consistent when he rejects Hegel's dialectic[29] – and then both men (Marx and Engels) accept it in its entirety. They seek, however, justification for dialectic in objective reality alone ('Nature is the test of dialectics').[30] But from nature, dialectic enters the brain (also part of nature) and so materialism finally comes to share the same method as idealism, which, strictly speaking, may be taken as a contradiction in the epistemological foundations of the entire system.

Is there such a thing as an 'objective', or should we say an ontological, dialectic? Is the world around us essentially dialectical? Can we accept the dialectical equations such as 'if feudal, pre-competitive monopoly is the thesis, and competition the antithesis, then modern bourgeois monopoly is the synthesis: this modern monopoly is said to negate feudal monopoly to the extent to which it entails competition, but at the same time it is a negation of competition to the extent to which it is a monopoly. Thus modern monopoly is a "synthetic monopoly, or a negation, a unity of opposites".'[31] Or Engels's famous 'butterflies negating eggs by springing from them' which is followed when 'they pair and are in turn negated', negation of the negation gives rise to hundreds and thousands of butterflies.[32]

On the one hand Engels writes 'any child can understand [dialectic], as soon as it is stripped of the veil of mystery in which it was wrapped by the old idealist philosophy'. And, Marx writes 'if there should ever be time for such work again, I should greatly like to make accessible to the ordinary human intelligence, in two or three printer's sheets, what is *rational* on the method which Hegel discovered but at the same time enveloped in mysticism'.[33] Apart from the sketch in his preface to the second German edition of *Capital*, Marx never took the trouble to elaborate on this (and perhaps the risk of doing so) and thus the marxist notion of dialectic comes mainly from Engels's courageous pen.

Yet, for all the brave words, however perceptive the author or incisive the exposition, it somehow has never amounted to the two or three pages envisaged by Marx. Not only does it never become so simple as to be understood by whatever child Engels had in mind but few areas of agreement on its essentials have been reached by writers then[34] or since. These sad truths have either plagued with contradictions the discourses of philosophers and students of dialectic or have been adduced in support of many conflicting theories in all areas contributing to the march of human progress. When we turn to our subject we must also try to discover whether dialectical laws are hidden beneath the surface of, in our case, international relations. And we will also have to examine with what validity or what exercise of the wide interpretative range available has made 'dialectic', 'dialectical method', and so on, household words in Soviet and East European vocabulary, as though by magical incantation they may conjure up and consecrate the details of the 'marxist' advance. Before leaving the particular source we will find it relevant and necessary to investigate such claims in regard to the dialectic and its uses as that which sees the contemporary principle of proletarian internationalism and peaceful coexistence – seemingly mutually exclusive concepts – actually to stand in 'dialectical relation' to one another.

That propensity of Marx to postpone elucidation of certain essentials is one of the major problems. Marx left most epistemological and historico-philosophical matters perhaps for a later stage in his life in order that he could avoid that *a priori*, abstract and dogmatic way of thinking which finds expression in ideological systems, and which he so despised. Thus in the event he left a great deal of exposition to Engels, who, in expounding it in the way that he did, contributed to the development of a comprehensive ideological system.

Engels's starting-point was the identity of nature and history (he calls the dialectic in history 'historical dialectic'). He perceived, however, a difference between the two spheres: nature is ruled by blind unconscious forces and nothing in nature takes place as a willed, conscious purpose, whereas the force in social history is always conscious man, acting with reason and passion for specific goals. However, 'the course of history is governed by inner general laws . . . on the whole, in spite of the consciously desired aims of all individuals, accident apparently reigns on the surface. . . . But where on the surface accident holds sway, there actually it is always governed by inner laws and it is only a matter of discovering these laws . . . [history] is precisely the resultant of these many wills operating in different directions and of their manifold effects upon the outer world.'[35]

In other words, Engels sees a pattern of general inner laws, a resultant of the conflict of countless wills; where this seems to be functioning as 'chance' it is due to our inability as yet to discern the laws. It is only when circumstances surrounding the appearance of 'chance' are scrutinised that the historical determining forces may be discovered: there are laws operative behind any expression of will and thus the role of the individual (or subjective factor) is considerably reduced.

Marx's statements, on the other hand, as has been observed, are not so straightforward. 'History does nothing, it "possesses *no* immense wealth" it "wages no battles". It is real living man that does all that, who possesses and fights; "history" is not a person apart, using man as means for its own particular aims; history is *nothing but* the activity of man pursuing his aims.'[36] 'World history would indeed be very easy to make if the struggle were taken up only on condition of infallibly favourable chances. It would on the other hand be of a very mystical nature, if "accidents" played no part. These accidents naturally form part of the general course of development and are compensated by other accidents. But acceleration and delay are very much dependent upon such "accidents", including the "accident" of the character of the people who first head the movement.'[37]

Desires and plans of individuals (continues Engels), far from flowing in one direction, cumulating in one movement and culminating in impressive events, run along numberless different paths, interacting with one another and modifying or cancelling each other out. Three final situations may possibly occur:

1 'These ends are incapable of realisation.'
2 'These results of many individual wills produce effects for the

23

most part quite different from that which was wished – often, in fact very opposite.'

3 'The ends of the actions are those intended but the results which follow were not intended.'

What happens in the actual situation is not – according to Engels – the product of human will. 'That which is willed happens but rarely . . . the conflict of innumerable individual wills and the individual actions in the domain of history produce a state of affairs entirely analogous to that prevailing in the realm of unconscious nature.'[38] From this it follows that the role of the human being is rather negligible in significance. The role of actors, the tasks of carrying out the dictates of economic development, are assigned to classes. 'When, therefore, it is a question of investigating the driving powers which – consciously or unconsciously, and indeed very often unconsciously – lie behind the motives of men who act in history and which constitute the real ultimate driving forces of history, then it is not a question so much of the motives of single individuals, however eminent, as of those motives which set in motion great masses, whole peoples, and again whole classes of the people in each people; and this, too, not momentarily, for the transient flaring up of a straw-fire which quickly dies down, but for a lasting action resulting in a great historical transformation.'[39]

Neither Marx nor Engels introduced a system into their plethora of 'social forces' and it becomes at times rather confusing and difficult to unravel. Particularly is this so when occasionally the very ground under our feet that seemed so solid and stable begins to tremble – thus Marx in the *Eighteenth Brumaire*: 'The existence and thereby collision, too, between these classes are in turn conditioned by the degree of development of their economic position, by the mode of their production and of their exchange determined by it.' This seems to suggest that the 'ultimate' driving forces are not the ultimate historical forces after all!

But it is not the vice of inconsistency so much as an indulgence of casualness, even carelessness, on the part of Marx (and Engels, too, elsewhere) and when again for example we read in the *Eighteenth Brumaire* that Napoleon 'swept away' the feudal system, or that (*Poverty of Philosophy*) 'Peter the Great overthrew Russian barbarism with barbarism', we may assume that it is a controlled 'carelessness' used in fact to simplify the argument. It would be unrealistic to expect that every time the theme of, say, Napoleon is developed, all the background reasoning should come in for similar attention. In this way 'Napoleon' or 'Peter the Great' become themselves concepts or symbols in a kind of shorthand, and the alleged schizophrenic discrepancies between Marx's theoretical considerations and actual historical case studies pointed out by some critics may well derive from a misunderstanding of this device. Indeed far from there being attempts to elevate the role of individuals there are many explicit cases of attempts to belittle their achievements. As Bober points out,[40] Marx's analysis, in the first volume of *Capital*, of the inventions of the eighteenth century seeks to demonstrate that they were due hardly at all to the work of single individuals. And elsewhere: 'it is still true that man proposes and God (that is, the extraneous force of the capitalist mode of production) disposes',[41] or, if it is true that a great man can lead to new deeds regardless of historical necessities, 'he might just as well have been born five hundred years earlier, and would then have saved humanity five hundred years of error, strife, and suffering'.[42] Acknowledging that each epoch needs a leader, Marx agrees with Helvetius that if it does not find him then it invents him.[43] That a great man appears at a given moment in a given country is pure accident.[44] Suppress him and a substitute will come. Napoleon was an accident and in the absence of a Napoleon, somebody else like him would have appeared.[45]

Thus Marx and Engels, in this respect certainly ahead of their time, perceive the world scene as a stage inhabited, despite the jargon, not by 'the high-sounding dramas of princes'[46] as individuals, but by social forces not necessarily identified with nations, states, or state leaders.[47]

Geographical conditions and environment receive very little attention, and that only through their effect on the mode of production. Marx repeated several times in *Capital* that where nature is too abundant and man is treated like a child he does not develop himself as much as where the geographical conditions are harsh. Engels goes so far as to acknowledge blatant differences in mental capacities caused by natural influences (the small brain of Indians in New Mexico as a consequence of vegetable diet; in contrast, Aryans and Semites in certain regions of Asia had a milk and meat diet, hence a superior brain).[48]

Rather than the direct influence of environment on man in the man-nature interaction it is more the work of man that influences

25

him. 'By thus acting on the external world and changing it, he at the same time changes his own nature and develops his slumbering powers.'[49] What man is depends on his production,[50] only variety of work can develop the many sides of human ability and character.[51]

Thus there is man, the subjective factor, against the background of objective conditions, and the relationship between the two, especially from the point of view of drawing a clear line between Marx's and Engels's ideas, is – with the best will in the world – difficult to establish. Whatever the differences in detail, both Marx and Engels often take refuge in the concept of 'law' and many of the explanations that one would want to hear get subsumed under this hazy notion. Reference to 'laws' are indeed so frequent that an explicit definition would be very helpful, but the nearest to a definition ('law, this inner and necessary connection between two seeming contradictions')[52] seems to us too restrictive to meet the demands that both Marx and Engels make on it.

To be more specific, the concept of 'law' as opposed to 'driving force' is in the first place not adequately differentiated, and in Engels's *Feuerbach*, for example, the two concepts are virtually indistinguishable and seem to merge. Second, the fact that the laws of nature and of history are treated as identical also creates a problem. However, it may well be taken as a logical consequence of materialism where economic development is considered to be a natural process. Marx and Engels believe that history or for that matter social science can become as rigorously controlled a discipline as is natural science. Indeed the chief criterion for the former's 'scientificality' is whether it (social science) can or cannot define its 'laws', the laws of historical development, to the same extent as natural science discovers its 'laws'. Engels certainly goes much farther than Marx in the identification of and drawing direct comparisons between natural laws and social laws. Marx's social laws on the other hand sound much less rigorous: alternatives are not excluded and decisions are conditional; it does not necessarily follow that the outcome must be unconditional. Thus Marx's 'laws' seem to have more the character of tendencies on an imaginary continuum at the farther extreme of which is the 'law as a necessary connection between two seeming contradictions'. Third, many of Marx's statements are in a form that could be understood not only as law but also as a statement of historical principle, as, for example, 'the history of all hitherto existing societies is the history of class struggle' (*Manifesto*), which can be understood as either:[53] in other words, either of two conceptions which coexist.

Fourth, neither Marx nor Engels is sufficiently clear in his distinction of basic and derivative laws. Although this may not seem to be all that important it is, to say the least, confusing. For instance, it is rather surprising that Marx fully accepted the allegation of his Russian critic who maintained that Marx's method admitted of no general laws or abstract methods. Marx in his reply agreed, and said that *Capital* contained only special, not general, laws of history. Engels, in sharp contrast to this, refers to 'general laws' rather freely: 'What therefore is the negation of the negation: An extremely general – and for this reason extremely comprehensive and important – law of development of Nature, history and thought . . . I bring them all together under this law of motion', comments Engels and goes on to say that although 'this most general law does explain the particular processes of development it does leave out of account the peculiarities of each separate individual process'.[54]

One could go on like this pointing out discrepancies or inconsistencies all of which suggest that whatever the meaning of Marx's and Engels's concept of law it would probably be rather different from standard contemporary notions. When reading Marx and Engels this should be borne in mind.

As has been suggested above, the difference between Marx's and Engels's ideas can often be accounted for by reference to the differences in their characters: Engels 'volunteers' to formulate in a concise way something that the more erudite Marx could have agreed with in principle (and there is biographical evidence to show that he did read a great deal of Engels's work and did not disapprove) but would have been rather reluctant himself to put into formal terms. He had a strong dislike for rigid definitions, and would regard as still 'metaphysical'[55] and 'speculative', or consider as working hypotheses, what for Engels has already become conclusions in embryo. It would, however, be wrong solely on the basis of his evidently less (than Engels's) enthusiastic embrace of their hegelian 'turned upside down' dialectic to reject any connection between what has now been labelled dialectical materialism and historical materialism;[56] which is to say, between his philosophy and actual social research.[57]

Differences between Marx and Engels notwithstanding, it would be very difficult to justify any argument that sought to diminish the value of dialectic in Marx's writing. Dialectic after all is the premise of Marx's methodology, or, as Isaac Deutscher put it, 'the grammar of marxist teaching', and that Engels himself judged to be 'our best working tool and our sharpest weapon'.[58] It is, of course, one thing to reject the validity of dialectic as an objectively existing force, i.e. its ontological existence; and quite another matter to argue that the grounding of 'historical materialism' in 'philosophical materialism . . . does not necessarily entail the further step of suggesting that human history is set in motion and kept going by a "dialectical" process of contradiction within the material basis'. Lichtheim thinks that such a conclusion does not follow from either the materialistic principle or the 'quasi-Hegelian picture Marx sketched in the 1859 Preface'[59] and the outline there of the successive stages leading from antiquity to communism. 'The notion of dialectical law', says Lichtheim, 'linking primitive communism, via slavery, feudalism and capitalism, with the mature communism of the future, was once more the contribution of Engels who in this as in other matters bore witness to the unshakeable hold of Hegel's philosophy upon his own cast of mind.'[60]

In our opinion, despite the differences between Marx and Engels, Marx's basic scheme remains hegelian: to understand the world is to perceive its energising principle; to grasp the form working dialectically through things towards an ultimate harmony that represents the full flowering into existence of the truly real. This scheme remained fundamental even to Marx's thought. The dialectical framework gave Marx the framework for his dialectical concept of history, on the one hand, and on the other it provided him with history's temporal and moral climax, and thus with the fundamental moral assumptions for his work.[61]

His belief in society's progress through successively higher stages to the 'truly human' society and morality of communism implies objective, eternal and immutable moral standards for appraising successive stages of development. From this belief it follows that a spate of denunciation of exploitation, privilege, etc., must flow. This kind of combination of the analysis of society in conjunction with moral judgments which we find in Marx is certainly not an exclusively marxist phenomenon, hence it is less than convincing to attempt to repudiate Marx's claim of objectivity on the grounds that his findings proclaimed the doom of existing society.[62] Marx regarded himself as an objective and dispassionate social analyst and attacked critics of the social order who attempted to find solutions to social problems through appeals to justice; who conjured up fantastic pictures of future society and called them Utopian. It was in order to draw a clear line between themselves and the 'Utopian' socialists of the beginning of the nineteenth century that Marx and Engels decided to style themselves 'scientific', their objective being to study social relations and the industrial system of the mid-nineteenth century so as to reach by similar paths propositions as valid and reliable as those made in relation to chemistry or physics.

Clearly this conception seems to eliminate the distinction between *fact* and *value*. The fact that thought is socially determined may appear to destroy the autonomy of moral judgment and indeed of all judgments, including 'those judgments which constitute Marx's own theory, so that there is no longer any point in asking whether it is true or false'.[63] This is obviously a problem not only for marxism, but for all deterministic theories and in a broad sense for any scientific theory in psychology or sociology.

The dialectical element of the law of social evolution is so significant because it is by a dialectical process that the abolition of private property and classes, that is to say socialism, will be finally realised in its ultimate form. Only an appreciation of the operation of this process could have led Marx to conclusions that certain developments *will* or *must* take place, rather than that they only *ought* to take place. It is only by taking the notion of dialectic into account, however scattered its exposition may be, that we can understand this conviction of Marx that he cannot only explain the past and the present but also predict the future. Marx, if nothing else, is always a scholar and to fail to acknowledge this link in the intellectual chain of his reasoning is, in effect, to accuse him of permitting most serious gaps and weaknesses. If in fact we do not accept dialectic as the mainspring of his thoughts and reasoning then the words dialectic, contradiction, inevitable, imminent, historical necessity, in the final analysis, etc., would appear to be introduced in order spuriously to authenticate an argument or would otherwise seem to violate their context. Of course had Marx been our contemporary, he would have been obliged, by way of presenting his argument in an acceptable form, to have occupied himself with a great deal of formulation and elucidation, whereas in his writing, conjecture, illustration, proof and evidence are presented at times as though they were on the same plane. The effect of the passage of a century in this context, as in the others, must be borne in mind.

The apparent inconsistency of predictions, sometimes couched in terms of imperative and at others subject to qualification give rise to arguments about Marx's normative orientations. Self-consciously and explicitly Marx's ultimate goal is freedom and the perfection of mankind (in the sense of freedom being a 'recognised necessity') towards which there winds a difficult path via the nearer, secondary, goals of proletarian revolution (abolition of exploitation), the overcoming of anarchy, and inefficiency and waste (in capitalist production). Only in this way will a classless society be brought about and a level of civilisation reached in which all men will be masters of their social and physical environment.

How accurate Marx's predictions have been is largely a matter of interpretation. As to his short-term predictions and 'prophecies', Bernstein was one of the first to point out how many of them went awry. The evolution of the capitalist system took a different shape from that which Marx anticipated, the middle class was not eliminated, the theory of increasing misery was proved to be wrong in so far as the standard of the working classes rose and continues to rise. His ideas on contemporaneous events may well excite our astonishment and sometimes a reflection perhaps of ('scientifically') dissimulated chauvinist sentiment; thus his support of Germany in the war against France in 1870, and his view that Germany might leave out the historical stage of bourgeois supremacy in the transition. Marx's prophecies almost always proved to be unfortunate and Engels admitted towards the end of his life that sometimes they had been 'overstatements'.

In view of all this, how is one to understand what Marx himself said in the second *Thesis on Feuerbach*? He stated: 'The question whether objective [*gegenständliche*] truth can be attributed to human thinking is not a question of theory but is a *practical* question. In practice man must prove the truth, that is, the reality and power, the this-sidedness [*Diesseitigkeit*] of his teaching. The dispute over the reality or non-reality of thinking which is isolated from practice is a purely scholastic question.'[64] In passing, one is tempted to ask whether this same formula would itself not act as a guillotine for Marx and Engels on the basis of their numerous 'errors' in prediction. And should not this application be decisive in their exclusion from occupying honoured places at the inception and elaboration of an ideology? As in so many other areas the post-Marx generations, beginning with Lenin, contrived to transform weakness into strength and changed even this into a *diabolus ex machina*. Since this particular question is so crucial for all latter-day Marxist-Leninists, we feel justified at this point in anticipating our next chapters with the following comments.

From Lenin onwards, by way of amplifying the substance and implications of the second *Thesis*, the 'salvaging' of marxism has been achieved through the concept of social practice which becomes the decisive verificatory criterion of theory. In fact the concept of practice (in the dialectical relation of theory and practice) becomes central to the whole subsequent ideological development. The conclusions of theory must be correlated with the achievement of practice based on theory.[65] If practice (a conscious activity of man which influences the world, events, and causes their change) brings results different from those suggested by theory, then the theory is wrong, and untrue (truth being defined as the correspondence of our notions with objective reality). And the corollary: the theory corresponds with truth as objective truth and must be proven by the ultimate and highest criterion – practice. Thus theory and practice are regarded as basic philosophical categories depicting the spiritual aspects of socio-historical processes of perception and transformation of the world, and are two basic sides of a unified, specifically human, reflection of the world. Their relative separation is of great importance but must not be made absolute.

If the concept were to be rigorously applied many of the theories of Marx and Engels would have to be totally rejected and forgotten, as would their authors. But this built-in safety-valve in the theoretical system explaining and/or justifying errors,[66] a real *deus ex machina*, has enabled the doctrine to survive its failures and conferred upon it those self-perpetuating qualities that are integral parts of the base of any ideology. This extenuating concept itself rests on two premises:

1 Practice is a criterion of both an absolute and a relative nature, absolute inasmuch as all that is proved by practice is objective truth, and relative in the sense that practice in any historical epoch cannot fully confirm or contradict certain theoretical assumptions: only future practice can do this.

2 There are two kinds of truth: absolute and relative, both of them being understood as two mutually supporting aspects of the process of discovery of objective truth. They, that is to say absolute and relative truth, cannot exist without one another and each of them presumes the existence of the other. Truth can be reached only through relative truth, in which a grain of

absolute truth can be found. But absolute truth in this sense has not yet been attained. Approximation to it will proceed as mankind, through a process of sifting relative truth, accumulates progressively the grains of absolute truth.

Does not, therefore, the second *Thesis on Feuerbach* directly spur on the continuing revision of doctrine in accordance with ceaselessly evolving objective reality? How otherwise, if the corrective factor of practice is denied, could the theory retain its relevance?

Lenin, for one, did not hesitate to rely on this crucial relationship and his contribution to Marx's doctrine differed from it so much that 'marxism' had to be restyled 'Marxism-Leninism'.[67] Apart from Lenin, contemporary marxism used this formula to so arbitrary a degree that the basic tenet of historical materialism has been gradually abandoned. Theory was divorced from practice and, instead of discovering the dialectic in it, the dialectic was imposed on practice.[68] The interpretation of history became '*une scholastique de la totalité*' and the theory of action '*une pratique terroriste*', banishing everything that was in disagreement with its principles.

In order to justify this dogmatic scheme, which is purely an *a priori* one, contemporary marxism seizes upon and attaches itself to vulgar materialism. The dialectic of history is interpreted as one empirical fact among others, impressing itself on the mind in the way that 'colours cause a photo-chemical reaction on the retina'.[69] Dialectic, as we have remarked, is imposed upon history, rather than its discovery being achieved through painstaking analysis. Historical materialism becomes a static 'ideology' which is 'officially revised' only if its divergence from the practice becomes embarrassingly obvious. Attempts are no longer made to prove and justify the necessity and universality of dialectic; its validity is assumed.

This basic contradiction in contemporary marxism devalues the work of Marx and Engels since in this sense, above all others, Marx and Engels were themselves not marxists.[70] But let it also be said that without this contradiction perhaps few shreds of marxism would have survived and the ruling ideology of the East would have to have a different, less legitimate, label.

At this point we leave the epistemological question. If the attention paid to this aspect may seem to have been unduly close, it is, in our view, no closer than the intimate relationship between it and the thought of Marx and Engels would warrant.

There are reasons to believe that Marx intended a much broader conception than that to be found in his legacy. In 1903 Kautsky, in *Neue Zeit*,[71] published for the first time that project which Marx had outlined in 1857 when he returned to his interrupted theoretical studies. The scheme that Marx had in mind at that point is significant in its originality and breadth of conception:

1 The abstract characteristics common to all forms of society, taking into account their historical aspects.
2 The main constituent elements of the internal structure of bourgeois society, upon which the basic social classes rest – capital, wage labour, and landed property. Town and country. The three great social classes. The exchange between them. Circulation. Credit.
3 Crystallisation of bourgeois society in the form of the State. The 'unproductive classes'. Taxation. Public debt. Public credit. Population. Colonies. Emigration.
4 International relations of production. International division of labour. International exchange. Exports and Imports. Exchange.
5 The world market and crisis.

Although he did not keep faithfully to the letter of this scheme, the main line of development is sufficiently clear: the historically grounded general sociology[72] (*sub* 1); the sociology and political economy of capitalist society (*sub* 2); the theory of state with its internal and external functions (*sub* 3); and, last but not least (*sub* 4 and 5), the theory of international relations, their economic foundations, the world market as a unifying scheme and the concept of crisis, on which probably the theory of conflict, or change in general, could rest.

This project can be regarded as one of the earliest attempts to depict society as a structured whole (albeit previously a bourgeois society) and on that basis to explain social change both in terms of its occurrence in individual societies and in terms and at the level of their interaction. It is with this notion in mind that Marx's writing is sometimes regarded as a pioneer work in the field of structural-functional analysis.[73]

A noticeable revival of interest in Marx's theoretical scheme has been the subject of recent comment[74] and contrasts with its declining intellectual appeal as a political creed. In consequence we shall dwell on the subject in a later chapter. Part of our purpose in interposing

Marx's own project of the theoretical structure of his works at this juncture is to draw certain necessary inferences before proceeding. It may be remarked that the projected scheme seems to be far removed from the dogmatically constituted 'component parts of marxism'[75] based on Engels's interpretation and further modified by Lenin. With the project before us nothing would seem to be more alien to Marx's way of thinking than that partitioning of his doctrine into 'self-contained' units neglectful of their interactions that has characterised its appropriation by the East. Indeed, Marx and Engels have some-times been castigated for failing to distinguish between individual disciplines, apparently unaware that in the traditional sense each one may exist autonomously and boast its own method. The fact that for Marx and Engels they flow into one dialectical method is regarded by critics as far too general and imprecise.[76]

When Lenin characterised marxism as a unity of three parts, 1 dialectical materialism and historical materialism 2 political economy and 3 scientific socialism (later called scientific com-munism to accommodate also the theory of transformation from socialism to communism), one has to wonder, once again, whether even in this context Marx would not have said that he did not want to be a 'marxist'. In this tripartite division the vast doctrine has become perhaps more manageable but also more susceptible to vulgarisation and departure from Marx's original thought.[77]

The fact that there is no particular monograph in which Marx and Engels may be said to have concentrated exclusively on the pheno-menon of international relations, and that their references to international relations must be sought mainly in that part of their doctrine called historical materialism,[78] does not in itself indicate that Marx and Engels were unaware of international relations and their importance, or that they would have been disinclined to have devoted more attention to them. It might indeed be thought that such an awareness is implied in the framework of Marx's 1857 project. If Marx had lived longer or had found time to write about them he would certainly have had no inhibitions whatsoever about doing so. Not only was he convinced that there were no serious barriers in the way of human knowledge, but the surmounting of present ones he regarded as imperative. 'Science should not be an egoistic pleasure. Those who are fortunate enough to be able to devote themselves to scientific work [and he regarded himself as a scientist *par excellence*] should be the first to apply their knowledge in the service of humanity.'[79]

The world in general, rather than international relations, plays a very important role in all of their studies. Quite understandably, at least until 1848, he and Engels restricted their interest to European affairs. Eurocentrism continued in their later outlook but their interest widened – amazingly for their time – beyond European boundaries. In 1852 Marx wrote to a friend: 'One could not choose a better time to come into the world than this moment. Both of us shall have had our heads chopped off or be shabby with age by the time it is possible to go from London to Calcutta in seven days. And Australia, and California, and the Pacific Ocean! The citizens of the new world will be unable to imagine how small our world was!'[80] The world as a global system could alone provide the framework within which the realisation of Marx's vision could take place; state divisions are temporary and in the long run unimportant. These, Marx for the sake of his argument can forget, and, as in *Capital*, regard the world as a potential integral unit; the whole world is treated as if it were 'one nation' and, so conceptualised, easier for him to study than its parts.

The divisions of mankind into states and nations, which will here be referred to as horizontal divisions,[81] are derivative, an epiphenomenon of the vertical divisions into classes. It should be noted, however, that in his youth, Marx, like Hegel, at first emphasised the state, and only later did he develop the concept of class (cf. the familiar statement, 'Man is the world of man, the state, society').[82]

The somewhat tortuous windings of the path one has to follow through his work in search of the concept of international relations – derivative as they are thought to be in terms of their origin and importance – may be best embarked upon at that traditional juncture where we first meet the 'quasi-hegelian picture'[83] of historical materialism that Marx sketched in the 1859 *Preface to a Contribution to the Critique of Political Economy*.[84] It is perhaps the only place where Marx provided the outline of his theory in its essential entirety. From this outline it is made very plain that classes, and by no means nations or states, are the basic units for investigation and it is the struggle between classes, not international conflict, that focuses the attention. (It is worthy of note that neither state nor nations, nor international relations are even mentioned.) Marx's theory traces a pattern in the historic class struggle moving through successive stages in the evolution of society as determined by conflict: Asiatic, ancient, feudal, capitalist and socialist. Marx anticipated any later critic who

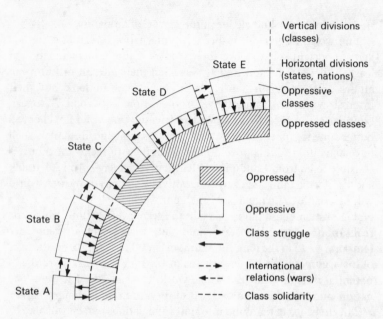

Figure 2 Horizontal and vertical divisions of mankind according to
          Marx and Engels

might point to the apparent incompatibility of some of the discrepancies in the development sequence with the dialectic. He made it very clear[85] that 'these abstractions have in themselves no value whatsoever', they can only serve to 'facilitate the arrangement of historical material', and that 'they by no means afford a recipe or a scheme'. Thus partly admitting that this scheme is nothing but a research framework, and well aware of the inconsistencies within the pattern, Marx concentrates on the capitalist society, that is to say, the 'present' of his and Engels's time which they regard as the last historical form of the antagonistic society.

The emphasis that Marx placed on economic structure was by no means new and notions in that regard had already quite a pedigree when he came to write on the subject. Marx's contribution to an economic tradition established by his precursors was the context within which the economic structure was placed. This was a context of historical development and within that matrix he attempted to classify human societies in terms of their own economic systems. Where international relations come into this picture will be obvious from

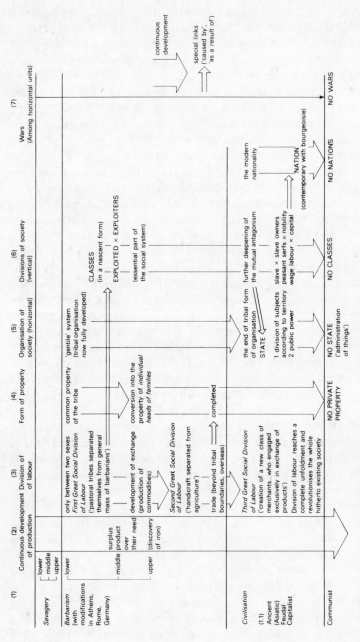

Figure 3 Marx and Engels's periodisation of human history

Figure 3 where two separate periodisations of the development of mankind are related (i.e. Marx's quadruple division from the Preface (column 1.1), and Engels's division (following Darwin-Morgan 1) into the stages of savagery, barbarism and civilisation, each subdivided in its turn.[86]

Although production was now regarded as the main determining factor, at least since barbarism, Engels admits[87] that before that there were other determinants such as the complex rules governing sexual reproduction that had nothing to do with material production. However, this 'darwinian-morganite addition' to Marx's thesis of historical materialism does not concern us here. Figure 3 spans the period from barbarism to civilisation,[88] from which point the marxian periodisation (ancient, Asiatic, feudal, modern bourgeois) follows. 'Asiatic' fits only imperfectly into this system. In a letter of much later date[89] Marx is clearly aware that owing to the absence of private property, the Asiatic system of production lacks an intrinsic dialectical factor of internal change and so does not conform to the dialectical pattern. He reaches the conclusion that the missing precipitant (of change) in static, unchanging Asiatic society must be found elsewhere – European colonialism. However inhuman and objectionable on moral grounds, this will be the instrument of socialist victory and the trigger of change even in these areas – a fact that understandably finds no favour with maoists. As for the onset of the communist revolution, he argued, elements of the European proletariat[90] would be obliged to assume control of some colonies to set in train the necessary preparations for independence.

In all other respects, the division of labour that reflects the development of production is, in Marx's own words, conceived of as being 'one of the chief factors in historical development up till now'.[91] This is so both within the state and in the international arena, since both state and international relations are the results of the concept of division of labour. The question inevitably arises as to how such potent and far-reaching developments can flow from this one notion and we turn for an answer to Marx's own definition and argument. He writes of this division of labour concept as a 'fixation of social activity, this consolidation of what we ourselves produce into an objective power above us, growing out of control thwarting our expectations, bringing to naught our calculations'.[92] At that initial stage of production where a surplus product is first achieved,[93] which is to say in tribal communist society, classes, albeit in embryonic form, come into existence. 'The first great cleavage of society into an exploiting and an exploited class . . . continued during the whole period of civilization.'[94] From this premise the argument proceeds: the common property of the tribe is gradually transformed into the private property of the individual heads of families as a result of which class divisions are strengthened. Reinforced by two further 'great social divisions of labour', the development of private property is completed and, acting in parallel with the transformation, the antagonism between the two classes reaches a pitch where only the institution of a state is a viable alternative to unremitting class struggle. The state as an organisation of the most powerful, economically predominant class replaces and differs from the tribal kinship form of organisation in the organisation of its subjects along territorial lines, and the creation of a public power which is no longer tantamount to the totality of an armed population. It is readily to be remarked that this resembles in no way Hegel's deification of the state; indeed the very opposite: the state that we have here is another form of human alienation, 'a machine for keeping down the oppressed exploited class'. Far from being a power forced upon society from without, the state exists as an admission that society has 'become entangled in absolute contradiction with itself'.[95]

Marx wrote modestly to the effect that he had not been responsible for the discovery of classes since 'long before the bourgeois historians had described the historical development of this class struggle and bourgeois economists the economic anatomy of the classes'. He credits himself in his own words only for proving:

1 That the existence of classes is only bound up with *particular, historic phases in the development of production.*
2 That the class struggle necessarily leads to the *dictatorship of the proletariat.*
3 That this dictatorship itself only constitutes the transition to the *abolition of all classes* and to a *classless society.*[96]

It is unfortunate that he did not leave us a definition of class. Probably aware of the fact that a concept so crucial to his theories should be given adequate treatment, he set out to devote an entire chapter to the subject in the manuscript of *Das Kapital*. His illness and death intervened and such few references as he was able to draft including his question 'What constitutes a class?' were taken up and answered later by his successors, and, among them, Lenin.[97] Otherwise we are left to scan Marx's own very ambiguous context: a context that has given rise to many conflicting interpretations and reconstructions of 'race', 'psychological', 'cultural' and other such definitions.[98]

But this is to emphasise marginal factors where beyond any doubt economic criteria are decisive for this concept of class. The dialectical contradiction emanating from the economic relationship between the two basic classes provides the main lever for development. 'Every advance in production is at the same time a retrogression in the condition of the oppressed class, that is, of the great majority . . .: each new emancipation of one class always means a new oppression of another class.'[99]

A 'psychological' factor, however, does come into the argument in two-stage form *'an sich – für sich'*. This factor was first introduced by Moses Mendelsohn (1729–86) and then further elaborated by Kant and Hegel: the progression is from the stage of mere potentiality (*an sich*) as in for example a seed, to actuality (*für sich*) – the seed changed into a flower. *Klasse an sich*, therefore, is that stage where the class exists in terms of sharing certain economic characteristics, with conflict potential which is, however, only a necessary condition (*conditio sine qua non*) for the transformation into *Klasse für sich*, which is to say the clear perception of a shared interest and common antagonism *vis-à-vis* other classes, together with the necessary knowledge for promoting these interests.[100]

The class consists of individuals but only in so far as they 'have to carry on a common battle against another class; otherwise they are on hostile terms with each other as competitors'. On the other hand, the class in its turn achieves an 'independent existence over against the separate individuals' so that the latter find their condition of existence predestined, hence have their position in life and their personal development assigned to them by their class, and become 'subsumed under it'.[101] Thus the class is seen not as a mere aggregation of the individuals of which it consists, but is a unit of a different, qualitatively higher nature.

Every society is ultimately stratified into two basic organised classes. There are other classes and strata, and Marx gives their number variously as two or five (in *Eighteenth Brumaire*), or four (in *Manifesto*). However, they are of lesser importance and gravitate towards the basic dualism. Although later in his studies, Marx took greater account of the multiplicity of society this dualism remains basic to his thinking on the subject. Classes are never regarded as immutable monolithic formations but are forever changing and developing, while one common element remains the integrative force. Another stage of development of the social division of labour[102] created the situation where 'the state was invented',[103] as an institution that would perpetuate not only the newly rising class division of society, but also the right of possessing class to exploit the non-possessing classes and the 'rule of the former over the latter'. [104]

The historico-economic sequence leading from division of labour, through private property to classes each one emanating from the other, calls for a further step in the sequential line of development – the state. The state apparatus was not known in tribal society where there were no soldiers, gendarmes, or policemen, no nobility, kings, regents, prefects or judges, no prisons, no lawsuits – and where affairs still contrived to run smoothly. [105]

The horizontal division into states, nations (and Marx and Engels use these two together with 'country' interchangeably) is thus only a surface projection of the basic conflict between classes and serves only to conceal the real struggle underneath. 'The state is only a transitional institution which is used in the struggle, in the revolution, to hold down one's adversaries by force, it is pure nonsense to talk of a free people's state.'[106] Indeed, Marx thinks a people's state would be a contradiction in terms. The use of the word state should therefore be discontinued and Marx suggests the German '*Gemeinwesen*', or the French '*commune*'. Marx himself, however, does not consistently observe this stricture and asks for instance in the *Critique of the Gotha Programme*: 'What transformation will the state [sic!] undergo in the communist society?'[107]

Whatever the semantics of Marx's position might be in this regard, the reasoning behind the eventual disappearance of the state as we understand it is not difficult to follow. The state is an expression of political power, there will be no more political power properly so called, since political power is 'precisely the official expression of antagonism in civil society'. [108] The proletariat seizes political power and turns the means of production into state property.[109] But in so doing it eliminates itself as proletariat, eliminates all class distinctions and class antagonisms, and eliminates also the state as state. Society, thus far based upon class antagonism, had need of the state: that is to say, of an organisation of the particular class which was for the time being the exploiting class, an organisation for the purpose of preventing any interference from without with the existing conditions of production, and therefore, more specifically, for the purpose of forcibly keeping the exploited classes in a condition of oppression to correspond with the given mode of production (slavery, serfdom, wage labour). Or, to put it another way: 'the state was the official representative of society as a whole. . . . When at last it has become the real representative it has also made itself redundant . . . state interference in social relations becomes, in one domain after another progressively superfluous, and it extinguishes itself of its own accord. . . . The state is not "abolished", *it dies out*.'[110] The whole machinery of state will be put where it then belongs: 'into the museum of antiquities, by the side of the spinning-wheel and the bronze-axe'.[111]

There is nothing immutable about the so-called socialist society, pointed out Engels,[112] like all other social formations, it should be conceived of as being in a state of constant flux and change. 'The crucial difference between it and the present order consists naturally in production organised on the basis of common ownership by the nation of all means of production.' Between this communist society and the capitalist society there is, however, a period of revolutionary transformation, to which Marx and Engels devote some attention (more than to the actual outcome of the revolution). The transition breaks down into three stages:

1 The period of revolutionary dictatorship of the proletariat, when capitalist strongholds are destroyed and new institutions introduced.
2 Socialism as a first phase of communism. The new institutions are consolidated, still bearing features of capitalism, the dictatorship of the proletariat continues 'stamped with the birthmarks of the old society from whose womb it emerges'.
3 The second phase of communism, communism in the proper sense of the word, based on the principle 'from each according to *his* capacity, to each according to his need' as a motto.[113]

In a communist society, accumulated labour is but a means of widening, of enriching, of advancing the life of the labourer and society, 'an association, in which the free development of each is the condition for the free development of all'.[114] Communism is the beginning of true human development in that scale of progression or ascent of man from the kingdom of necessity to the kingdom of freedom.[115]

To the bare concept of state-political power in the early works in general, and in the *Manifesto* in particular, Marx later added a dimension of state-political machinery for class oppression. The state continues as an apparatus of social enslavement even when it tends towards state capitalism and assumes the ownership of parts of the industry. The employers, however, remain bourgeoisie and their oppressive dominion is merely extended in scope.[116] Beyond these conclusions and the concept of political power confined to the state there is little or no attempt at this stage to identify central power nodes, to isolate individual power holders, to enlarge on additional (non-coercive) functions the state might perform, or to distinguish other organisations wielding influence on the decision-making process.

Although the state is a resultant of economic situations, there operates between the two an interaction analogous to that between superstructure and basis.[117] That is to say the state is not an altogether passive derivative. It reacts on economic phenomena and can influence them in the sense of retarding or accelerating the effect of economic forces (for example through such instruments as protection, free trade, financial measures, and so on). However, in Marx and Engels's perception it can never substantially modify the irresistible economic currents.

The capitalist system above all is in the very forefront of Marx's interest. He sees its operation all around him, and although he admits that there are certain differences ('it is different in the Prusso-German Empire from what it is in Switzerland and different in England from what it is in the United States'), their shared characteristics, 'based on the same modern bourgeois society, only one more or less capitalistically developed',[118] are what matters. With this in mind we can understand that neither Marx nor Engels should have developed any classification of the countries of their contemporary world. 'Advanced' countries (obviously West European), 'backward' but beginning to develop their modern economies (Russia, Turkey), and 'backward and stagnant economically' (without much chance of development unless influenced from outside), these are perhaps the broad categories of Marx and Engels's thought in this regard. Marx's terminology concerning his non-European studies is even more primitive: 'barbarian', 'semi-barbarian', 'the East', 'nations of peasants', are labels he very often uses in this regard.

Nations are also historical, ephemeral units, although their derivative position is made far less clear than in the case of states. Sometimes the intricacy of the argument results in confusion of the two concepts while in other contexts the terms 'nation' and 'state' are used interchangeably from the outset.

The appearance of nations in Europe is conceived as a development that paralleled the appearance of the bourgeois class (Figure 3, column 6) whereas with a clear distinction made between nation and nationality, the latter is regarded as being much the earlier in origin – a view that would appear to find expression in such passages as: 'unproductive as these four hundred years appear to have been [until the ninth century] they, nevertheless, left one great product behind them: the modern nationalities, the refashioning and regrouping of West-European humanity for impending history. The Germans in fact had infused new life into Europe . . . raising new nationalities out of the muck of the Roman world.'[119]

Since nations do not relate readily to the central concept of class, any acknowledgment at all of their existence must have been difficult to extend. Although he referred to them as 'these imaginary units',[120] Marx rather unfairly never hesitated to ascribe certain characteristics as general attributes to individual nations.[121]

The intractability of the problem is clear yet a theoretical link between the concepts of state and nation had to be established. With a certain ingenuity a common denominator was found: in any historical period there was always one class whose own advantage coincided with the 'national interest' which is ultimately reducible to the interest of society in the improvement and better exploitation of the means of production. At that point class met nation.[122] The dominance of a ruling class had national justification as long as it served economic progress and there is indeed an expression for it: 'a national class', which describes the phenomenon of the proletariat raising itself to the position of a 'national class, constituting itself as the nation'. Until that point, however, the proletariat 'in England as in France, in America as in Germany . . . was stripped of every trace of national character';[123] workers have no nationality. The bonds of class also transcend national boundaries and the fiction of belonging to a state and/or nation is a privilege of the ruling class alone.

Marx and Engels are certainly not theoreticians on nationalities. Descriptions of national and racial problems as 'natural' features, 'innate characteristics' which will be done away with historically; of race which 'is itself an economic factor'[124] are among their most obscure statements.

Some of the most widely agreed criteria of nation and national appear to leave both Marx and Engels unimpressed. When within the International a question from the discussion on the subject arose as to whether the German-speaking members should have a section in the International, Marx was much against the idea, on the grounds that linguistic distinctions were 'arbitrary'. As an example he pointed to Jews and Saxons living in Hungary who were trying to preserve 'an absurd nationality within an alien country'. The language factor was certainly not a sufficient guarantee of national unity.

Nor were territorial claims based on historical rights sufficient. In 1871, when Prussia demanded the cession of Alsace and Lorraine by France on such grounds, Marx was known to have made remarks against such claims and the justification adduced in their support.[125] Similarly, he regarded as 'altogether an absurdity and anachronism to make military considerations the principle by which the boundaries of nations are to be fixed': 'If this rule were to prevail, Austria would be still entitled to Venetia.' If this were the criterion 'there will be no end to claims, because every military line is necessarily faulty, and may be improved by annexing some more outlying territory.'[126]

However, his attitude to the national question changed a great deal during his lifetime as he came to realise[127] that nations were a fact and had to be treated as such. They certainly were no fantasy. In 1871 Marx denied that the 'unity of the nation' would be disturbed by the victorious proletariat. So the dictum from the *Manifesto*, 'the working men have no country . . . we cannot take from them what they have not got,[128] had certainly come in for some modulation. Moreover, the importance of national feelings could not be ignored and had to be taken account of in drafting political programmes. Indeed it transpired that national sanction for political action was a matter of requirement: 'the working class must organise itself at home as *a class*. . . . In so far as its class struggle is national, not in substance, but as the *Communist Manifesto* says, "in form".'[129] Besides, national boundaries, as much as any other of the horizontal divisions, suffered continued erosion at the hands of the capitalist system itself as 'national one-sidedness and narrowness' came increasingly into collision or obstructed the path of development of the capitalist mode of production.

The principle of national self-determination and the interpretative gloss placed upon it by Lenin in particular, is in Marx virtually non-existent. Its accordance by Marx is on a highly discriminative basis and dependent mainly on the potential of the nation or nationality concerned: 'The very first conditions of national existence' included 'large numbers and compactness of territory', and additional requirements, according to Marx, were resources, ability, specialisation, so as to facilitate the creation of a rich and proliferated society.[130] Thus the right to separate statehood would belong only to nations capable of developing modern economies. And certainly as far as Marx was concerned it was to be denied to small nations, and to the Austrian Slavs in particular, unless they were incorporated within a greater Pan-Slav empire.

Marx acknowledges national discrimination only as a form (albeit minor) of human oppression since the principal source of it is, again, class exploitation. 'Hungarians shall not be free, nor the Poles, nor the Italians as long as the worker remains a slave.'[131] The separation of Ireland from England was not possible, because of the economic dependence of Ireland, a circumstance to be doubly deplored since Marx denounced the 'most abominable reign of terror' of England in Ireland.[132] National movements should and could be, therefore, channelled in such a way as to run parallel with the international aims of socialism.[133] In case of a clash, the latter must of course take precedence.

Division of labour as we have already remarked has its expression not only 'inside a nation'[134] but 'these same conditions are to be seen (given a more developed intercourse) in the relations of different nations to one another'. According to Marx, 'the whole inner organisation of nations with their international relations' is nothing other than 'the expression of a particular division of labour' bound to change with changes in the division of labour.[135]

In the same passage Marx is very indignant with Proudhon, who, although he was aware of division of labour, did not see its consequence, which is to say the world market. The world market is conceived to transform the whole world in due course into one global capitalist stage where the inherent contradictions are now more intensive than hitherto. 'This market has given an immense development to commerce, to navigation, to communication by land. This development has, in its turn, reacted on the extension of industry; and in proportion as industry, commerce, navigation, railways extended, in the same proportion the bourgeoisie developed, increased its capital, and pushed into the background every class handed down from the Middle Ages.'[136]

The inherent need for larger and larger markets for the placement of its products drove the bourgeoisie over the whole surface of the globe, 'It must nestle everywhere, settle everywhere, establish connections everywhere.'[137] 'As the world is round, this seems to have been completed by the colonisation of California and Australia and the opening up of China and Japan.'[138] Thus, 'in the 16th century, with the opening of a world market . . . the modern history of capital begins'.[139]

Engels goes into even greater detail: 'Large scale industry has brought the peoples of the earth into relations one with another, has transformed the hundred-and-one small local markets into one huge world market, has everywhere introduced civilization and progress, and has arranged matters in such a way that when anything happens in the civilized countries, the events have their repercussions in all other lands. Suppose, e.g. the workers of England and of France were to win their liberty today, this would cause revolutions to occur throughout the world which in course of time would lead to the emancipation of all other workers likewise.'[140]

What is this world market, 'this power which so baffled the German theoreticians?', asks Marx. He explains it in terms of its being an alien power, a 'pressure which was conceived of as a dirty trick on the part of the so-called universal spirit but it is', he goes on, 'nothing of the sort'. He understands it as a mere extension of the contradictions of the capitalist system to a wider plane. . . . The bourgeoisie, as a result of its power and natural tendency to expand, draws all, 'even the most barbarian nations into civilization' (i.e. civilization of a bourgeois nature). All nations, rather than become overwhelmed and crushed, must adopt the bourgeois mode of production and thus become bourgeois themselves. And just as it had created a hierarchy of dependence within its state (town on country, etc.), 'so it has made barbarian and semi-barbarian countries dependent on the civilized ones, nations of peasant on nations of bourgeois, the East on the West'.[141]

Apparently, the world market will continue to exist alongside the capitalist division of labour and private property, and therefore also with the state. Only after the communist revolution, which will start off with abolishing private property, will 'this power' (the world market) be dissolved: 'the various national and local barriers will be dissolved and the individual will be brought in practical connection with the material and intellectual production of the whole world'. Alienated powers, be it classes, states, nations, or world market – derivatives of the division of labour – stand between man and nature and, since he has to act through them, he is enslaved by them. The communist revolution by sweeping them all away will enable man 'to control and master these powers'. Inevitably we ask ourselves whether in this allusive context Marx believes that they will not be abolished but rather become transformed in a manner analogous to the process of 'dying out' of the state. We will search in vain for an answer.

The states are seen as being pushed into interaction in international relations by the same forces that brought them into existence – those generated by the capitalist system. Capitalist production simply has to expand into international relations since by that agency alone lies its future hope for development. Understandably, therefore, international relations are seen at one and the same time as contributing to the expansion of the capitalist system and also intensifying the contradictions within the system that will ultimately engineer its downfall. In this manner will the communist revolution be heralded whose society will know no classes, no states, no world market, *ergo* no international relations.

International relations, as long as class conflict is a determinant of their processes, will have a twofold thrust and nature:

1 The bourgeoisie has to fight not only with the other classes within its state, but, in the international sphere, will be in perpetual conflict with 'the bourgeoisie of foreign countries'. (The international relations of capitalist countries are a result of 'foreign policies in pursuit of criminal designs, playing upon national prejudices and squandering in piratical wars the people's blood and treasure'.)[142]

2 Marginally, however, a certain degree of inter-state (inter-bourgeois) co-operation is indicated, although unlike the proletariat, the bourgeoisie has by no means the same degree of international coherence which would prevent them from fighting each other across national frontiers. The bourgeoisie can temporarily unite only against its worst enemy, the international proletariat. 'The bourgeoisie . . . is already linked up in brotherhood against it [international workers' movement] with

the bourgeois of all other countries – and Herr Bismarck's
international policy of conspiracy!'[143]

A conflict having the nature of the first category can subsequently
assume the features of the second: 'after the most tremendous war of
modern times [this apropos of the French-Prussian War of 1870],
the conquering and the conquered hosts should fraternise for the
common massacre of the proletariat – this unparalleled event does
indicate, not, as Bismarck thinks, the final repression of a new society
upheaving, but the crumbling into dust of bourgeois society. The
highest heroic effort of which old society is still capable is national
war; and this is now proved to be a mere governmental humbug,
intending to defer the struggle of classes, and to be thrown aside as
soon as the class struggle bursts out into civil war. Class struggle is no
longer able to disguise itself in a national uniform, the national
Governments are as one against the proletariat.'[144]

On the other hand, the degree of class cohesion enjoyed by the
proletariat is in inverse ratio to that of the bourgeoisie. Their typical
inter-class attitude is one of loyalty: 'The proletariat has in all
countries one and the same interest, one and the same enemy . . . the
proletarians are, in the great mass, by nature without national
prejudice, and their whole upbringing and movement are essentially
humanitarian, anti-national. Only the proletarians can destroy
nationality.'[145] (Here nationality means obviously the state or
national distinction where they do not coincide.) On the other hand,
there is evidence to show that Marx realised that the Irish worker, for
example, hated the English worker (a sign of false consciousness).[146]
This is a case of a marginal attitude that can be conquered by
improved knowledge and enhanced consciousness of class.

As far as international relations are concerned it may well be
appreciated that Marx believes them to be in a state of 'constant battle'
and this conflict theory forms an integral part of his attitude. Wars are
strongly denounced by both Marx and Engels. War existed on the
inter-tribal level long before the emergence of the state but 'the wealth
of neighbours'[147] (the economic nexus once again) 'excited the greed
of the peoples who began to regard the acquisition of wealth as one of
the main purposes in life'. Accordingly the character of tribal wars
changed from simple 'avenging aggression' or as 'means of enlarging
territory that had become inadequate', to a 'regular profession',
waged for the sake of 'plunder alone'.

Marx and Engels accepted the common distinction between just and unjust wars; all being unjust except:

1 The war of the enslaved against their enslavers, the only justifiable war in history.[148]
2 Defensive wars of various kinds.[149]

Offensive wars are unjust, even in the case of a victorious proletariat attempting to 'force blessings of any kind upon any foreign nations'.[150] If this were to occur, the proletariat would undermine its own victory in so doing (sic!) except in cases where considerations of defence were involved. But Marx realises that to deprive the nation of the power of offence means to deprive it also of the means of defence[151] and his conclusion that 'you must not only garrotte but murder' suggests a complete pessimism as far as doing away with wars in a capitalist society is concerned.

Since revolution then as now falls into a conflict category of its own – and from the marxian point of view into the sub-category of justifiable wars (those waged by the enslaved against their enslavers) – we will devote some attention to it. Before doing so, it is necessary to pause a moment to examine the eve of the revolution, the activity ultimately leading to the revolution and the international workers' movement from the point of view of international relations.

In the *Address on the Civil War in France*, in particular, Marx developed the concept of an international labour movement, the rationale for which lay in the fact that the bourgeoisie, locked in 'constant battle with the foreign bourgeoisie', is compelled to solicit help from the proletariat who, dragged thus into the political arena by an element for whom they will act as future 'gravediggers', will be instructed by the class in the elements of its own general and political craft. Furthermore, it was envisaged that at the time when the decisive hour draws near, 'a small section of the ruling class cuts itself adrift and joins the revolutionary class'. This small section would contain some of the 'bourgeois ideologists, who have raised themselves to the level of comprehending theoretically the historical movement as a whole'.[152] (In this way the role of Marx and similar ideologues both of proletarian and of non-proletarian origin is explained.) To be able to fight at all, the working class must be organised:

1 First of all at home as a class, since its own country is the

immediate arena of its struggle.[153]

2 But, continues Marx, 'the framework of the present day national state', e.g. the German Empire, is itself in its turn economically 'within the framework' of the world market, 'within the framework' of the system of states. National and international are inseparable: 'Every businessman knows that the German trade is at the same time foreign trade and the greatness of Herr Bismarck in the national German sense obviously 'consists, to be sure, precisely in his pursuing a kind of *international* policy'. To talk, therefore, says Marx about the internationalism of the proletariat only in terms of '*international brotherhood of peoples*' without 'a word . . . *about the international functions* of the German working class' means a serious reduction of the meaning of internationalism of the proletariat.

The element of strength that the proletariat automatically possesses is a numerical one. It was the realisation that their efforts are doomed if they are incoherent that 'prompted the working man of different countries assembled on September 28, 1864, to found the International Association', which was conceived as a co-ordinating centre of an advisory nature, and which would 'intervene in the foreign policies of their respective countries, watch the diplomatic acts of their governments, counteract them, if necessary, by all means in their power to combine in simultaneous denunciation, master mysteries of international politics and vindicate the simple laws of morale and justice, which ought to govern relations of private individuals, as the laws paramount of the intercourse of nations'.[154]

Although Marx claimed[155] that the International was an attempt – the very first one – to create 'a central organ' in this first historical form, it remained 'nothing but the international bond'[156] between the most progressive working men throughout the various countries of the civilised world. The members of the International were conceived 'naturally' to stand in the forefront of any class struggle and act as its vanguard, but the international activity of the working classes would not in any way depend on the existence of the International Working Men's Association. The international workers' movement was seen to constitute an objective factor which governments, in order to stamp out, 'would have to stamp out the despotism of capital over labour – the conditions of their own parasitical existence'.[157] The subjective factor, their organisation, was not seen to be so crucial. Thus Engels could say with some truth after the fall of the Paris Commune and the dismemberment of the International Association, 'today the German proletariat does not need any official organisation, either public or secret', since the 'simple self-evident interconnection of like-minded class comrades suffices, without any rules, boards, resolutions or other tangible forms'. The day to day growth and increasing menace of the 'athletic figure of the German Proletariat', already foreseen by Marx in 1844, would be capable by itself of 'shaking the whole German Empire to its foundations'.[158]

Thus Marx and Engels conceive of a sequential development for the international workers' movement whose structural formations in the first stage would be characterised by sects, justifiable (historically) so long as the working class is not yet ripe for an independent historical movement.[159] The sects were succeeded in the next stage by an international association whose path had been cleared by history which 'had already smashed sectarianism'. And yet it was the disruptive activity of sects within the International which destroyed it, thus bearing evidence of history's repetitive process and testimony to Marx's dictum: 'What is antiquated tries to re-establish itself and maintain its position within the newly acquired form.'[160]

After 1871, however, with the International largely a spent force,[161] a further stage was reached in the development of the movement. In spite of the expulsion of Bakunin in 1876 the endless squabbles between him and Marx had made apparent the many internecine cleavages and its deterioration (as Engels put it) to a 'naïve conjunction of all factions' resulted in its dissolution in that year. The successor organisation, this time founded without Marx's assistance in 1889, once again took on the aspect of an international organisation as an institution. In so doing it reverted to that earlier institutional concept prior to the interim period (1872–89) of an emphasis on objective development at the expense of subjective organisation. A simultaneous advance might thus be understood to have taken place, not only forward but also upwards – taking place, as it were, on a spiral.

But wherever the emphasis, whether structured institutionally or objective and structurally amorphous, no power could deny to the proletariat its rightful place. In the long run even war itself would retreat[162] before the alliance of the working classes of all countries. The united international proletariat will be capable of something without historical precedent: as capitalist governments rush headlong 'into fratricidal feud', the proletariat, as demonstrated in the Franco-German war, will 'send each other messages of peace and goodwill'. In contrast to the old society with its economic misery and political turmoil, the new (communist) society will have peace as an international rallying cry 'because its national ruler will be everywhere the same – Labour'. The International Association was seen as a pioneer of this New Order.[163]

Marx set standards of analysis of revolutionary movements and of comparative[164] revolutionary studies that sociologists since have been hard put to match. He conducted a survey across the entire spectrum of social change, and the perceptiveness and relevance of its insights and central features are only now appreciated. In so far as these have a bearing on international relations both in our present understanding of these and in the disputed place occupied by international relations in Marx and Engels's thinking, they are of direct concern to us at this point. Disparity in the pace of development between the material productive forces and that of existing relations of production was understood to cause a deterioration into conflict at some point and initiate an epoch of social revolution.[165] Thus revolution attends the transition from one mode of production to another. The concept of revolutionary change means here that a new set of relations of production come into existence (in contrast to a mere evolutionary change which would not qualitatively change their nature). All previous revolutions (i.e. between antiquity and feudal system, feudal system and capitalist system) were only 'political' revolutions, in which one class gave itself the fiction of representing the interests of the whole of society. It was, however, only a question of redistributing power, without basically affecting the scheme of exploited versus exploiters, whether the former were slaves, serfs, or proletarians, and the latter slave owners, nobility, or capitalists. Thus 'in all revolutions up till now the mode of activity remained unscathed and it was only a question of . . . a different distribution of labour to other persons'.[166]

In contrast to all previous revolutions, the communist revolution would not be based on any such fiction and so in a real sense it would have ceased to be 'political': 'the communist revolution is directed against the preceding mode of activity, does away with *labour* and abolishes the rule of all classes with the classes themselves', the reason being, and however complicated this may sound, that 'it is carried through by the class which no longer counts as a class in society, is not recognised as a class, and is in itself the expression of the dissolution of all classes, nationalities, etc., within present society'.[167] This is necessary, Marx goes on to say, since the *ruling* class can be overthrown in no other way but by revolution; alone in that way can its successor class get rid of 'all the muck of ages and become fitted to found society anew'.

Out of this basic outline, many 'operational' questions arose. First of all there was the question of the co-ordination of national and international revolutionary movements or, in other words, how to go about starting the revolution. Marx and Engels seem to be quite consistent on this issue: the struggle will be in 'form, though not in substance' primarily a national struggle inasmuch as the proletarians of every country 'must, of course, first of all settle accounts with its own bourgeoisie'.[168] As late as 1875 this strategy that assumed the 'immediate arena' to be their own country remained unaltered, although given 'the interconnections of the world market', there were clear indications that the organisation of the struggle would have to encompass the international dimension as well.[169] Second, in answer to the question as to whether the revolution was to be violent or whether circumstances could smooth its path without recourse to violence there was a certain equivocation. The dictates of the *Manifesto* certainly prescribed violence: (communists) 'openly declare that their ends can be attained only by the forcible overthrow of all existing social conditions. Let the ruling classes tremble at a Communist revolution.'[170] Although the inflammatory nature of the *Manifesto* must be taken into account similar remarks can be found scattered throughout other works, as, for example, *Class War in France*, *The Eighteenth Brumaire* or *German Ideology* which were not published until much later. 'Combat or death; bloody struggle or extinction. It is thus that the question is irresistibly put.'[171] And as late as 1867, in the first volume of *Capital*, there appears the famous dictum, 'force is the midwife of every old society pregnant with a new one'.[172] But it takes no particularly discerning reader to perceive Marx's distaste for violence, which he regards as an often necessary but avoidable evil. Thus he welcomed the fact that the leaders of the Paris Commune were 'chosen by universal suffrage'.[173] 'We shall proceed against you [i.e. the capitalist governments] by peaceful means where possible, and by force of arms if necessary.'[174] 'We know that the institutions, the manners and the customs of the various countries must be considered, and we do not deny that there are countries like England and America, where the worker may attain his object [i.e. the capture of political power] by peaceful means. But not in all countries is this the case.'[175]

Third, the question as to where Marx and Engels expected the revolutionary outbreak to occur poses itself. In this respect they had to change their predictions several times. Initially (before 1848) it might take place in France, but the central stage would be highly industrialised England with the rest of the world waiting in the wings for their cue. After the failure of the revolutions of 1848, and the non-participation of England in these, although this pattern had to be changed it never became bold or decisive. Sometimes Germany assumed the central place in their hopes but a more favourite locus appeared to be France. Obviously in order not to discourage the Russian marxists, Marx, late in life (1882) in a preface to a Russian edition of *Manifesto* considered Russia as 'the starting-point to communist development' but made this quite clearly contingent on the eventuality that 'the Russian Revolution becomes the signal for a proletarian revolution in the West, so that both complement each other'.[176] Marx and Engels must often have been taken aback as developments failed to come into accord with the belief that the rise of political tension would parallel that of economic development and that the most economically developed country would hence become the revolutionary epicentre. Prediction after prediction failed to materialise, although on occasions, when at last the integers seemed to have fallen into place, they felt that they could 'almost calculate the moment'.[177]

A fourth question following that of operational milieu concerns the anticipated chain of events as forces unleashed drove outwards from the centre. 'Empirically, communism is only possible as the act of the dominant peoples "all at once" and simultaneously, which presupposes the universal development of productive forces and the world intercourse bound up with communism'[178] or 'this is to be a universal revolution, and will, therefore, have the whole world as a field for operation'.[179] There are many more references to this particular feature regarding the dispersion of revolutionary force and momentum to the ends of the earth to show that the development was absolutely taken for granted. Revolution would be world-wide. Perhaps, admits Engels,[180] 'it will start in all the civilised countries of the world, or at least in Great Britain, the United States, France and Germany, but at one and the same time. It will take a longer or shorter time in each of these countries, according to the degree of industrial development in the respective countries, and in doing so the rest of the world will be influenced so that their development towards the same revolution will be hastened. Every social reform remains a utopia until the proletarian revolution and the feudalistic counter-revolution measure swords in the world war.'[181]

One is prompted to enquire from whence the conviction arose in the minds of both men that the revolution must inevitably assume global dimensions and that no alternative course of action existed. 'In societies as in nature, nothing takes place in isolation. Everything affects and is affected by every other thing, and it is mostly because of this manifold motion and interaction that one is unable to see the simplest things.' Large-scale industry, the world market, 'has linked up the peoples of the earth . . . so that each of them is dependent on what happens in other lands. Further, the social development of all civilised countries has become so similar that everywhere the struggle . . . between the two classes upon which the issue depends, has become the dominating struggle of the day. . . . This is to be a universal revolution.' And – 'the revolution is imminent'.[182] The problem as they saw it was not so much whether the revolution would have a world character as in trying to anticipate the main obstacles it would encounter on the way. If communism wins in Europe, and capitalism continues in Asia, wondered Marx in a letter to Engels, 'is it not bound to be crushed in this little corner, considering that in a far greater territory the movement of bourgeois society is still on the ascendant?'[183] It was concluded that the two systems would have to face each other as irreconcilable enemies. The chain of reasoning is not difficult to follow, but more important to our purposes is the fact that it is from these conclusions and by following the reasoning that leads to them that we derive our information and our notions on their theory of international relations.

Raymond Aron has said that Marx's work is like history, 'equivocal and inexhaustible'.[184] While in agreement with Aron's simile and choice of adjectives one could add that Marx's work is also 'inexhaustibly equivocal'. Since there are so many questions immediately arising out of an investigation of Marx and Engels's 'theory of international relations' and its implications, to say that there were 'unresolved tensions' among them[185] is putting it mildly.

The first comment that one could make is that the communist revolution took place in a country where Marx and Engels would least have expected it, and contrary also to their expectations it certainly did not assume world-wide proportions. Since in the area where it took place it was required to coexist alongside its irreconcilable enemy, the capitalist system, the basic components of the original vision of Marx and Engels – particularly those with an international relations bearing – had to undergo a transformation at the hands of Marxism-Leninism that changed it almost beyond recognition. The nature of the contemporary environment and that of the international relations that emanate from and take place within it offer a most serious challenge to the original ideas of both men. If we revert to our horizontal-vertical matrix (Figure 2) the nature of this challenge may be made clearer. In the light of what has been said above on the subject let us now examine more closely the validity of the divisions (horizontal-vertical) and discover the degree of consistency in their interaction.

Marx's vision of the unity of human society undivided by alienated dehumanised powers and built on the total rejection of vertical divisions into classes would seem necessarily to lead to a rejection of the horizontal divisions. Although Berki attempts to show that it may not make sense in terms of Marx's thought to talk about non-antagonistic diversity[186] Marx himself makes it clear that the possibility of such a development could not be excluded. In *Capital, III*, Marx admits as conceivable the possibility that although the economic basis may be uniform, its surface reflection might show 'infinite variations, and gradation . . . in its appearance, natural conditions, race relations, outside historical influences, and so forth'. More puzzling, or more enlightening, depending on the viewpoint, is Marx's and subsequently Engels's reference to a particular passage in the *Gotha Programme* which they both generally criticised in harsh terms. The passage in question refers to 'the elimination of all social and political inequality' as one of the objects of the German workers' party. The criticism offered to this by both Marx and Engels coincided, with slight variation. Instead of this 'indefinite concluding phrase', Marx would have substituted 'with the abolition of class distinctions all social and political inequality arising from them would disappear of itself[!]'.[187] In a letter to Bebel Engels enlarges on this idea: 'Between one country and another, one province and another and even one locality and another there will always exist a *certain* inequality in the conditions of life, which it will be possible to reduce to a minimum but never entirely remove. . . . The idea of a socialist

57

state as the realm of *equality* is a one-sided French idea resting upon the old "liberty, equality, fraternity" – an idea which was justified as a *stage of development* in its own time and place . . . but which . . . should now be overcome, for it only produces confusion in people's heads.'[188]

Were Marx and Engels in fact distinguishing between two kinds of 'social and political inequality'?

1 That which will 'disappear of itself' with the abolition of class distinctions.
2 That which is the result of 'certain' inequality in the conditions of life which will be always, albeit in a minimal form, present.

But these inequalities by definition could not be 'political'. Engels gives an example of differences in geographical conditions. ('Alpine dwellers will always have different conditions of life from those of people living on plains.') Are we to understand that geographical conditions as a part of the social basis[189] will have a direct effect on the ('surface') superstructure? (In capitalist society the function of the environment was acknowledged only through the mode of production.)[190] Could the 'geographical divisions of labour' not develop into another 'fixation of social activity'[191] which could achieve an independent existence over and above individuals, forced upon them and by which they were shackled (i.e. the 'definition' of alienated power)?

In any case in this context it might be observed that Marx's attitude towards the division of labour appears to have been a little unrealistic, if not to say inconsistent. Advocating as he does amateurism, he sees as an ideal in the communist society a situation where each individual will be able to do 'one thing today and another tomorrow, to hunt in the morning, fish in the afternoon, rear cattle in the evening, criticise after dinner' without ever becoming 'hunter, fisherman, shepherd, or critic'. Is it possible that Marx could have attributed such diversity to the human intellect, such an equal distribution of faculties? Or was it a clumsy, imperfectly thought out notion having some relevance to the position of individuals only, and without application to the communities – whatever they might be called – into which society was to be organised? And yet Marx seems always prepared to draw this parallel between the levels where the individual interacts, and the level of international relations as if the same rules operated and were applicable at both levels: 'the simple laws of morals and justice, which ought to govern the relations of private individuals, as the rules paramount of the intercourse of nations'.[192] Nor can the idea of such mutually applicable laws be easily contradicted. Even if the envisioned communist society contrived to achieve such a state of wealth that some of the consequences of the division of labour would vanish altogether one can hardly conceive of an end to the division of labour on that wider international or inter-community scale – which would in any case counter their notion of 'universal interconnections'. Engels himself talks about the separate existence of 'countries, provinces, localities' possessing a certain degree of inequality. But surely once one admits the separate existence of communities the central moral argument against diversity on whatever grounds is in jeopardy. Clearly after the communist revolution the world would have to be organised and it is difficult to see how this organisation is to be accomplished without some 'administrative' units[193] on the horizontal level. In the total absence of vertical divisions (i.e. classes), after the communist revolution, this new division of labour – and indeed it would have to be a division of labour on a horizontal level – would come very much into prominence by contrast with those periods when international relations were a mere projection of all-determining vertical divisions.

In particular Engels failed to show an absolute coincidence of classes and states on the one hand, with wars on the other. In an attempt to bring historical materialism into harmony with Darwin's theories of evolution, Engels in *The Origin* admits that prior to that fraction of human history covered by historical materialism, forces other than class struggle did exist. Although it would be reaching too far to compare the stage of primitive communism with that of the communism of plenty, we may still justifiably regard as significant Engels's admission that inter-tribal warfare, long before the emergence of classes and states, flourished with 'the cruelty that distinguished man from animals'.[194] 'War was as old as the simultaneous existence alongside each other of several groups of communities.'[195] Where 'no treaty of peace existed' wars were waged for such reasons as 'avenging aggression', 'enlarging the territory', etc., where motivation could not derive from (as yet non-existent) vertical divisions. The assumption that the abundant communist society of the future would eliminate 'pure human greed' is based on the premise that private property (hence vertical divisions) are tantamount to 'all evil in human nature'. If we accept this even with reservations, we have to accept the possibility of conflicts even on the horizontal level.

Marx's condemnation of vertical divisions in society is quite unequivocal, unlike his attitude to those on the horizontal. In the aftermath of the communist revolution and period of dictatorship of the proletariat, the state – and hence inter-state relationships – would have to exist. And what is more, it is assumed (by 'communist colonial policy')[196] that the fraternal assistance of the proletarian state will be extended to other states to help them accelerate their own revolutions. Even if the revolution were not to sweep across the world a decisive war was expected to follow its advent (in this context it is not quite clear where Marx's statement regarding the victorious proletariat 'forcing any blessing on any nation'[197] fits).

Anticipated developments following in the train of the revolution further reveal Marx's projection. There are three possible alternative situations that may follow upon the period of the dictatorship of the proletariat.

1 Unity of mankind with no vertical and horizontal divisions
   (horizontal non-antagonistic being negligible).
2 Continuous horizontal diversity with tendency to:
   2.1 continuous inter-unit relations, despite the internal
       structure of the units;
   2.2 absorption of all units in one or more larger 'nations'.

Marx seems not to have taken seriously, nor rejected out of hand, the last alternative (2.2). At least judging from the incident that he describes to Engels in a reference to Lafargue, who, 'by the negation of nationalities . . . appeared, quite unconsciously, to understand their absorption into the model French nation'.[198]

It is more difficult to decide whether Marx and Engels favoured the remaining alternatives (1 and 2.1).

The notion of the unity of mankind with no vertical and horizontal divisions seems to be one of the basic assumptions of Marx's philosophical system. The four aspects of alienation: man alienated from nature (alienated labour), from himself and his own activity (self-estrangement), from his 'species being' or from his being as a member of the human species (objectification of man's species life), and from man (alienation from another man),[199] can only be overcome within the context of a global framework and in their totality, otherwise human nature 'remains captive to it and infected by it'.[200] '*Communism* as the *positive* transcendence [*Aufhebung*] of *private property*, as *human self-estrangement*, and therefore as the real *appropriation of the human essence* by and for man; communism therefore as the complete return of man to himself as a *social* (i.e. human) being – a return become conscious, and accomplished within the entire wealth of previous development. This communism, as fully developed naturalism, equals humanism, and as fully developed humanism equals naturalism; it is the *genuine* resolution of the conflict between man and nature and between man and man – the true resolution of the strife between existence and essence, between objectification and self-confirmation, between freedom and necessity, between the individual and the species. Communism is the riddle of history solved, and it knows itself to be this solution.'[201] Universal human emancipation[202] can be achieved only after the 'positive transcendence of all estrangement – that is to say, the *return of man from religion, family, state, etc.* [author's italics] to his *human*, i.e. *social* mode of existence'[203] when he is delivered from these 'alienated powers'. 'Not the gods, not nature, but only man himself can be this alien power over man.'[204]

Berki suggests that horizontal antagonism may be inferred particularly from some of Marx's early writings. '*Private property* is . . . the product, the result, the necessary consequence of *alienated* labour, of the external relation of the worker to nature and to himself.'[205] The point Berki tries to make is that one can extend the basic scheme of society divided by the existence of private property to cover a wider area. He thinks only 'two shifts' of the theory are necessary:

Instead of Marx's

whole nation (community, society) . . .	the whole world of societies
based on private property . . .	based on ownership by a group or part of a whole.

The 'internal structure' (without private property) of each of these societies, says Berki, is immaterial, and ownership by society would mean the exclusion of others from this ownership. The antagonism among those horizontal groups would derive from the existence of 'private property' in this extended sense. The conclusion appears inescapable, he asserts: 'an economically integrated world still consisting of separate nations is, whatever the internal structure of these nations, a *capitalist world*'.[206] The solution (Berki's) will be seen to be based on an assumption that Marx's thesis of absolute dependence of international antagonism on domestic strife cannot be accepted.

This conclusion seems to be corroborated by another, more common, argument in Western literature: the 'disappearance' of dialectic. Marx speaks of communism as the true beginning of human history, in contrast to the conflict-ridden 'human prehistory', but would it not confirm the accusation that Marx's dialectic was after all only epistemological, with no ontological counterpart, if all of a sudden in communist society the dialectical forces ceased to operate? If on the other hand new stages of human conflict obeying the laws of dialectic were to be unfolded in the aftermath of communist revolution, Berki's suggestion would imply a mere shift of the dialectical forces onto a different (higher?) level. Otherwise the notion of communism would – as has been pointed out many times – devalue the whole point Marx and Engels were trying so hard to make. Engels's statement: 'if all contradictions are once and for all disposed of, we shall arrive at so-called absolute truth – world history will be at an end . . . [but] it has to continue, although there is nothing left for it to do – hence, a new, insoluble contradiction',[207] is not particularly helpful.

The two polar attitudes traceable in Marx's work (1 and 2.1)[208] are nowhere explicitly reconciled by Marx and the only thing which it is possible to establish is that he tended to move across the continuum towards the second attitude: that is to say from the early vision of men in an undivided world, which undoubtedly runs throughout his work and imparts a moral climax to his theories, to the gradual, and reluctant acknowledgment of the existence of some horizontal divisions even after the communist revolution. The acknowledgment, if at first a matter of strategical expedience, becomes later due to the realisation that the existence of horizontal divisions, be they nations or other administrative units, is not so simply reducible to a derivation from vertical divisions as the theory would have wished.

CHAPTER 3

Theory of international relations in the East

> The Golden Age is the most unlikely of all dreams that have
> been, but for it men have given up all their life and strength. . . .
> Without it the people will not live and cannot die.
>
> Feodor Mikhailovich Dostoyevsky

In the course of dealing with Marx and Engels's ideas on international relations in the previous chapter, we tried to unravel some of the intricately woven strands of the theoretical tapestry. Thus, following the necessary prefatory remarks, we offered a reconstruction of their thought concerning 'the nature, conduct of, and influence upon, relations among individuals or groups operating in a particular arena . . . and . . . the nature of, and the change factors affecting, the interaction among them'.[1] We drew attention to the position of the two thinkers in relation to such central areas as: what groupings are perceived to operate in the world arena, their role, mode of interdependence and operation; what is the nature of that world arena in which they move, relate to one another, and generally have their being; what are the forces that maintain, disrupt, and transform that world, and, finally, the question as to the nature of such change – and degree of human control thereof. Perhaps, therefore, as we now broach the question of international relations theory in the East such doubts as the reader may have had as to the respectability and length of the theoretical lineage in that part of the world – or indeed as to whether the work of Marx and Engels did incorporate a theory of international relations at all – may already have been dispelled.[2]

As we now turn to consider the theoretical constructs of the Soviet and East European part of the world we make the further observation that, in addition to the intricacy of Marx and Engels's writings on the subject of international relations, no small part of the resultant

63

interpretative confusion has been a result of the fact that the translation of theory into practice has been in the hands of generations of political leaders, rather than by scholars in the same line. It is thus not difficult to understand the emphasis placed by some Western writers on the pragmatic aspects of the doctrine and its usefulness to the policy-maker as an instrument for the opportunistic manipulation of the environment and events, rather than a prism through which to interpret the world.

With these considerations in mind, we shall turn in the present chapter to an investigation of the various ways in which generations of Marx's 'heirs' have from their variously oriented theoretical or 'practical' standpoints superimposed their own referents on the original doctrine and have interpreted and reinterpreted it accordingly. We will discuss first Lenin then Stalin and will proceed to a consideration of contemporary Soviet Marxist-Leninists. Limitations of space will preclude more than a brief reference to maoist marxists, although it is fully realised that the maoist theoretical contribution would warrant quite as much attention as that which we propose to give to their Soviet Marxist-Leninist counterparts. Similarly, and again mainly for reasons of space, we omit the Western marxists as well as various other schools of thought who claim Marx as their intellectual progenitor.

At this point a brief comment in regard to how profound the difference in theoretical positions, and how long the road that has been travelled between Marx as the original point of departure and the Soviet Marxist-Leninists as the last way station along the route, might be in order. The divergent conclusions of the lone scholar abstracted from his world of ideas and those of a power elite having reference to, and operational sway over, a great part of the globe are difficult to grasp and bear in one's mind, much less hold together in sufficient proximity to facilitate comparison. Broadly speaking, we would suggest that the main difference between the theories of Marx and those of contemporary Soviet Marxism-Leninism is that, in parallel with its maoist counterpart, the latter is an ideological paradigm of theory of international relations, while the former – Marx's thoughts drawn together into an integrated whole – takes the form rather of a reformist social doctrine. Immediately we are again involved in the question of definition of some central terms. Theory – as we have shown in Chapter 1 – was one such term; doctrine and ideology (as in our present context) are others. It follows also that related notions such as 'culture' and 'value structure' and, logically, the mutual relationships of all of these terms assume a variety of forms. In these circumstances, and short of devoting entire chapters to summarising and surveying the more common Western usages, the only sound course of action would seem to be to follow Bertrand de Jouvenel's advice and simply decide for ourselves the meanings to be ascribed to such expressions.[3] Special difficulties arise in this present context since part of our task must of necessity be the establishment of some correspondence between the concepts and terminology as used by both sides.

We meet least difficulty when we attempt first of all to deal with the term 'doctrine'. We propose to use it to signify a type of theory *sui generis*: the distinction between theory and doctrine is not seen to rest on differences of substantive content but rather on attitudes towards propositions and the role assigned to them. Where propositions are regarded simply as the product or as the hand tools of scholarship – that is to say where they are related solely to intellectual activity – they will constitute a theory. Where, however, they become a guide to action, they will be taken as more likely to constitute a doctrine.[4] In illustration let us briefly recapitulate Chapter 1. We identified there four functions of theory[5] and now, faithful to those distinctions, let us suggest that the type of theory which claims not only taxonomic, explanatory, and predictive powers but also a controlling function, would conform to our definition of a doctrine. Accordingly, Marx's and Engels's theory is pre-eminently a doctrine: a claim that might be even more persuasively argued if the central position it occupies with such facility at the ideological heart of an entire political movement is borne in mind. And, in this vexed question of terminology we can go no further without attempting to discuss the much used, abused, and confused term, ideology.

Daniel Bell in an amusing selection of examples of Western uses and abuses of the word demonstrates the near meaninglessness of the term ideology and makes it abundantly clear how difficult it would be to arrive at any widely accepted Western agreement on the subject.[6] This is not to overlook a certain agreement as to the *functions* of ideology, which are generally seen as a provision of a counter model of the particular society (or explanation of what is wrong), a Utopian model (or how the society should be reassembled), and an action-oriented model (an operational plan for the destruction of the old society and the realisation of the ideal). Recognising the marginal value of 'definitions', we propose here to approach the notion of ideology from a Marxist-Leninist angle. We will hope in so doing to establish a correspondence or terminological bridging between the two sides and also to throw light on Western confusion on the subject. We shall do this under the following headings: 1 Ideology, social consciousness, culture, and value systems. 2 Ideology and the political system. 3 Ideology and theory or doctrine. 4 Ideology as a paradigm of theory of international relations.

1   Ideology and social consciousness, culture and value systems

The basic explanation of these terms is to be sought within the formidable structures of Marxism-Leninism in those parts of dialectical materialism dealing with epistemology which, in order to avoid confusion with 'bourgeois' theory, is referred to as gnoseology.[7] Gnoseology is simply another name for epistemology, and our proposal to use the term here is consistent with established usage in Marxist-Leninist writing – it appears also in some English translations of that literature. Although the Marxist-Leninist approach to ideology via social consciousness, social existence, among other concepts, brings with it its own uncertainties it has not gained the attention in the West that it deserves, and some explanatory attempt here is therefore not out of place.

It is the problem of oversimplification – and consequent distortion – to which we have referred in regard to Marxist-Leninist textbooks in the East rather than the complex highly specialised expositions that so often puzzle the West that afflicts the general reader in the Soviet Union and East Europe. The complexities of Marxism-Leninism are elucidated frequently in collectively written (to the point of anonymity), often oversimplified but accessible textbooks that undergo periodic re-edition. There are very few communists on any level of the Party hierarchy who would have actually acquired their knowledge of Marxism-Leninism from the original works. This may be attributable not only to the degree of relative difficulty involved but also to the great divergences from these sources of current Marxist-Leninist thought. The difficulty we shall experience then derives in large part from the fact that standard Soviet and East European textbooks go either to extremes of oversimplification and impart no more than a smattering of the subject, or are directed at a more formally trained readership. These latter texts, mainly monographs and articles in philosophical journals, explore and debate controversial issues arising from virtually all aspects of the following exposition. In an attempt to clarify the problem we offer the gist of the argument in the form of a chart and the accompanying text should be read as its legend. [8]

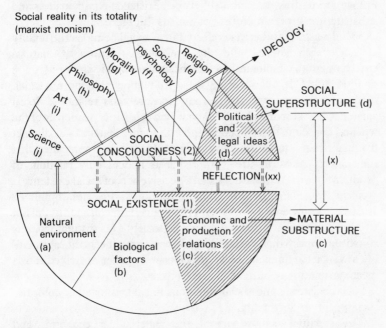

Figure 4 Marxist-Leninist 'gnoseology'

Marxism-Leninism (and we should emphasise that the following account is more leninist than marxist) [9] claims to be monistic in that, unlike some other philosophical schools, it recognises one social reality and not two substances. Thus the distinction it makes between material and spiritual (ideal) is claimed to be gnoseological (which is to say, epistemological) not ontological and absolute: the sole purpose of the distinction is to enable an identification of the primary and secondary role of the two substances to be made. Thus Marxism-Leninism distinguishes between social existence and social consciousness where social existence is primary in so far as its priority of origin and importance is concerned: social existence is *reflected* by social consciousness. Partly as a result of inconsistencies in Marx's own usage of the term there has been and continues to be some confusion[10] as to the meaning of social consciousness, the most prevalent error being to confuse it with such terms as 'material substructure' (c), or even with ideology itself. It is mainly a Lenin innovation to draw the parallel between existence-consciousness and substructure-superstructure. Let us consult Figure 4.

Social existence (otherwise referred to as social being) is the totality of society's material life and relations (comprising natural environment (a), biological factors (b), and economic and production relations (c)).[11] In a class society these production relations into which men enter in the process of production are class relations. Social existence is that social phenomenon which exists independently of the will and consciousness of people and is therefore material – as distinct from spiritual – in nature. From Figure 4 it will be appreciated that the material substructure, comprising as it does only relations of production (c), is only a part, albeit a decisive one, of social existence.

Social consciousness is the totality of ideas, theories, opinions, attitudes, knowledge, emotions, etc. of a certain community, class, stratum, group, or indeed of the whole society's (as distinct from its constituent individual parts) consciousness that reflects the 'spiritual' life of a society. As such, social consciousness cannot be arrived at by a mere summation of individual consciousness.

Social existence and social consciousness taken together comprise social reality in its totality.

The spiritual counterpart of the material (or economic and production relations) substructure taken in conjunction with the material substructure, is alluded to as *social superstructure* (d), which term designates only those ideas (and institutions) of social consciousness that reflect the given relationships of production on which the existence of the social superstructure rests and is entirely dependent (i.e. political and legal ideas). The interrelationship between these terms – social existence, social consciousness, and material substructure – and social superstructure is indicated in Figure 4. The actual relation of social superstructure to material substructure (x in Figure 4) consists of the quintessential features of the life of society that act as determinants of the specific socio-political system. In precisely what way this reflection of social consciousness and social existence operates (xx in Figure 4) or finds its reflection in social superstructure and material substructure is not altogether clear and is a subject that continuously attracts and exercises Marxist-Leninist philosophers.[12] For our purposes it will have to suffice to say that 'reflection' denotes not only causality (as in for instance social existence taken as a cause – with social consciousness the effect, and, in like manner, the effect (social superstructure) being produced by material substructure (the cause)), but by 'reflection' is supposed to be meant also special creative human activity, somewhat in a functional sense – rather than being confined in meaning to a copy or simple mirror image. In this connection it will be noted that both social consciousness and social superstructure exercise considerable 'feedback' on social existence and material superstructure respectively and thus their dependence is far from complete.

Where, in all of this, does ideology fit? Ideology is defined by Marxism-Leninism as a system of ideas and opinions (not necessarily theories since one can refer also to the ideologies of primitive peoples and of those less sophisticated ideas) held by *a certain social class or group about society as a whole*. Its purpose is to defend the interests of a class, to enhance its social position, or even to disturb the position of other classes and groups. Marxism-Leninism stresses, however, that not all ideas, opinions, attitudes, etc. included in social consciousness are necessarily ideological. Political and legal ideas are by their very nature bound to be so, but not necessarily is this true of other parts of social consciousness.[13] Thus for example science (j in Figure 4) should under certain circumstances have the capacity to become ideology-free and by virtue of this capacity assumes a special position within social consciousness.

Let us interrupt at this stage the flow of the Marxist-Leninist argument to return to a few comparative observations. In the first place it might be agreed that even this first glance at Marxism-Leninism justifies some tentative conclusions regarding the vexed question of terminological equivalence. Thus we would conclude, in full awareness of the wild terminological disorder prevailing in the West,[14] and with the proviso that the range of equivalence is over a select number of Western meanings, that social consciousness comes closest to the Western notion of 'culture'. If, for example, we take culture to mean a set of orientations of individuals within the society, encompassing their command of facts, their emotions, as well as their values, the Marxist-Leninist concept of social consciousness and the

Western concept of culture would be very near one another. Similarly close would be Almond and Powell's definition of political culture as a 'psychological dimension of the political system consisting of attitudes, beliefs, values and skills'.[15] Again in Schurmann's analysis we find a tolerable basis of comparison. Central to this writer's notion of 'culture' is the acknowledgment of a delicate interrelationship with ideology. Significant also is his identification of value structure as the conceptual compilation of values shared by most members of a society created over a period of time which is, during the revolutionary period, superseded by artificially created ideology. The coexistence and interaction of the old value structure and the new ideology in a dialectical relationship creates Schurmann's culture.[16] Clearly this is not altogether incompatible with the approach of the Marxist-Leninists which, in our understanding, sees social consciousness as designed to comprehend a similarly broad spectrum of views, opinions, etc. of all classes and strata within the given society: incorporated too within that approach is the notion of a flexible and constantly changing relationship and interaction with ideology. However, it is to be noted that the line drawn between ideology and culture does not always coincide with the Marxist-Leninist line of demarcation between social consciousness and ideology. The inclination to employ this quality of being shared by a particular social group or a whole community as the touchstone in determining whether beliefs, ideas and attitudes are ideological or not is shared by Plamenatz, who offers 'a generally accepted definition of ideology [as a] set of closely related beliefs or ideas, or even attitudes characteristic of a group or community'.[17] It would seem then reasonable to say that culture (as much as social consciousness) is generally regarded as a broader term in encompassing ideology or ideologies within it. And in this respect at least, there would be no grounds for difference between the Marxist-Leninist understanding and that of the West. But, these broader areas of compatibility aside, the Marxist-Leninist analysis differs fundamentally from many of its Western counterparts in so far as it takes account of the social conditioning of both ideology and social consciousness and considers them as derivatives of social existence (the lower semicircle in Figure 4). This view – that all ideas are conditioned, or indeed class conditioned and socially determined – is not unknown in the West but has been explored fully by only a few Western scholars, among them Scheler, Durkheim, Sorokin, and Mannheim.

The fact that emphasis on the social conditioning of ideology finds favour with Marxist-Leninist writers is understandable and its essential place in the chain of Marxist-Leninist reasoning becomes clear as we prepare to follow the next step in the argument, namely, the epistemological/sociological explanation of ideology which lies at the very heart of the rationale that gives to the proletariat a leading role in society.

2   Ideology and the political system

Given the epistemological explanation of the nature of ideology and social consciousness and the construction that places these as derivatives of social existence, the premises or assumptions of the Marxist-Leninist argument are as follows: that the proletariat is a uniquely privileged class; that the conception of society, and of the course of social change that favours the interests of the proletariat, are the only 'true' constructs; that, alone among classes, it is the destiny of that class to comprehend the course of social change and rise above false consciousness (that is to say a set of mistaken ideas shared by a group or sometimes by even a whole community).[18] This unique position allocated to the proletariat – and justified in terms of its standing in a special relationship to the means of production – has been embraced by generations of Soviet leaders as a vindication of their rule. Some Western scholars on the other hand have based their rebuttal on the same unimpeachable source – Marx's writings and his own emphasis on the social conditioning of ideas. Mannheim, for instance, noted that Marx's conclusion in regard to the special position occupied by the proletariat is not quite in keeping with the rest of Marx's doctrine, and indeed the reference does seem to present something of an inconsistency if not an outright contradiction: 'Marx, by claiming for his own theory a privilege he denied to others, showed that he did not fully understand why it is that thought about human behaviour is necessarily "relative".'[19] Thus Mannheim seems to evade the actual marxist argument as to why the proletariat's ideology should be exempted from the same 'relativist' treatment and why marxists would argue that the proletariat's unique position is fully consistent with the rest of the doctrine. In summary this argument rests basically on philosophical and moral grounds: there derives from the traditional marxist collectivist explanation of the nature of man[20]

71

the conclusion (on the basis of historical and dialectical materialism *in toto*) that only in a society with no private property, division of labour, or alienation (communism), can man for the first time achieve freedom and assert himself as a species. The proletariat, which is instrumental in the attainment of this, the objective moral goal of mankind as a whole, already represents and is the champion of interests that will be within the grasp of mankind once it has achieved communist society. The proletariat may thus be said to have already assumed a unique position. It should be reiterated that this moral argument is the actual rationale of the political system itself. The fact that the ascendancy of the proletariat is subject to considerable modification (if not indeed negated) when its privileged position is usurped by the party of the proletariat is of course another matter altogether – and one that is not without some justification in Marx.[21] However, it will be more appropriate to discuss more exactly how this shift was effected and rationalised in the section on Lenin.

In summary, and if we might here anticipate that section, let us review the Marxist-Leninist argument so far. Ideology is a system of ideas held by a certain class or group about society as a whole. Because it forms part of social consciousness – which is regarded as being determined by social existence – and because the crucial part of social existence is material substructure, comprising relations of production, it is conceived by logical progression that only the proletariat's ideology is the true one. Others are distorted, false. Thus the leading role of the proletariat's vanguard (the Party) becomes axiomatic and the cornerstone of the closed-circuit political system. This shift of emphasis to the Party, complete with philosophical accoutrements, has had the apparent effect of reducing concern for the relevance of questions that once clamoured for attention. These, such as the relationship between Party and proletariat, policies of recruitment to Party membership, and the whole question of Party organs, internal mechanisms, and institutional framework, assume now a very secondary position. In spite of the anomalies, the privileged position of the proletariat is jealously guarded and it is one question that is endlessly rehashed in all Marxist-Leninist deliberations. Moreover, although we would seek in vain in Marx's writings for the notion of the proletarian party wielding such political leadership in the aftermath of the revolution, the attribution of such power has become an integral part of the system and flows directly from Lenin's adaptation.

Characteristically, this is the terminal analytical point for the Soviet analysts while it represents the starting-point for Westerners. The former rehearse endlessly the whys and wherefores, and the explanations/justifications of the foundations of their political system while the latter concentrate on the analysis of the end-product, the system itself. We too, at this juncture, will 'change trains', leaving the Soviet analysis for the conclusions of Western sovietologists. The political system that emerges after the proletarian revolution, wherein Party is merged with state, and itself acts (in combination with an elaborate police apparatus) as a coercive instrumentality for enforcing conformity with an ideology that permeates every last cranny of the life of society, has been labelled 'totalitarian'. This description[22] by Western analysts denotes an East-West departure point where the philosophical justifications of Marxist-Leninists end and the socio-political institutions and techniques of ideological indoctrination and compulsion begin.

The totalitarian model as a conceptual approach to the analysis of the Soviet and East European political systems is, however, generally recognised to have had serious shortcomings – mainly because it was insufficiently flexible in its outline to permit account being taken of changes that occurred after Stalin's death in 1953. By focusing on the alleged overwhelming concentration of power in the higher echelons of the Party structures there was no room in the model for consideration of the intra-societal conflict and change from below. Nor, within the parameters of the totalitarian model, could the emergence of secondary power nodes and the development within the allegedly monolithic Soviet bloc of international relations among the bloc members be accommodated. The greater flexibility of some more recent conceptual approaches appears to have met with greater success in comprehending such recent developments; Barghoorn's 'almondian' analysis of Soviet society in which the author describes Soviet political culture as 'ideological-partisan, elitist and subject-participatory'[23] is one such model which is, in our opinion, a more useful framework of analysis. The Party's assumption of the leadership of society is implied in Barghoorn's 'elitist',[24] and his 'quasi-messianic political set[25] refers of course to the Communist Party, an elite whose inner elite arrogates to itself alone the right to formulate the official and authentic version of Marxism-Leninism. This is precisely the phenomenon which in the opinion of many marxist revisionists has placed the whole future development of Marxism-

Leninism at serious risk: the fact that Marxism-Leninism has become an amalgam of officially recognised theoretical pronouncements, has lost its capacity for response and hence the capability to develop in sympathy with change. It has become static in an environment undergoing fundamental change and, shielded from the revitalising, regenerative processes of criticism and scrutiny, the once dynamic earth-girdling and universally applicable message has been gradually transformed into the abstract dogma of a secular religion. The relationship, or rather reflection of social existence and social consciousness – to return to the Marxist-Leninist terminology – has been severed; its functioning interrupted.

The 'ideological-partisan' element in Barghoorn's framework of analysis turns on that demand by the Communist Party for total submission to the movement that leaves no room for partial, selective, or qualified commitment to the politically functionalised truth. And, finally, the culture is seen to be 'subject-participatory[26] inasmuch as it describes the subordinate relationship of all citizens to superiors next higher in one or more of the chains of command, and whose obligation it is to do their best to promote the performance of the collective to which they belong and advance its prescribed goals and objectives.

In this context we should note the crucial functioning and high priority assigned to programmes of political socialisation.[27] Barghoorn, among other commentators, has remarked on the Communist Party's having set in motion one of the most systematic overt political indoctrination programmes ever known in terms of educational institutions (from primary schools to universities) as in the political training of adults. This has as its sole object: 'to inculcate, reinforce, and when necessary, modify political beliefs and attitudes and with other channels of political communication to deepen the support for current Party policies by interpreting them in accordance with officially approved Marxism-Leninism'. In human terms it might even be said that the very elaborateness and explicitness of the ideology exercises a certain appeal since it lends definition and symmetry to the bewildering amorphousness of human experience, thus providing to those individuals (including the leaders) who may be uncertain or confused about their own ideas, a framework of identification and reference. From this framework 'escape is costly and difficult', as Almond tries elsewhere to demonstrate with examples of 'indoctrinated' Communist Party members in the West European countries, since, when Marxism-Leninism becomes one's only code, one 'has to destroy this-self to find a new one'.[28] Whether this syndrome applies only to extreme cases or to all, it becomes increasingly obvious that in the world of the intellect the same language is no longer spoken and nowhere is this more true than in that East-West culture division which has become one of the most significant and real divisions of the contemporary world.

The approach to Marx's doctrine and the way in which it is treated by the 'ideologues' (that is to say the extent to which it is incorporated into or suppressed from current ideological trends) is determined entirely by the political rulers and is certainly beyond the reach of permitted academic research. Indeed the ideologically based social practice has often been in overt contradiction to Marx's basic propositions. Significantly, this is less so with the ideas of Lenin, whose contribution to Marxism-Leninism receives a disproportionate share of emphasis and attention in contemporary political writing. Despite this, and since it is also the marxist part of Marxism-Leninism that is conceived to legitimise their rule, the leaders will insist on presenting themselves as the most authentic exponents of Marxism-Leninism. Indeed much of the insistence on the ideological basis of the East European culture can be traced to this concern and consideration for legitimisation. If it were otherwise the strict application of some of Marx's ideas (for example the belief in the overwhelming revolutionary solidarity of the world proletariat) to the approach and elucidation of world affairs could lead to serious mistakes.

Thus we can see, particularly against the background of ruling elite characteristics (closed, self-selective, self-perpetuating, etc.) that political power in the East is not based on a notion of legitimacy afforded by competitive political parties and universal suffrage in constitutional democracies but derives its 'legitimacy' from ideological considerations (the moral mission of achieving communism). In spite of the widely claimed notion of representation and accountability – that remains no more than a slogan – the mandate of a majority of the population is neither asked, given, nor required. That mandate is assumed under the rubric of ideological leadership. Hence the unending battle to preserve the authenticity, integrity, and authority of the ideology. Bearing this in mind, much that seems to be no more than meaningless 'quotation-mongering and political iconography'[29] that is sometimes seen in the West as a proof of the total inability of the leaders to think for themselves begins to make sense.

For the political rulers a dilemma presents itself at this juncture and a course has to be charted between the submission of the official version to free and critical discussion[30] or, on the other hand, run the risk of that version's over-sanctification. With the former course the attendant hazard might be ideological disintegration and the emergence of pluralism of interpretation incompatible with the required political monolithism. With the latter, there is the ever-present danger of an unrevised ideological statement becoming obsolescent and, at an increasing number of points, overtly irrelevant. As Brezhnev himself pointed out at the 24th Congress of the CPSU, 'the repetition of old definitions when they are outlived, incapability or unwillingness to adopt new approaches to new problems, all of this is damaging to our cause and creates additional possibility to disseminate revisionist distortions of Marxism-Leninism. The criticism of bourgeois and revisionist attacks on our theory and practice is more convincing if it is based on the creative development of social science and Marxist-Leninist theory.'[31]

In other words, the Soviet leader is here admitting quite explicitly the undermining effect that irrelevance could have on legitimacy, and that a failure to adapt would facilitate political '*coups d'état*' by rivals whose challenge would be offered in the name of restoration of ideological purity. Clearly any admission of obsolescence in the ideology, even if merely implied in the corrective measures designed to align it with the actual environment, could bring its own dangers; to this delicate task of realignment communist leaders have had recourse to such devices as the supplementation of ideological areas perceived to be lagging or deficient. These supplementary or interpretive variations are rationalised by appropriate quotations from the 'classics' and this practice has been facilitated and credibility lent by the ample interpretive range of which the ideas of Marx and Lenin are capable. It was after all from this very looseness in the conceptual fabric that allowed Marxism-Leninism to spring from marxism to be succeeded by stalinism, and to be returned to 'pure' Marxism-Leninism – and for each to lay claim to be more or less in direct line.

3   Ideology and theory or doctrine

The question now raised as to the relevance of marxist doctrine to the theories and postulates of his 'heirs' must wait for an answer until the distinction between, on the one hand, theory and doctrine and, on the other, ideology is clarified.

First of all ideology may be said to be analogous to a theory about politics or a doctrine. Moreover, both are clearly political in orientation and it would be as much a contradiction in terms to speak of a non-political ideology as it would be to refer to a non-political theory of politics. Each stands in a slightly different relationship to philosophy; for whereas theory may be regarded as an offshoot of a political argument, ideology has a philosophical content.[32] Thus, doctrine or theory and ideology are related and yet are at one and the same time distinct – the distinction becomes clear when we apply tests of comprehensiveness and consistency.[33] Surprisingly, a considerable agreement is apparent between Western and Marxist-Leninist analysts when the question of distinguishing between doctrine and ideology is discussed. Acknowledged by both is the fact of the inherent limitations of doctrine, limitations that result from its author's confinement within temporal limits and the inevitable imprecisions or ambiguities that flow from it and which an ideology – a day to day guide to action – cannot afford. Thus Brzezinski's comment repeats basically Lenin's own ideological creed that stresses the importance of being true to the 'spirit of the teaching' rather than to the letter.[34] It is however in this same quotation that Lenin goes on to say that the 'spirit of the teaching' is the 'marxist method of research'. It will be recalled from the previous chapter that this method of research (which is obviously the dialectic) is not only difficult to understand but the difficulty is compounded by interpretative confusion. Thus, to argue that Marx's contribution to the creation of an ideology lies in the provision of the dialectical method for it is not particularly meaningful. And yet Lenin's tradition in making this questionable distinction persists to this day. A recent statement by a Marxist-Leninist philosopher when repeating this distinguishing feature sees the 'marxite' (or 'marxian') approach as one searching for 'the philosophical ideas of Marx in the authentic shape, in their historical setting, which can be imitated and his phraseology copied'.[35] This 'copying of a highly individual style and unrepeatable approach to the problems of his particular time' is then seen to be quite futile. Instead, the true approach advocated is the so-called 'marxist orientation' which denotes 'the organic continuity of marxist real innovation as well as that of other representatives of the movement'. Thus, the partisans of the same ideology manifest different standpoints by 'agreeing on the basic issues, on points of view and on main objectives', but at the same time 'retain the freedom to confront this heritage with the state of the world today, with the development of modern science and culture and with the historical experience acquired since the time Marx formulated his ideas'.[36]

Thus it seems obvious that both Western and Eastern theories are agreed on three distinct and separate types of Marx-inspired or Marx-oriented approaches: marxian, marxologue and Marxist-Leninist. The marxian would try to 'imitate' and 'copy' Marx's highly individual style and, irrespective of change in the time intervening between Marx's and his own particular period, would seek to draw direct answers from Marx's teaching. A marxian approach to international relations for example would, strictly speaking, be that of disregard and profound inattention leading (if professed by a political leader) to constant breaches and the refusal to acknowledge international law, and the existence of nations, states, and interests based on them. The marxologue, on the other hand, concerned primarily with clarification of Marx's doctrine, would study Marx's thoughts within the framework of Marx's own time and particular historical circumstances without attempting to apply them to an understanding of his own time. Thus, the marxologue, after establishing the precise degree of Marx's disregard for international relations, states, and nations, would be best try to analyse why in his particular historical circumstances Marx felt the way he did. And finally, the Marxist-Leninist will extract from the works of Marx and Lenin the 'spirit of their teaching' and apply it freely to the problems of his own time, building in the process a colossus of changing ideas which, if presented as being shared by a class (or other social group), would be described by both West and East as ideology.[37] But of course this is precisely the nub. The root of the problem for the Western analyst (that is to say sovietologist or Marxist-Leninist theoretician/ apologist) is to answer the question as to who determines what exactly is meant by 'the spirit of the teaching' and how is the 'consent on the basic issues, points of view, and main objectives' to be arrived at. In the answer will lie also the key to understanding the difference between Marx's theory of international relations and that of the present Soviet Marxist-Leninists. In other words and with regard to our present study of theories of international relations it would mean determining who is to be credited with the task of unravelling Marx's complicated, often ambiguous, writing on the subject and deciding which parts remain of relevance and interest to the contemporary international relations theory of the Soviet world. The answer most often given by Western analysts is of interest since it seems to partake in some respects of Marx's own attitude and begins with the postulate that the movement's current ideologue must exercise, as well as an interpretative function, a controlling influence over it. Thus the intra-ideological struggles portrayed as being waged to preserve ideological integrity are by definition functions of, and coincide with, the political power struggle. *Ergo* (the Western argument would continue) considerations of ideology-making are necessarily of secondary importance: the victor determines future direction and course of action. Had, for example, Trotsky emerged triumphant instead of Stalin we might have expected to have been confronted with an entirely different ideological content – though the power implications would have been the same. From this it would appear to follow that such explicitly ideological theories of international relations as Marxist-Leninist ideology contains are useless. We now turn to a commentary of the extent to which such appearances may prove deceptive.

4   Ideology as a paradigm of theory of international relations

As has been suggested it is something of a paradox that in some respects the conclusions of a number of Western analysts revive Marx's own disdain for ideology. Where Marx used the term loosely and often under the rubric of false consciousness ideology gained a new respectability with Lenin that persists to the present day. Compare this with the pejorative connotations[38] attributed by Western political theorists who often refer to ideology as something which 'they' (the East) have while 'we' do not. Or, more recently, the era of ideology as a factor instrumental in assisting certain stages of political and economic growth which, once completed, the ideological schism narrows or neutralises. The two political systems are supposed to grow increasingly to resemble one another as ideology gives way to the rationale of advanced technology. Indeed, both of these opinions lead to the conclusion that in our field (theory of international relations) the utility of Marxist-Leninist ideological insights into an understanding of Soviet practice of international relations is quite negligible.

One might therefore be excused for asking why bother with an ideology, the content of which is so arbitrary and the congruence of which with the ideas of Marx, Engels, and Lenin depends only on compatibility with the requirements of the political leaders – especially since it has been agreed by many marxist revisionists and sovietologists that the most probable pattern of change in the East will be the broad persistence of the present system rather than a pattern of responsive, experimental reforms, along a spectrum ranging from liberalisation to democratisation. There is every indication to suggest that the Soviet political system as described above is not likely to undergo any dramatic change in the near future. Important questions arise here to which answers must be attempted: Is the West right in assuming that whatever is written on the subject of international relations by Soviet writers may be ignored? Can we conclude that all explicitly ideological theories of international relations – i.e. theories of international relations contained *within* an ideology – are *a priori* condemned to non-importance? In answering such questions we should on the other hand remember from our glance at the Soviet theory of knowledge that all social theories are supposed to be by definition ideological. And the question that flows from that proposition – is not the 'bourgeois' theory of international relations (which means any theory coming from the pen of a Western author) also by definition ideological in the Soviet Marxist-Leninist view? And, if there is no unity of opinion as to what constitutes a theory of international relations, which one of the existing theories would be the one representative of the pluralistic Western ideology?

Although there does seem at face value to be a strong case for giving up the attempt to come to grips with Soviet international relations theory on this basis[39] there are a number of considerations that render it not only of academic interest but of pressing Western concern to investigate further. In the first place we cannot expect an analysis of the transformation of thinking on international relations and accounting for all of the ideological vicissitudes, beginning with Marx through to contemporary Marxism-Leninism, from a Soviet pen. Furthermore, broad as it is, even a first glance would indicate that the concept of international relations, cutting one might say right across the ideology, might be a better, more revealing and even embarrassing index of change in Soviet marxist thinking. And how otherwise are we to assess the extent to which contemporary Marxism-Leninism may have departed from Marx's original doctrine? But these questions aside (and the following three sections, whose substance may be said to lie in the study of the history of ideas, will be devoted to finding answers to them), there is still another reason as to why the reader should bear with us as we attempt to make such an assessment. We believe that there is a basic inconsistency in Western attitudes to ideological phenomena in general and to Soviet thinking on international relations in particular. On the one hand we can trace without difficulty an unusual awareness in Western research of processes of political socialisation operative in the Soviet Union – a conclusion indicated by these sample analyses of which we have given a résumé above. On the other hand we detect a somewhat casual assumption that the foreign policy-makers are completely immune or in some way exempt from the socialisation process. In our opinion such attitudes reveal a total lack of understanding of the real situation and show little regard for the fact that for instance a person like Brezhnev is a product of that selfsame socialisation process, and in order to reach his present pinnacle has been called upon to prove on innumerable occasions that he knows his 'scriptures' by heart and that he has totally 'internalised', and has identified himself with, the Marxist-Leninist *Weltanschauung*. This Western attitude further ignores a fact that seems self-evident, namely, that Brezhnev and the Soviet leadership believe that communism is the answer to humanity's problems. One further apparent inconsistency that is very likely is the propensity of the Western policy-maker to liken himself too readily to his Marxist-Leninist counterpart: forgetting entirely that the thinking idiom of Nixon, Ford and Carter and other leaders may be as alien to Brezhnev as Marxist-Leninist patterns of thought are to Western power incumbents. The cultural and political background of these leaders is totally different and the values that they may at first sight seem to share would in most cases turn out to carry no more than superficial (and possibly misleading) resemblance.

In other words and to repeat, we are convinced that the West and the East each uses language that is at crucial points incomprehensible to the other, and dichotomous attitudes are rooted in incompatible systems of thought. No interested observer, be he student of Soviet foreign affairs, policy-maker, international lawyer, or diplomat, is unaffected by interpretative problems or is not plagued by confusion when the analysis of contemporary Soviet thinking on international relations is called for. A catalogue of instances deriving from Western

81

literature on all of these subjects, and expressive of responses ranging from bewilderment to outright, even dangerous, misunderstanding would not be difficult to compile. The time is surely past when serious students or practitioners in these fields should be at an interpretative loss when crucial parts of the Soviet ideology require to be transcribed into the Western idiom: or are we to continue so readily to label as 'contradictions', dishonesty, or lies, simple misunderstandings that stem from a lack of familiarity on the part of Western writers with another idiom and mode of thought? At no point can ideological considerations be dismissed in the process of transcription and in this regard a comment by a leading Western sovietologist may be cited. Brzezinski points out that to dismiss ideology as 'an irrelevant criterion to an understanding of the political conduct of Soviet leaders . . . would be to assume that it is possible to build up a large organisation ostensibly dedicated to certain explicit objectives, in which individuals are promoted on the basis both of their professional ability and their demonstrable ideological dedication both in which an inner sanctum operates, makes decisions with a complete disregard of the ideological principles of the movement, indeed remains immune to the constant pressures for ideological justification, and cynically disregards the official creed'.[40] Nor should it be difficult to show that notions torn out of the close-knit context of Marxism-Leninism (and subjected to Western interpretations) are not always 'contradictions' when viewed within the framework of Marxist-Leninist ideology where they properly belong.

In summary then let us recapitulate our 'working' assumptions for the following three chapters: the thesis first of all that Soviet Marxism-Leninism does contain its own theory of international relations as distinct from the theory of international relations of Marx to which it frequently bears only generic resemblance; that the two theories exhibit a number of different characteristics; that although the Marxist-Leninist theory of international relations is not the product of a scholar, and is full of ambiguities (perhaps because ambiguity is unavoidable), it is however more comprehensive and consistent than Marx's original doctrine. Although explicit attention to theory of international relations as a special field of inquiry has been paid only recently,[41] Marxism-Leninism always comprehended within itself such a theory. Because of the intensity of the political socialisation process no part of Marxist-Leninist ideology can be left out of an analysis of any Soviet or East European policy. And certainly, as far as the Soviet understanding of the world and their attitude towards international relations are concerned, a quite precise understanding becomes mandatory.

The formation of a Marxist-Leninist corpus of doctrine in its present shape has a history that goes back to Engels, who simplified and popularised some of Marx's ideas. Although not always acknowledged in the West, Lenin made his own brilliant contribution to the process and his adaptation of Marx's doctrine into what has been called Leninism was to become a cornerstone of Marxism-Leninism. The ideological structure possesses a quite remarkable inner logic despite the convenient vagueness of the formulations and bears still the marks of Lenin's intellectual stature. Perhaps we should set aside Stalin's theoretical deficiencies (accepted no less by the East than by the West) that sometimes obscure the fact that it was Stalin who was personally responsible for putting the Soviet Union in the centre of the capitalist map. Although the question as to the extent to which Lenin's thinking would have inclined, or perhaps converged with that of Stalin had not his death intervened, must remain unanswered, it does seem unreasonable particularly in view of Stalin's bridging position that such theoretical contribution as he made should be ignored. However inept his theory, and however 'non-theoretical', it is nevertheless deeply embedded in the contemporary Soviet model of international relations, and quite apart from Stalin's unquestionable triumphs in, particularly, the practical field of foreign affairs, it is equally certain that the theory of international relations of the present-day Soviet Marxist-Leninist cannot be understood without the 'theoretical bridge' that he also supplied.

And so our course over the next few chapters would appear to be not only logically charted – proceeding from Lenin by way of Stalin's 'theoretical bridge' to Soviet Marxism-Leninism – but also it seems temporally there will be a rough coincidence between basic periodisation of the Soviet theory of international relations.

Lenin

> To ignore the changes which have taken place . . . and to
> continue advocating the old solution by Marxism, would mean
> being true to the letter but not to the spirit of the teaching . . .
> without being able to use the Marxist method of research to
> analyse the political situation. Those times and today . . . differ
> in the most obvious way.
>
> Lenin

It will have become clear that between them Marx and Engels left the
next generation of proletarian leaders with an enormous body of
doctrine which was difficult to read, difficult to get hold of
(particularly in foreign languages) and, notwithstanding its remarkable encyclopedic conception, remaining the 'encyclopedia of an
inexact science'.[1] It is hardly surprising that from this abundant
source so many conflicting interpretations and political orientations
should have been derived.

Although it has since been claimed that he did not read some of
their works[2] Lenin was extremely thorough in his studies of Marx and
Engels, and he regarded their teaching (referred to already as
marxism) as an intellectual system 'comprehensive and harmonious'
and as 'an integral world outlook'.[3] He believed he could see in the
work of the two men a direct continuation of the best in the teachings
of the greatest thinkers of the past and ascribed to their doctrine
values of an almost divine nature: it is 'omnipotent because it is true'.[4]

Omnipotent it certainly was, in its profound ambiguity which could
somehow accommodate departures called for by the requirements of
that reality which Lenin had set out to change. Despite all attempts on
the part of contemporary marxists to prove to the contrary, there were
major differences between Marx and Engels on the one hand and
Lenin on the other. Those consisted largely of background,
education, and political role, and although a Soviet marxist would
inevitably allude to the contribution of Marx and Engels to the
Internationals (that of both men to the First and of Engels also to the
beginning of the Second), unlike Lenin they were never direct
political leaders of any consequence. Brought 'by the historical tide' to
the leadership of the Russian Social Democratic Labour Party, Lenin
contrived the no mean feat of retaining that leadership until his death,

adding also in that period to his manifest political skills and astuteness, qualities that marked him indelibly as a brilliant exponent of the theoretical art. It is to be regretted that even now Lenin's theoretical works are not given the attention that they deserve, and to charge his philosophy as an exercise in 'expediency' (Merleau-Ponty) and his policies as 'realpolitik' are overstatements that would seem to argue a certain lack of understanding.[5]

Lenin was genuine in his reluctance to abandon traditional marxist formulas. But when no other course offered and discrepancies between the theory and the reality of particular political situations taxed his patience he was eventually obliged to re-examine the theoretical principles. Even then he believed such a reappraisal to be dialectically justified: 'Our struggle cannot be understood at all unless the concrete circumstances of each battle are studied. But once that is done, we see clearly that development does indeed proceed dialectically, by way of contradictions . . . [which] . . . must never be confused with the vulgar trick of justifying the zigzags of politicians . . . with the vulgar habits of lumping together particular statements, and particular developmental factors, belonging to different stages of a single process. Genuine dialectics does not justify the errors of individuals, but studies the inevitable turns, providing that they were inevitable by detailed study of the process of development in all its concreteness.'[6] It is to be conceded, however, that a careful reading of some of his *a posteriori* dialectical interpretations of past events shows how difficult it is to draw the line at the 'vulgar trick of justifying the zigzags of politicians' and how delicate the task of remaining within the flexible parameters of 'genuine dialectics'. Nor have the difficulties in precisely locating and treading this narrow line grown less with the years: there is little point in arguing with a marxist as to the extent to which leninism represents a deviation from Marx and Engels and not a 'mere dialectical incorporation into the theory of the further development of the historical process' since Marx. But of the 'actuality of the revolution', as Althusser refers to it, there could be no doubt and the inescapable fact that Lenin operated within that 'future' which Marx and Engels could only adumbrate brought an altogether new dimension to his perceptions and interests. In this new operational milieu he was less concerned with the 'past' and accepted historical materialism (i.e. of both Marx and Engels) without reservations. Confronted with the manifold problems of the 'present', a primary task was to develop Marx's somewhat antiquated theories (although they were still supposed to have remained valid for their own time) and make them operational. Every aspect of the doctrine had to be examined and reinvested with fresh relevance so that they might meet the challenge of a radically changed environment.

No aspect was in more urgent need of refurbishing than that of international relations for which, as we have observed, both Marx and Engels expressed nothing but contempt. Quite clearly they had consigned the notion to the affairs of capitalist nations and had relegated it in their work to scattered allusions loosely strung together in the expectation that the future would witness the actual demise of international relations. But with Lenin the 'future' had arrived and, far from diminishing in importance, international relations for the infant Soviet state and its leaders had acquired a new immediacy and, in certain areas, even a sense of urgency. 'Comrades,' Lenin pointed out to the Sixth Extraordinary All Russia Congress of Soviets, 'from the very beginnings of the October revolution the main question that has faced us is that of foreign policy and international relations.'[7] The 'actuality' of the present had overtaken the doctrinal past and caught it completely unawares. Instead of the cataclysm spreading outwards in revolutionary waves to break on the most distant shores Lenin found himself stranded and struggling for survival on that selfsame strand that had borne the first tidal shock. Nothing in the theoretical 'support system' availed him in such a situation since the doctrine had not provided against the contingency. Lenin was now thrown back on his own theoretical resources which as it was to transpire were fortunately more than adequate to meet the challenge.

Perhaps we might be excused a digression at this point in order to trace the turns of the theoretical path that enabled Lenin to lead the movement to more secure ground. It should first of all be made clear that even in the midst of his problems he had nothing but acclaim for his great intellectual progenitors. His respect and reverence for Marx and Engels is made quite clear time and again in his largely polemical writings (forty-five volumes in all).[8] In contrast to his 'idealist' contemporaries and political opponents, whom he generally regarded as 'blockheads', 'nitwits', and professors of 'armchair gibberish', Marx and Engels are quoted as if they had written another gospel. For his philosophical substance Lenin draws mainly on Engels, whose *Anti-Dühring* is 'the book with seven seals . . . for the modern theory of knowledge'.[9] His main philosophical work,[10] *Materialism and Empirio-criticism*,[11] was designed to fill the gaps in marxism in this respect and it is arguable that in achieving this purpose Lenin's thesis in certain aspects goes beyond the work of both Engels and of Marx.[12] At one such important juncture Lenin's work turns on the restoration of the validity of the dialectic in its materialistic sense which had come under strong attack as a result of the new scientific discoveries at the beginning of the twentieth century. In his rebuttal of the critics' argument that matter does not follow the universally valid dialectical processes, Lenin makes a very important distinction. He distinguishes between matter as a philosophical category (unchanging, 'absolute', and bound with the thesis of existence and objectivity)[13] and the scientific concept of matter (undergoing a ceaseless process of change commensurate with the development and deepening of scientific knowledge). It will be appreciated that from this argument it follows that a parallel distinction must be made: between philosophy with its subject-matter as a philosophical category, and the sciences which subscribe to the concept of matter in the other sense.

Matter is a philosophical category.[14]
The sole property of matter with whose recognition philosophical materialism is bound up is the property of being an objective reality.[15]

Ergo: Philosophy is not a science and is distinct from the sciences, philosophical categories are distinct from scientific concepts.[16] However, there is a special link between philosophy and the sciences represented by the materialist thesis of objectivity. ('The concept matter . . . epistemologically implies *nothing but* objective reality existing independently of the human mind and reflected by it. But dialectical materialism insists on the approximate relative character of every scientific theory . . . it insists on the absence of absolute boundaries in nature.')[17] Indeed it was already Engels, says Lenin, who stated explicitly that 'with each epoch-making discovery even in the sphere of natural science (not to speak of the history of mankind), materialism has to change its form'.[18] In this way, therefore, the subject of philosophy becomes considerably reduced and the diminished discipline proceeds along the age-old dichotomy of materialist and idealist[19] and in the grey area between 'various shades of agnosticism'. Or, as it is succinctly put by Lenin: 'Nomenclature may change (that is always possible) but the issue remains the same: being and thinking, matter and sensation, physical and mental

87

remain the ultimate, the most comprehensive concepts'[20] (of philosophy). And, he adds, the main epistemological question revolves around them, inasmuch as it tries to answer the question whether the 'source of our knowledge . . . is objective natural law or properties of our mind, its innate faculty of apprehending certain *a priori* truths, and so forth.'[21] This, Lenin postulates, is the central epistemological question and not 'the degree of precision attained by our description of causal connections, or whether these descriptions can be expressed in exact mathematical formulas'.

In this respect philosophy remains a constantly repeated variation on the same theme but beyond this there is no real change and the main philosophical propositions of materialism and idealism have been handed down to us unaltered since they were first formulated by the Greek philosophers. Philosophy serves then as an epistemological basis for the sciences (social sciences included) which themselves are in a constant state of flux. That being so it follows that in this sense the new discoveries in physics and chemistry are merely 'another *corroboration* of dialectical materialism'.[22] Thus philosophy merely 'reflect[s] the tendencies and ideology of the antagonist classes. . . . Recent philosophy is as partisan as was philosophy two thousand years ago. The contending parties are essentially – or by a weak-minded non-partisanship – materialism and idealism.' According to Althusser[23] this simply makes Lenin's philosophy into the practice of political intervention in thinly disguised theoretical form. There is no such thing as non-partisanship in philosophy which 'is only wretched mashed servility to idealism and fideism'.[24] It is because of that, Althusser maintains, that Western philosophers have such disrespect for Lenin's 'philosophy'. In other words, as Lenin reiterates throughout the volume of *Materialism and Empirio-criticism*, philosophy has no history because it has no object in the sense that other sciences have.

Lenin's contribution to the marxist theory of knowledge – neglected as it was by both Marx and Engels – is crucial and on the two above occasions when reference has been made to some aspects of Soviet Marxist-Leninist epistemology[25] we were in fact anticipating this section on Lenin. Thus, no matter how much he 'confuses the ontological and epistemological categories' and realism with materialism,[26] stalinism or contemporary Marxism-Leninism neither rectifies nor abandons his epistemological assumptions. Consequently, in chapters that follow we shall again find ourselves returning to Lenin – albeit through the pronouncements of his heirs. For the sake of completeness, although we have already touched on the theories in question, let us repeat that Lenin added to classical marxism what has been described as the copy theory of knowledge whose central argument might be briefly stated thus: sensation and consciousness are reflections of the external world; since the image cannot exist without an imagined original, therefore the external world must exist. Knowledge is then essentially a reflection or copy of reality. Beyond the fact that it is a 'qualitative transformation' the precise nature of this 'reflection' is not quite clear. As R. T. de George says, the argument is 'straightforward, naïve and simplistic. Lenin, characteristically, is 'wasting no time on subtleties'.[27] Following Engels, Lenin sees mind as the highest product of matter, and consciousness as a product of the brain. Their relationship is that of correspondence and our ideas are supposed to *correspond* to the external world (rather than convey it through hieroglyphic symbols). From that it follows that knowledge is always relative (because the world is of an inexhaustible nature). Practice is the only test of knowledge – and if our perception of an object is incorrect our attempt to use it will be unsuccessful. Thus Lenin distinguishes between absolute and relative (and objective) truth – a distinction that has been taken over, lock, stock and barrel, by his successors.

It is directly from his copy theory of knowledge, however, that by virtue of a new emphasis on practice as the only verifying agency of theories, there comes the possibility of departure from the doctrine of Marx and Engels. Admittedly – as Lenin himself is ready enough to point out – the concept of practice received some emphasis (from Marx in 1845, and from Engels in 1888 and 1892)[28] but the fuller elaboration of this *'salto vitale method* of philosophy, that is to say, *the leap* from theory to practice'[29] remains to the politician-theoretician Lenin to accomplish. The argument as we have outlined it above goes on: In the dialectical unity of the theoretical and the practical activity no theory can be 'true' if not verified continuously in action. Lenin proposed that 'every law is a truth only approximately';[30] this world and these laws are fully 'knowable to man but can never be known to him with *finality*'.[31] He pushed it even further: in relation to the notions of determinism of Marx and Engels; that is, to the previously held thesis that the relationship between objective and subjective in history is dependent on the 'objective' factor,[32] the leninist 'departure' was almost diametrically opposed. Where his marxist predecessors held for example that economic conditions were changing of themselves and that the revolutionaries could only await patiently and trust to the processes of historical inevitability to create the necessary objective preconditions of revolution, Lenin offered the alternative – that theory is inseparable from action, and that action taken in the absence of theory is 'blind'. 'Without the revolutionary theory there is no revolutionary movement',[33] spontaneity must be combated: 'the greater the spontaneous upsurge of the masses and the more widespread the movement, the more rapid, incomparably so, the demand for greater consciousness in the theoretical, political, and organisational work'.[34]

From the new perception of the role of the subjective factor, itself derived from the new emphasis on practice, there follows a long series of new emphases, among them the primary task of the revolutionary which is to obtain the most exact scientific knowledge of contemporary reality. (Hence, incidentally, the slogan appearing everywhere on the walls of schools and other educational institutions: 'To learn, to learn, to learn'. (Lenin))

The perception of the role of the individual also underwent change: the idea of historical necessity is not in the least undermining the role of the individuals. When the activity of an individual is being appraised what matters is 'What conditions ensure the success of his actions, what guarantee is there that these actions will not remain an isolated act lost in a welter of contrary acts?'[35] In other words, what kind of organisation is required to channel individual action to revolutionary advantage and ensure that they become combined to promote the outbreak and to further the objectives.

Yet another link in the chain of changed emphases, Lenin's concept of the Party, not only resulted in a split of the Social Democratic Party of Russia,[36] but constituted another major contribution to marxism. Although its pertinence to the present context may be questioned it will be appreciated that this concept also plays an important part in understanding the role of international actors. Indeed, a party, understood as a section of class, introduces the notion of subdivisions on the vertical scale. Notice also in this context the concept of the International, the organ of the international workers' movement, based on the same idea, that is to say, the vertical unit spreading across national boundaries.

From his rather pessimistic attitude regarding the capability of the proletariat to fulfil what Lenin considered to be its historical mission,[37] and from his perception of the revolutionary period of 1905 when the proletariat managed to rise spontaneously and organise itself into Soviets (only to be 'led astray' shortly afterwards by the reformists and bourgeoisie), Lenin began that formulation of his concept of the Party which was to have such a profound influence on both theory and practice. His argument went as follows: it happened time and again during their lifetime that Marx and Engels had ample opportunity to observe the objective revolutionary conditions falling into place. Yet more often than not, although a revolutionary situation migh be said to have arisen, the expected outcome – the revolution – might well not materialise. Lenin's argument would then seem to be borne out: that from the existence of the objective situation it does not necessarily follow that the subjective factor will come into conjunction and thus make the outbreak inevitable.[38] In other words the proletariat may not yet be capable of making decisions; decisions that would bring revolutionary goals within their reach. Marx himself was rather equivocal on this point having said on the one hand that 'the workers' emancipation is their own achievement' and their movement is an 'autonomous movement of the immense majority'. On the other, Marx also lauded (*Manifesto*) the communists for being 'the combating vanguard' capable of awakening the class consciousness of the working class, averring that its strength lay not in numbers but in 'knowledge and determination'. It was this latter aspect that Lenin chose to elaborate more fully and derived from it the concept of a tightly knit, disciplined, and centralised party. It was seen to interact dialectically with the otherwise dispersed, spontaneous, and uncontrived (and also easily misled) mass (the unmobilised remainder of the class). The latter was conceived to have its class consciousness developed only in incipient awareness form (*an sich*) whereas the Party, consisting as it did of the most advanced section of the class and armed with marxist theory, was deemed capable of accomplishing the transformation of the consciousness (*für sich*) of the whole class.[39]

The dialectical relation between Party and class excluded the possibility of both dangerous extremes: it precluded the development of any elitist attitude on the part of a 'sectarian party' cut off from the rest of the class, just as much as it prevented the elements characterised by spontaneity from ignoring the direction of the vanguard group. 'In the struggle for power,' writes Lenin, 'organisation is the only weapon the proletariat have.' The capitalist system, itself based on anarchic competition, produced disunity also within the ranks of the proletariat. But it is only when organised that the proletariat will 'inevitably' become an 'invincible force', and that can be achieved only through ideological unification around the principles of marxism and through the material unity of organisation, not otherwise.[40] 'Without such organisation [i.e. political party] the proletariat will never rise to the class-conscious struggle; without such organisation the working class is doomed to impotency.'[41] An interesting shift, it will be remarked, from Marx and Engels's concept of the role of the individual: 'not a single class in history has achieved power without producing its political leaders, its prominent representatives, able to organise a movement and lead it . . . we must train people who will devote the whole of their life, not only their spare evenings, to the revolution'.[42] We must not of course discount the genuine efforts to broaden the inter-Party democracy already in operation especially after 1905: such developments as, for example, the wider application of the election principle and also concern for the rights of a minority within the Party. But our main concern here is to emphasise the completely new approach to the concept (and role) of the subjective factor in general and of the Party in particular. As will be shown later, these new ideas had repercussions on the perception of the roles of actors in international relations.

With the emphasis on a search for new theories if the old ones do not work, and citing for 'authorisation' Engels's statement that the laws of economic life are not unchangeable from one historical epoch to another, Lenin proceeded to re-examine a capitalist system that featured new phenomena unknown to Marx and Engels. The fruits of his research was given in *Imperialism as the Highest Stage of Capitalism*,[43] a work that gave the widest currency to a term already used before although seldom by Marx and Engels: 'imperialism'.

The first conclusion to emerge was that with the onset of this new epoch in the history of capitalism (retaining the main characteristics of capitalism) all of the contradictions inherent in the capitalist system were thrown into sharp relief ('when certain of its fundamental characteristics began to change into their opposites').[44] While the class content remained the same,[45] the form of the struggle (inter-class) followed its course of ceaseless change and was seen to have entered a new phase. Details of the economic analysis and the transformation of capitalism to its highest stage as described by Lenin are sufficiently well known; it is the consequences of this process that chiefly concern us in the present context. The revolution would not take place simultaneously in the most developed countries or indeed on a world scale but would begin in one country (the 'weakest link of the chain') and the rest of the world would follow suit. This most surprising conclusion Trotsky and Lenin derived from the 'absolute law' of capitalism that the latter claimed to have discovered: *the law of uneven capitalist development.* Unlike the situation in Marx's time where a more or less even rhythm of capitalist development was assumed, it was now postulated that economic development in the imperialist stage functions from one sector of production to another, and from one country to another, in an uneven manner. Thus the imperialist system, like a giant mosaic, is seen to be composed of heterogeneous elements, and stands at every new phase of its development at a crossroads of contradictions. Had the development followed the path predicted by Marx and Engels, capitalism would never have reached this stage. However, having escaped self-destruction in its own 'insoluble contradictions' and as a result of the non-appearance of the awaited revolution, capitalism not only survived but flourished and moved to a new stage. The theory had been wrong, indeed it could hardly have been expected to take into account all of the variables – some of which had not even existed at the time. And it was left to Lenin to provide a new, more widely encompassing revolutionary perspective: imperialism, through the creation of monopolies and financial capital spread across the world in search of new markets and new resources. For the first time in history the world was so completely divided up that only repartition would be possible in the future.[46] Free enterprise capitalism (the name used since then to designate the variety of capitalism described by Marx and Engels) lost its free competitive element, its having been replaced by the direct opposite: the capitalist monopoly ('before our eyes, creating large-scale industry and forcing out small industry, replacing large-scale by still larger-scale').[47] Competition, regarded as such an important feature, was transformed and moved to another level: shifting from its previous position within the horizontal units (its residual presence there being of negligible import) to relations among horizontal units – the capitalist states – and thus entering the field of international relations. The competitive struggle did not, therefore, 'vanish' but took a new form in which the protagonists of the class struggle were no longer classes within the states but they themselves became states.

Lenin goes as far as to classify the states (again with frequent and indiscriminate use of the terms, nation, state, country, government)

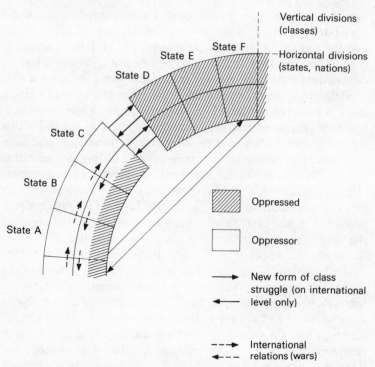

Figure 5 Horizontal and vertical divisions of mankind according to Lenin

into two main groups: the oppressed and the oppressor. In so doing he resumes the analysis begun by Marx and Engels (who noted themselves an emergent process of polarisation of states)[48] and now comes to rather far-reaching conclusions.

Thus these rare allusions by Marx and Engels became links in the chain of reasoning which Lenin now applied to the rethinking of the new era. The proletariat of the oppressor countries (England in particular) might stand to share in the capitalist super profits, a factor which could blur their perception of their role and confuse their class consciousness. On the other hand the workers of the oppressed 'backward' countries would be just as oppressed as a century before. The vertical and horizontal divisions were now seen to intermingle in a hitherto unprecedented manner.[49] Just as the bourgeoisie overflows the horizontal boundaries of its own state and becomes an imperialist class spread over all the globe, so the working class is subjected to a similar process. On that continuum that runs through the various degree of class consciousness there were always divisions within that class in any particular country, but now this subdivision, so to speak, overflows the horizontal boundaries and establishes itself on the international level. No longer do the classes within states, but states (the backward ones) themselves, assume class consciousness, now on a world scale. The proletariat of the most developed capitalist countries, once regarded as the leader of all humanity and the potential 'gravedigger' of its oppressors, with the development of capitalism into imperialism undergoes a shameful transformation from 'revolutionary aspiration to trade union consciousness and from the latter to "social chauvinism" '.[50] The class war within advanced capitalist states has virtually ceased, and the Second International through its identification with the bourgeois class in its chauvinistic struggles, having been seduced by nationalist sentiment into unity with that class, ended in complete fiasco.

Thus leninism, by offering another optimistic perspective of the revolution when the one before had ceased to be practicable, may be seen as an attempt to enable a fresh start. The vertical (classes) scale whose complementary association with the horizontal divisions of both states and nations (or nation-states) had been so reluctantly acknowledged by Marx and Engels, receives a most profound shake-up, the outcome of which is to throw into prominence the horizontal state divisions which now assume a completely new, much less despised place in the theory.

Lenin, of course, was not the only proletarian leader who was trying to rethink the new era. Kautsky ('the renegade') thought that the number of great powers on the international scene would decrease and that they would eventually become organised as a kind of 'super imperialist bloc' whose frictions would be resolved by recourse to instruments and processes other than war. Lenin's concept of the uneven development of capitalism refutes this 'nonsense' of Kautsky's, described as 'the joint exploitation of the world by internationally united finance capital'.[51] In Lenin's view the now less developed countries would be more rapid in their imperialist development. This differential development rate would lead to major wars between the imperialist blocs since 'once the relation of forces is changed, what other solution of the contradictions can be found under Capitalism than that of force'.[52] Needless to say, this new theory saw

95

tsarist Russia as a cynosure of events, and since revolution could no longer be regarded as imminent in the advanced capitalist countries, backward countries like Russia would now have to fulfil the historical mission of the proletariat. The proletariat of the capitalist countries, ran the implications of Lenin's law, is now corrupted to such an extent that not only did it encourage the imperialist governments to go to war in the first place but it was later quite unable to see its historical duty, which, according to Lenin in 1914, was to change imperialist war into civil wars in their respective countries. The imperialist wars, however savage, are not any longer, he believed, destroying the capitalist system (their main objectives being invariably only the further redistribution of the world). The outcomes of such wars merely bring readjustment of the capitalist *status quo*, while the basis of capitalism remains intact. The element that would be the agency of its destruction must come from without. It was Lenin's belief that the destruction of imperialism must now take place on a world scale (and on this point coincided with Marx and Engels) but would do so through a sequential development of a phased revolutionary process.

The law of uneven development dictated to him a twofold methodological principle:

1 He had to abandon Eurocentrism completely and instead conduct his search for the clues to the new revolution elsewhere than in the most developed capitalist countries.
2 He had to go beneath the surface and try to discern the real role played by each element in the system by, for example, breaking classes along the lines of their own internal stratification as suggested by their respective environment, and by their interaction with that environment as well as with the rest of the system.

For the purposes of this analysis, Lenin divides the countries of the world into three broad categories, according to their envisaged role in the forthcoming revolution:[53]

(a) Semi-colonial countries such as China and all other colonies;
(b) the East European countries, above all Russia;
(c) the hitherto leading capitalist countries of Western Europe and the USA.

Sub (a) This group certainly cannot initiate the revolution but it is already deeply (although indirectly) involved in the preparation of the proletarian revolution. Their territory was swamped by foreign imperialists in search of additional resources whose exploitation demanded the establishment of the fundamental elements of industry and the basic commercial substructure (railways and mines in particular). This process creates *inter alia* a national bourgeoisie as well as an infant proletariat. The new national bourgeoisie, motivated by national feeling, would soon come into conflict with the colonisers, and the proletariat, similarly motivated, would lend their temporary support. In this struggle the remnants of the old feudal system would be disposed of. The proletariat of these countries will have to exert themselves to retain their own independent organisation and the proletariat of the developed countries will join them in their efforts. The socialist revolution in these countries will have to proceed by way first of all of the bourgeois (anti-feudal) revolution.

Sub (b) In the East European countries and Russia (described as 'backward') society was still in its feudal stage, the economy based on agriculture and with industry confined to a few towns. The foreign oligarchies of the advanced countries lent massive sums of capital, most of the profits from which went to the borrowers: the indigenous national capitalists. With a view to increasing their profits even further, the national bourgeoisie tries to modernise industry and in so doing becomes increasingly indebted to the foreign imperialists. A paradoxical situation is created whereby the economic basis of capitalism which conditions and precipitates a bourgeois (anti-feudal) revolution is not paralleled by adequate development of a new capitalist superstructure with which to correspond. The Russian bourgeoisie, smaller in number than their East European counter-parts, is also supported and exploited by the foreign imperialists, but because of the false appearance of its national independence, degenerates before becoming established. By way of contrast the modernisation of industry creates a proletariat which, albeit small in number in proportion to the total population, is highly concentrated. With war as its background and forcing-bed it matures politically much faster than could be expected in normal conditions. And so, very soon, it gives evidence of its capability of taking the place of the bourgeoisie in the leadership of the revolution. When the objectives of the bourgeois revolution are achieved (as for example the end of the

97

autocracy of the tsar) the proletariat's work is not done and its further aspiration will be the achievement of the socialist (anti-capitalist) revolution. 'From the democratic revolution we shall at once and precisely in accordance with the measure of our strength, the strength of the class conscious and organised proletariat, begin to pass to the socialist revolution. We stand for uninterrupted revolution. We shall not stop halfway.'[54]

The only possible ally for the proletariat that was at hand was the peasant, who, however, had traditionally been regarded as having strong bourgeois tendencies because of his land ownership, and Lenin's attempt to justify his choice of revolutionary ally was regarded in marxist circles as strongly reactionary. Events seemed to bear him out in 1917 when the theoretical validity of the thesis of permanent revolution (that is to say the transformation from the bourgeois into the socialist) was proved to work. The February revolution, initially a spontaneous insurrection of the workers supported by the peasant members of the tsarist army, opened the path to parliamentary democracy. (Lenin speaks of a constitutional assembly until after the October revolution.) In the event, however, the bourgeois class by entering into a compact with the aristocracy showed a total incapacity for coherent action. They had then to be defeated by the proletariat led by the Bolsheviks who took over what the February revolution had achieved and finally seized power in October. Thus the first rupture in the imperial front had indeed taken place, as predicted by Lenin, in an autocratically governed backward country where imperialism in its extended form (from the countries where according to Marx and Engels the revolution was supposed to take place) had created a disequilibrated situation the bringing of which back into balance had outstripped the adjustment capabilities of the system – and demanded the remedial action of revolution. That the action involved not only a bourgeois revolution but, flowing directly from it, a socialist one, was significant. The first rupture was, according to Lennin's expectations, going to have most dramatic consequences, since it must remind the proletariat of the West European capitalist countries of their 'historical mission'.

Sub (c) Thus in the capitalist countries the victory of the Russian proletariat was expected to stir revolutionary feelings dormant since before 1914. The working class there was divided into two main groups: the proletarian aristocracy confused by the sense of well-being conferred upon it by sharing in capitalist profits, and the rest of the working class, not possessed as yet of a clearly defined class consciousness. Needed in both cases was the application of some sharp external stimulus – now supplied in the Russian Revolution. Although there existed also an objective situation ripe for the revolution in these areas, the perceptions of the proletariat were not as yet attuned. Lenin hoped that the exploited masses engaged in the war would show their willingness to go on fighting and would turn their arms on their exploiters in a civil war: an aroused sentiment would prevail and would gain in intensity from feelings of class solidarity when they saw the imperialists of their own countries involved in an attempt to crush the Russian Revolution. Therefore, thought Lenin, in the wake of the Russian experience the European revolution could not long be delayed. In these circumstances, the newly fledged Soviet state had to preserve its proletarian power not only in its own defence but also in the cause of the further revolution. To serve that purpose as well as to gain the time necessary for consolidation, peaceful international relations with the capitalist world had to be entered into. There was wide disagreement over this issue, since to many it was inconceivable that such a compromise was even possible. Nevertheless, in the event Lenin was able to justify the conclusion of the treaty with Germany,[55] on unfavourable terms, while simultaneously the Soviet state tried to encourage and assist in all possible ways the European proletariat to make the most of the post-war crisis situations.

Lenin based his theoretical considerations on a radically different interpretation of superstructural phenomena which, as, for example, in the case of state and nation, had been taken by Marx and Engels to be mere reflections of the state of the economic basis on which they rest. Lenin's conclusion, however, was that imperialism caused 'irregularities' not only in the foundations but even also within that superstructure. In the first place, he argued, the economic basis, because of its intrinsic inclination to multiply its capital, interfered with the bases of the capitalist states abroad and thus artificially accelerated their development. A classical example of this process at work was Russia where, within the archaic agriculture-dominated basis, Western imperialism had forced the development of small industry into a very modern sector.

In the second place, after the occurrence of the communist revolution in Russia a new superstructure was artificially installed

99

upon a basis which was still predominantly feudal. (Where normally the basis was thought to precede and influence the superstructure.) The Soviet state showed not the least correspondence with its still 'backward' basis; in terms of time the synchronism in economic development being of the order of several centuries. To ensure that the Soviet state could survive at all, in this exercise in 'asymmetry' it had to 'bridge' the gap between itself and the basis by establishing a firm control over the economy.

In the third place, as has been suggested, the new socialist super-structure, apart from playing a crucial role in the development of its own basis, exercised a considerable influence on the superstructure of other capitalist states in order to encourage within them a proletarian movement.

And so the superstructure is now seen to play a dramatically different role from that accorded to it by Marx and Engels. Not only is the role of the individual, the organisation of the proletariat, and the subjective factor in general, seen to be influential but now even the state performs a role, and a most active one at that, in lieu of and alongside the 'driving forces' described by Marx and Engels.

Let us now take a closer look at what these new ideas concerning the superstructural phenomena (the state and nation in particular) consist of, what new roles are allocated to them, and what their destiny is conceived to be.

Marx's general theory of state, expounded in terms of its history, and economic and philosophical foundations in the context of historical materialism is taken over lock, stock and barrel by Lenin, who, here as elsewhere, causes it to be 'extended to the concrete'.[56] Although the main theoretical work on state was completed in 1917 (*State and Revolution*), Lenin continued writing on the subject – in particular in *The Proletarian Revolution and Renegade Kautsky* (1918), and '*Left-wing' Communism – an infantile disorder* (1920), among others. It becomes clear from these works that the state in the phase of imperialism is conceived of as remaining an instrument of class domi-nation having at its disposal a vast apparatus of repression composed of army, police and bureaucracy. Whatever the claims of democracy it remained an instrument for the maintenance of hegemony over the majority by a minority class.

Lenin agreed with Marx and Engels that this state would eventually disappear and indeed accepted the notion of the process taking place in the two-phased pattern outlined by Marx and Engels. At least he agreed with what he thought Marx and Engels had meant: Engels, asserts Lenin, could not possibly have thought that the bourgeois state was going to 'wither away'.[57] What must be construed is that Engels meant it was to be abolished by the proletariat in the course of the revolution. Withering away or dying out described the expected demise of the proletarian state or 'semi-state' and in that context, according to Lenin, all references by Engels to the 'withering away' or 'dying down of itself' referred clearly to the period after the revolution.[58] In other words, the dictatorship of the proletariat became the touchstone of the concept of communist revolution. Lenin maintained that only the recognition of the dictatorship of the proletariat and not the mere recognition of class struggle was what made a marxist a marxist.[59] In the presence of such a dictatorship the state was to perform a repressive function *vis-à-vis* the bourgeoisie, since although deprived by the revolution of its economic means, the bourgeoisie would remain for some time considerably better organised than the proletariat, unversed as was the latter in the complexities, and inexperienced in the running, of a state. Therefore it was legitimate to deprive the bourgeois element of its democratic right (now for the first time at the full and untrammelled service of the majority of the people). The proletarian state under the dictatorship of the proletariat was to be the first state in history that would openly and without taint of hypocrisy acknowledge that it was itself still a class instrument of class oppression. Democracy in any case is seen to be a meaningless notion, since it is always a class democracy and 'proletarian democracy is a *million times* more democratic than any bourgeois democracy; Soviet power is a million times more democratic than the most democratic bourgeois republic'.[60] Lenin attacks Kautsky for claiming that the idea of the dictatorship of the proletariat 'rests upon a word of Karl Marx's in his letter of 1875'.[61] It would be ridiculous to think that Marx and Engels were naïve enough to imagine the total disappearance of the state after the communist revolution; we are not Utopians writes Lenin, 'we do not "dream" of dispensing *at once* with all administration, with all subordination'.[62]

Apart from its repressive function under the dictatorship of the proletariat, the state will have to assume new functions, such as educating the masses, overcoming their fragmentation and inertia, teaching them discipline and preparing them for participation in the life of the state. This, says Lenin, is what Marx must have had in mind when referring to the Paris Commune – a phenomenon that represented the first form of the dictatorship of the proletariat ever as 'a working not a parliamentary body'.[63] The Party, needless to say, is to play the most prominent role in the running of the state's affairs. Thus, willy-nilly, the merger of the Party and the state is acknowledged, albeit only as a temporary measure.

The concept of nation becomes in the leninist gloss considerably more complicated and full of additional unresolved tensions. Since indeed the three separate slogans 'the eventual amalgamation of all nations', 'absolutely direct, unambiguous recognition of the full right of all the nations to self-determination', and the 'complete equality of all nations' do not easily fit together. It might almost be said that they are contradictory.

For Lenin, the national units were basically a transitory historical category bound to vanish eventually, and to him 'eventually' is the key word. But, in the meantime, they were part of the reality; nation-states were the universally accepted form of political organisation and had to be treated accordingly. There was therefore a delusory quality to nationalistic feelings which could confuse people to such an extent ('Scratch some communists and you will find a Great-Russian chauvinist')[64] that they might prevail (and in fact did so on the outbreak of the First World War) over class feelings. And so, looking for potential allies he made it quite clear that to 'champion the interests of every oppressed nationality or race, of every persecuted religion, of the disfranchised sex, etc.' could only be to the advantage of the workers' movement.[65]

It would be quite uncharacteristic of Lenin to want to antagonise useful allies whose aspirations could easily be incorporated (as short-term goals) into the Bolshevik programme. In the long run, he expected that the nations would volunteer to form a free federation which would lead to a merger, and within these terms of reference he distinguished between the nationalism of small and large nations and, like Marx, came down heavily and without reservation in favour of the larger since they could apply themselves more successfully to the tasks of economic progress than could the smaller.

Endorsement of the right of national self-determination, clearly implying an equality of all nations, their size and economic potentialities notwithstanding, went no further, however, than political expediency demanded, and was intended as little more than a slogan or catch-phrase. Particularly was this so when in 1913 its meaning was extended by the Party to engross also 'the right to secession and formation of an independent state'. An independent proletarian state yes, but not another autonomous *class* state.[66] Although the following statement belongs to an earlier date it would appear, in our opinion, to have remained as the indelibly etched motto of nationality theory and practice: 'Every nationality's right to self-determination simply implies that we, the Party . . . must always unconditionally *oppose any attempt* to influence national *self*-determination from without by *violence or injustice*. While at all times performing this negative duty of ours (to fight and protest against violence) we on our part concern ourselves with the self-determination of the *proletariat* in each nationality rather than with self-determination of peoples or nations.'[67] In other words the real content of the concept of the right of national self-determination and the right to secession and formation of an independent state should rather have read 'the right of the proletarian class to national self-determination and statehood'. The first half of the above statement clearly indicates that national oppression in any other case should still be taken advantage of for promoting class goals, and thus the Bolsheviks accepted the role of guardian to all oppressed nationalities. After all, Lenin himself asserted that this guardianship should (conditionally) be written into the party programme since from the strategic point of view 'all possible and even conceivable combinations' must be taken into account.[68]

The right to national self-determination, and the like, goes hand in hand with the concept of proletarian internationalism or, in other words, a reminder that it is the class difference that ultimately counts. In the dialectical unity these opposite sides of the same coin are flexible enough to accommodate all shades of attitude. The resultant of two dialectical processes are two concepts: the movement having as its goal the creation of nation-states in the first instance, and the other, produced simultaneously, the tendency to break down national (state) barriers. Both concepts derived encouragement from the increased flow of international relations, an impulse which, though galvanised by capitalism, would continue and gain strength after the creation of the socialist states. Hence two dialectical policies: national self-determination and the right to secession on the one hand and proletarian internationalism on the other. With the growing emphasis on the latter it might be expected eventually to predominate.

The International which stems from and works in the cause of proletarian internationalism is conceived to be both the instrument and also the focal point of the struggle of the oppressed peoples throughout the world. Just as clearly as Lenin saw the nascent revolution in the micro-scale of the Russian state he anticipated the consummated revolution in a macro-cosmic context along analogous lines. Against this background the International was an extension of the concept of the Party on to the world scale, and charged with the task of joining the 'communist parties into one world party'. In pursuit of its main objective of institutionalising the proletarian links, the Third Communist International (founded as soon as the international situation permitted in March 1919) was entrusted with two immediate tasks:

1 Co-ordination of the support of the East European proletariat for the new Russian Soviet state now menaced by civil war from within and foreign intervention from without.
2 Planning of joint operations and tactics by which the proletariat of the Western countries could come to power in the next series of communist revolutions.

As far as the question of war was concerned Lenin's attitude was again influenced by political expediency but he coincided at least in terms of general interpretation with that of Marx and Engels: war is an inevitable corollary of the division of society into classes and can be abolished only with the classes.[69] Only when the bourgeoisie of the whole world and not merely of one country (sic) is 'finally vanquished and expropriated' will it be possible to 'consign all armaments to the scrap-heap'.[70] Until that time comes, however, wars are inevitable and socialists could not be opposed to all of them 'without ceasing to be socialists'.[71] Lenin certainly was without any doubt neither opposed to war as such nor to the use of force in general and took great pains in collecting all of the statements of Marx and Engels containing the 'panegyrics on violent revolutions'.[72]

Like Marx and Engels, Lenin explained wars in terms of class antagonism.[73] Every war is but a continuation of policy by other means[74] and in this light it should be judged. Thus the character of the war does not depend on 'who the attacker was, or in whose country the "enemy" is stationed; it depends on *what class* is waging war, and on what politics this war is a continuation of'.[75]

Employing a similar method to that of Marx and Engels, Lenin classifies war in a manner that might be presented as follows:[76]

1 *Legitimate and just wars*
  1.1 In international relations
     1.1.1 national wars by colonial peoples against their
          imperialist oppressor;
     1.1.2 wars of future socialist states (written in 1916)
          against the attempt of the bourgeoisie of other
          countries to crush the socialist state (since the revolu-
          tion according to Lenin will not take place simul-
          taneously all over the world but in phases), i.e.
          defensive wars (never explicitly offensive ones).
  1.2 Within the state civil war 'is just as much a war as any other'.
     Naturally in a preponderantly class interpretation of society,
     class wars (and all wars are believed to be of a class nature)
     are treated in the same manner whether they occur between
     the states or within them. Civil wars, in every class society,
     are the 'natural, and under conditions inevitable, con-
     tinuation [and] development of the class struggle'.
     'Revolution is war',[77] obviously regarded as a special
     kind of civil war since Lenin no longer expected a revolu-
     tion proper to scourge several states simultaneously.
2 *Unjust, imperialist.* 'Rapacious, predatory, reactionary' wars
  of the oppressive classes against the oppressed were waged
  amongst imperialists in quest of their goals.

In terms of these categories, therefore, the First World War was
classified by Lenin as a typical example of war belonging to the second
group. The war was fought by both main belligerents as an imperialist
war, which is to say one waged by capitalists to determine the division
of profits arising from world domination, to secure the appropriation
of markets for the deployment of finance capital, and to accomplish
the subjugation of the weaker nationalities.[78] However, although it
was fought purely in the interests of the 'rapacious capitalists' who
alone stood to be enriched by it, the war could not be ended 'at will'; it
was not a product of will but of half a century of world capitalist
development, or the meeting point of its many arteries, capillaries,
and interconnections. The only sure end to war was the transfer of
state power to the proletariat, to 'save mankind from the horrors of
war and endow it with the blessing of peace'.[79]

Class antagonisms, according to Lenin, cannot be resolved by
means other than the use of violence. In support of this view Lenin has

recourse to the authority of Marx and Engels, to their 'proud and open proclamation of the inevitability of a violent revolution' and underlines that '*this* and precisely this view of the violent revolution lies at the root of the entire theory of Marx and Engels'[80] (yet another of Lenin's overstatements, contrived to serve contemporary propagandist purposes).

In the meantime, until after the victory of the proletariat, the latter, like any other oppressed class, has to strive to acquire arms and to learn to use them. If it does not, it 'deserves to be treated like slaves'.[81] The logic of this conclusion is not difficult to follow: there is no other escape from the class society but through resort to arms; the state is an oppressive class instrument, which is to say the oppressor class is always armed; hence the proletariat must also arm. To Lenin the conclusion is 'such an elementary truth that it is hardly necessary to dwell on it'.[82] And now he proceeds to argue the corollary: disarmament prior to the victory of the world revolution, as a social idea 'and not an invention of some crackpot', can only be the product of exceptionally 'tranquil' conditions that might occur uniquely in a certain state that

1 Is small.
2 Has been for a long time out of the main stream of world events and hopes to remain that way (for example, Norway).

Such conditions create an objective social environment in which the idea of disarmament may bring a certain measure of success 'to the petty bourgeoisie of petty states'. Although it may well be successful, the striving towards disarmament is reactionary and based entirely on illusion, for, 'in one way or another, imperialism draws the small states into the vortex of world economy and world politics'.[83]

In the event Lenin's predictions proved to have been remarkably accurate inasmuch as the October revolution did take place in the 'weakest link of the chain', and gave rise to a new situation by which, inconceivable though it would have been to Marx and Engels, the socialist state *de facto* joined in international relations with the club of capitalist states and began to coexist with them. To begin with, 'peaceful coexistence' was a notion that no more occurred to Lenin or other communists than it had to their illustrious forebears. In fact it was apparently not Lenin but Trotsky and Chicherin who originated the term and during Lenin's lifetime a more common expression was *mirnoe sozhitelstvo* (*lit.* peaceful living together in cohabitation) rather than *mirnoe sosushchestvovanie* (*lit.* peaceful coexistence) which only since December 1927 received official sanction and came into sole use; the subtle semantic difference suggesting a more stable and less transitory state of affairs.[84] Whoever was the author of this now so important term, it is certain that one of the reasons for the obvious hesitation in concluding the treaty of Brest-Litovsk with Germany must have been the strong conviction shared by Lenin and those others that the remaining states of Europe were on the verge of communist revolution. In such circumstances it must have seemed pointless to attempt to bring the relations of the Soviet state into correspondence with the rest of the world – especially by way of such traditional capitalist diplomatic instruments as treaties. Further, the first actions of the Foreign Commissariat consisted of somewhat non-conventional attempts to discredit and embarrass the imperialist governments. The publication of the texts of the secret treaties concluded with tsarist Russia, and diverse encouragement of disaffection of the international proletariat in their various countries, were earnest of an intention to proceed other than by way of 'peaceful coexistence'.

In the end it was probably as an expedient to gain time to consolidate that they were impelled to sign the Brest Litovsk treaty of 1918. 'If our forces are obviously small, the best means of defense is to retreat into the interior of the country',[85] wrote Lenin and, should the wisdom of this formula be doubted, he advised a reading (as he frequently advised elsewhere) of 'old Clausewitz'. Therein might be found ample confirmation of the fact that to effect a heroic retreat is just as important as the launching of heroic assaults. In any case, he averred, the second socialist revolution was bound to come, and this time it 'will be world-wide in its scope'.[86] Acceptance of the notion of 'peaceful coexistence' came gradually, was adopted as a very temporary measure, and drew strength in inverse proportion to the inevitable weakening of confidence as time passed in the revolution's immediate future. Predictions in this latter regard tended to increasing vagueness and lack of conviction:

1918: The socialist revolution in one country alone is inconceivable.[87]

1920: The world socialist revolution [is] being delayed.[88]

May 1921: We have made the start. When, at what date and time, and the proletarians of which nation will complete this process is not important . . . the ice has been broken; the road open, the way has been shown.[89]

December 1921: I do not know whether this is for long, and I do not think that anyone can know.[90]

All these statements were made in the context of assessing international affairs and were invariably prefaced by: 'our forecasts and calculations were proved to be correct [!] . . . we received considerable support of another kind, not direct support'.

Always dependent of course on the definition and purposes of 'peaceful coexistence' there was no fundamental obstacle in the path of such a relationship being established and indeed it followed from many of Lenin's statements about the time of the conclusion of the Brest-Litovsk treaty that, by definition, a socialist state did not 'in general reject military agreements with one of the imperialist coalitions against the other'. It will be remarked, however, that such agreements were only entered into where the following conditions were fulfilled:

1 The agreement would not undermine the basis of Soviet power.
2 The agreement would strengthen – its (Soviet) position.
3 The agreement would frustrate the attacks of any imperialist power.[91]

Already by the conclusion of the Brest-Litovsk treaty commercial relations were viewed in a different light, hampered in their operation though they might be by allied intervention and economic blockade. On this subject Lenin emphasised that there was no reason why a socialist state could not do business indefinitely (!) with capitalist countries. 'Socialist grain tastes the same as any other grain, does it not?',[92] he asked, and pointed out that there was no objection to 'taking capitalist locomotives'.

Although Lenin spoke of peaceful coexistence at an earlier date, until 1920 it was no more than a propagandist slogan implying that there would have to be peaceful coexistence after the successful revolution. The beginning of the period of peaceful coexistence is conceived to have started only after three years of fighting on both the national and international fronts and Lenin indicates his puzzlement as to how to interpret the development in recurrent reference to 'the establishment of something in the nature of equilibrium . . . temporary and unstable but nevertheless an equilibrium'. Functioning at something less than his dynamic revolutionary strength, he again speaks of success, in that 'we have entered a new period, in which we have, in the main won the right to our international existence in the network of capitalist states'.[93] But he is now reaching for it, and sounds more and more uninspired on the subject of international relations as if the removal of the world revolution from his intellectual grasp had left only the consolation of internal affairs, the world reduced to cliché.'

Stalin

> It would be ridiculous to expect that the Marxian classics should have elaborated for our benefit ready-made solutions for each and every theoretical problem that might arise in any particular country fifty or one hundred years afterwards, so that we, the descendants of the Marxian classics might calmly doze at the fireside and munch ready-made solutions.
>
> Stalin

The portrait of Stalin if drawn in all of its practical and theoretical aspects over three decades would occupy a large canvas. Perspective might vary but an adequate appraisal could hardly take in less than the world revolutionary movement in general – the weaknesses and strengths of which Stalin to a large extent epitomises. In approaching an assessment of the achievements of one of the most influential (and successful) political leaders and military strategists of this century, it would be curious indeed if there were to be unanimity of views or if the issues debated were small. The 'Stalin question'[1] poses itself not so much in regard to an assessment of his practical achievements, but centres rather on the controversy surrounding the extent of Stalin's theoretical contribution and/or the extent to which Soviet ideology as we know it today is owed to his influence. At this point we would refer the reader to previous chapters[2] from which the impression might have been gained of ideology and theory as two partially overlapping circles. They are not mutually exclusive: 'theoretical' is not

109

necessarily 'ideological' while a glance at the partial overlap of the two circles suggests also that 'ideological' does not necessarily have to comply with the requirements of 'theory'.[3]

Stalin's practical achievements hardly come into question. It was during his reign that the Soviet Union's position on the map was consolidated and, as culmination of the breakout strategy initiated at Rappallo, she emerged from the Second World War having shattered the 'capitalist encirclement'. Joined now by a group of East European countries in her socialist 'camp' (or 'socio-economic system') the Soviet Union ushered in a new era. This much is largely to be placed to Stalin's credit balance, a fact that is gradually finding acknowledgment even within the Soviet Union where in the course of the Twentieth CPSU Congress the slightest possibility of such 'rehabilitation' was banished for the next twenty years. It is noteworthy, despite the accusations levelled by his critics,[4] that the practical consequences of Stalin's achievements have lasted. Irrespective of the answers we may find to such questions as whether he did or did not understand foreign affairs, whether or not his foreign policy was pursued in accordance with some distinctive stalinist doctrine, or whether his utterances comprised an incoherent jumble of undistinguished, often contradictory *ad hoc* formulas designed to meet the immediate and temporary needs of the movement and yet satisfy the demands of orthodoxy, the achievement is clear for all to see. And yet it remains an astonishing fact that (though for obviously different reasons) while no major publishing house in either the USA or the USSR within the last twenty years has authorised publication of Stalin's work, the pronouncements of his critics and enemies (of Trotsky in particular) have in that time met with no such reticence and have been distributed far and wide. If claims were to be on the basis of influence alone a reluctant publisher would be obliged to contend with a recent assessment that asserts that Stalin's thinking has influenced some billion people across the face of the earth, and most particularly in China, Vietnam, Korea, and Albania are the effects still marked. To that assessment we might add the rider that Stalin's influence on contemporary Soviet thinking, and particularly on the subject of international relations, is considerable. An influence that crystallised not from any explicit formulation of theories but emerged rather in a seemingly haphazard fashion from a bulk of practice – the theoretical linkages, associations, inferences and conclusions left to later generations to draw.

110

In this section we do not aspire to resolving the 'Stalin question' and will neither offer any new assessment, nor attempt an appraisal of Stalin's varied policies in the field of foreign affairs. Least of all will we undertake the undoubtedly thankless task of showing Stalin to have been a philosopher and thinker in the Marx, Engels, and Lenin moulds. By narrowing the aims of the section to the discovery of a theoretical bridge between Lenin on one side and the contemporary Soviet Marxist-Leninists on the other, we hope not only to open up access to the Stalin contribution but also to avoid the mistake of crediting contemporary Soviet Marxist-Leninists with a greater insight and theoretically innovative role than their contribution would warrant. The main span of our bridge will join two seemingly irreconcilable times and theoretical positions. We have implied the non-theoretical content of Stalin's contribution in the sense that his theory was subordinate and subject to the vicissitudes of practice. Endowed by their author with no heuristic value Stalin's theoretical positions served rather as political rationalisation and justification for manoeuvres already executed. Nevertheless it was during the stalinist decades that the last stages in the process of transforming doctrine into ideology were completed and, as a corollary, there took place a transformation at depth in Soviet thinking on the subject of international relations. Indeed, as we shall contend, Soviet theory of international relations is to a degree more stalinist than it is either leninist or marxist. But that is to anticipate the argument.

Following the pattern of the sections on Marx and Lenin we shall, before proceeding to a reconstructrion of Stalin's 'theory' of international relations, begin by glancing at Stalin the political philosopher. It should be remarked here that there is no complete collection of Stalin's writings. Of the sixteen-volume edition planned by the Marx-Engels-Lenin Institute, only thirteen volumes (to end with his writings of January 1934) were published before the task was interrupted with Khrushchev's disclosures in his secret report to the 20th CPSU Congress. The concluding three volumes have never appeared and his writings in general were declared *libri prohibiti* although (or possibly *because*) they bore a striking resemblance to texts that appeared in the post-Stalin era. In contrast to his distinguished predecessors in the ideological line, Stalin, despite efforts throughout his lifetime to assume the marxist ideological mantle, had neither the capacity for speculative thought nor had the training for, nor inclination towards, philosophy in general. One area

111

in which his efforts were crowned with success was in establishing himself as an arbiter of the widest possible range of social subjects and in managing gradually to eliminate discussion on social theory. Significantly enough, the process was attended by the elimination of political opponents – who were invariably accused of being representative also of erroneous theoretical positions. Thus, with controversy already a thing of the past, each of the turning points of 1929, 1931 and 1938[5] was followed by another turn of the screw in the process of extinguishing theoretical debate. From the year of the purges and for more than two decades, Stalin's pronouncements on social issues held sway.

Broadly speaking, two periods can be discerned in the development of social theory. The first period begins with the October revolution after which marxism for the first time in history became an official philosophy and was elevated from the obscurity of clandestine communist organisations to become the subject of university courses. With this new-found respectability there began an academic dialogue, the participants in which (marxist more often than not) cited in support of their rival opinions and in refutation of those of their (other marxist) opponents, the works of Marx, Engels, and Lenin.

We have sought to show in previous chapters to what extent ambiguity and the consequent possibility of conflicting interpretation is as much an inherent and characteristic part of marxism as is any of that doctrine's more positive aspects. In the field of philosophy such controversy centred on the meaning of dialectical materialism with, essentially, the emphasis placed either on the dialectical content (Deborinists) or on the materialist part (mechanists). The controversy that surrounded the notion of building socialism in one country and the question as to the degree to which its attainment would be contingent on world revolution raised, beside the main issue, a plethora of questions associated in varying degrees with it. High on this list came such weighty considerations as: the possibility of a division of the world economic base into two parts (capitalist and socialist); the ramifications of such a dichotomy for superstructural phenomena – touching as it must on international law and international relations characterised by some form of coexistence, this last leading in turn to speculation as to the nature of a capitalist world that might coexist with the socialist state. Needless to say the results of such speculation were inconclusive, and in any case the dialogue was

112

terminated from above by a political decree whose issuance established a precedent which, confirmed at intervals since, marked the end of the doctrine-to-ideology shift outlined above (pp. 76–9). It was thanks to this initial period of relatively unfettered opinion, however, that Stalin was obliged to give grudging recognition to the very theses that he sought to eliminate – and formulated his own theories (as antitheses) accordingly. Again responding rather than taking theoretical initiatives the formulation of stalinism received an impetus and shape from the growing emphasis on the socialisation process whose implementation placed a primary importance on the necessary teaching media – among them textbooks. In this context Stalin himself supervised work on the most important text of all, the *History of the Communist Party of the Soviet Union (Bolshevik): Short Course*, which appeared in 1938 and included one section (Dialectical and Historical Materialism), the writing of which was attributed directly to Stalin himself. The *Short Course*, together with the earlier and most important *Problems of Leninism*,[6] became prescribed reading for millions of Soviet and east European citizens and profoundly influenced generations of Stalin's subjects. Although the virtues of simplifier, populariser, and commentator may not be the stuff to engender a particularly high regard, these do none the less have an indisputable function whose non-fulfilment would have left some sectors of the contemporary ideological position without an explanation.

Although in the latter part of the second period (after 1938) Stalin countenanced a certain amount of marxist debate,[7] the only theoretical works of substance in this period were his own.[8] Of those, most far reaching in importance was a collection of five letters appearing in *Pravda* in 1950, which influenced profoundly the subsequent development of social theory. It elaborated the notion of relative independence and the active role of superstructure phenomena apropos of the discussion as to the epistemological placement of language in either social coexistence or social consciousness. In the year before his death there appeared finally his *Economic Problems of Socialism in the USSR* (1952) which, despite his attempting therein to modify the notion of the independence of superstructure *vis-à-vis* substructure, failed to disturb trends that continue today.

Although, as we have implied, Stalin's limitations as a philosopher are self-evident, the basic philosophical postulates to which he subscribed bear examination. Like many men of action (including

Lenin) he brought a certain refreshing, not to say essential, pragmatism to bear on a new generation of theoretical problems. The abstruseness and ambiguities of the writings of Marx and Engels had compounded Lenin's problems of theory, added to which was the fact that these writings concerned themselves largely with the onset of the communist revolution and, in its aftermath, the establishment of socialist society. Left thus stranded, to all theoretical intents and purposes, Lenin had acknowledged his debt but had proceeded to justify his theoretical departures by a new emphasis on the corrective function of practice.[9] Central problems therefore remained as Stalin's legacy – with no theoretical blueprint bequeathed for their resolution. Reminiscent too of Lenin's unfailing respect for the marxist 'classics', the similarity in approach was equally apparent in the departure from all of them *in the name of practice*. This respect for the classics coupled with a boundless admiration for Lenin's updating and adaptation of them – coloured above all by an overriding pragmatism – is apparent in his definition of leninism as 'Marxism of the era of imperialism and the proletarian revolution'. And again, in more specific terms, as 'the theory and tactics of the proletarian revolution in general, the theory and tactics of the dictatorship of the proletariat in particular'.[10] The pragmatism that is central to any understanding of Stalin's approach is brought to our attention in a typically inadvertent formulation when Stalin defines social theory as: 'the experience of the working-class movement in all countries taken in its general aspect'.[11] Taking the operative notion as 'generalised experience' Stalin would thus seem to emphasise the pragmatic aspect of theory with a consequent degradation of its heuristic *a priori* value to a mere 'giving the movement confidence, the power of orientation, and an understanding of the inner relation of surrounding events . . . to understand the present and future direction'.[12] Yet at the same time he still explicitly subscribes to the absolute gnostic position of Marx and the assumption of total knowability of the world, when he suggests that 'theory could not confine itself to *explaining* the world [authors' italics], that it must also change it'.[13] Be that as it may, Stalin's theory is representative in the main of *post facto* justifications and explanations devised to re-establish doctrinal continuity following some departure or innovation. With certain provisos it is therefore not difficult to have sympathy for those of Stalin's critics who charge that his actions rested on no firm preconceived theoretical ground, or that as far as action in the domestic or international spheres is concerned his theories remained no more than *post festum* apologetics. Although this reading of Stalin's theory can be fully justified the provisos mentioned are threefold: in the first place it is to be remembered that Stalin was still fully committed to the construction of a communist society, a vision which – however distant – still beckoned, even as it had his predecessors. In quest of the objective the distinction is drawn between short range and long range, between tactic and strategy, and we should not be surprised if in order to attain that distant objective a tactical deployment is made which in the short run may well appear to go counter to the achievement of that goal. For, as we have asserted, beyond the marxist vision Stalin's inheritance contained no blueprint or route map and the task of charting such a route was left entirely in his own hands. A formidable task that to most would have seemed daunting; but even here Stalin's pragmatism asserts itself and comes to his rescue as he seeks to adapt to the realities of his situation and to transform weakness into strength. The *Short Course* emphasised the notion of the 'moral-political unity' of society that has prevailed to the present time: by way of this convenient notion the moral ideal (the achievement of communism) and the political system (communism) are made to merge and thus any action performed by the Communist Party (or by Stalin on its behalf) is by definition moral and may assume the moral approbation of society.

A second consideration that should be borne in mind is the fact that even a *post facto* justification when added to the growing corpus of Marxist-Leninist ideology itself becomes an organic part of the myth which, in the 'internationalisation' process, conditions the minds even of those whose destiny carries them to supreme power. Thus leads the path from *a posteriori* rationale to *a priori* reasoning behind some future action in Marxist-Leninist policy. One final consideration to be taken into account before dismissing Stalin's theoretical approach is the grounds on which he himself justified the monopoly of the Party (and later his own) in policy formulation. In this context he could cite once again the eleventh thesis in the *Theses on Feuerbach* with its emphasis on the absolute gnostic epistemological position in endorsement of the Party prerogative in this respect.[14] For Stalin's purposes the chain of reasoning begins with Lenin's taking his stand in regard to the total knowability of the world. If the subject is right no insurmountable obstacles lie in the path leading to that objective and, here again, it is the Communist Party alone that, having the wherewithal to brush aside such obstacles, holds in its keeping the key by which that future will be unlocked – Marxist-Leninist theory. But inceasing vigilance must be exercised and a regular check carried out to ensure that the theory continues to relate to a practice and environment that are in constant flux. A theoretical formula that was correct for and in complete correspondence with the exigencies of one epoch may be incorrect and fail to correspond – or indeed find itself in direct contradiction to – the requirements of the present day. 'Consequently, the two different formulas corespond to two different epochs in the development of society, and precisely because they correspond to them, the two formulas are correct, each for its own epoch.'[15] This leninist relativisation of truth, it will be appreciated, offers wide scope and the opportunity to depart with impunity from classical doctrine and precepts since, although the classical marxist solution is a blatant contradiction of that of Stalin, the correctness of both can be asserted. From this assertion virtually all paths lead to Stalin's theoretical monopoly: the concept of the withering away of the state, for example, though a valid perception for another time, no longer holds true. When the Soviet state is subject to capitalist encirclement, and an intensification of the class struggle within the state, it is clearly the time for reinforcement rather than a weakening of the state dictatorship of the proletariat.[16] The Party likewise must, if anything, be strengthened so as to be able to face the build-up of centrifugal pressures from within the state and of disintegrative pressures from beyond its frontiers. Thus the Party cannot permit itself to acknowledge any criticism since such criticism argues a loss of unanimity, and from there it is a short step to a position that regards anyone initiating or encouraging discussion within the Party as a traitor to the working class. It is to be observed that although Lenin presaged such a development at the Tenth Party Congress (1921) at which freedom among communists to criticise was removed, the unanimity formula is of more recent vintage. Only along these lines can a party be strong enough to determine what is 'true' in every sector,[17] and from the requirement of full unanimity it seemed to follow that the ultimate repository of truth resided in that person whom the Party entrusted with its leadership. In this way was the power monopoly justified and the implications went beyond the frontiers of the Soviet Union to apply equally to the international workers' movement. Since the Soviet state was the only one to have been successful in its advocacy of interests *common* to the international workers' movement as a whole it could feel justified in requiring the submission of all communist parties to the dictates of the Soviet Party – and ultimately to those of Stalin. In this sequence is to be found in abbreviated form the 'theoretical' justification for what was after Stalin's death to become known as the 'cult of personality' – that consisted essentially of a further shift to the very extremity of subjectivism on the objective-subjective continuum. With this shift towards the subjectivist end of the continuum entered by Lenin we see a continuous process of exclusivism involving the progressive contraction of that privileged group who alone can aspire to be 'right' in the quest for 'truth': thus the process leads from the working class to the Communist Party, from the Party to its central power structures, from the power structures to an inner elite, leading ultimately to the leader of that elite who is thus justified in his assumption of supreme dictatorial power, not only within the Soviet state but in regard also to the international workers' movement at large, in relation to whose communist parties he stands as puppeteer. Yet as we have suggested, even with the subjective emphasis developed to the point of caricature and reinforced in its distortions by the new requirement of unanimity, these conclusions or inferences bear a semblance of continuity with Lenin's teaching.

It was part of Stalin's ambition to display philosophical genius, and having contrived the elimination of all possible rivals he was indeed in a position to receive graciously the accolades which, thanks to the dogmatism preached in the name of leninist *partiinost*,[18] flowed bounteously from all quarters. 'When only one man was recognised as having the right to scientific creativity, all that was left to the others was to comment, popularise and – admire.'[19] From the point of view of lasting influence Stalin's efforts met with varied success depending on the area surveyed. Just as much as it is possible to say that his influence on historical materialism was profound, his handling of dialectical materialism on the other hand evinced a naïve confusion and lack of understanding. Of the former influence clear traces remain to this day while from the latter area most of his contribution has been excised from the received doctrine. As we have pointed out, attempts to grapple with the meaning of 'dialectical materialism' gave rise to serious controversy throughout the 1920s, the controversy resulting in the emergence of two conflicting schools; proponents variously of dialectics *or* materialism. Bochenski observed with some insight that the dualism remains and that the tendency to come down on the side of either one or the other has become endemic to marxist interpretations. His description of the emphasis on dialectical or on materialist as hegelian or aristotelean respectively is apt.[20] Stalin gradually eliminated both of these schools – the aristotelean mechanists first followed by the hegelian Deborinists – and took it upon himself to produce a strange hybrid. This consisted of a confused marriage between dialectical materialism and a hegelian (although Stalin was a confirmed anti-hegelian), basically idealistic reinterpretation of historical materialism, which had the effect of separating dialectical from historical materialism. This verdict[21] on Stalin's 'contribution' invites closer investigation.

To deal first with dialectical materialism, it might be remarked that Stalin opens his discourse with a most unusual division into dialectical method and marxist philosophical materialism – an analytical framework that has since been abandoned in favour of that suggested by Engels. He would seem to indicate by his reduction of dialectics to dialectical method that he sees no need to distinguish between them. According to Stalin the principal features of the dialectical method are an awareness of (a) the general interconnectedness of all nature (b) the state of continuous flux and change in nature (c) the onward and upward movement in nature; quantitative changes leading to qualitative (d) all phenomena possessed of integral contradictions, negative and positive sides, so that the struggle between old and new is inherent in all phenomena and forms the basis of development. Thus, according to the dialectical method any phenomenon under investigation should be considered in terms of its interrelationship with the rest of nature, seen in a state of constant development and change (notably through quantitative changes leading to qualitative ones) and identification of the internal contradictions of each phenomenon (social in particular) should be sought (in its negative as in its positive sides, in its old and its new aspects). In Stalin's interpretation, Engels's three laws of dialectics become reduced to two: the interpenetration of opposites, and the transformation of quantity into quality. In this context the very important one, that of the negation of the negation, is significantly absent as is any mention of the concept of freedom and necessity, causality, etc.[22] In this way the concept of the dialectic, ubiquitous in its application across the whole marxist panorama, is reduced to describing the mechanical relationship of contradictions (a simple enough function compared to the obscure esotericism of Marx's treatment) with little of heuristic value to its name. In Stalin's interpretation to say that something is 'dialectically' related means little more than the restatement and description of a relationship without saying much more about it.

Similar confusion attends the relationship of dialectical and historical materialism: where on the one hand Stalin seems to subordinate historical materialism to dialectical materialism, implying that the former is a derivative of the latter, he at the same time builds an intellectual barrier between the two by introducing certain notions into historical materialism which have no direct parallel in dialectical materialism. We refer primarily to the introduction into historical materialism of 'non-antagonistic contradictions' in society without a corresponding introduction of 'non-antagonistic contradictions' within matter in dialectical materialism. The assumption in the marxist classics, and restated by Stalin as the expected mode of development, was that the development of nature (matter and society) through the conflict of contradictions would generate its momentum by way of violent clashes. His version of dialectical materialism, however, was not confronted by the selfsame question that had already exercised Engels,[23] namely, what happens to these dialectical contradictions once the construction of the socialist society has been achieved? Or, in other words, the proponents of the contradictory standpoints in a class society being classes what then, once these classes had been eleminated, was to become the motive force (or 'engine') of the development? Stalin's answer to the problem of how to reconcile the dialectic and its perpetual application in the absence of contradictions in conflict was as follows: in socialist society there are no longer antagonistic classes in the sense that they stand in a different relationship to the means of production, and although classes still continue to exist (working class and agricultural workers), their relation to each other is no longer of an antagonistic nature. Since the tensions between antagonistic classes from which flowed the main developmental surges were now gone,[24] the dialectical source to feed and power the continuing development of socialist society has to be looked for elsewhere. There still remained such mere differences as the above-mentioned urban-rural schism and these, together with a new surrogate dialectical force (the state), comprised Stalin's answer to the theoretical dilemma. The state was the answer in so far as in its new role it had now become capable of staging a 'revolution from above', which is to say a revolution initiated by the state itself but

119

carried out from below by the masses. Addressing himself to those comrades 'who have an infatuation for such explosions as that the law of transition from an old quality to a new one by means of an explosion', Stalin pointed out that such explosions are attributable neither to language nor to 'some other social phenomena of a basal or superstructural character'.[25] Where hitherto the state had been conceived of as being a mere superstructural phenomenon supposed only to follow development of the economic basis and having only a very limited feedback in its own right, in order to explain the strong emphasis and the enhanced role allotted to it Stalin now proceeded to distribute over other areas the stress he placed on the subjective factor. Among the first to receive this new stress was the active part of theory which, as we have shown above, led to a fresh corroboration of the omnipotence of the Party. Thus the whole of the social super-structure and social consciousness, together with their respective relations to economic basis and social existence, have to be reinterpreted so as to cause to emerge the newly perceived active role of social superstructure and social consciousness. In other words, superstructural phenomena now no longer merely follow develop-ments taking place in the economic basis but can exercise significant influence over them. A new importance is attributed also to the function of state and, together with a reinterpretation that recognises the independent development of social consciousness, opens the way to discussion about the functions of law and morality in a manner that classical marxism had not known. Social consciousness in its development may lag behind the development of social existence in regard to which Stalin speaks of the 'survivals of capitalism' (such as capitalist morality, interest in religion, and so on). The outcome of the decision to shorten artificially this lag by the direct inculcation into people's minds of socialist values led to a new emphasis on indoctrination.[26] In this connection we might remark a shift also in the identity of 'motive forces'. In the idiom of classical marxism, these had referred to economic forces alone whereas in the stalinist version 'motive forces' encompassed such factors as patriotism and mutual friendship of Soviet nations. Thus, in addition to placing an unprecedented stress upon superstructural phenomena he succeeded in placing in jeopardy the very core of historical materialism itself – the classical marxist couplings of social consciousness – social existence and social superstructure – an economic basis which in the Stalinist reinterpretation had virtually lost its meaning.[27] Stalin's theoretical edifice was 'crowned' by the suggestion in *Marxism and Linguistics* that certain phenomena do not necessarily fall within either of these dichotomised notions but may lie somewhere 'outside'.[28]

The net result of the subjectivist emphasis, which in Stalin runs through the whole of historical materialism, is the separation of historical materialism from dialectical materialism. Marx emphasised the unity of his teaching as a whole, and we have tried to show in Chapter 2 that the distinction between historical and dialectical materialism is alien to Marx and originated in the works of his successors.[29] In Stalin's version the dichotomised pairs of historical materialism are moulded quite obviously to follow a similar dichotomy in dialectical materialism but if the equivalent of categories of matter-mind in historical materialism display characteristics that are without parallel in the dichotomy matter-mind in dialectical materialism (that is to say if a corresponding stress on matter cannot be placed equally on material existence – or, for example, if the discovery of 'non-antagonistic contradictions' in historical materialism has no parallel in dialectical materialism; if some elements are seen to be outside of both substructure and superstructure while all phenomena are comprehended in the matter-mind division in dialectical materialism), then dialectical and historical materialism are separated and the unity of marxist teaching considerably disturbed. These innovations by Stalin – that is to say, his contribution to historical materialism in the sense of an idealistic interpretation of its categories unparalleled in dialectical materialism – are part of the Soviet Marxist-Leninist inheritance which so far the ideologues have not been able to expurgate. Such excision would involve either rethinking dialectical materialism so as to make it compatible with historical materialism, or attaining the same end by removing the incompatible elements from historical materialism. The former course would involve tampering with the basic assumptions of physics, chemistry, and other natural sciences while the latter would require the renunciation of a considerable part of their own social practice.

The heart of what has become known as stalinism was what could be described as a new 'theory' of international relations, erected upon the new practice of an infant Soviet state that found herself in the middle of a hostile capitalist ring. That this, Stalin's major innovation, should have been in the realm of international relations theory was in itself something of a paradox in view both of the inbuilt

121

disrespect for international relations in classical marxism and of the doubts we have already expressed concerning Stalin's theoretical competence. In this latter regard it will be made clear that as far as using the word 'theory' to describe the advance is concerned the reservations persist and are valid. To begin with, the new theory of international relations, widely recognised by its designation 'socialism in one country', and with its complementary notion of 'capitalist encirclement', cut right across the marxist intellectual structure. Furthermore, since Stalin continued to utilise marxist terminology and vocabulary it is only in conjunction with and within the framework of the theory itself, that the new meanings conferred by Stalin upon such terms as state, nation, class, socialism, etc. can be fully appreciated.

Characteristic of Stalin's approach, the fact of socialism in one country (or, more correctly, the prospect of that eventuality) was the eventuality coming prior to the theoretical formulation – an example of an already existing situation conspiring to bring theory into line. In the event the Soviet example had either not been followed by other countries or attempts to do so had been short-lived.[30] Thus the emergence of a theory of socialism in one country came hard on the heels of the environmental realities – and had soon become the only way of explaining the non-materialisation of that envisaged further stage in world revolutionary development (the immediate attachment of other socialist states). Weakness had been transformed into strength, relevance and marxist continuity had been established and, typically, a virtue had been made of necessity. At least in theory the possibility of a socialist state flourishing in the midst of a capitalist agglomeration without 'degenerating' into one of them had been recognised. In his time too Lenin had been confronted with the problem of relating simultaneously to the classical marxist past and bygone theoretical inconsistencies as well as to his own revolutionary time and place. Then, in extricating himself from the dilemma and to justify the fact that the revolution had broken out in the 'weakest link' of the capitalist chain instead of in the (anticipated) most highly developed capitalist countries, he had rested his theory of imperialism on the newly discovered 'law of uneven capitalist development'. Now, as in these earlier circumstances, the theory of socialism in one country served for Stalin the same purpose of establishing theoretical continuity with the past, as had Lenin's theory of imperialism. Both theories derived from the same law of uneven capitalist development and with the crisis of relevance again negotiated the situation was (again thanks to an adroit leadership) retrieved. As once before, when the successful outcome of the Great October revolution had set the Soviet state firmly on the 'right' path to communism, theoretical confirmation was now available to show that developments in the Soviet state were both compatible with, and indeed offered a vindication of, marxism.

Now, however, 'ratification' of marxism's validity had been achieved largely at the expense of Lenin's theoretical approach, over which (particularly in regard to the area of international relations theory) Stalin showed a marked inclination to compromise. Lenin's expectation had been that the onset of the world revolution would not be long awaited and though its development might proceed by stages it certainly would not be contained within the boundaries of one country. Though it might well 'begin with brilliant success in one country' it would then go through agonising periods, since final victory is only possible on a world scale, and only by the joint efforts of the workers of all countries.[31] Indeed without support from the rest of the world the Soviet success was conceived in the long run to be condemned to failure: 'there is no *other* alternative: *either* Soviet government triumphs in every advanced country in the world, *or* the most reactionary imperialism triumphs. . . . One or the other'.[32] Numerous such statements would seem to leave no doubt as to Lenin's theoretical standpoint in this respect. The socialist state in isolation would be condemned to disintegration either as a result of military aggression or because of internal economic weakness. This assumption (of the approaching *end* of international relations) seems to have been an integral part of Lenin's thinking on international relations. It followed from the expected division of the world in the post-revolutionary era into new units of a different nature from states, that strictly speaking there would be no need for theories of inter-national or inter-state relations. Fortunately for Stalin, however, the ailing Lenin towards the end of his life made statements that were either confused or lent themselves to misinterpretation. From one of these in particular Stalin contrived to take full advantage. We refer to Lenin's article 'On Co-operation': 'indeed, the power of the state over all the large-scale means of production, political power in the hands of the proletariat, the alliance of this proletariat with the many millions of small and very small peasants, the assured leadership of the peasantry, etc. – is this not all that is necessary to build a complete socialist society out of co-operatives, out of co-operatives alone, which we formerly ridiculed . . . is this not all that is necessary to build a complete socialist society? It is still not the building of socialist society, but it is all that is necessary and sufficient for it.'[33] It seems odd in the light of what we may assume Stalin was seeking that he did not fully exploit in support of his theory a clearer statement by Lenin along the same lines in the article 'On our Revolution': 'if a definite level of culture is required for the building of socialism . . . why cannot we begin by first achieving the prerequisites for that definite level of culture in a revolutionary way, and *then*, with the aid of the workers' and peasants' government and the Soviet system, proceed to overtake the other nations?'[34]

On the basis of these few lines from the article 'On Co-operation', which is to say some fifteen lines taken out of the forty-five volumes of Lenin's work, Stalin claimed that the socialism in one country doctrine was fully compatible with the relevant articles of the marxist legacy and the authenticity of its pedigree to have been thus established. Thus Stalin had become the first marxist writer to formulate a theory of international relations that would not explicitly incorporate a theory of the *end* of international relations and in so doing started a tradition that continues to the present day. Although in Lenin's time international relations had undergone something of a rehabilitation it is to the reign of his successor that we look for their elevation to an incomparably higher place in Soviet theory. Where in Lenin's perception international relations became a field where the class conflict took place Stalin went beyond this to a point where international relations became a subject around which the struggle for power raged and controversial issues in the domestic environment were all to a greater or lesser extent reflections or derivatives of international developments and relationships. Those others of the Bolshevik old guard who persisted in their commitment to Lenin's teaching in its more radical (that is to say world revolutionary) form received short shrift for their failure to adapt their theoretical standpoints to the tide of history whose direction of flow Stalin had so correctly gauged. Stalin might well ask of what use were the failed predictions of a trotskyist or to what end the auguries of doom told by such pessimists when, in practice, support for the Soviet state by the victorious revolution in the rest of the world was not forthcoming. It was Stalin, characteristically sardonic, who levelled at Trotsky's theory of 'permanent revolution' the jibe of 'permanent hopelessness' and in so doing underlined his own enduring pragmatism. Unlike Trotsky, Stalin's first concern lay with the actualities and practice of the Soviet state: Trotsky's lay with intellectual integrity, and loyalty to the tenets of orthodox ideology.

It was in his adroitness of manoeuvre and flexibility of attitude, that could so easily be taken by his opponents for cynicism and the dexterity of the opportunist, that much of Stalin's strength lay. In this context it should be emphasised that he himself at the beginning was by no means certain as to the probable duration of the socialism in one country phase and, even as the doctrine received its first enunciation, he suggested then, as subsequently, his preparedness to move in any other direction, and perform a complete about-face if need be.[35] With Lenin's confirmatory and encouraging allusions as blessing, proponents of the 'socialism in one country' doctrine began to come together towards the end of 1924, although unequivocal acceptance of the possibility of the establishment of socialism in a single country did not meet with full endorsement until the Fourteenth Party Conference meeting between 27 and 29 April 1925.[36]

We would contend that the theory of 'socialism in one country' inaugurated a new era, and although it no longer constitutes part of official Soviet policy the year of its enunciation (1924) may be regarded as a point of departure in Soviet theory that leads directly to contemporary thinking on the subject of international relations. Some brief account of the reasons for this opinion should perhaps be given at this point.

The challenge of 'socialism in one country' in all of its implications to the fabric and very foundations of marxism made redefinition and doctrinal revision (or need for 'adjustment') at a commensurately fundamental level unavoidable. The redefinition of 'socialism' alone was clearly a matter of urgent concern as indeed was the need to identify that variety of socialism that could take root 'in one country' alone. Could such a (capitalist-encircled) 'one country' be placed in juxtaposition with the rest of the world? What was the nature of the changes that this 'one country' would have to undergo in her domestic structure (in terms of the standard definition of state and nation) so as to rationalise marxism's becoming 'domesticated' within the perimeters of one horizontal unit (nation-state)? What kind of restraints would this form of 'domestication' impose upon marxism whose perspectives and frontiers were global? And, finally, what model of the world could possibly be conjured up to represent the marriage of

Lenin's model of imperialism to Stalin's 'socialism in one country'? Such questions demanded immediate answers, the urgency stemming from the need to dissimulate the highly embarrassing fact that the socialist state was to be built 'coexistent rather than subsequent to capitalist society, as the competitor rather than the heir of the latter'.[37] Since it is at times difficult to distinguish between the dependent and independent variables, the logic of the argument in these answers is not always easy to follow. The path of the avalanche that swept across the doctrine changed much of it beyond recognition. We can trace, and may even recognise, familiar landmarks in the new configurations; it is when we try to isolate individual fragments that first set the mass in motion or identify internal lines of thrust that we meet with difficulty. However straightforward the task may sound to the logic-attuned Western ear the logic of the theory of socialism in one country is the logic of the avalanche and as such does not yield easily to ordinary Western processes of analysis.

Following roughly the sequence of questions as they suggested themselves above we might say that the prerequisite of the application of the concept was to be the modification of the meaning of socialism itself. As opposed to the achievement of some modified, watered-down version of socialism, was it indeed possible for a 'small island' in the middle of a 'capitalist sea' to achieve a true socialist state untainted by its surroundings? Answers to such questions could not be postponed since upon the outcome of the discussion as to what was and was not possible, and in regard to what the face of socialism would look like in this beleaguered situation, depended the extent to which the theory would be valid or invalid, defensible or indefensible.

In the advance on the ultimate objective, Marx, Engels, and Lenin had predicted a sequential development in which the transformation from capitalism would occur in three stages: the period of revolutionary dictatorship of the proletariat would lead to socialism (as a first phase of communism) which would give way in turn to the achievement of communism in the full and proper meaning of the word.[38] Stalin must not only claim the conformity of his own plans to that outline but bring persuasive evidence to show that his line of development was consistent with the main marxian programme. Along lines determined for him by the 'domestication' of marxism he introduced sub-phases into the second and third stages in so nebulous and indeterminate a way as to allow himself scope for redefinition as and when it became necessary, as well as latitude to terminate or

126

introduce successive stages. The two sub-phases of socialism in the new programme were: 1 the complete victory of socialism and 2 the final victory of socialism. These two phases would be duplicated in the final advance on communism thus: the complete victory of communism and the final victory of communism. The attribution of, respectively, 'domestic' and 'world-wide' to these sub-phases would have been more exact since those descriptions would have corresponded more closely to what was intended. Such a description would also have served to make quite clear a central feature of the theory: the fact that the advance from the victory of socialism to the attainment of communism in the domestic context could be made directly without awaiting the 'final' victory of socialism on a world-wide basis. The necessity for the subdivision of the state had been thrust upon Stalin by the fact of 'capitalist encirclement' and it was against that background that the attainable in his perception must remain as a domestic ('complete') socialist victory, or socialist system. Only by the replacement of that background by a situation of 'socialist encirclement'[39] could the victory of socialism enter the 'second degree' and become final (world-wide). Although these notions were given some prominence in Soviet writing up until the early 1950s one derives the gist by implication rather than from any attempt during that time at clear definition,[40] and in a speech by Mikoyan in 1956 they were in any case finally declared to be obsolete and to have been superseded.

As we have suggested above, the expedient of introducing sub-phases left it to Stalin alone to decide on the moment when he could declare the construction of socialism in its first complete stages to have been accomplished. The declaration was forthcoming in 1936 with the statement 'socialism has now become a fact', and by way of proof promulgated a new socialist constitution. As to the prospect of building communism he stated to the Eighteenth Party Congress in March 1939 that it was even possible for one country in isolation to build a complete communist society – as the stage following that of 'complete' socialism. Thus there begins to assume definite form the vision of a communist state [sic] – an apparition which would no doubt have astonished Marx and Engels for whom 'socialist or communist state' would have seemed *contradictio ex adjecto*.[41]

In the process of redefining and reshaping socialism Stalin had to answer the question as to whether, given the marxist postulates of the indivisibility of world economy, the surgical cuts involved in the operation could be justified. While it is possible to assert that even in this respect Stalin merely presses Lenin's theses to their (arguably) logical conclusion it is worth remembering that the difference between Lenin and Stalin in their diagnosis of the nature of the socialist state *vis-à-vis* the hitherto assumed monolithic capitalistic economy was (to use the marxist jargon) qualitative. While Lenin appears to have viewed the Soviet socialist state as a more or less temporary but malignant tumour on the body of the capitalist world and anticipated the cellular spread[42] of the infection, Stalin concludes that the tumour is merely benign, is in (conceptual) isolation from the capitalist body, and therefore no longer anticipates an acute over-all infection. A conclusion of far-reaching (and practical) consequence to be sure but one whose appropriateness he seems in his treatment of the condition to deny. The simile suggested by his approach to the condition is rather of a healed area (socialist state), permanently isolated from the rest of the diseased capitalist body. In this perception may be seen the origin of Soviet attitudes and thought patterns that have prevailed in the field of international relations since.

However, if the representation of Stalin's innovations in terms of metaphor presents little difficulty, their theoretical justification in terms of historical materialism and marxist political economy is a different matter altogether. Trotsky, basing his thinking on the traditional marxist assumption that the capitalist system was most fatally undermined by the contradiction of its world-wide nature and economic scope in conflict with its exclusively national political structure, found it impossible to reconcile the approaches of Stalin and Marx in this area. Socialism alone could resolve this fatal contradiction because socialism, according to Trotsky, was based on the international economic unity of the socialist classes; and so it was precisely in socialism's obligatory application across the face of the earth that lay one of its main distinguishing features.[43] A scaled-down socialism was a contradiction in terms. In Trotsky's view, therefore, the infant Soviet state had no real choice: or, to put it more precisely, it had the choice of either engendering the immediate support of world revolution ('permanent revolution') or perishing.[44] Trotsky rejected totally the notion of the 'domestication' of socialism and compared its absurdity to the games of children: 'Up to the complete world victory of the world proletariat, a number of individual countries build socialism in their respective countries, and subsequently out of these socialist countries there will be built a world socialist economy, after the manner in which children erect structures with ready-made blocks.'[45]

An area of similarly fundamental nature that went without theoretical resolution in Stalin's time emerged from problems associated not only with the question of the divisibility or otherwise of the economic basis but also of that question applied to its 'reflection' in superstructural phenomena – which is to say the nature of the rules governing the conduct of relations in international law between capitalist and socialist states. When we bear in mind contemporary Soviet international relations typology[46] it is interesting to note in this context that until they were peremptorily silenced 'from above' the discussion among Soviet international lawyers anticipated that of their successors – our contemporaries. The argument turned on Marx's dismissal of all law as class law and an instrument of the ruling class. Furthermore, as a corollary to Marx's negative attitude, Soviet international lawyers faced the extremely difficult theoretical question as to how one single corpus of law could possibly bind diverse social systems. We should emphasise that, then as now, the concern manifested in regard to international law came in the wake of the practical realisation that, despite all previous expectations, relations with the rest of the world would stand or fall by the degree of expertise developed in international law and in the field of diplomacy. Interest was given a boost also by the failure of less conventional methods (the Comintern for example) of handling international relations. It might also be borne in mind in this regard that, quite irrespective of Marx's contempt for law, the new Soviet federation soon after its inception embarked upon the negotiation of treaties, arranging the terms of peace, and dealt with the settlement of boundary disputes.

The debate that centred on Marx's attitude to law produced three schools of legal thought which, although soon reduced to silence, presaged contemporary Soviet attitudes (some of which appear today practically unmodified), and are therefore worthy of a brief mention. The first school, and that most faithful to the classical marxist position, was that represented by the Communist (Sverdlov) University of Moscow which designated the teaching of international law as superfluous and removed it from its curriculum. The textbook in international law of the time drew attention to the pressing need to destroy the theory of state and national sovereignty in all of its historical configurations, 'from Bodin to Hobbs through Rousseau and Montesquieu, to Jellinek, the Mensheviks and social revolutionaries'.[47] The statement was probably motivated still by expectations of an impending world revolution to which eventuality both Rousseau and Montesquieu would have had very little to contribute. In opposition to this legal nihilism there appeared two schools, one led by Korovin and the other by Pashukanis. Both of these agreed that superstructure could not be automatically dismissed along nihilist (classical marxist) lines and that indeed it evinced something of a *new* nature. Accordingly there was perceived to have come into existence a 'new system of legal relationships'.[48]

The Korovin school espoused the view that the involvement of the Soviet state in international relations with capitalist states does not by virtue of being so involved become deprived of its natural place in the non-capitalist superior social order. Nor do such transactions imply concession to the capitalist system because international relations are conceived of as being of a *new* type. The superstructural reflection of the meeting of the bases on which the two systems rest is also new in nature being neither capitalist nor yet fully socialist. When to this argument there is joined the expectation of an inevitable 'socialist-wards' drift culminating in the ascendancy of that system, we have a conclusion not far distant from that reached by Soviet theory in our own time. One, in other words, that takes full cognisance of the possibility of the two systems existing in protracted coexistence and suggests a confident anticipation of the development of those distinct types of international relations to which we have referred. In this regard it was assumed that international relations between capitalist states would continue to be pursued along the old well-trodden paths while international relations between capitalist and socialist states would exhibit uniquely new and unprecedented characteristics. Since at the time he was writing there was only one socialist state (the Mongolian development minimally influencing the situation) Korovin does not identify relations between socialist states as a separate and distinct type of international relations, but the theory makes explicit provision for such a development: 'The deeply rooted fundamental differences of the legal and social order of capitalist society on the one hand and socialist order on the other entails a manifold and substantial alternative of legal norms governing mutual relations between bourgeois countries and the socialist ones.'[49] From these assumptions there derived a negative attitude to the admission of custom and precedent as a source of international law. This attitude, still traceable in the contemporary approach, saw custom arising as a result of *usus longeavus* and *opinion necessitatis* and would be, by definition, of a capitalist nature. It followed therefore that the only meaningful source of international law that would bind both capitalist and socialist states was treaties: 'watching each other closely, the two participants, the USSR and the "Capitalist State", met on the strictly limited grounds of mutual agreement of a conventional character, only to return at once each to his own principles. The sacred formula so dear to every adherent of international law, that of the "common principles of international laws", has only rarely been made in Soviet treaties, most frequently in those with Germany, and has been of inconsiderable practical importance.'[50]

It was precisely here, in this area dealing with the bases on which the establishment of a socialist-capitalist international relations dialogue was to rest, that the school represented by Evgenii Pashukanis[51] parted company with that of Korovin. This rival school rested its challenge on the contention that there is no such thing as an international community of values. That, accordingly, as far as sources of international law are concerned, both custom and treaty may be regarded as on a par since they merely provide an outline whose content is supplied by each system in accordance with its own values. In comparison with Korovin's handling of main questions, the school failed to come up with adequate answers and to this extent may be regarded as a theoretical regression. Yet another stand taken by one of Korovin's critics, Andrei Sabinin, advocated that the fullest possible improvement be achieved through the exploitation of the existing system, much along the compromise lines followed during the period of NEP. In the early 1930s both Korovin and Sabinin came in for violent criticism[52] which received official endorsement in a resolution of the 1931 Congress of Marxist Theoreticians of Law that labelled Korovin as a 'pseudo-marxist' and Sabinin as 'bourgeois'. Thenceforward theoretical answers were to be sought elsewhere than in Pashukanis's notion of filling capitalist institutions with socialist content.

In the mid-1930s it was Pashukanis's 'turn' to be criticised for maintaining that the law of the transitional period was still a bourgeois edifice – albeit tenanted by socialist content – and that this law should begin its gradual 'withering away' immediately. The main critic of both Korovin and Pashukanis during the period after 1937 was Andrei Vyshinskii whose failure to put forward a substitute theory for either school[53] gave rise to a situation that might justifiably be described as a period of theoretical crisis during which Soviet practice advances, while marxist theory in its explanatory or even justificatory function is conspicuously lacking.

With 'socialism' redefined (though neither empirical nor theoretical evidence as to its attainability in one country had been forthcoming) and with the removal in one way or another of some awkward questions posed by historical materialism, the way was open to Stalin to reconstruct the theoretical model of the world, designate the principal actors, and establish the nature of their interrelationship. We will hope to show as we analyse Stalin's new model the extent of the modification as well as the redefinition of such major notions of historical materialism as state and nation occasioned by the newly perceived constellations. Indeed, the model will occupy for the remainder of this chapter a pre-eminent place since it is by reference to it that we consider to be the most satisfactory method of establishing perspective and the necessary connections between such concepts as Lenin's imperialism, 'socialism in one county', 'capitalist encirclement', and the 'two camps doctrine'.

The hybrid growth that resulted from Stalin's joining Lenin's model of imperialism with his own 'socialism in one country' resulted in some strange features, not the least strange of which being the fact of its acceptance over the long term – an acceptance that would seem to have run counter to Lenin's anticipated short-run expedient. In contemporary Western jargon the 'solution', deriving from global structural dependence, was incorporated as a third pole[54] into Lenin's 'classical' model of bipolar structural dependence. Due to the relative weakness both of this third pole (socialist state) and of the exploiting (capitalist) states they, in Stalin's perception (and in reality), became locked in a new triangularity which has been a major feature of Soviet thinking on international relations ever since. Indeed, one might argue that the Soviet state which was intended to act as a 'solvent' functioned instead as a 'catalyst' in regard to the continuing existence of that bipolarity that it was supposed to remove for ever. But that is to anticipate conclusions before identifying the premises and subjecting these, together with their interrelationships, to analysis.

In the first place we should make it clear that Stalin has taken over Lenin's theory of imperialism *in toto* and endeavours throughout the course of his career to sustain its major characteristics oblivious of the

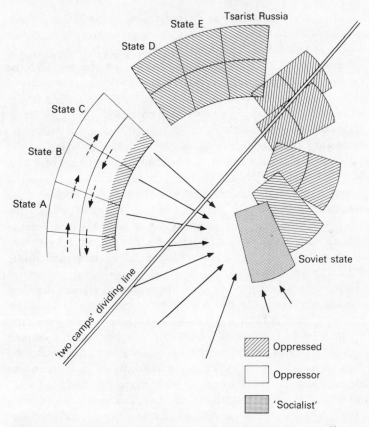

Figure 6 Horizontal and vertical divisions of mankind according to Stalin (1).

fact that from the moment when the third 'pole' is introduced revision of that theory automatically follows. And so he conceives of the world as falling into two major groupings: 'exploiting countries' (which is to say developed capitalist countries), and 'exploited countries' (which is to say underdeveloped countries and colonies). As the reader is aware, it was in the interaction between these two divisions that Lenin located that irreconcilable contradiction and focus of class conflict for the period of imperialism – thus relegating, at least temporarily, into a position of secondary importance the proletariat in capitalist countries. In Stalin's revised version both groupings of states retain their internal bipolarity of classes (exploited and exploiting), and continue thereby to exhibit an internal (class) contradiction – which his third pole addition (socialist state) does not possess. As described above, contradictions within the socialist state, if they exist, are conceived to be of a different non-antagonistic nature, and the internal dynamic deriving from the mutually opposed interaction of classes central to the operation of the dialectic is supplied in the socialist state 'from above' by the strong state itself.

In addition to these three major participants in his triangular relationship there operate what Stalin describes as 'allies' of the Soviet state located in each of the original two groupings of states. These 'allies' are twofold and consist in the developed countries of the proletariat and, in the underdeveloped countries and colonies, of the oppressed peoples.[55] The very existence of the newcomer to the model (socialist state) is a function of the resultant of all of the contradictions operative within the model. But now let us look more closely at the relations taking place among all of these participants outlined above.

First of all a new type of interrelationship to replace the class contradiction within the two original groupings of states had to be invented. Since (and here was the whole point) the socialist state could no longer be said to be exploited, Lenin's explanation in economic terms of relations between exploited and the exploiting states no longer obtained. 'We must build our economy as an independent economic unit based mainly on the home market',[56] declares Stalin, admitting at the same time that some residual economic dependence of the Soviet state on the world capitalist economy was still present, though in his view offering no longer the slightest impairment of that state's autonomy. Thus, rather than demanding explanation, the new phenomenon of schism in the world economy is accepted as axiomatic with the open acknowledgment of the fact that a still weak Soviet state is obliged to 'resort to economic manoeuvring and utilizing economic contacts with capitalist countries . . . but only within the limits useful to the USSR', so that the hazard of the USSR slipping back into economic dependence and becoming once again 'an appendage of the world capitalist system'[57] is avoided. The theory was plausible; the way in which in practice an economically backward Soviet state was to avoid slipping back was less clear. We have it on Lenin's own testimony that he clearly regarded state monopoly capitalism as the 'complete material preparation for socialism'. Seen, in other words, either as some sort of 'ante-room' of socialism or in some sense the historical stage that inevitably must precede the advent of socialism.[58] In this context, in fact, Lenin once went so far as to say that 'state capitalism would be a step forward . . . if we were capable of obtaining a state capitalism in Russia within a short time, this would be a victory . . . our saviour. If we would have it in Russia, then the transition to full socialism would be easy and certain. For capitalism is a system of centralisation, integration, control, and socialisation. And this is precisely what we lack.'[59] And this is precisely what Stalin adopted as his own; not a state capitalism, but 'state socialism' (although he of course does not use the term). His answer then to the problems arising from the predicament of 'capitalist encirclement' involves a redefinition of the proletariat's internal 'allies', an enormous emphasis on the accelerated development of industry and agriculture (an unlimiting stress on heavy industry and on collectivisation of agriculture as the vehicles), and each sector of the advance controlled and implemented by a strong centralised state – itself controlled by (not to say tantamount to) a powerful tightly knit Communist Party.

The details of the argument used in the redefinition of the proletariat's allies, or that incorporating the peasant – along lines suggested by Lenin – more fully into the socialist orbit need not detain us here except in two respects. The first of these is that it was used as the main counter-argument to Trotsky's concept of permanent revolution which would have joined inseparably the fate of the Soviet state with the vicissitudes of the world revolution. By way of contrast – and with the help of such internal allies as the peasant – Stalin sees a strong possibility of 'going it alone' and using the resources of the Soviet state itself instead of relying on outside help: 'According to Lenin,' maintains Stalin, 'the revolution draws its forces chiefly from among the workers and peasants themselves; whilst, according to Trotsky, the necessary forces can be found only "in the arena of the world proletarian revolution" '.

The second aspect of the argument that might claim our attention here is the inclusion of the peasant into the marxist equation, a development that allowed Stalin to hold less in the centre of his attention the course of events in the semideveloped countries and colonies; for as soon as the peasant can be regarded as a revolutionary force, a more detached approach to 'letting them get on with it' could be adopted without the harassment of having to contrive any particular policy towards that part of the world. Hence the argument

135

provided at one and the same time grounds for the rejection of Trotsky and for the inclusion of the peasant as a revolutionary ally. Assigned this enhanced role both within the 'exploited' countries and, above all, in the Soviet state, the dictatorship of the proletariat and peasantry was soon to become a dictatorship *over* both of them with each controlled rather than controlling.

The notion of state in its post-revolutionary manifestation also demanded redefinition if in contravention of classical marxist expectations it was quite obviously not withering away. In fact the nihilist approach and 'withering away' formula of Engels had already undergone qualification at the hands of Lenin[60] but now, with the fading prospect of *final* (world-wide) victory for communism replaced by the expectation of prolongation of the first phase of communism, the formula was abandoned altogether. Were Engels's formula to be applied in the way originally intended, Stalin maintained, it would mean that the Communist Party of the Soviet state would have to take 'steps to bring about the speedy withering away of our state, to dissolve state institutions, to give up a permanent army'.[61] He argued that for precisely the same reason (capitalist encirclement) as had required a new stage of socialism to be formulated, so was now required the formulation of a new concept of state: 'in a condition of capitalist encirclement, when the victory of the socialist revolution has taken place only in one country, while capitalism rules in all other countries, the only country of the victorious revolution must not weaken, but in every way strengthen its state, the state institution, the intelligence organs, and the army, if this country does not wish to be crushed by the capitalists' encirclement'.[62] With some justice one might thus conclude that a new concept (of the strengthened state) is imposed on Soviet theory by virtue of the perceived danger of extinction at the hands of incomparably more powerful capitalist states: in other words, a preferred course of action to reliance on the operation of external factors – which is to say the world revolutionary movement. Despite superficial resemblances and indications to the contrary, however, these capitalist states still remained different in kind to the new socialist state: while the capitalist state remained the oppressive instrument of one class (exploiters) and held coercive sway over the majority element of the society (exploited), the state in the socialist mould underwent a complete transformation whereby it was no longer an instrument controlled by a minority but was now in the hands of the majority, with only 'non-antagonistic' solutions requiring to be handed down 'from above'. Therefore, although the stress placed on the state in socialist society remained extremely strong Stalin was able to argue drastic differences existing not only between the socialist state and its capitalist counterpart but differences associated also with its stage to stage development. According to Stalin the capitalist state had two functions: an *internal* function which Stalin described as 'the main function' which would 'keep in restraint the exploited majority', and an *external* function which, while 'not the main function', would 'extend the territory of its class, the ruling class, at the expense of the territory of other states, or defend the territory of its own state from attack by other states'.[63] During the first period of its existence the socialist state was obliged also to retain both functions. In circumstances of 'capitalist encirclement' no particular justification was required for the retention of the second (external) function but for the retention of the first (internal) function cause had to be found and in this regard it was postulated that it was necessary, by whatever means, to repress hostile sections of society.[64] As suggested above, the second (external) function would be effective throughout the period of capitalist encirclement in the course of which the first (internal) would be subject to considerable modification. Such modification, it was anticipated, would emerge as the neutralisation or elimination of hostile classes proceeded to the point where its function would become 'protecting socialist property from the thieves and pilferers of the property of the people'.[65] In addition to these two functions the Soviet state from its inception assumed a third role: 'the work of economic organisation and cultural education' by which there was added to the broad front of the socialist advance an 'economic dimension and a cultural revolution'. This third function became increasingly important and was soon to be styled 'the main function'.

Stalin's handling of another central sector, the national question, may also be ascribed to that emphasis on centralism and elimination of centrifugal tendencies that derived from a real, or certainly perceived, external threat. One of Stalin's first forays into the realm of theory had been in this area[66] and his first assignment in the Soviet government was that of People's Commissar (1917–22) of Nationalities Affairs. During that period his handling of the nationalities was characterised by ruthlessness up to and including genocide,[67] an approach whose explanation might be found either in his own theoretical work or may be inferred from environmental pressures. Apart from considerations that made expedient policies of rapid centralisation, these pressures included the debilitating action of certain elements in the infant state as well as their potential hazard as 'clients' of members of that hostile capitalist ring.

We would suggest three areas in which as early as 1913 Stalin gave some indication of an intention to depart from previously held marxist views. There was the question first of all of definition of a nation. While his marxist predecessors showed more caution in offering a comprehensive descriptive definition Stalin did not hesitate: 'A nation is a historically constituted, stable community of people, formed on the basis of a common language, territory, economic life, and psychological makeup manifested in a common culture.'[68] As Stalin himself immediately went on to point out, one result of defining nation in this way is that 'it is only when all these characteristics are present together that we have a nation'.[69] In practical terms, in the absence of all of the prescribed characteristics, this would mean denying to many national groupings who might regard themselves as nations the possibility of being considered such. Ethno-religious groupings such as Jews would not be deemed to constitute a nation, nor would such entities as colonial peoples without a viable economic existence be so considered. Such a definition lent itself to a great deal of arbitrariness in the interpretation of its vague terms, but perhaps an even more serious blow struck at the right to nationhood was Stalin's welding of the concept of nationalism to that of the bourgeoisie: 'the national struggle under the conditions of *rising* capitalism is a struggle of the bourgeois classes among themselves. Sometimes the bourgeoisie succeeds in drawing the proletariat into the national movement, and then the national struggle *externally* assumes a "nation-wide" character. But this is only so externally. In its *essence* it is always a bourgeois struggle, one that is to the advantage and profit mainly of the bourgeoisie.'[70] *Ergo*, nationalism, it would seem to follow from this argument, is an anomaly *after* the socialist revolution has been accomplished – when it has become an anachronism to be combated. Despite feigned fidelity to and dutiful repetition of some early leninist statements in regard to the right of self-determination and the equality of all nations[71] yet a further blow was delivered with the adoption of the principle of international solidarity of the workers (i.e. class considerations) which was construed as an essential ingredient in the solution of the national question. And, further, that the stress was to be placed on *regional*[72] autonomy of crystallised units (as opposed to national), the unity of such groupings deriving from the workers (from below) of all nationalities. The national groupings to which they adhered were disregarded.

This basic anti-national attitude and approach was inconsistent and completely at variance with Stalin's attitude to the Russian nation which as Lenin had feared was already on the way to a position of privileged national status. One suggestion has been that as a result of the prominent role allocated to the proletariat in marxism and to the fact that that element was less weak in the Russian than in the other nations that joined in the Soviet state, it was in consequence not only the Russian proletariat but also the Russian *nation* that gained such prominence as to enable it to defy both the repeated commitment to the equality of nations and also to confound notions of proletarian internationalism. Lenin himself had been well aware of the dangers inherent in Great Russian chauvinism but after his death nothing could be done to stop it. Soon the Great Russian *nation* assumed both a most privileged and a superior position *vis-à-vis* all other nations, first of all within the Soviet state, and shortly within the whole world proletarian movement, whose interests it came to be assumed to represent.

Thus the negative attitude to nationalism deriving from the perceived bourgeois connotations of nation incongruously linked with a distorted priority given to the Russian nation as the leading nation of the proletariat (paradoxically by Stalin who himself was not a Russian) soon led to a redefinition of proletarian internationalism itself:[73]

> He is an internationalist who unreservedly, unhesitatingly and unconditionally is prepared to defend the USSR, because the USSR is the base of the world revolutionary movement, and it is impossible to defend, to advance this revolutionary movement without defending the USSR. Whoever thinks of defending the world revolutionary movement without, and against, the USSR, goes against revolution, and must slide to the camp of the enemy of the revolution.

In other words, instead of subordinating the interests of the USSR to the interests of proletarian internationalism – and its extension of interests on the world scale – proletarian internationalism itself was now subjected to domestication and subordinated to the interests of 'one country' which, although of a 'higher order', could still be claimed to constitute no more than one horizontal unit.

Hand in hand with this development and, it might be said, following more or less automatically upon it, came the domestication of the Comintern. Had the leninist parallel of the relationship of class to Party been followed, the Comintern, as the representative of all workers and their interests (designated by Lenin as 'the world party of the proletariat'), would have been placed at the centre of that movement. This place however was now usurped as the interests of the world proletarian revolution were subordinated to the interests and preservation of only one proletarian *state* – a state artificially located at the centre of the world proletariat movement, represented falsely as the homeland of all workers, its capital masquerading as their class capital.[74]

The central position of the USSR (and within it of the Russian nation) thus foreshadowed soon became a matter of fact, and Soviet practice, for no better reason than that she alone had so far been successful in orchestrating the pre- and post-revolutionary score, laid claim to the blueprint that all subsequent communist revolutionary practice was to follow. Trotsky seemed to have been aware of the danger and like Lenin, who showed awareness of Russia's backwardness and need to 'catch up' in respect of general civilisation and culture, believed that the USSR was unsuitable as a permanent leader of the world communist movement:[75]

Our country is still very backward, our country is barbarian . . . but we are defending this bulwark of the world revolution since, at this moment, it is the only one in the world. When another stronghold is erected in France, or in Germany, then Russia will lose nine-tenths of its significance, and then we shall come to you in Europe to defend this other, more important stronghold. It would be sheer absurdity, Comrades, to think that we consider this Russian revolutionary stronghold the centre of the world.

While Lenin paid a great deal of attention to the Comintern, encouraged its smooth functioning, and enjoyed the lively ideological debates on its platform, Stalin treated it from the first with disrespect. Soon, as the link between the USSR and the Comintern proved an embarrassment to his diplomatic activity with the capitalist states, it came to represent something of a nuisance. Instead of the World Congresses of the Comintern its presidium gained in importance, and for at least as long as it suited his convenience he saw to it that there was a preponderance of Russian representation throughout its various organs. As we have suggested, the decline of the organisation was manifest in a loss of interest in its congresses, and in this regard the record speaks for itself: while Lenin was still alive in the first four years of the Comintern's existence four World Congresses were held, all of them attended and addressed by Lenin himself. In the twenty years[76] that followed Lenin's death there were but three congresses; at the end of this period Stalin himself was responsible (in 1943) for the dissolution of the Comintern. In addition to this attenuation, the role of Lenin's 'World Party of the Proletariat' was changed so as to provide a rostrum for the enunciation of Stalin's views on matters of Soviet domestic and foreign concern: paradoxically the Comintern had come to be more involved in purging the communist movements of dissidents rather than in engaging battle with the capitalist states. As a consequence the Soviet state – allegedly of a different nature but remaining still a state (horizontal unit) – assumed the distinct and rather asymmetrical place that Lenin had envisaged for the Comintern, namely the epicentre of the (vertical) class scale. Indeed the Programme of the Comintern admitted these self-imposed limitations and declared dependence upon the Soviet state when it proclaimed as a duty of the international proletariat the furtherance of the state (sic) interests of the Soviet Union, and the theoretical confusion was compounded in its attitude to the USSR: 'The working class of the world now has its own state, the exclusive Fatherland of the international proletariat.'[77] That the Soviet state would have wished to perform both of these roles – relating as a state (horizontal unit) through traditional (diplomatic) channels to other states, and as the self-appointed centre of the international proletarian movement usurping the originally intended role of the (vertical unit) Comintern, is not a doubt, but when the clash came, as inevitably it must between these two contradictory functions, it was resolved unequivocally in favour of the adoption of a state posture. Although there is no agreement amongst sovietologists in this regard,[78] it was when the too apparent link between the Soviet state and the Moscow-located Comintern headquarters began to hinder the smooth functioning of Soviet inter-state relations with capitalist countries that the Comintern went to the wall.[79] Whether the final dissolution of the Comintern came as a result of Stalin's changing priorities or derived from the theoretical impasse that lay at its heart it is certain that, particularly after 1933, references to the Comintern in Stalin's foreign policy speeches and reports dwindled and faded to nothing. Further-more, by the time of the last World Congress in 1935 the derussifica-tion of Comintern personnel had become a simple and undeniable symptom of its ebbing life.

As it transpired, the dictatorship superimposed by the CPSU and Stalin on the proletariat and peasantry of the Soviet Union also extended to a dominion by the USSR over foreign communist parties. Broadly speaking, the world proletarian movement was held in thrall, to be animated intermittently by its Moscow masters as and when Stalin saw fit. Trotsky relates in what contemptuous regard Stalin held this Soviet creature and the potentialities of the world proletarian movement in general. [80] If it was left to the Comintern, Stalin allegedly asserted, a revolution would be awaited in vain for ninety years,[81] by which was implied the containment of the revolutionary potential of the proletariat within the capitalist countries. Certainly such contain-ment, coupled with an already remarked non-existent policy and lack of direction afforded to 'colonial revolutions',[82] would tend to lend substance to his gloomy prognostication. And yet, in the circum-stances suggested above, Stalin's policy (or non-policy) of 'following' rather than issuing revolutionary directives to these areas was not without merit. Indeed, in areas where the proletariat was small or non-existent and the peasantry already playing the role of revolu-tionary ally, a policy of *laissez-faire* could be theoretically justifiable since in such circumstances, it might be argued, the peasant mass was naturally 'ripening' and the revolutionary dynamic generating 'of itself'. Left to a large extent indeterminate were Stalin's views as to where precisely the next revolutionary outbreak might be expected to occur. While paying his official respects to Lenin's theory of the weakest link in the chain he defined that link so loosely that, had it snapped at any time or in any part of the world, it would have occasioned him no particular problem of theoretical justification – or of repudiation.[83]

Thus, if we were to engage again in an assessment of the emphasis apportioned by Stalin to the various parts of the (now become) triangular world model we would have to admit that the class units – upon which an aspiring marxist theoretician must be expected to rely heavily – are shabbily dealt with. By containing the revolutionary proletariat in the developed countries (including its organisation, the Comintern) and by effectively excluding from his theoretical (and practical) perspectives the underdeveloped countries and colonies, the area left within Stalin's focal range would seem to be the part of the triangle that remains – the capitalist states. The process of exclusion is easy to follow, and from this point it proceeds to deal with the revolutionary mass – the proletariat in the developed countries was 'unable to render us direct and decisive assistance' while the build-up of the 'immense reserve for our revolution' (and 'reserve' may be taken as the operative word) among oppressed colonial peoples and underdeveloped countries was described as being 'very slow'.[84] The digression from this exclusivist assessment only became manifest in the deliberate and formidable efforts to mobilise all domestic resources while exploiting capitalist conflicts and contradictions. It is as if, by repudiating Trotsky's argument and criticisms, Stalin had repudiated also classical marxism. As it is, his theory of international relations falls quite clearly into two sections: one in which he tries rather painstakingly to establish a continuity with the marxist heritage (and it is to this end that the content of socialism in one country and capitalist encirclement are obviously developed), and a second part in which he reverses direction and conveys an impression of discontinuity. In other words, having contrived in the first part to redefine the principal terms of marxism, he then, contrary to all our expectations, offers a most un-marxist theory of inter-*state* relations. The very conventional language and conceptualisation in which the theory is couched is relieved only by a marxist 'touch' in the shape of explicit moral approbation of the Soviet state as opposed to all others.

If then we were now to chart on Figure 7 the scope of Stalin's international relations theory the full implications of his direction might be appreciated. Eurocentric once again, Stalin looks unwaveringly in the direction of the capitalist states and in his conceptualising he does not stray from the assumption of two, and only two, sets of relationships. With the understanding and manipulation of the interaction between these two sets of relations in sight we have clearly arrived at the heart of that theory of international relations upon which basis rested Stalin's foreign policy formulations. The first set of relations has to do with 'capitalist conflicts and contradictions' in their domestic operation and international ramifications, and the second set refers to relations between the Soviet state and the capitalist countries. The remainder of this section will be devoted to an investigation of each of these two sets of relations, and we turn first to that of intra-capitalist conflicts and contradictions.

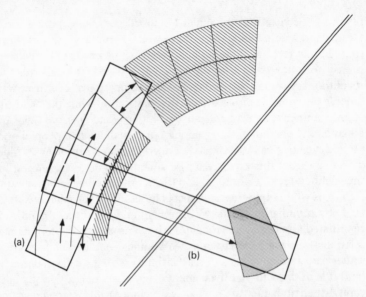

Figure 7 Horizontal and vertical divisions of mankind according to
Stalin (2). The narrowed range of Stalin's history of
international relations: (a) International relations among
capitalist states and capitalist contradictions generally.
(b) International relations between capitalist states and
the Soviet Union

In subscribing to the notion of intra-capitalist conflict and
contradictions Stalin's fidelity to the analysis of Marx and Lenin is
established, but he then proceeds to depart from them both. For
Lenin and Marx the *fact* of intra-capitalist contradictions had become
something of a taboo, and of course theories denying these contradictions are therefore rejected. In this context we have already noted
Kautsky,[85] who had been the subject of a bitter attack by Lenin; and
Eugen Varga, who when he too touched on a notion that has since
become axiomatic to Soviet thinking on international relations was
similarly castigated during Stalin's time. These notions, which have
now become constants of Soviet thinking and with which we have had
reason to become familiar, were concerned with the explicit commitment to a conviction that the capitalist system must of necessity breed
intra-capitalist contradictions and that these, although ultimately
fatal, may for temporary purposes (such as to resist the international

proletariat) be overcome.[86] That in the context of these contradictions there should be some divergence between Marx's conclusions and those of Stalin is to be expected. Initially at least, Marx, for example, anticipated neither the emergence from the irreconcilability of these contradictions of a socialist state nor that its survival would depend on (and its integrity stand or fall by) policies derived from them.

Describing the conflicts and contradictions among the capitalist states as an 'ally, intangible, impersonal, but for all that an extremely important one',[87] Stalin, we may surmise,[88] meant the contradictions:

1 Between the proletariat and bourgeoisie within the individual capitalist countries.
2 Among the 'ruling classes' of the imperialist powers struggling for the conquest of foreign territories.
3 Between the imperialist powers and their colonial and dependent peoples.
4 Between the victorious powers and the vanquished in which the former seek to retain the *status quo* while the latter are revisionists.
5 Between the capitalist states and colonial dependencies over former colonial territories.
6 The contradiction between the two (capitalist and socialist) camps.

Following Lenin, Stalin agreed that in the final, terminal stage of the existence of capitalism, which is to say imperialism, the intra-capitalist conflicts reach their highest pitch. Stalin added as an accelerating factor in this process the existence of the Soviet state which, by such considerations as the reduction in size of the capitalist market and attendant adverse influences on production, sharpens the pitch and further precipitates the capitalist disintegration. Unlike the situation that obtained in Marx's time when free enterprise capitalism capable of 'normal' functioning had the facility of recovering at regular intervals from the periods of crises to which it was equally regularly[89] subjected, this regenerative mechanism in the imperialist stage of capitalism no longer operates. Thus, instead of a short developmental cycle with a relatively brief stay at the bottom of each downturn, imperialism's condition now is one of perpetual crisis. Such is the meaning of the term 'general crisis of capitalism' still extant in Soviet marxist terminology to describe a plight that will occupy not a year or two but the entire epoch. During that space of time the parallel development in the socialist socio-economic system – destined to be the historical successor of capitalism – is one characterised by forward motion and growing strength. And so, regardless of intermittent periods of capitalist stabilisation,[90] the relation of the Soviet Union with the capitalist countries is essentially based on relations among the capitalist countries and is a function of their inner contradictions.

It was Lenin who began this tradition of making the very existence of the socialist state contingent upon the existence of contradictions within capitalism: 'Our existence', he observed at the Eighth All-Russian Congress of Soviets in December 1920, 'depends, first, on the existence of radical split in the imperialist Powers.'[91] But it was left to Stalin to carry the tradition of his mentor to a logical (and more practical) conclusion that had the flavour, so to speak, of a Soviet 'divide and survive': 'The whole purpose of the existence of the People's Commissariat of Foreign Affairs is to take account of these contradictions, to base ourselves upon them, and to manoeuvre among these contradictions.'[92] But how, one might well ask, could such an emphasis be reconciled with the placement, frequently reiterated after 1919, of these relations (between capitalist and socialist states) at the hub of world affairs? Even given a new type of domestic structure an onlooker would have been forgiven the impression that the Soviet state's internal situation was assailed from so many sides and its very survival so problematical that to ascribe such prime importance to the relationship with capitalist countries – much less place so arrogant an emphasis upon that relationship – seemed contrived and unrealistic. The theoretical justification of the predominance (in theory) of the socialist-capitalist relationship over intra-capitalist relationships was supplied in the 'two camp doctrine': 'The world is definitely and irrevocably split into two camps: the camp of imperialism and the camp of socialism . . . [and the struggle between them] . . . constitutes the hub of present-day affairs, determines the whole substance of the present home and foreign policies of the leaders of the old and the new world'.[93] However small and weak relative to the capitalist states the Soviet state might have been, this doctrine assigned to the relation between them a chiliastic nature and thus, by seeming to create for the Soviet state a category of its own, pre-empted any supposition that placed it among the ordinary run of states. For such it was not: not only did it have the clear potential to survive and flourish but it represented the first stage in the advance of communism – in the achievement of whose world victory it still expected to be instrumental. Essentially then the two camp doctrine was based on a set of axioms: first of all on the ultimate irreconcilability of the two camps and, second, that one of these (whose identity was known) was already condemned to perish. In other words a zero-sum situation with victor and vanquished predetermined. The victor after all could hardly be the one whose terminal disease had already been diagnosed (and no marxist would deny the fatal and irreversible processes of the capitalist disease) and for the relief of whose crippling internal ailment there existed only one nostrum – and that beyond his reach. To Stalin's international theory the two camp doctrine represented a salutary, if vestigial, reminder of class origins. In other words, if all the other vertical (class) allies were indeed to be ruled out, at least the vertical (class) nature of the Soviet state remained to sound enough of a class echo. Despite changes of emphasis, already presaged or initiated during Stalin's reign, the two camp doctrine with some subsequent refinement has passed into contemporary Soviet hands virtually intact.

But there remained one term still to be supplied before the theoretical conundrum could be answered. The missing term to the problem as to how the infant Soviet state could enter into this irreconcilable conflict with any hope of victory was found in the theory of peaceful coexistence. If, as we suggested at the outset, the relationship between socialist and capitalist states could not be one of dependence as had been postulated between the two major groups of Lenin's theory of imperialism, peaceful coexistence described the only conceivable alternative – and one that was later to be deliberately selected as the theoretical base of Stalin's policies. At first, however, peaceful coexistence supplied a short-range tactical need and only when the world revolution failed to eventuate were its terms of reference extended so as to comprehend the longer range political objective; in other words, when that power which had been expected to prevail found itself locked in a precarious equilibrium of weakness then was it deemed expedient to settle (temporarily) for coexistence. The expediency of the approach may be inferred from frequent reference to the notion of 'true' peaceful coexistence attainable only after the world-wide victory of communism had been achieved or, indeed, to the reality already in evidence within the Soviet federation.

There, and there alone, Litvinov asserted, the member nations lived in a condition of true peaceful coexistence:[94]

> The Soviet Union is entering into the League today as a representative of a new socio-economic system, not renouncing any of its special features . . . the idea in itself of an association of nations contains nothing theoretically unacceptable for the Soviet state and its ideology. The Soviet Union is itself a League of Nations in the best sense of the word, uniting over two hundred nationalities, thirteen of which have a population of not less than one million each, and others such as Russia and the Ukraine, a population running into scores of millions. I will make so bold as to claim that never before have so many nations coexisted so peacefully within a single state.

We find, however, that this original interpretation of peaceful coexistence was gradually abandoned and peaceful coexistence has since tended to become a blanket description of Soviet attitudes towards the *capitalist states*. The question remains as to whether the vaunted notion deserved the equally oft-repeated accusation of propaganda slogan or whether it also held some genuine explanatory content. Some brief comment here might help to throw light on the subject.

To put it in its crudest form, Stalin's task was to strike a balance between two variables: between a weak Soviet state requiring 'respite' for reasons of survival and consolidation, and capitalist countries, themselves riddled with internal contradictions.[95] In the first stage of 'coexistence' Soviet policy towards the capitalist states had to be 'peaceful' from sheer necessity. No other course but peaceful coexistence could give that needed 'breathing space' that was of such concern to the early leadership. Moreover, some measure of economic co-operation, if not necessary, was also highly desirable in this first period. Apart from the obvious advantages deriving from such co-operation the opportunity to aggravate intra-capitalist contradictions would doubtless be afforded. This then would be the rationale of that first period of 'peaceful coexistence' that was marked otherwise by Soviet participation in the International Economic Conferences at Geneva in 1922 and in 1927 and by the conclusion thereafter of numerous trade agreements. By 1925 success in the economic field had been consolidated and sanctified by political action to such effect that every major power in the world except the United States had

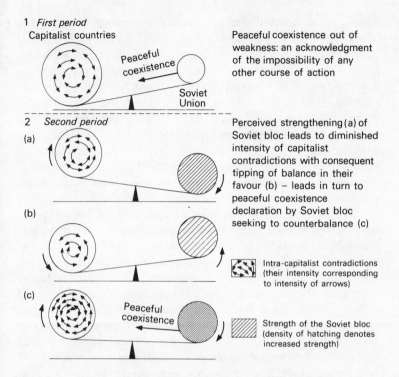

Figure 8 The first two stages in the development of the concept of 'peaceful coexistence' as an equilibrating factor between the 'two camps'

extended diplomatic recognition to the Soviet Union, who, with increasing seriousness, took a formal part in international relations. As we have suggested, a preference for this course was apparent at an early date and was pursued at the expense of such options as engagement in the adventures of the international working-class movement or in the independent (of Moscow) activities of the Comintern. The political actions[96] that paralleled and consolidated economic initiatives were crowned by the entry of the Soviet Union into the League of Nations in 1934 – described by Lenin, only a few short years before, as 'a pack of wolves who are all the time at each other's throats'.[97] It seemed now that there was no area too sacrosanct to be above compromising: no economic, political, or ideological element too profane to be sacrificed on the altar of day to day circumstance. Relieved thus by 'peaceful coexistence' of the need to launch against the arch-enemy that frontal assault that marxism demanded, and committed to conciliatory policies and expedient diplomacy, Stalin ensured survival and the respite necessary for consolidation. With the exception of the Spanish Civil War there was little meddling in the international affairs of others while a rather unexpected facility on Stalin's part for lavishing his diplomatic attentions with ideological abandon resulted in such unholy alliances as that with the Nazi regime in 1939. It is hardly surprising, particularly after the breach of peaceful coexistence principles represented by the military aggression on Poland, the Baltic States, and Rumania among others, that every opportunity was taken to debate types of aggression and the moral dimension. Invariably the conclusion produced moral exculpation of the Soviet Union and established the fighting of 'just wars' as the Soviet Union's enviable prerogative. It was determined also at this time that, regardless of the Soviet Union's embracing the principle of peaceful coexistence, a world riddled with capitalist contradictions could not avoid war, and in these circumstances Stalin used Lenin's distinction between just and unjust wars to condemn those waged by imperialists and to consecrate certain others: 'Wars that are not wars of conquest but wars of liberation, waged to defend the people from foreign attack and from attempts to enslave them, or to liberate the people from capitalist slavery, or, lastly, to liberate colonies and dependent countries from the yoke of imperialism.'[98] Even so, there is to be remarked in this period a pronounced preference for the uncomplicated security of peaceful coexistence than for military adventurism, however 'just' or sanctified such adventures might be.

In the aftermath of the Second World War there was in the enormous tasks of reconstruction that faced the Soviet Union little indication at first of a balance that had in fact undergone subtle change. Nor was there any suggestion that the prolongation of the respite thus far permitted by the two camps and peaceful coexistence doctrines was still, along with their theoretical underpinnings, a matter of urgent need; for the attention of the West had been diverted for a significant period of time and she faced identical problems of recovery and reconstruction: identical restatements of the pre-war two camp doctrine were still to be found but in fact, if not officially, capitalist encirclement was at an end. Although the appearances remained, quite radical change in the balance of force and transfer of initiative had taken place, at depth. Theory now responded, at first sluggishly then with increasing sensitivity, to practice and the passage of events. Capitalist encirclement was in the process of giving way to 'socialist encirclement', a configuration in which the Soviet Union no longer stood alone but had been joined by a group of European (and soon Asian) countries, participants in the socialist system. The two camp doctrine, from which the theory of peaceful coexistence derived its meaning, underwent successive modification as attempts were made to cause it to conform to the two camp concept of the 1920s and 1930s: 'Two opposite political lines, two camps – the camp of imperialism and anti-democratic forces, whose chief aim is the establishment of a world-wide American imperialist hegemony and the crushing of democracies: and the anti-imperialist, democratic camp, whose chief aim is elimination of imperialism.'[99] Resemblance to that earlier configuration was coincidental: the world had revolved on its axis since the thirties and to bring theory and practice again into conjunction, peaceful coexistence had to be infused with fresh meaning so as to reflect accurately the new relationship between the socialist and capitalist camps in the post-war years.

Now, according to Stalin's analysis of the conduct of the capitalist states in the Second World War, although the contradictions between the socialist and capitalist states were 'theoretically' still more important and remained at the heart of the world development, contradictions among the capitalist states had become stronger.[100] Adduced in evidence of the accuracy of this conclusion was the intensity of the struggle among capitalists for markets and the desire to crush their capitalist rivals, a struggle more bitter than that between them and the USSR. What other construction could be placed for example on a situation where the Anglo-French-American bloc, instead of joining with Hitler to crush their arch-enemy the Soviet Union, entered instead into a coalition with her? And so, all appearances to the contrary notwithstanding, whereas wars among capitalist countries were still inevitable, wars between capitalist and socialist countries were now regarded as *not inevitable*.[101] The contradictions endemic in capitalism were deep-rooted and efforts to arrest their operation were foreordained to failure. Sure in this knowledge such attempts at European integration as the Marshall Plan, Schumann Plan, Council of Europe, Organisation for European Economic Co-operation, etc., were met with a tolerant disdain. But this reinterpretation did not go unaccompanied by corresponding problems of theoretical formulation. If, for example, the capitalist-socialist contradiction was central and of them all the most irreconcilable, did it not follow that this apportionment of 'irreconcilability' inclining towards and having a main bearing on intra-capitalist dilemmas meant a corresponding decrease in the 'irreconcilability index' when applied to that original socialist-capitalist conflict?

However such questions were to be answered, there derived immediate practical advantage from this theoretical shift when translated into foreign political action. It could be expected, for example, to convey to the 'progressive democratic forces' within the capitalist world that they would wait in vain for a Soviet frontal assault. By allowing the perceived contradictions within these countries to take their natural, disruptive course, and by giving assurances of peaceful intent, the Soviet Union's policy of passivity would itself contribute to the contradictions a new more highly explosive dimension. It followed also that such a policy of laying disproportionate stress upon capitalist conflict and the notion of the inevitability of another capitalist war[102] would more effectively annihilate the capitalist camp than could be hoped for from a costly assault on capitalism by the socialist states. That capitalist contradictions must lead inevitably to yet another war[103] and that such an inter-capitalist war would be highly advantageous to the communist cause was not in doubt:[104]

> The facts of history cannot be ignored. And the facts show that as a result of the First World War Russia dropped out of the capitalist system, while as a result of the Second World War a whole series of countries in Europe and Asia dropped out of the capitalist system. There is every reason to assume that a third world war will bring about the collapse of the world capitalist system.

While assuming a generally passive international posture the USSR subscribed over these years to efforts made by the world community in regard to disarmament. Adequate support for such a posture was to be found in Marx's analysis of the political economy of capitalism wherein reference had been repeatedly made to the 'regenerative' function of the war industry for the whole capitalist economic system. It was no large step from that realisation to the perception of an appropriate strategy on the part of a socialist system that required no such boost. Through 'peaceful coexistence', and support for such of its adjuncts as disarmament, there was denied to socialism's rival system the remedial, or booster, effects that would otherwise have flowed from the adoption of more vigorous initiatives. By removing herself as capitalism's whipping boy the USSR might also expect capitalism's internal contradictions to intensify to an increasingly sharp pitch.

The theoretical justification of peaceful coexistence seeks to retain a continuity with the leninist position on these questions and Stalin's typically bluff endorsement bears the hallmarks of that arrogance often associated with ignorance: 'Clausewitz substantiated in his words the familiar Marxist thesis that there is a direct connection between war and politics, that politics gives birth to war, that war is a direct continuation of politics by violent means.' Stalin, as Goodman points out, had failed to appreciate that Clausewitz was neither in a position to have 'substantiated the familiar Marxist thesis'; nor indeed was correct in referring to 'a marxist thesis' at all, since Clausewitz's work *On War* was written only in 1818, the year of Marx's birth![105] Held simultaneously with the above views was Stalin's professed belief in the feasibility of a peaceful proletarian revolution at however distant a remove.[106] Thus the Marxist-Leninist position on the use of violence remained fundamentally unaltered, continuing as it did to assert that peaceful coexistence would be deployed as a tactical device operative in the short term. As a result of the discovery of the atomic bomb and its implications for the international situation that Stalin could not begin to anticipate, it fell to Stalin's successors, and to Khrushchev in particular, to revise these conclusions so as to bring them more closely into conjunction with the situation. That the record of Stalin's views on these subjects is sometimes less than clear may well be due to the (possibly deliberate) dissimulation of the implications of the qualitatively different nature of violence in the atomic age – an understandable dissimulation at a time when the Soviet Union did not herself possess the atomic weapon.

Stalin, however, had a foretaste of a number of problems which in their developed form were to be visited on his successors. The discovery of a continuity in the theoretical and practical answers produced by the successive generations to issues of a like nature should not surprise us, and at points is so striking that we are driven to acknowledge the fact that Stalin's death in 1953, sometimes taken as a theoretical datum point, constituted either a most arbitrary one or no point of departure at all as far as stalinism is concerned.[107] It is fitting

153

in the light of this appreciation of marked continuity that we conclude this section with a glance at one such important theoretical problem which, though receiving only rudimentary formulation in the stalinist period, provides a direct link between Stalin and his successors.

In regard to the changes effected by the Second World War on the socialist vertex[108] of the triangular model of international relations, Stalin's pronouncements were significantly (and characteristically) lacking in commitment to any one theoretical position. There can be no question but that the Red Army and its Generalissimo presided over the birth of what was later to be described as a new type of international relations. Nor can there be doubt as to the fact that this type of international relations then in process of crystallisation from among the emergent 'socialist socio-economic system' located both in East Europe and in Asia exhibited a nature very much *sui generis*. Questions pose themselves as to the reason for silence on such a subject. Was it attributable to theoretical indecisiveness? Did the theoretical implications arising from the multiplicity of communist states pose too great problems of compatibility with the theory of 'socialism in one country'? Was it held indeed to challenge the very existence of that theory? Or in the face of such a challenge did doubts remain, one might well ask, as to whether the theory of socialism in one country was still strong enough to meet the challenge of the new practice of 'socialism in several countries'?

We have tried to show that there was a clear and natural tendency for both the theory and practice of socialism in one country to lead to the 'domestication' of the once universalistic 'transnational' and vertically (class) oriented doctrine of classical marxism – a tendency that had already led to the generation of a strong Russian nationalism. Evidence for such a tense interaction – between Russian nationalism and universal communism – became indeed increasingly manifest as soon as other countries joined the USSR on its path to socialism. Irrespective of whether the process of joining her was in a spirit of slavish emulation or accompanied by reservations and criticism of Stalin's theory and practice of socialism in one country, it led after Stalin's death to doctrinal and political developments that signposted a number of 'different roads to socialism', and that spawned those tendencies to polycentrism with which we are now familiar. The tradition of anti-Great Russian chauvinism has of course a longer history than the emergence of a socialist bloc and the etching of its more modern features we may trace to the first years of the federation of the Union Republics of the USSR.[109] That such centrifugal tendencies with their potential easily discernible at an earlier date should not have led the countries concerned to have sought and found[110] in 'socialism in one country' earlier doctrinal justification for separatism is attributable to the unassailable hegemony of the USSR over the period concerned. In the absence of a significant challenge to that ascendency neither the non-Russian Soviet Republics, nor the crippled Comintern, nor the first incipient polycentrism of the Yugoslav-Soviet split could hope to reinvest with meaning the universalist features of the marxian vision; and not until a major socialist state was in a position to offer a real challenge to the USSR and to its leadership of the international workers' movement could such changes be made. The opportunity (and the Chinese challenge) was forthcoming after Stalin's death – although both sides claimed that the origins of the dispute lay in the stalinist period. In this context it will further be recalled that up to Stalin's death no consistent theory relating to what has now come to be called the Third World had been advanced. Stalin, as we have seen, had made no real distinction between the capitalist countries and their colonies and so his Asian and Chinese policies at best were generally of an *ad hoc* nature, responding to the march of events rather than to any preconceived pattern systematically pursued. At worst, towards these areas on the perimeter of Stalin's control his policies were marked by indecision, inflexibility, and, not infrequently, by lack of interest. The Chinese were thus enabled to offer their challenge, which from the start purported to make good the post-leninist deficiencies and supplant the ideological bankruptcy of stalinism: 'The Chinese working class has to shoulder the grave responsibility of rendering assistance to the working class and working people of capitalist countries in the world, especially the colonial and semi-colonial countries in Asia and Australasia. The victorious Chinese working class cannot, and should not, evade such an international responsibility.'[111]

The structure and functioning of the expanded socialist system had been determined by the dictates of its main power centre and its evolution would continue to depend on the countervailing pre-ponderance exercised by one or other of its parts – rather than emerge as a product of the contribution of each member. That a superficial 'international communist system' existed already during the era of the Comintern can be argued, but such appearances notwithstanding –

and although the organisation as originally conceived was to have been the epicentre of a network of vertical (class) units designed by Lenin to become the 'world party' – this was misleading. The grand design as originally projected had been betrayed by the special relationship between the Comintern and the Soviet State, by the CPSU's maintenance of a far-flung net of bilateral relations between itself and other communist parties throughout the world, and by the Russians' resolute discouragement of other communist parties entering into relationships of a like nature if the CPSU were to be excluded. In 1944 as German and Japanese power withered and as the Soviet Red Army crossed the 1939 frontiers of the Soviet Union it became obvious that there had been no power willing or capable of interrupting the transformation of these territories into 'Popular (or Peoples') Democracies'. This process, invariably taking place in the daunting presence of the Red Army, was completed with the areas' incorporation into the Soviet conception of a socialist camp, or commonwealth, or socio-economic system, as the new grouping came to be referred to. In the present context the question as to whether the motives for the Soviet expansion were economic, strategic, or ideological is of secondary concern: the point here being made is that whatever the motivation or intention with regard to the 'liberated' territories, Stalin's aversion to spontaneity on the part of communist parties in their revolutionary development appears to be fully justified by the permissible limits within which their transformation to socialism was required and their evolution circumscribed. In other words, by whatever category of dictatorship of the proletariat it was to be known,[112] it could be carried out only along lines consistent with Stalin's views on revolution – which is to say 'from above', following a phased (and rigidly controlled) development. In a manner reminiscent of Stalin's earlier methods in establishing the Soviet regime in territories that were to become constituent parts of the Soviet Federation, a way was opened by 1947[113] to the stalinisation of all the 'liberated territories'. A further element of irreversibility was introduced with the refusal by the Soviet Union to allow the occupied territories to participate in the Marshall Plan in 1947. Neither from outside nor from within the socialist grouping did there present itself at this point any possible challenge to the Soviet position. A new type of international relations had emerged for which, with the possible exception of the vassal-overlord relationships of feudalism, there was no historical precedent. It is worth remarking that it is that system with its stern hierarchical pattern of fiefs, inescapable obligations, allegiances – and controls – that relations among socialist countries have most tended to resemble.

In what sense, one might wonder, is the perception of the emergence of a new type of international relations justified? As has been suggested above new features were certainly exhibited. Among these and due to the centralist structure of the popular democracies was the undeniable and sizeable reduction in volume of the actual amount of international contacts on a personal and official level. In contrast to this decrease went hand in hand the complexities arising from the superimposition upon normal diplomatic relations channels of a new inter-party communications network. The resulting web of relations among the participant states was predictably more intricate and possessed of characteristics not found in conventional inter-state diplomatic intercourse. No exchange has ever taken place on the inter-party level of accredited representatives with functions set forth and publicised – though Party observers and representatives are seen and usually heard at other party congresses and the summit meetings of the communist leaders have become much more common than is the case on the inter-state level. It remains true to say that the usual assumption that inter-party transactions are engaged in is based on the absence of any statement to the contrary. To compound the confusion of the echelons (Party and state)[114] we might observe that in addition to their incomplete merger there is also to contend with the fact that ambassadors and representatives of those states who do carry on diplomatic relations dispense with traditional usages of diplomacy and intervene without hindrance in inter-party matters.[115]

Towards the multilateral type of relations among the socialist countries some attempt at an approach was made in the stalinist period. Moreover, at Party level the evidence suggests that the informal Party transactions and the confusion we have referred to owed much to Stalin's influence. We need not look far to discover examples of his distaste for formal organisation nor, as we have indicated, can it be presumed that bloc solidarity suffered as a result. The new Communist Information Bureau[116] he treated with as little respect as he had its predecessor, the Comintern. The reasons for the Yugoslav-Soviet split are dealt with exhaustively elsewhere[117] and it will suffice for our purposes to draw attention again to the essential unity of the bloc during the stalinist period and to the fractional nature of the tremor that radiated outwards from the titoist experience. The

1948–9 schism might indeed be viewed as much in the light of the plans of the Yugoslav leader and of G. Dimitrov for the establishment of a large South Slav federation as seen in terms of a threat to the stalinist monopoly of bloc leadership. But apart from this area of ideological dispute there was a quite extraordinary measure of unity within the bloc at this time as well as a high degree of pro-Stalin and pro-Soviet loyalty. A restrained friendship with the Chinese Republic further marked this period of intra-bloc relations. On the official state organisational level the stalinist era saw the foundation of the Council for Mutual Economic Assistance (CMEA)[118] which, despite structural weakness and chronic inefficiency, represented formal acknowledgment of intra-bloc economic co-operation.

The surprising degree of intra-communist stability achieved between the dissolution of the Comintern and Stalin's death in 1953 was a result solely of Stalin's personality, of stalinism as represented particularly by the theory of socialism in one country – and, not least of all, to the ruthlessness of methods too well documented elsewhere to warrant further chronicling. The theory itself served the dual function of giving the illusion of fundamental depth to what was essentially a superficial solidarity and further warded off for a significant period of time the evils of polycentrism. Ideological integrity was thus preserved intact with only one minor *de facto* alteration having to be made which, as Isaac Deutscher puts it, consisted of the extension of the theory of socialism in one country to the theory of socialism in 'one zone'. The task of keeping the illusion of universalism and the true proletarian 'transnationalism' of Marxism-Leninism has proved increasingly difficult since 1948. As long as the theory in its extended (zone) form could be preserved the illusion might be maintained, but soon after Stalin's death and the official termination of 'socialism in one country' the end of the chapter of monolithism of the international working class movement had also been written.

Soviet Marxist-Leninists

> Instead of transforming the world, it is the Soviet Union which has been transformed.
>
> Aspaturian

Although in terms of time the post-Stalin period is shorter than that spanned by Stalin's reign, the proposal to deal with the period in one section and under only one heading might, we realise, afford room for criticism. It is, moreover, a much more diversified period not only in terms of variety and contrast at the political leadership level but also in terms of the developing momentum of world events. It is as though the wheels of history turned faster and ever faster, their passage marked by a complexity of developments and events that would defy comprehensive analysis.[1] The standard method of coping with the task of converting a disorderly pile of past events into meaningful history – which is to say some division in terms of time and of ruling personalities – is of course a remarkably hazardous one. Thus, the placing of too great an emphasis on events or on the advent of new leaders may be part of the legacy of historicism whereby such is the distracting diligence of the search for turning points that it is carried out often at the expense of underestimating areas of continuity and the quality of persistence – which in our case go deep into the very nature of politics and of international relations.

In this present context then, while acknowledging a certain arbitrariness in the choice of the death of Stalin as a milestone, we will try to avoid some of the pitfalls by following those observers[2] who have seen as important the quality of continuity in certain aspects of 'destalinisation' well before Stalin's death and who see persistence in many features of 'stalinism' beyond 1953.[3] Of the major problems his successors were called upon to grapple with few had not been given a 'dress rehearsal' during Stalin's reign. The Sino-Soviet split followed lines not at all dissimilar to those along which the fracture with Yugoslavia had run, while adumbrated in the Yugoslav experience was the subsequent drive to 'national communism' or 'separate paths to communism' whose complicating influence on the later ideological problems necessitated no fundamental change in Stalin's theoretical framework. It will have been appreciated that the doctrinal dialogue of the later period also traced its origins to the stalinist years, and most notably to those debates of 1947 and 1950 to which he lent such personal stimulus. This personal involvement in matters of theory had had the effect too of 'freeing' certain aspects of the hitherto too deterministically postulated superstructure and resulted in an impetus imparted to the development of the social sciences on the one hand, and, on the other, in a shift from more violent methods of social coercion and control to an emphasis on the role of indoctrination in

159

the process of the 'building of socialism'. But at the same time certain aspects of the future remained of necessity hidden, among them the consequences of the nuclear age whose advent Stalin witnessed but the fuller impact of which lay in wait for a later generation. Similarly, although the burgeoning strength of the Soviet state and globalisation of her power had its origins in the stalinist era, the implications of this phenomenon were left to a future leadership to appreciate and explore.

Beside such areas of persistence and continuity, 'points of departure' or 'milestones'[4] as represented by Stalin's death or, for that matter, Khrushchev's ouster and replacement in 1964, may be seen to dwindle in relevance; and it is to such factors as the onset of the nuclear age, of the globalisation of Soviet power leading to vast changes in the thinking on international relations that we look for the real matrix within which developments of the post-Stalin era are embedded and lent cohesion. Despite the undeniable multi-faceted features of the post-Stalin era, we feel therefore that the common denominators are sufficiently strong to justify stress on continuity rather than abrupt change of direction – and on a chapter structure to correspond.

We now enter an era of dramatically enhanced importance in terms of thinking on international relations. Whereas until now theorising on international relations had been implicitly contained within the broad framework of the marxist *Weltanschauung* it now for the first time assumes an explicit form of its own. No longer merely a by-product or side issue restricted to consideration by, and subject to pronouncement on the part of the political leaders alone, the subject gradually assumes during this period an aspect so broadened as to comprehend the world as a whole, and boasts an autonomous character in its own right – to take its place within the integrated Marxist-Leninist intellectual structure. And so, despite polycentrist forces operative within the Soviet bloc, the strength and influence of the Soviet Union increases and parallels the expansion of the theoretical field. There was indeed some justification for Khrushchev's comment at the beginning of this period: 'International relations, spread beyond the bounds of relations between the countries inhabited chiefly by peoples of the white race, are now beginning to acquire the character of genuinely world-wide relations.'[5]

The new importance ascribed to the theory of international relations cannot be dissociated from the no less new version of the concept of peaceful coexistence which now in this period, as a 'concession to the nuclear age',[6] is reinterpreted and charged with new meaning. It goes without saying that in view of their desire to establish in this area as elsewhere theoretical continuity, Soviet Marxist-Leninists would certainly deny such a revamping; they would for the same reason repudiate with equal vehemence Stalin's part in the process claiming that peaceful coexistence 'of states with different social systems' is not a stalinist but a leninist concept, that it has always been, and remains the general line of Soviet foreign policy.[7] Be that as it may, we maintain that although the label remains unaltered the conceptual content has undergone drastic change. Just as the doctrine of 'socialism in one country' is taken to epitomise the Stalin era, so it might be said peaceful coexistence, new furbished, characterises the period since – despite Brezhnev's description of the most recent period as that of 'developed socialism'.[8] Where at an earlier time the Soviet State was perceived to be 'encircled' by an allegedly hostile ring of capitalist states – and peaceful coexistence was taken mainly as an objective description of an undesirable equilibrium – in this latter period the concept has become a policy norm. Which is not to say that the interpretation of the concept runs smoothly throughout the post-stalinist years. We shall devote some space in this section to the vicissitudes through which the concept passed (and continues to pass) and in this context the perceptions that determined its distinctive form in its khrushchevian incarnation, important though they undoubtedly are, will be dealt with simply as one such stage of development in its history.[9] A useful preamble to our taking a closer look at the component parts of contemporary theory of international relations in the Soviet sphere might consist of a brief survey of the conceptualisations that emerged from the 20th CPSU Congress. These taken together offered a new picture of the world which throughout this period has remained a basic scheme for the Soviet understanding of the world. The main propositions to emerge from the Congress deliberations were as follows:

1 The period of 'capitalist encirclement' was declared terminated and the Soviet Union was thereafter conceived to be surrounded by friendly socialist states in Europe and Asia – the totality of which amounted to one-third of the land area and population of the world.
2 In addition to the numerical growth of the socialist camp another

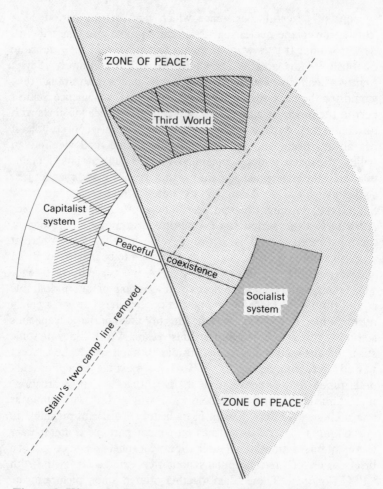

Figure 9 Khruschev's 'zone of peace' modification of the Soviet
model of the world

major change in the world relationship of forces was deemed to
have taken place with the removal of that stalinist-demarcated
line that had divided the world so ominously into the two camps
of socialism and capitalism (see Figure 9). The division had been
an exclusive one which is to say that all states were conceived to
occupy either one side or the other of the divide. In 1956 this
dogmatically postulated dichotomisation gave way to an equally

decisively drawn triangular model of the world and the acceptance of the notion of a group of countries taking up a position 'in between' the capitalist and socialist camps (that occupies, in terms of the triangular model, the third vertex of that triangle). This 'in-between' group consisted mainly of those newly independent countries which Stalin's rigid designation as capitalist would have alienated. A diplomatic bonus also accrued from this revised (1956) picture since the removal of these countries from the capitalist camp simultaneously reduced restraints on diplomatic activity towards them. Otherwise, with these countries regarded as capitalist, such activity must necessarily have been subject to corresponding inhibitions. The divisions of the world, now redrawn to correspond with the broadening horizons of Soviet interests and activity, permitted the countries of the Third World to become a legitimate object of Soviet diplomatic attention, and the balance of world forces could be described as having undergone further advantageous change. The Third World and the socialist camp were now together linked in a 'vast zone of peace' which included 'peace-loving states, both socialist and non-socialist, of Europe and Asia.[10] This new delimitation led to the jubilant claim that the zone of peace embraced the 'majority of the population of the planet', and the triangular conceptualisation of the world[11] has remained the characteristic feature of the entire post-Stalin period.

3   Further to the division of the world on the basis of states, or rather of groups of states, in addition to the 'zone of peace' consisting as we have seen of the socialist states and Third World countries, there was identified yet another 'ally' (if we may use a leninist term) in the shape of the 'labour movement in the capitalist countries'.[12]

These three forces – the process of identification of which is another of the characteristics of this entire period – constitute a conceptually interesting phenomenon since two of the 'forces' are of a state nature while the third, deriving as it does from the vertical (class) axis, is not – a fact which as recently as the 25th CPSU Congress Brezhnev corroborated in his reference to the 'militant alliance of the main revolutionary forces of our day'.[13]

4   To complete the revised outline of the world picture we note that

as a result of the assuredly disastrous effects of a nuclear exchange and (not less importantly) as a consequence of these changes in balance that favoured the socialist camp, the thinking on war has been revised. The reader is here reminded of the leninist dictum that wars would exist as long as imperialism exists – and the stalinist qualification. It will be recalled that Stalin took for his first step the proposition that wars were 'fatally inevitable' among the capitalist countries; and for his second, that they were no longer inevitable between the socialist and the capitalist countries. Khrushchev in turn revised this view to meet the imperatives of an era when 'imperialism [is] no longer an all-embracing world system'[14] and when 'mighty social and political forces' had come into existence 'possessed of formidable means, to prevent the imperialists from unleashing war'.[15] More importantly, among the imperatives that Khrushchev was obliged to acknowledge, was that invention (atomic bomb) 'which does not observe the class principle'.[16] For, as he was constrained to point out, 'the first to suffer in the event of war would be the working people and their vanguard – the working class',[17] and went on to argue that in the event of the outbreak of war – hitherto regarded in the case of 'just wars' as a morally positive element – the very objective of human history would suffer defeat. There would be 'no victor'.[18] Paradoxically, as remarked above, that defeat of the main objective (communism) could well be at the hands of its proponents when the zero-sum conflict postulated between socialism and capitalism with a historically preordained victor would end on a depopulated planet.

In other words the revised attitude to wars rested on the premise that their outbreak was no longer a matter of 'fatal inevitability' – a conclusion which applied not only to the socialist-capitalist conflict but also to the world as a whole.[19] The very nature of nuclear war rendered meaningless the distinction between wars among capitalist states on the one hand and between capitalist and socialist on the other. The expectation that a nuclear war – even one that broke out initially between capitalist states – could be confined to these states without the involvement of the socialist bloc was clearly unreasonable. One wonders whether Khrushchev's use of the word 'fatal'[20] was not of major significance in this respect. Certainly the new line was more consistent with the traditional Soviet posture as the main self-declared advocate of peace. Indeed it could be said that the power of the new nuclear weapon, so assuredly annihilative of mankind as a whole, when coupled with ideological insistence on the inevitability of war, had introduced something of a paradox. It certainly presented with a problem the belief in the communist future of mankind – a future that any single nuclear exchange could negate.

Before mentioning one further point let us say that the four above-mentioned propositions to emerge directly from the 20th CPSU Congress in 1956 (in respect of 'non-encirclement', in respect of the replacement of the two-bloc image by the triangularity of (state) blocs, in respect of the triangularity at one remove (class) of 'progressive forces', and, finally, in respect of the non-inevitability of wars) seem to us to be readily identifiable throughout the period we have now under consideration. A fifth point that would seem to follow by logical extension of the revised attitude to war embodied a development that more than any other separated the Khrushchev era from that of the present Soviet leadership. The development to which we refer was concerned with the question of the actual *desirability* of wars and their position within the Marxist-Leninist revolutionary arsenal. The resultant dilemma was real and deserves comment.

Whereas Khrushchev (perhaps still grappling with the ramifications of the nuclear phenomenon) seems to have regarded as undesirable *all* wars, including local wars of Third World national liberation,[21] the present Soviet leadership has made a clear distinction between general war and local wars.[22] It seems clear that under stress and in contrast to the present leadership Khrushchev overreacted and, in arguing that 'there are only two ways',[23] oversimplified the issue. From this we might infer that despite his 'zone of peace' innovation Khrushchev seemed still to share Stalin's view of a world divided into two hostile camps that could be freed from their historical and irreconcilable encounter only through the victory of one. And, as the later khrushchevian corollary had it, the one to emerge in triumph would be the socialist camp providing (and only providing) that both sides exercised restraint. Khrushchev's concern was therefore that the Soviet Union and other socialist countries should avoid violence, and local wars (so susceptible he believed to escalation into general war) should be eschewed. It would follow that such risks as were taken at

Berlin and Cuba must in his view have fallen into the easily controllable category. In sharp contrast the present leadership feels less inhibited and relatively secure in the belief that the 'balance of world forces'[24] has already shifted in their favour. In other words, there is no longer a precariously poised balance in existence between the two camps but rather a state of disequilibrium in which the United States and other major capitalist countries are seen to be in an advanced state of decline.

As the Soviet categorisation of wars on the basis of their 'inevitability' and of their 'desirability' became crystallised, so by way of the alteration in the linkage between imperialism and war the need for the revision of the connection between war and world communist revolution was perceived. This latter concept was the step leading to that final stage (communism) – the ideal in which reposed the very legitimacy of Party leadership and to which was owed their explicit commitment. In these circumstances the obstetric instrument of violence that had traditionally been regarded as midwife to the new communist society was suddenly possessed of too sharp an edge – an edge that might in the process of delivery inflict a mortal wound on the infant communist society. As we have observed, it seemed to follow that the main features of revolutionary strategy should assume a non-violent mien, and ready to hand was the concept (peaceful coexistence) that already occupied a place in the marxist lexicon. Born in the era of stalinist weakness, the early definition reflected the circumstances of its birth when it had been peaceful coexistence that accepted (sometimes apprehensively, occasionally wishfully) the assumption of the *inevitability of wars*. But in contrast to that time of necessity when it had the character of a short-term tactical expedient, the notion in the post-Stalin version had quite clearly become a *strategy*[25] for world revolution: a strategy whose development would deliver progressively the world to communism.

Khrushchev, still overwhelmed by the likely consequences of *any* war in the nuclear age, quite clearly overstressed the peaceful content of the concept so as to make of it a sort of preservation of the *status quo* instead of a strategy of communist revolution; a curious attitude indeed in the light of the divergence between his pronouncements on the subject and his actions. And in any case, the present leadership has affirmed the fact that peaceful coexistence cannot by any stretch of the imagination be taken to mean an end of wars. As distinct from Khrushchev's statements, some of which dealt with the concept *in isolation*, and gave rise to consequent misunderstanding, the present Soviet leadership has structured other types of international relations around peaceful coexistence,[26] and far from promoting it as an aim in itself, it is seen as just one part of their theory of international relations. The concept has become a means to (certainly not an objective of) world revolution.

These major changes lead to the attribution of a (qualitatively) new importance to international relations and a situation where they can no longer run counter to the operation and processes of the world revolution: instead it is *through* international relations that the transformation of the world is to be effected. If Lenin's horizontalisation of the class conflict to produce an emphasis on international relations (with stress on wars as its corollary) had meant a dramatic upsurge in the importance which international relations began conceptually to play within Marxism-Leninism, these developments reinforced the change of attitude towards the subject and gave it momentum. The surprise that Marx would unquestionably have felt on learning that states had become protagonists in the class conflict would doubtless have turned to astonished disbelief were he now to have been apprised of the important role international relations were suddenly expected to play within the Marxist-Leninist intellectual structure.

Before we take a closer look at the emergence of theory of international relations as a separate field of academic interest, let us reiterate two further essential features of this period that we have broached: first, the changed status of the Soviet Union in the international arena and, second, the changed nature of the Soviet leadership. Without special attention being paid to these two aspects, the new status of thinking on international relations could not be fully appreciated.

1   The changed Soviet posture

In parallel with the transformation of Marxism-Leninism from a humble reformist social doctrine to a fully fledged ideology, the USSR underwent a gradual change from its equally humble beginnings to its final global extension. Small wonder that Stalin, in control of a great power after the Second World War, and prior to the advance to superpower status under Khrushchev, had not been able to divest

167

himself of the 'encircled mentality' of the besieged early years. Nor was he called upon, though in possession of the nuclear weapon, to make the doctrinal adjustments which Brezhnev and Kosygin and a new generation of (globally attuned) ideologists would have to make.[27]

This parallelism in Soviet development is one of the most interesting aspects of its changed posture – the rise from weak state status to global power presided over by an ideology – in parallel flux. Aspaturian with characteristic perceptiveness has pointed to the globalisation of Soviet power as the factor that brings into sharpest relief the contradiction that results from what we have described as the 'domestication' of marxism by a state unit, and has drawn our attention[28] to the tension-producing potential of such a development. We have already considered such a potential[29] and have seen one such major tension source in the interaction of demands created by the two roles which the Soviet Union from its inception had to play: first of all, that of a state, finding her bearings alongside the other states despite an initial commitment to destroy the institution of such (horizontal) units; and second, as ideological epicentre of the vertical (class) line, committed to the role of promoting the proletarian (class) revolution. In that context we suggest that the tension factor must heighten as the Soviet Union, increasing in power as a state, was faced more and more frequently with contradictory choices to correspond with the growing divergence of the two roles. A further point made by Aspaturian is worth noting, namely that at certain stages the roles may not be in conflict but may, on the contrary, converge and mutually reinforce one another. An instance of such a convergence is to be seen in the early stalinist years when the leadership of the international workers' movement acted as a surrogate for Soviet weakness as a state power. The possibility of the operation of the converse process must also be recognised when, as we have indicated, the growth of Soviet power might detract from her importance as a leader of the international workers' movement.[30]

We would in this last regard disagree with the description of the process as the 'deideologisation' of Soviet foreign policy and treat cautiously Aspaturian's proposition that, as the Soviet Union becomes a global power, its foreign policy becomes largely (not completely) deideologised since (he argues) 'maximisation of possible diplomatic gains in the non-communist world dictated a minimisation and dilution of the ideological content of Soviet foreign policy.'[31] To be sure such developments as the sacrifice by the Soviet Union of local communist parties in return for diplomatic gains in the Third World, or the diversion of scarce resources from domestic and bloc development for use as economic bribes for the purpose of seducing newly independent Third World countries might be cited in support of the propositions. But on the basis of such evidence other constructions are possible. If, in describing this process, Aspaturian were to mean by 'deideologisation' either 'deleninisation', or 'destalinisation' (or even 'deradicalisation') of Soviet foreign policy then one would have to agree. If however he means a process that foreshadows as a logical conclusion Soviet foreign policy's becoming devoid of ideological content then we would offer an alternative description: that of an ideological revision and 'stretching' so as to accommodate fresh diplomatic initiatives and a new Soviet posture. The ideology is adjusted and reformulated, while continuing to inform and guide foreign policy.[32]

Such a need to introduce very serious ideological adjustment manifested itself during the Khrushchev period and ensuing developments should be regarded in that light rather than interpreted merely in terms of his personality, or of the apparent contradictory nature of his policies, the ambivalence of his goals – or even of opportunism, or irrationality. With the reformulated ideology as counterpoint Khrushchev's policies reached into every corner of the globe. Where Stalin had been keenly aware of Soviet weakness, where he had substituted for an adventurous continental policy bloc expansion along lines of physical contiguity – and had always been ready if challenged to turn aside and direct his attentions to 'the weakest point' the internal development of USSR), Khrushchev, presiding over an inestimably stronger state (and bloc), was capable of challenging the United States as leader of that other bloc for preponderance. This challenge, in conjunction with his claim to the right to intervene in any part of the world, signalled the removal of those self-imposed constraints that had hitherto placed some areas beyond the theoretical and operational reach of Soviet foreign policy. And it is to be emphasised in this context that in contrast to these erstwhile voluntarily accepted restrictions, Khrushchev, while proceeding to devise bold global strategies that reached out across oceans and continents, sought not only recruits to the 'camp' but aimed also at the enhancement of the Soviet diplomatic posture. It

169

would not be going too far to say that inasmuch as 'capitalist encirclement' (and 'socialism in one country' as its adjunct) influenced and characterised the Soviet theory of international relations in Stalin's time, the concept of 'deencirclement'[33] influences and is characteristic of the post-Stalin era.

2   Change in the nature of Soviet leadership

Although the process that relates ideological adjustment to corresponding change in the Soviet Union's world status would seem in our view to be of primary importance it would be a mistake to underestimate the nature of the personality of the political leaders. We have to recognise the significance of the fact that all of Stalin's successors, Malenkov, Khrushchev, Bulganin, Kosygin, and Brezhnev, never again joined theory with practice in the manner of Marx and Lenin.[34] For Lenin, leadership had meant the roles of chief ideologist, principal organiser of the Party, founder of the movement itself, and top administrator of the state[35] joined in a merger in which his power depended less on the actual institutions than on his own personal qualities and authority. In an attempt to imitate his illustrious predecessor Stalin contrived to maintain this amalgam, not so much as a function of his personal qualities but as a complement to the absoluteness of his rule. We have remarked on his mediocrity as a philosopher and thinker generally: the profound and lasting mark he left on Soviet Marxism-Leninism is attributable not to his remaining the chief ideologist of the movement, but to the fact that he achieved a position from which he could physically silence any other contender. With the denunciation of his rule as a 'cult of personality', however, a split was introduced that has not since been mended. No effort was spared to avoid the emergence of another such 'cult' and, by destroying the myth of Stalin's infallibility, Khrushchev had eliminated the possibility of any other leaders – whether of the calibre of a Marx or a Lenin – becoming the object of such personal veneration.[36] Although the link between political leader and ideologist remains very strong, the practice has been established whereby political leaders are no longer at one and the same time by definition top ideologists.

The effect of these internal 'structural' changes, that resulted in the intensification of focused thinking on the part of a large group of people on the subject of international relations, led in due course to the 'subject's' advancement to fully elaborated academic discipline.[37] In this way, and for the first time in the history of marxism, one of its major paradoxes has become gradually resolved. We refer to the obvious discrepancy beween a marxism that aspires at every point of its development to contain a comprehensive world view (*Weltanschauung*), on the one hand, and a lack of explicit formulations about the way in which the world is (and has not ceased to be) organised on the other.[38] The discrepancy had become too glaring. The injury done both to the doctrine and to the reality where the former continued to predict the near obsolescence of international relations while the continuing existence of a Soviet state (sic) and other socialist states unashamedly – indeed enthusiastically – attested the fact that the reality had become too painful to contemplate.

Lenin's own precedent had of course seemed to allow for the provision of a major 'addition' or 'contribution' to the theory so as to rectify the anomaly, but somehow the field of international relations proved too daunting and theorists, lesser in stature than Lenin, were deterred from following that particular lead. The implications that must flow from any discussion as to the theoretical existence or non-existence of international relations were too far-reaching, and too profound. And so, in this field that remained so neglected, a situation that amounted to a virtual theoretical taboo was perpetuated, and remained, even while Stalin was giving a general boost to the social sciences. Even in the 1950s when the conclusion was reached that responsibility for the 'discovery of the laws of socialism' (since communism would not arrive automatically but would have 'to be built')[39] lay with the social sciences the memory of the stalinist treatment of heretics remained strong. Any discussion of such delicate subjects as the concept of state, or international relations, might easily infringe the permitted limits within which social science research was contained – and bring speedy retribution.

Although one could speak about a new-found 'freedom' of academic research, the limits set were still restrictive by any Western standards, and research in the social sciences was confined within the Marxist-Leninist framework as currently determined by the Party. The continuing limitations (although the relaxation was, by stalinist standards, a near revolution), coupled with the 'psychological' trauma of the personality cult, caused the Soviet academia to take a long time to recover and to begin to think for themselves.[40] Nevertheless, for the first time new officially recognised parameters afforded scope for rational argument, and the departure from repetitious paraphrasing of an official political line led to a considerable increase in the number of people involved in the field and to the establishment of an un-precedented number of academic institutions. The first harbinger of change in the field of international relations was in the form of a discussion immediately after Stalin's death on the need for military rethinking necessitated by the changed nature of war in the nuclear age, and by 1956 the emergence of international relations as an independent field of enquiry in the wake of the 20th CPSU Congress was assured. Thus, statements made in Western literature to the effect that the rapid development of international relations theory in the United States, in the United Kingdom and other West European countries had 'so far at least, under the communist regimes, no parallel'[41] were correct only in the narrow sense of the east not as yet having autonomous departments of international relations within its universities. Prior to 1956 in regard to work in that field there could have been justification in this attitude, but even in this regard the assessment was oversimplistic. Soviet research during this pre-1956 period[42] was focused on the history of international relations rather than on current events and problems, and in this connection there was published annually until 1956 collections of international treaties and a profusion of propaganda booklets paying tribute to Stalin's unerring statesmanship.

To whatever stimulus we might attribute the subsequent develop-ment it would be true to say that in addition to the continuous *implicit* theory of international relations that can be reconstructed from the thinking on world revolution of all Soviet political leaders, the existence of a discipline of international relations in the East by the 1960s is certainly to be recognised.[43] While in the earlier period the research could be confined to the writings of the individuals Marx, Lenin, Stalin, in this later period the net must be cast considerably wider. In addition to primary sources that embrace the works and pronouncements of the political leaders, commentaries,[44] resolutions of communist party congresses, documents of the international com-munist summit meetings and the writings of an army of theoreticians of varied standing must be consulted. Apart from monographs (individually or collectively written) theoretical articles appear in a number of journals whose relatively recent profusion of numbers underlines the suddenly heightened awareness of the complexity of the subject under discussion. Among these publications should be

172

mentioned the monthly *Mirovaia Ekonomika i Mezhdunarodnye Otnoshenia*,[45] one of the organs of the Institute of World Economics and International Relations.[46] This Institute was established for the purpose of continuing the work of Varga's Institute of World Politics and World Economics that, together with its publication *Miroovoie Khoziaistvo i Mirovaia Politika*, was dissolved after Varga's disgrace in 1949.[47] Two other journals explicitly devoted to international relations deserve mention: *Mezhdunarodnaia Zhizn'* (since 1954) and its counterpart *International Affairs* appearing in English (Moscow). Other journals not explicitly concerned with international relations but devoting substantial space to the subject are: *Voprosy Istorii* (Problems of History), *Voprosy Filozofii* (Problems of Philosophy), *Kommunist*,[48] and *Problemy Mira i Socializma*, published in its English version under the name of the *World Marxist Review*. Nor would these constitute an exhaustive survey of publications on the subject. Some idea of the focusing of interest may be gained from the three-hundred-page bibliographical handbook of International Relations by V. V. Yegorov.[49]

Research into the international relations field in the late 1950s and early 1960s was still predominantly synonymous with the examination of direct and specific inter-state relations and was centred in the university departments of history and of international law where, curiously enough, it often encountered as hostile a reception from these disciplines as was met in similar circumstances by the theory of international relations in the West. The hostility was due in the main to its failure to distinguish itself in methodological terms from other subjects and to its omitting to use techniques used in other social science fields in the East such as game theory, communications theory, and cybernetics. However, unlike the comparable situation in the West, opposition was overruled from above. Questions that demanded immediate attention differed from those that exercised the ideologically, non-monolithic West, and involved such areas as the structure of Marxism-Leninism and the potential and scope of international relations theory therein. Indeed the possibility of supplementing or modifying such hitherto sacrosanct subjects as historical materialism and scientific communism could not be dismissed:[50]

Is it necessary to constitute a political science in the communist countries? . . . We do not question the fact that there must be a

173

theoretical scientific reflection of politics. The problem is elsewhere: is it necessary to constitute a new scientific branch – political science – or indeed a whole complex of new scientific disciplines, or is there a sufficient platform and an adequate framework provided by some of the disciplines within the established system of social science, or a conjunction of several such disciplines (scientific communism, theory of state and law, sociology, etc.)? The answer would have scientific-institutional consequences.

We might add that although numerous proposals have been put forward,[51] answers to these important questions had not yet been found. Regardless of what these answers might be, what *has*, however, emerged is an acute awareness of the urgency that attaches:[52]

> The explanation that modern marxist classification of the science has not yet been formulated does not remove the social urgency of examining political questions which, in modern society, assume greater and greater significance.

And so the trend that had appeared at the 20th CPSU Congress continued without serious deviation and, in the event, due to a further realisation shortly to strike the leadership, was destined to receive regular and powerful boosts. That realisation was of the need to carry the ideological battle into the enemy camp, an advance spearheaded by the promotion of serious research into 'bourgeois' and revisionist ideas. In this context Brezhnev's words at the 24th Congress are illuminating:[53]

> We live in a situation of permanent ideological war which is conducted against our country, against the world of socialism by imperialist propaganda using very sophisticated and efficient technical methods. All devices for influencing the thinking of people which the bourgeoisie has at its disposal, press, film, radio, are being mobilised to confuse the people, to put into their heads an image of almost paradise-like life in capitalism, and to denigrate socialism. The special feature of the class struggle in the international arena in this contemporary historical epoch is above all the fact that it becomes more and more acute in all areas, in economics, social relations, international politics, ideology, and culture. [In

these areas a] desperate fight between the dying-out world system of capitalism and the world socialist system is taking place . . . the theoretical-ideological fight which began within the last few years against bourgeois 'marxologists' and revisionist elements, who try to advocate the 'renaissance' and 'new interpretation' of marxism, pluralism in marxism and advocate synthesis with non-marxist teaching – this fight must continue.

To conform with section structure so far we should now, after this glance at the historical origins of the Soviet theory of international relations, proceed to an analysis of its parts. In that context a preliminary look might be taken at what is referred to as the assumptions and research orientations of Soviet theory. Or, as we would refer to them, ideological parameters that seem to be 'axiomatic' and which, while demarcating the bounds of Soviet theorising about international relations, at the same time set aside and delimit areas for rational discussion. One of the most coherent expositions of such axiomatic parameters comes from the pen of Professor Yelena Dmitrievna Modrzhinskaya,[54] a member of the Institute of Philosophy of the Academy of Sciences of the USSR. Although the content of this exposition belongs to Professor Modrzhinskaya it is completely consistent with that which is stated and restated at intervals throughout the (Eastern) literature on international relations. Here then, the opportunity might be taken of establishing an outline of Soviet theory by reassembling Modrzhinskaya's original content within a point-by-point format [55] as follows:

1 The theory of international relations is based on the general principles of Marxism-Leninism, most particularly on leninist methodology and dialectical materialism.
2 International relations theory is part of historical materialism and scientific communism.
3 The theory of international relations is defined as a theory that examines the economic, political, ideological, legal, diplomatic, and military relations (in that order) among nations, states, systems of states, basic social economic and political forces, and organisations acting in the world arena (some definitions, for example that of Longin Pastusiak, also include 'cultural' relations[56]).
4 International relations theory is interdisciplinary in so far as it

175

requires close links with economists, international lawyers, politicians, philosophers, historians, and publicist-international-alists ('Mezhdunarodniks').

5 Class relationships play a decisive role, the type of international relations being determined by the nature of existing economic formations, and by the economic and political interests of the governing classes.

6 International relations can be correctly understood only as part of, and indivisible from, its unity with domestic policy.

7 Marxism-Leninism provides the key to the scientific understanding and control of the subjective factor in the life of society: international relations are not fatalistic, the scientific approach to the analysis being based upon the realisation of their *objective* basis, the existence of which does not depend on the will and wishes of the people and which determines in the final analysis the nature of international politics as well as of the *subjective factor* (which is to say the activity of the masses, of classes, parties, governments, states). It determines also the ideological expressions of their class interests.

8 The crucial influence in the world arena is that of socialist international relations.

9 The following are the main areas on which international research should concentrate. (Because of the implications of point 6, there is a basic difference between the international relations conducted within socialist countries and those conducted within capitalist ones; the research topics also are divided into two groups.) As follows:

1 *Those concerning socialist international relations*
   (a) The analysis of international relations of socialist states.
   (b) The role of the subjective factor in the development of a new type of international relations – which is to say socialist international relations.
   (c) An analysis of the unity between the domestic and the international politics of the socialist countries.
   (d) The parallel relations of various forms of the class struggle in the world arena.
   (e) The influence of the socialist community (commonwealth) on the entire system of international relations, and on the developing countries in particular.

176

(f) The analysis of neo-colonialism as opposed to socialist internationalism with its fraternal aid to the developing countries.

2 *Those concerning capitalist international relations*
   (a) The analysis of contradictions in capitalist international relations (believed to be possible only from the positions of Marxism-Leninism).
   (b) The question of war and peace, one of the most serious problems of our time.
   (c) Analysis and criticism of bourgeois concepts of international politics – a task of primary importance since in the first place such theories are presumed to 'provide the basis' of reactionary imperialist politics and tend to dissimulate their true appearance; and, in the second, works on international relations produced by bourgeois ideologists draw a false picture of the USSR and its international politics. Such attempts must be constantly resisted. The analysis of concepts of contemporary capitalist international relations theory should concern itself with the revelation of their ignorance of the objective laws of social development and of the class struggle which is the essence of politics. It should draw attention to the manner in which Western theory of international relations confuses analysis and description, substituting falsely the latter for the former.

In summary, may we then reiterate that the Soviet theory of international relations is in its philosophical assumptions firmly committed to dialectical materialism as a part of historical materialism and scientific communism, and with them accepts the further commitment to the recognition of class relations as the determinant of inter-state relations. And so, the actors in the world arena consist of states and class-determined systems of states, as well as 'basic social, economic, political forces' (clearly derivative also from class). It is, then, the political, ideological, legal, diplomatic, military and cultural interactions of all of these that constitute the province of international relations theory and with which it concerns itself on an inter-disciplinary basis. The class analysis of international relations – particularly the assumption of the unity of domestic and international politics – leads Soviet theory to distinguish among types of international relations based on the various subjects of the relations rather than the 'object' with which the particular relation deals.

Since an understanding of the general approach is in our view of central importance, the remaining part of this chapter will be devoted to examining the outline in greater detail. In the first of two parts, therefore, we shall attempt a summary of contemporary Marxist-Leninist philosophy, without some understanding of which we could hardly hope to understand the subject's epistemological and methodological assumptions. In other words we are discussing, in terms of Modrzhinskaya's analysis, points 1 and 2. In the second part will be outlined the framework of its conceptual model of the world, that is the divisions between states, systems of states, and classes, with the analysis of the various types of relations that take place among them. This outline will cover the remaining points of the Modrzhinskaya framework.

1   The philosophical/epistemological assumptions of the contemporary Soviet theory of international relations

Let us say at the outset that despite attempts to 'destalinise' over a period of two decades, the nature of the stalinist implant into the body of Marxist-Leninist philosophy remains effectively intact[57] – a fact that is well attested in various texts, and specifically in the major philosophical compendium of the post-stalinist era, namely the *Osnovy Marksistskoi Filozofii* (Fundamentals of Marxist Philosophy) as well as V. Afanasyev's *Scientific Communism*.[58] These works, whose distribution was in the millions[59] and on whose chapters on both dialectical and historical materialism we base the following survey,[60] replaced Stalin's *Short Course* and *Fundamentals of Leninism* as the major textbooks used widely not only in the USSR but also in translation throughout the countries of the socialist bloc. A glance at Konstantinov's footnotes reveals neither any reference to Stalin nor a direct quotation from his works. As a matter of fact, most citations derive either from Engels's *Anti-Dühring* and *Dialectics of Nature* or from Lenin's *Materialism and Empirio-criticism*. In these circumstances our earlier insistence on extending to Engels the same respect as that accorded Marx may be appreciated. The decision to incorporate a section on Lenin comes also into this category since it is from these two rather than from Marx that the intellectual lineage of contemporary Marxism-Leninism can most clearly be seen to derive. The reader may therefore find it useful at this point to refer to these sections for we shall proceed now not by way of essential similarities but by establishing main departures from the works of both Engels and Lenin.

As Richard T. de George has commented[61] Soviet philosophy in the dogmatic and rigid form in which it is to be found in the writings of Engels and Lenin makes no contribution whatsoever to the solution of those problems that have confronted marxism since the doctrine was first enunciated. Nor does it come to grips with such central questions as arise from rapid developments in the sciences in recent times. Nothing substantial is to be found, for example, on the important implications of the discovery of the theory of relativity or quantum mechanics that open up the whole question of Marxist-Leninist philosophical consistency. Satisfactory answers to the question as to what extent these discoveries challenge the validity of dialectical materialism have not been given. The attempt to argue in extenuation of contemporary Soviet theory that each successive discovery in the natural sciences brings fresh ratification and verification of the dialectical laws has been unconvincing and is at best a half-hearted response to Western philosophy's rejection of the notion of dialectics on the grounds of philosophical incompatibility with modern scientific development.

Dialectical materialism is returned directly to Engels and Lenin, its reinterpretation following closely these original lines, while historical materialism remains very much stalinist. Here then is the source of the schism between historical and dialectical materialism and we might well ask ourselves why, despite assurances to the contrary,[62] it is permitted to persist. Dialectics is defined in the new textbooks as 'the theory of universal connections, of the most general laws of development of all reality . . . [and] . . . *a method of cognition* and *guide to action*'.[63] 'Knowledge of the general laws of development' (the text goes on to explain) 'makes it possible to analyse the past, to understand correctly what is taking place at present and to foresee the future.'[64] While accepting the assumption of universal interconnectedness, Marxism-Leninism endorses the leninist acceptance of causality as the basic form of interconnection. Thus, by recognising all phenomena as necessarily subject to causality Marxist-Leninists acknowledge that the world is 'ruled by necessity'. This necessity, in nature as in society, reveals itself in 'laws'. A law is defined as 'a profound, essential, stable and repeated connection of dependence of phenomena or of different sides of one and the same phenomenon'[65] – hence, 'knowledge of the laws of objective reality helps us to understand the causes of events and therefore constitutes a reliable basis for man's purposeful activities'. The notion of determinism, another key concept of marxism, is to be understood as a 'recognition of the objective character of universal connection, the causative determination of phenomena, the rule of necessity and regularity in nature and society'.[66] The main dialectical laws are, in their post-Stalin interpretation, first the law of transition of quantitative into qualitative change (described as the *dialectical law of development*) which is conceived to operate in all of the processes of nature, society, and thought.[67] The transition of a thing, in other words, is by way of the accumulation of quantitative modification, and it is the prescriptions of this law (totally repudiated by Stalin) that govern the change in things from one qualitative state to a different new state – that change described as a leap in development.[68] The 'leap' signifies a break in the gradualness of the quantitative change of a thing: it describes a sharp turn, a radical change in development.[69] These leaps occur – here again in contradistinction to Stalin's dialectics – in social development as well but (we are informed) although they are there 'relatively rapid' compared to the preceding periods of gradual accumulation of quantitative modifications, the rapidity of their incidence varies, depending upon the nature of the object and the conditions in which the leap occurs.[70]

The second dialectical law focuses not on development but on an analysis of the sources of development and in so doing is sometimes seen to express the 'essence of dialectics'.[71] This is the *law of dialectical contradiction*, or the *law of unity and conflict of opposites*. By 'dialectical contradiction' is (in Marxism-Leninism) understood 'the presence in a phenomenon or process of opposite, mutually exclusive aspects which, at the same time, presuppose each other and within the framework of the given phenomenon exist only in mutual connection'.[72] In this way in nature, in social life, as well as in human thought, developments are supposed to proceed in such a way that 'opposite, mutually exclusive sides or tendencies reveal themselves in an object; they enter into a struggle which culminates in the destruction of the old forms and the emergence of new ones'.[73] Once again there is a hark back to Lenin whose statement 'development is the "struggle" of opposites' is adduced by contemporary Marxist-

Leninists.[74] Thus all development is taken to be 'contradictory in its essence'[75] which means that at any given moment a thing or process 'retains its identity and at the same time ceases to retain it'.[76] It contains within itself its own 'antithesis, a "negating" element which prevents it from remaining inert and immutable'.[77] The contradiction is eventually resolved in a 'qualitative change of a thing'.[78] Before that resolution comes about, the stability of a thing presupposes a 'certain balance or equilibrium of opposites' which can by definition be only 'temporary and relative'.[79] It is because of this awareness of the 'internal contradictoriness of all things and phenomena' that Soviet Marxism-Leninism makes the lofty claim to possession of 'the key to the comprehension of self-movement and development [which leads to the conclusion that] the dialectical concept of development does not require any supernatural source of motion'.[80]

The stalinist distinction between antagonistic and non-antagonistic contradictions is retained in its entirety. Antagonist are those contradictions between 'oppressors and oppressed, exploiters and exploited' (which is to say at the present stage between the 'working class and the capitalists') which will not disappear until after the capitalist class has been 'abolished as a class by either peaceful or non-peaceful means, i.e. until it has been deprived of political power and of the means of production, and thereby of the very possibility of exploiting working people' – a development which can take place only by way of a socialist revolution.[81] In a classless society, that is one from which the surviving remnants of class distinctions have been removed, there remain still non-antagonistic contradictions regardless of the 'coincidence of basic interests of classes and social groups'. These, however, can be resolved without the class struggle (on which the resolution of antagonistic contradictions depends). As in the case of antagonistic contradictions, resolution of these (non-antagonistic) will be 'through the joint efforts of friendly classes of all social strata, under the leadership of the Marxist-Leninist Party'.[82] These contradictions are 'connected with the rapid growth of the material and cultural requirements of the people; [they are] contradictions between the old and new, between the advanced and the backward; they are contradictions between the requirements of the members of socialist society and the still limited material and technical facilities'[83] and it follows, therefore, that with the development of material and technical resources their removal can be accomplished without difficulty.

By way of contrast once again to Stalin's version there is joined to the first and second dialectical laws[84] a third major dialectical law. This is the *law of the negation of the negation* which is seen to follow logically from the 'operation of the law of the unity and struggle of opposites'[85] – which is to say from the second dialectical law. As has been suggested above, Stalin clearly did not find the logic of the third law's deriving from the second sufficiently persuasive as to engage his attention. This third law describes the 'law-governed replacement in the process of development of an old quality by a new one, which comes into being within the old' . . . a phenomenon that occurs often in the process of the 'transformation of a thing into its opposite'.[86] But the chain of development does not cease when one phenomenon is 'negated' – the new phenomenon contains within itself new contradictions which in the course of time lead to a further 'negation'. Thus, no negation may be said to sever or terminate the chain, each 'negation' itself being in turn 'negated'.[87] The operation of a law by which viable elements are preserved from the destruction of the old – and a certain degree of continuity thus maintained – facilitates comprehension (and rationalisation) of such processes as the takeover by a socialist society of the 'old bourgeois culture'.[88] It will be observed too that since it is always the obsolete that is negated and the sound and viable preserved, the development is always progressive and suggests the dictum, 'development is progress'.[89] Taking as example from historical materialism the replacement of the primitive-communal tribal system with no exploitative features by no exploitation in a socialist society, it is argued that social development proceeds not in a 'circular course, or a straight line, but a *spiral*' whereby some features of the past are reproduced at an 'immeasurably higher level'.[90] This is not to preclude the possibility of the occurrence of deviations from the spiral: 'zig-zags or regression', as well as periods of 'temporary stagnation' that might describe the nature of such deviations – which are invariably overcome in the long run.

Questions might well be asked as to the actual deployment and use of these 'laws' and, particularly in the event of their content and nature varying from one instance to another, whether they retain any relevance at all. We are, however, assured that these dialectical laws provide the 'scientific method of cognition and of practical trans-formation of the real world'.[91] They are regarded as *'pointers for research'*[92] and no matter what subject of the social sciences is broached it is with these laws in mind that an approach should be made. The injunction would of course apply to an approach to the theory of international relations and there the researcher has not only to accept marxist determinism with its assumption of an organised, basically non-chaotic nature ascribed to international relations, but in his explanation of international affairs he should have distinguished these dialectical laws and taken them into account. It is an exercise, it will now be appreciated, that would have involved him in the further assumptions of the universal interconnectedness of all things and processes, in the transition of quantitative into qualitative change (with its leaps), in the assumption that everything contains the elements of its opposite as suggested by the law of dialectical contradiction (together with the sometimes difficult to grasp distinction between antagonistic and non-antagonistic contradictions) and, last but not least, in the negation of the negation. This latter suggests a chain development through the negation of opposites by way of an upward, progressive, spiral. Later we shall trace these 'pointers' as they manifest themselves in the actual theory of international relations and will attempt an evaluation as to the extent to which they help or hinder the elaboration of that theory. For, international relations theorists, like all other social workers, are obliged to formulate the laws that govern the objective development of their subject – a necessary undertaking since (as is frequently reiterated) to understand the movement of the world is in effect to formulate the laws of its objective development. In order to use dialectics in the process of cognition, the textbook enjoins us, it is necessary to have a complete 'mastery of the principles of dialectics' and to couple it with a 'profound knowledge of concrete facts and circumstances'. Thus, research ought to begin with a 'most careful and thorough study of each concrete situation' and only after that preliminary study can it be discovered 'how and in what form dialectical laws operate'.

The theory of knowledge is practically word for word that postulated by Lenin with strong emphasis once again on certain aspects of the corrective function of practice, on the rather vague theory of *reflection* of objective reality in the human mind, on the distinction between absolute and relative truth,[93] and on the basic belief in the ultimate knowability of the world. It is pointed out that with the mastery of the laws of development comes an ability to establish trends of development and to foresee the course of events, although in this context the textbook advises that only the general direction of historical development and not actual details are foreseeable. [94] But even though the conferment of a final form as well as the setting of time limits to many social processes are subject to the influence of a multitude of fortuitous circumstances that 'cannot be foreseen even by the most brilliant mind', [95] it is clear to Marxism-Leninism that general tendencies and the broad lines of the development of international relations (such as the victory of one system over another) can be predicted. With that done the filling in of the details is of lesser importance.

Historical materialism, as we have noted, remains more or less in the form in which it was taught in Stalin's time. Historical materialism studies society as a whole, concerning itself with the most general laws of social development and of life. These general laws are objective, independent of man's will and consciousness, and operate in a different manner to that of their counterparts in nature. This, we are told, is due to the fact that in a social context it is more difficult to trace regularities largely because of the variable operation of the human element which is 'endowed with consciousness and will-power' and which pursues goals. [96] This is not to deny the fact that even the development of society is a process governed by laws and subject to a certain historical necessity independent of the will and consciousness of man. The task of the social scientist is to 'discover the nature of this necessity, to find out what laws determine the development of history and how they operate'. [97] By way of qualification of the implications of this statement, however, we read that 'historical laws themselves, without people, do not make history': [98] 'They determine the course of history only through the actions, the struggle, and the consciously directed efforts of millions of people.' [99] In other words man uses his knowledge of social laws (knowledge seen as an insight into necessity) to achieve his own ends. If we might offer an analogy it is rather like a blind man who ventures into a room alone and attempts to pinpoint the location of some of the objects in the room so as to avoid stumbling into them.

By establishing the size of the room and the location of the objects he becomes progressively 'free' to move about; that freedom is restricted by the 'necessity' of the position of some of the objects and the possibility of moving others to his advantage. An alternative situation that might help throw light on the meaning of knowledge as 'insight into necessity' could be that of the pilot equipped with radar information in regard to his flight path. Within the constraints of that knowledge he is 'free', which is to say free from the hazard of collision with other planes or from that of proceeding in a direction other than that selected.

Our Soviet text reiterates once again that the main factor of social development is the growth of the forces of production. Marx's notion of a productive process resulting in certain relations of production characterised by forms of property is fully retained as is his assertion that the masses are the makers of history.[100] It is the productive activity of the masses that is the decisive factor in the life and development of society, but individual leadership is also regarded as part of that objective necessity.[101] With Marx the Soviet Marxist-Leninist maintains that the conception of the leaders as driving forces is an illusion: the course of history being determined by the struggle of large social groups, by classes, and masses. Deprived of this mass support leaders are without a source of strength.[102] Moreover, 'unrestrained adulation of a leader, exaggeration of his merits' (or, in other words, the cult of the individual), instils in the masses an erroneous idea that their tasks can be performed by the leader and not by themselves. This error may lead to passivity and the 'freeing of the rank-and-file members of the socialist movement from the duty of thinking, of showing initiative, of creating, and of actively influencing the course of events'.[103] Apart from that, the cult of the individual (an explicit reference to Stalin) undermines democracy and so shifts the centre of gravity of leadership as to have it rest on the decision of a single individual.[104] At this point the textbook proceeds to a detailed analysis of Stalin's personal traits and summarises the damage for which he was responsible. However, the historical mission of the Party continues to be endorsed.[105] Another important notion that receives deliberate stress – but comes in for significant qualification – is the concept of the weakest link(s). Because of the existence of the socialist system the socialist revolution can now take place in practically any country regardless of its weakness or strength;[106] a circumstance that makes the term 'weakest link' something of a misnomer. An unfortunate dimension of arbitrariness is given to the recognition of such revolutions as socialist.

Editions of Marxist-Leninist textbooks published after the 22nd CPSU Congress offer as a culmination of the otherwise stereotyped repetitiousness of the historical sequence[107] a definition of communism. The 1961 Programme of the CPSU (the third in the history of the Soviet Communist Party) attempted to supply this glaring omission whose seriousness as regards the whole Marxist-

Leninist intellectual structure may be appreciated. Designed as a portent of the approach, and on the eve of the transition to communism, it expatiates on the merits of that society and offers a guide to the route that is to be taken to ensure successful entry into that final stage. The Programme defines communism thus:[108]

> Communism is a classless social system with one form of public ownership of the means of production and full social equality of all members of society; under it, the all-round development of people will be accompanied by the growth of the productive forces through continuous progress in science and technology; all the springs of co-operative wealth will flow more abundantly, and the great principle 'from each according to his ability, to each according to his needs' will be implemented. Communism is a highly organised society of free, socially conscious working people in which public self-government will be established, a society in which labour for the good of the society will become the prime vital requirement of everyone, a necessity recognised by one and all, and the ability of each person will be employed to the greatest benefit of the people.

Although this is possibly the longest definition of communism ever attempted, it deals extremely loosely with the concept. Setting aside the vagueness one discerns two main themes: the consecrated importance of the notion of communism and the conferring upon it of a multiple role. In this latter regard it is conceived on the one hand to act as a moral goal as well as a moral criterion[109] while on the other it is described in terms also of its qualities as a political system. What is to happen to the moral ideal with the establishment of communism as a political system is not at all clear. Further confusion is caused by suggesting different usages of the term communism and failing to give some clear indication as to any one sense in which it is to be understood. As in Marx's time the definition remains a negative one, that is, it states what is *not* to be rather than offering a blueprint of what will be. Considerable scope is left therefore for supplementary elaboration – and, alongside that, the potential for arbitrary interpretation in practice. Nor is it at all clear on whose shoulders the task will rest of deciding that society has entered communism: as it stands, there is the distinct possibility that (as in the case of socialism in Stalin's time) a simple declaration will suffice. That the promulgation of communism must rest with the Communist Party goes without saying but as to which group or individual within the Party will take it upon itself/himself to perceive and announce the advent of the last stage is another matter. Quite clearly, the 'actual' will be tailored to match the 'ideal'. In this context a confusion of the functions of communism with the placement on the Party of the onus of filling in the details is presented as an advantage. The advantage is epitomised in the still widely disseminated stalinist notion[110] of the 'moral-political unity of the society' that expresses the merger of political aims with moral goals. In these circumstances it can be appreciated that while at least striving towards the still distant political objective[111] Party decisions and Party actions, whether internally or at international level, become, by definition, 'moral' and 'good'.

In this context too it is important to realise that the notion of communism is absolutely central to Marxism-Leninism. Of equal importance is appreciation of the fact that the present political leaders derive their very legitimacy not from adherence to the teachings of Marx or Lenin as such nor by reason of the doctrine's resting upon such illustrious authority, but from the shared commitment to the same moral goal (communism) as that perceived by Marx and Lenin.

Many Western writers, preoccupied with the notion of communism, brand Soviet philosophy as no more than a secular religion wherein fact merges indiscriminately with value.[112] Thus such bland 'factual' propositions as 'communism is the goal of all mankind' must (since they can never be empirically tested) appear to the critics as no more than high-flown professions of faith, instances of mere value falsely flying the colours of fact. However, it remains a fact that most systems of thought bear within themselves their own definition of truth and thus it does not seem fair that Marxism-Leninism be rejected solely on these grounds.

The first part of the Soviet 'scientific' affirmation that communism is a 'fact' refers to the assumption on the part of both dialectical and historical materialism that society's operation is in accordance with discoverable laws. The fact that these laws can be construed as leading historically from one type of a society to another[113] gives them further confidence in an ability similarly to predict 'scientifically' the coming of communism. In other words, as we have observed in a previous chapter,[114] the line between the elements of explanation and prediction remains for them (unlike for some Western theorists)

187

shadowy and indistinct. The situation then is that the occurrence of certain developments in the past and the existence of 'objectively' existing laws that derive from their pattern of occurrence is supposed to allow Soviet theorists to predict 'scientifically' the occurrence of certain events in the future. As with Marx, Lenin, and Stalin – and once again in contrast to most Western theorists – Marxist-Leninists give an affirmative answer to the question of the possibility of prediction in social theory, adducing in evidence of its scientific nature its capacity to control future events. Thus Soviet Marxism-Leninism still endorses the *factual inevitability* of the advent of the communist society. It is a future that awaits the whole of mankind.

Confidence in their ability to unravel the objective laws of development that lead to communism is, however, only the first part of the answer as to *why* communism is 'inevitable'. Recalling the marxian approach, the second part of a Soviet reply to Western criticism in this regard would be based on an analysis of human nature which, it is understood, can achieve fulfilment only within a communist society. The seeming paradox of this part of the rebuttal is where the justification of communism is made in terms of man, the 'most valuable entity in the world'.[115] Some explanation is therefore called for. We discover from their attributions to Marx's sixth *Thesis on Feuerbach* and to passages from the *Economic and Philosophic Manuscripts of 1844*[116] that Soviet theorists still understand human nature as a collectivist entity: 'the human essence is no abstraction inherent to each single individual. In its reality it is the ensemble of the social relations.'[117] A man is seen as a collective being, fully externalised – that is with no value of his own except that which derives from his place in a certain collective. Thus, paradoxically, the ultimate goal of marxism – to liberate man – can only be achieved within and through the collective. Only within the fully fledged communist society, runs the argument, is man able to be free, to develop all of his inherent human characteristics, and achieve universal happiness. Only in communist society can there be freedom of expression and, for everyone, universal justice and material abundance. Only within and through (and despite) the collectivity will his interests and those of everyone else for the first time fully coincide. Until that time, however, and in order that such a coincidence be achieved, these interests have to be shaped so as to ensure their convergence. Thus, from Marx onwards – and particularly when marxism came to be applied to social reality – it has contained a paradoxical (one might say 'schizophrenic') value system: one which rests on the proposition that on the way to the attainment of the desired end those same values might be denied that were once advocated and formed an inseparable part of the vision.

In the light of the above observations one could argue that the bulk of Soviet social science including the theory of international relations is devoted to the purpose of devising 'systems of levers' for the purpose of synchronising conflicting interests, and of transmission belts for the transference of these to communist society on a world scale. At that level all interests will not only have become compatible but will coincide.

This is the result – and a peculiar one – of the combination of two typically marxist concepts: the identification of the *objectively* determined triumph of the proletarian world revolution and, within it, a place assigned for the operation of a *subjective* foreign policy. The interplay, in other words, of the historical process teleologically conceived and of the international system, or so to say, the striking of a balance between the conscious activity of human beings on the one hand and the degree of distortion/faithfulness with which it reflects and assists the objectively given laws of history. In the discovery of compatibility in the incompatible the ubiquitous dialectic continues to play an important part although the constantly reiterated reference in Soviet literature – 'dialectically related' since Stalin's time – has not provided an explanation but rather at best a tautological restatement of the problem.

2 The conceptual model of world politics in Soviet Marxism-Leninism

A brief but important comment on bibliographical sources has to be made at the start of this section. Our 'reconstruction' of the Soviet theoretical model is based on a broad reading of a variety of Soviet and East European sources, and yet there is, so far as we know, not one among them that might be said to cover the Soviet theory as a whole. In these circumstances it is impossible that footnote references should be comprehensive. The problem is compounded by the strong tendency to repetitiousness in Soviet literature whereby without adding new insight a single idea culled from an important political document comes in for laboured perusal and debate. And so it might be argued that by structuring the argument on a close analysis of the foreign affairs reports that have emerged from all of the recent CPSU Congresses, as well as newspapers and journal articles, a picture of Soviet theory more complete, comprehensive, and consistent in its parts than has been achieved in the Soviet Union itself can be made to take shape. In this belief and in asserting the consistency of the parts of the picture thus derived we are sustained by the inclusion in the Soviet Constitution of a chapter on Soviet foreign policy that fully endorses our understanding and the analysis of Soviet theory as set forth in these pages.[118]

With that understanding we would draw attention once again to another major assumption of this work, namely, that ideology does profoundly influence thinking on international relations.[119] In this context and in the light of the conclusions reached so far in the text, we would go so far as to say that because of the high intensity socialisation process and the strong emphasis on training in Marxism-Leninism of the entire Soviet and East European populations,[120] the outline of contemporary Marxist-Leninist philosophy that we have sketched constitutes a *minimum* philosophical/epistemological background for both theorist and policy-maker. The career profiles of Soviet leaders and theorists, all of whom are either university[121] graduates or have been otherwise equipped with solid Marxist-Leninist education, amply bear out the claim. A contrary argument that would reject any connection between Marxist-Leninist philosophy and the actual decision-making and theory-making processes, and that sees Marxist-Leninist jargon as a mere propaganda expedient, runs into difficulty when it is called upon to explain how people whose education has been along such lines could find it possible to set their in-depth training aside and apply some other set of responses to their serious task.

That the attitudes and patterns of thought of those so trained should evoke at every turn of the discourse or argument the Marxist-Leninist vision should then occasion no surprise. No matter whether facility in the use of Marxist-Leninist terms and concepts are explicit or present as a 'subconscious' background, the philosophical postulates 'prefixing' *any* consideration of world politics are as inevitable as guides to the formulation of instruments of high political import as they are unmistakable in their influence on scholarly works. A glance once again at Modrzhinskaya's outline of the Soviet theory of international relations makes us aware of the extent of intellectual tie in for example references to the 'general principles of Marxism-

Leninism, in particular leninist methodology and dialectical materialism' which is seen as the 'basis of the theory of international relations'.[122] In this context Modrzhinskaya sees the theory of international relations as 'part of historical materialism and scientific communism'[123] and similar testimony to the dependence of theory of international relations on Marxism-Leninism is a commonplace in writing on the subject. A reference by Israelyan offers typical acknowledgment of the dependent association: 'complex, diverse and contradictory as world developments are, it would however be wrong to regard current international life as a chaotic and inexplicable agglomeration of chance phenomena. The *development of world affairs is subject to the general laws* [italics added] governing the development of human society which Marxism-Leninism has discovered. The Marxist dialectical method alone helps to account for all the complex and contradictory developments in international affairs today.'[124] How in practice one might ask does the philosophical indebtedness of the policy-maker and theorist influence Soviet international relations theory? And how can an understanding of this association help us to an analysis of that theory?

By attempting answers to two straightforward questions certain features are revealed that assist the analysis. There is the question first of all as to the place occupied by the dialectical method in international relations theory. In this connection we observe first the dialectical assumption that 'international affairs [are] a single whole in which separate events are mutually connected and determined'.[125] From this the conclusion derives that 'any diplomatic act or foreign policy step is inseparably bound up with a concrete and constantly changing historical situation which continually gives rise to new diplomatic acts and foreign policy events'.[126] We see also emerging from the practical application of dialectics to international affairs notions to the effect that 'quantitative shifts taking place on a world scale such as the increase in the number of socialist countries and the emergence of dozens of new states pursuing an anti-imperialist policy, result in qualitative changes in the aggregate of contemporary international relations'.[127] In Israelyan's own words the advantage of the application of dialectical method to international relations research lies in the fact that it 'shows the diversity and contradictory nature of international developments in their interconnection, interdependence and constant movement and the dialectical unity of all the counteracting factors'.[128]

191

Of similar importance is another fundamental assumption of historical materialism: namely the marxist doctrine of basis and superstructure which translates into the theory of international relations as the absolute dependence of foreign policy on domestic structure.[129] This leads to a twofold conclusion: first, that the class structure of any particular state profoundly influences (if not determines) the foreign policy of that state. Thus the foreign policy of each and every state should be assessed against the background of the class structure of that particular state. Hence Marxism-Leninism rejects point blank the concept of national interest which is construed always as class interest in disguise.[130] And secondly it would seem to follow that states of the same class structure, as a result of the basic coincidence in their economic structure (that is property relations and form of division of labour), are grouped together into 'systems', 'blocs', or 'camps'; groupings which, we might observe, are not necessarily formalised in any way. This division of the world into socio-economic systems (capitalist and socialist) has close affinity to the Soviet moral conception. Such indeed is the affinity that it is possible to see in the official recently promulgated 'moral code of the builders of communism'[131] a moral code also of international relations. Because of the inherent unity of all parts of Soviet Marxist-Leninist teaching [132] moral conception may therefore be said to lie at the very heart of those main characteristics of Soviet international relations theory which characterise and supply a basis of that strict *differentiation between types of international relations* to which we have already alluded, a differentiation made not according to the content but to the nature of the participant in those relations. It is to marxist ethics that we must look for the explanation of this participant-determined (as opposed to content-determined) international relations type. With this done we may then proceed to a more detailed analysis.

In terms of ethics marxism does not distinguish between goodness and the agency responsible for doing good; nor between wrongdoing and the perpetrator of the wrong. The distinction is between the agency responsible for right or wrong; the actions of the former are automatically deemed to be right while those of the latter are by definition bad and immoral. In other words, the same moral yardstick is never applied to the judgment of an identical action on the part of two agencies but rather the judgment is arrived at through the identification of the agency responsible. All important then in such a judgment are answers to the question as to what *class* (which, because of the link between domestic structure and foreign policy, means what *state*) and, with reference to the assumed broad similarity in the relationship between base and superstructure among certain states, what socio-economic bloc or system is identifiable as the agency responsible. Consider briefly the Soviet moral code, and particularly those areas having a direct bearing on international relations: 'Devotion to the communist cause; love of the socialist motherland of the other socialist countries . . . friendship and brotherhood among all peoples of the USSR: intolerance of national and racial hatred; an uncompromising attitude to the enemies of communism, peace and the freedom of nations; fraternal solidarity with the working people of all countries, and with all peoples.'[133] A glance only is needed to reveal quite clearly that the world is seen to be divided (in the language of the New Testament) into capitalist 'goats' and socialist 'sheep'. The Soviet understanding and model of the world fully coincides with this division whereby the world is divided sharply into two main socio-economic systems (capitalist and socialist) which are a 'spillover' result of the two basic antagonistic classes.

We are not surprised to discover once again when we turn to the notion of system that particular connotations attach to a notion that conjures up not a political alliance of states operating within the system of international relations but is rather 'a socio-economic, class, political community which determines the unity of the objective interests of its states in the struggle between the two systems'.[134] The two systems are 'offsprings'[135] of the two basic classes, and hence the Third World constitutes in this respect a category of its own. Khrushchev, with his modification of the stalinist two camp doctrine[136] through the addition of the 'developing countries' (or Third World) and their inclusion in his concept of a 'zone of peace', postulated a triangular model. The modification left Marxist-Leninist first principles relatively intact, and theory still remained indissolubly linked to them, since the state of flux in which the 'Third World' vertex clearly exists was still fully consistent with the basic notion of dichotomisation essential to the dialectic. The 'dialectical' dichotomy emerges once again with the (theoretical) resolution of the conflict between the two main systems over the Third World and replacement of the transitory triangular stage by bipolarity. The outcome of the struggle, it goes without saying, will be in favour of the Soviet system, a system which in its turn will give way to a monolithic communist world. Thus, with no main area of divergence, international relations theory parallels and at main points is dependent upon Marxist-Leninist general principles: the dichotomisation of the world into two 'contradictory parts' is as we have seen entirely consistent with dialectics and the conflict taking place in the world arena is construed basically as a zero-sum game with a historically and morally preordained victor – communism.

Let us now take a closer look at the major constituent parts of the Soviet model, consisting of the *capitalist world*, the so-called *progressive revolutionary forces* (that embrace *inter alia* the *Third World*) and the *socialist system* – in that order.

The capitalist world system once stretched across the world, represented the sole and then the determining factor in world affairs and, after its exclusive hegemony, continued to exert an all-powerful influence that went without serious challenge until 1917. Flowing from Lenin's 'law of uneven development of capitalism "in the era of imperialism" ' is the belief that the demise of that system will be the end result of a last fatal conflict with the socialist system as adversary. By this is understood not one major clash, but rather a period over which the two are locked in mortal combat – a period described as the 'general crisis of capitalism' and punctuated by two world wars and numerous lesser conflicts. The first stage had been ushered in by the post-First World War break-up of the capitalist system whereby, as a result of the Great October revolution, the first socialist state came into existence while the second stage started after the Second World War and the dramatic territorial extension of the socialist camp. The present, third stage, required no such upheaval as detonator but owed its relatively gentle beginnings in the mid-1950s to *qualitative* changes taking place in the 'world correlation of forces',[137] such as the ending of United States strategic invulnerability, the growing strength of the socialist bloc in economic, political and military muscle and, last but not least, the effective secession from the capitalist world of those newly independent states who favoured, however unrealistically, postures of genuine non-alignment. It is to be noted in this context however that, in the leninist tradition, no matter how weakened the capitalist world might have become, the analysis of its inner contradictions still plays a very important part in Soviet thinking.

It would seem that the 'balance' (or 'correlation') of the forces within the system still depends on the traditionally postulated inter-capitalist contradictions.[138] However, the emergence of the socialist camp and the Third World has resulted in the identification of fresh characteristics in the capitalist contradictions. It is assumed, for example, that the outbreak of armed clashes between capitalist countries is less probable than before. Furthermore, there is, against a background of mighty 'revolutionary progressive forces', a tendency for the capitalist powers to integrate both militarily and in economic formations under the aegis of the strongest – i.e. the United States. The process of economic integration, it is assumed, simply represents the logical result of the interlocking processes of monopoly capital – capital which long ago burst the confines of narrow national boundaries and embarked simultaneously on a course that would strengthen its position in the coming struggle with socialism. It is, in other words, due to the influence of both internal (capital) and external (anti-socialist) motives that the traditionally assumed irreconcilability of intra-capitalist contradictions seems to have lost some of its sharper features. No matter the extent of the amelioration, however, we are assured that these remain one of the most important 'assets [!] in the foreign policy formulations of the socialist countries and the art of using them is not to be neglected',[139] for the appearance of strength in such tendencies is misleading and 'neither the military nor the economic integration will eliminate them'.[140]

In a truly dialectical manner therefore the general crisis of capitalism is seen as being aggravated by factors that operate both from within and from outside the system: the system is on the one hand united both by the requirements of capital and by the shared ideology and practice of *anti-communism*[141] and is at the same time ridden by 'serious divergences and contradictions . . . that . . . enable the socialist countries to arrange relations with capitalist states in a differentiated way, striving for utmost efficacy of co-ordinated action in preserving general peace and averting a world thermonuclear war'.[142] The past decade, as Soviet commentators jubilantly note, has witnessed an unprecedented retreat on the part of capitalism on all fronts: 'The collapse of the monetary system, feverish inflation, the mounting inability of production, which has more than once resulted in slumps, and the problems of environmental pollution, which are becoming increasingly difficult, demonstrate the state of crisis of capitalist relations of production, and of the ineffectiveness of state-monopoly regulation to resolve'.[143] The 'destructive processes inherent in bourgeois economy lead to political upheavals'[144] and the 'progressive forces' located in that part of the world have been on the

195

increase. Soviet authors emphasise the intensification of the struggle of the working class and of democratic movements generally, which further distinguish themselves from those in the past by a more marked anti-imperialist stance as, for example, in the unprecedentedly broad scale of the strike movement.[145] The most interesting and most enthusiastically received feature of the new strike wave has been the increasingly close link of the elements involved with political demands. The strikers – according to the Soviet Press – progressively improve their techniques, the strike movement assumes an increasingly broad basis – and the processes of the scientific and technological revolution[146] march inexorably and in step.

This brings us to another dimension of the Soviet model – a model by whose configuration is comprehended much more than the three major systems or blocs alone. The sheer impossibility of bringing the notion of socialist 'sheep' and capitalist 'goats' into precise coincidence with the major systems (or for that matter with class structure) would, apart from any other consideration, suggest a broader, more encompassing theoretical framework. And so, in addition to discerning two basic socio-economic systems of states to which is joined the Third World, Soviet theory of international relations reaches for 'actors' on the international scene distinct from the conventional structure of states or coalitions of states. As a matter of fact this category of 'sheep' (sometimes referred to as *'progressive forces'* or as a *'militant alliance of the main revolutionary forces of our day'*[147]) is already perceived to be broader than the socialist system alone. Taking a leaf from the stalinist book in which 'allies' were similarly identified within the 'hostile camp'[148] these 'progressive forces' are located in the capitalist world (as the international working class together with other progressive anti-capitalist forces), in the Third World (the anti-colonial national liberation movements), and of course (as the third progressive force) the totality of the world socialist system.[149] The relations among the 'sheep' as defined by the moral code might suggest relaxation of the strictures of the code and the emergence therein of a certain humanism.[150] But exclusive as it is to the 'progressive forces' alone, and with the adoption of an 'uncompromising attitude' with respect to the 'goats', it is humanism of a limited variety indeed.

The process whereby these 'progressive forces' and particularly those located within the capitalist system grow in strength is described by Soviet writers as the 'democratisation of international relations', which is perceived as a subjective expression of the objectively given historical revolutionary process. However marked does this so-called 'democratisation of international relations' become, it is noteworthy that these contingents of progressive forces are subjected to a gradual process of dilution in terms of definition so that eventually they embrace any movement of an anti-imperialist – or even an anti-establishment – nature. This tendency for membership qualifications in the ranks of these progressive forces to become increasingly less stringent, unorthodox and arbitrary as the reach of the Soviet Union in global politics has extended has of course been commented on at various times. Thus the very category of 'progressive forces' so heavily relied on in the theory itself suffers from a vagueness of definition and in effect comprises a very wide and disparate (and also changeable as they fall in or out of Soviet favour) and unconventional conglomeration of the elements of one system (socialist), most of another one (Third World) and a considerable proportion of the capitalist system. Membership (if one can describe it in that way) once again only *predisposes* certain behaviour rather than indicates a united course of action.

We have mentioned above what is referred to in the West as the 'Third World' or, in Soviet parlance, the 'developing countries'. Of a basically similar nature to the 'progressive forces' – it having also formed part of the capitalist system – this area was originally described in Lenin's theory of imperialism. In that exposition the world capitalist economy once comprised two types of economy, namely, that of the few industrially highly developed states who, in Lenin's terminology, did the 'oppressing', and that of the less developed (the oppressed) whose economy was colonial in essence. Political revolutions in those concerned with dislodging the metropolitan rule were primarily directed towards the establishment of formal independence and as a rule did not go far enough in their elimination of residual capitalist economic influence. As the Programme of the CPSU puts it, unless the embryonic states 'put an end to their economic dependence on imperialism, they will be playing the role of the "world countryside" and will remain an object of semi-colonial exploitation'.[151] Contrary to the direction of modern Western theories, Soviet theorists maintain that imperialism constantly creates conditions of oppression and exploitation which not only perpetuate but even augment differences in levels of economic development. Thus the task – of 'liberation' – that confronts Third World countries is defined primarily in economic terms. Their basic motivations in the repudiation of imperialism should not be sought either in the sphere of superstructure, the sphere of ideology, or government, or in politics in general but rather in economic life – by that to be understood not the framework of economy of individual nations but economic life on a world scale. [152]

The socialist world system is seen as the most important of the 'progressive forces', and is defined as the 'social, economic and political community of free and sovereign peoples united by close bonds of international socialist solidarity, by common interests and objectives, and following the path of socialism and communism'. [153] The socialist world system originally comprised the USSR, Poland, Czechoslovakia, East Germany, Hungary, Romania and Bulgaria, [154] to which such countries as Cuba and new socialist states of Africa and Asia have been added. Its formation is described as a historical event second in significance only to the Great October revolution, and every advance is conceived to be at the expense of capitalism. Each accession of strength reflects a corresponding intensification of the general crisis of that system. As the inevitable and irreversible process of the general crisis works towards the end, so the socialist world system progresses and makes headway in what we have suggested is best likened to a zero-sum contest. It could not be otherwise for the ultimate victory is to the socialist side. [155] Ultimate is the operative word, because in the meantime the process of socialist integration becomes an immediate objective and one which is subject to the vagaries of the struggle with the capitalist system. [156]

As we have suggested elsewhere, a sense of timing, flexibility and a pragmatic adaptation to 'the realities' have been and continue to be an integral part of the approach. The Programme of the Communist Party of the Soviet Union points out that since socialist revolutions in contemporary socialist states took place at different times, and the economic and cultural levels of the countries concerned are dissimilar, therefore the non-simultaneous entry into the period of the full-scale construction of communism is to be expected. Nevertheless, the fact that the socialist countries are developing as members of a single world socialist system *enables them to reduce the time necessary for the construction of socialism and offers them the prospect of affecting the transition to communism – more or less simultaneously, within one and the same historical epoch.* [157] The socialist system, we are told, is by no means a 'temporary grouping or a military political bloc', but a 'new and qualitatively higher stage in the progressive development of mankind'. In fact the socialist community is seen as the prototype of the future organisation of the world – in which context Lenin is freely quoted: 'a voluntary union of nations – which precludes any coercion of one nation by another – a union founded on complete confidence, on a clear recognition of brotherly unity, on absolutely voluntary consent'.[158] A laudable sentiment indeed were it not for the ironic commentary provided by practice in the recent history of intra-socialist relations.

Our brief résumé would not be complete without a note on the place of communist parties which, contrary to what one might expect, are not regarded as an official actor in world politics.[159] We know that once come to power inside its society the party formulates the broad lines of foreign policy. Beyond that, however, the idea that the Soviet Union accepts the rules of traditional diplomatic transaction and carries out its official relations through the normal – i.e. state – diplomatic channels (a concession to the horizontal level) and not between the Soviet Party and its foreign counterparts requires qualification. With those countries where communist parties are in power (i.e. in other socialist countries) or with those where they exist, no matter in what degree of obscurity, the Soviet Union adds to the web of inter-state relations the intricate inter-party network. Thus a new and quite unprecedented type of relations (i.e. inter-party relations) has been added to the conventional intercourse of diplomatic institutions. Where the communist party is not in power, there are relations only on an inter-party level in addition to the parallel diplomatic relations with the (non-communist) government.

With the major constituent parts of the Soviet model set forth, a brief recapitulation at this stage will serve to underline once again the close linkage between Marxism-Leninism and the Soviet theory of international relations which manifests itself in the following axiomatic parameters:

1 The assumption that the world is basically non-chaotic, reinforcing belief in the possibility of reaching an understanding of world politics. Such an understanding becomes possible only when the dialectical laws controlling the world are discovered.
2 The assumption of mutual interconnections between and among all international events.

3 The assumption of what might be termed an absolute dependence of foreign policy on domestic (i.e. class) structure leading to the rejection of the notion that all states are directly comparable as 'neutral' actors. Their classification is instead on the basis of their predisposition towards certain courses of action which in turn depends on their belonging to a particular socio-political system.[160]

4 Following this basis of identification of major actors it may be appreciated that these are *no longer necessarily coincident with states*, and there is postulated instead a triangularity of 'socio-economic systems' (capitalist, socialist, and 'third'). This is overlapped by a second 'inner' triangularity of 'progressive forces' that exactly coincides with neither state nor class structure, and the concept of triangular overlap completes the essentials of the Soviet picture of the world.

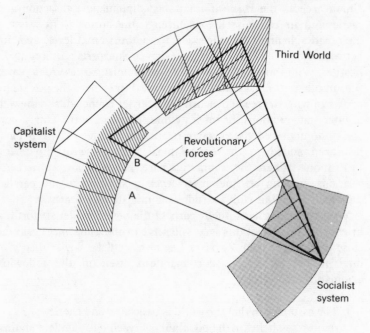

Figure 10 The two triangles of the Soviet model
A: the three 'worlds' (capitalist, socialist and Third).
B: the 'revolutionary forces' (socialist system as a whole and 'progressive elements' in the other two 'worlds').

5 The basic 'dialectical' dichotomisation of the world, and the assumption of the inevitability of conflict between the 'parts'. This dichotomy would seem to go some way towards explaining the oversimplified perception and sharp distinction between good and bad in the Soviet analysis generally.

6 The assumption that this conflict will ultimately take the form of one that (in Western terms of reference) might be likened to a zero-sum game with a historically and morally preordained victor – the socialist (communist) system.

7 Until that final outcome, however, and the ascendancy of one system it is believed to be in the arena of international relations – unconfined as in Marx's time to the domestic situations of states – that the conflict of world class antagonisms will work itself out.

8 Thus the Soviet theory of international relations arrives at what we would style a *participant determined typology of international (as well as other intergroup) relations*,[161] which is to say the categorisation of relations in the world arena not according to their content but according to *the identity of the actors* between whom these relations take place. The inclusion of participants other than state 'actors' in this categorisation helps to explain the description of Soviet theory of international relations as the sociology of international relations.[162]

It is this last parameter, namely our contention that one of the characteristics of Soviet thinking on international relations is within the framework of distinct categories of such relations, that requires elaboration. This is particularly so since expanded comment will be called for also in regard to the cluster of problems arising from this categorised thinking.

Commensurate with the many varieties of actors (states, 'progressive forces', systems of states) the logical requirement would be the operation of some nine categories of relations.[163] But before proceeding with the enumeration it should be noted that because of the basic dichotomisation of the world all of these relations ultimately may be resolved into the antagonistic conflict between socialism and capitalism; the separate categories of relations being to a large extent variations on, or derived from, that fundamental relationship. In fact in Soviet theory six or seven such types of relations so distinctly emerge as to warrant identification through the shorthand terms commonly used in Soviet parlance to describe them. In this way that of *proletarian internationalism* and its derivative *socialist internationalism* identify relations among the 'progressive forces' and among the socialist states respectively. *Peaceful coexistence* describes the relations that are promoted by socialist states towards states of the capitalist system and the 'capitalist-oriented' states of the Third World, while *anti-communism* describes the relations of capitalist states *vis-à-vis* the socialist. *Neo-colonialism* identifies the relations of capitalist states with respect to states of the Third World while the Third World response is described as *national liberation movement*. Last but not least, the label *capitalist contradictions* (with which we dealt above) is descriptive of the relations mutually engaged in by capitalist states among themselves.

It should be emphasised at this stage that in terms of the clarity and consistency of this system of conceptualisation in Soviet theory a great deal is left to be desired and some of the more obvious inconsistencies and shortcomings, some of them inherent in the approach (most notably the Soviet attitude to China) we shall draw attention to here. While it can be said that some sections of the model are more fully elaborated than others it is also to be remarked that each of these international relations types appears to have characteristics of its own which are not interchangeable with those of another type except in so far as they are quite clearly *hierarchically* ordered. That is, the 'lower' relation contains some but not all of the attributes and qualifications of the higher – a situation that in practical terms means the relationship may be downgraded or upgraded as international circumstances would seem to provide and the leadership determines.[164] The Soviet model corresponds in fact to that which in the West has recently been designated a structural dependence model, or that which postulates the close dependence of any one type of relations (and indeed the model as a whole) on all of the other relations categories each of which is similarly dependent. In the case of the capitalist versus socialist, the relationship is, to use their own word, a function of inter-capitalist contradictions.

Crucial also to an understanding of the Soviet model are those problems of a semantic or terminological nature which give rise to ambiguities and misconceptions, and these perhaps ought to be clarified before we proceed further. Such ambiguity might be said to apply to the subtle distinctions that are drawn for example between policy, the actual international relationship itself, and the 'state of international relations' or 'conditions of international relations'. Since the terminological confusion into which one might easily fall can here lead/has led to misunderstandings with far-reaching results we may, at the risk of seeming unnecessarily reiterative, redefine very briefly our own understanding of the Soviet terms as follows: The class nature of a state determines the fact of its belonging to a particular socio-economic system (socialist or capitalist). This adherence determines its general predisposition to behave in a certain manner adjudged positive or negative with respect to ultimate historical and moral criteria. Soviet theory equates this general predisposition with ideology as the expression of the fundamental interests of the classes whose instrument the state is.

Within the confines of this broadly determined ideological behaviour pattern the state formulates its politics both domestic and foreign although, we are reminded, politics should not be confused with ideology. Although ideology is a pervasive influence in politics it comprehends politics, is much broader in scope and, in contrast to the very essence of politics, permits of no compromise.[165] Soviet theory, while rejecting the notion of a distinction between domestic and foreign policy on the grounds that both are determined by class interests and therefore seem to be in complete accord with one another, nevertheless recognises other modes of differentiation. For example, policies are of two kinds: strategic and tactical. Policies that are *strategic* are deemed to be those in close accordance with the dictates of ideology and are basically long-term policies devoted to the achievement of such serious goals as the victory of communism and final defeat of capitalism, the success of the national liberation movement, etc. *Tactical* policies on the other hand are short-term policies: they are subordinated to the strategic and are designed to serve strategic purposes. To this end they also differ from strategic policies in their built-in provision for the deployment where necessary of such expedients as 'zig-zags', compromise, and outright retreat.[166] The distinction will have made it clear that peaceful coexistence, socialist and proletarian internationalism, and the rest of the underlying principles of international relations types quite clearly come under the heading of strategies.[167] It is important to note further that as the implementation of a specific policy proceeds and triggers a response from the recipient, or target, the relationship thus produced or, so to speak, the resultant, taken in conjunction with the general correlation of forces that prevails at the time, signifies the 'condition' or 'state' of international relations.[168] Obviously, in establishing this 'state' of international relations those relations engaged in between the two major parts of the world model, the socialist and capitalist, must play a paramount role. And as a matter of fact the reciprocal interaction between peaceful coexistence and anti-communism provides a good example of the way in which the resultant is used to identify this 'condition' or 'state'. The resultant of the interaction between peaceful coexistence and anti-communism (and to these we shall return in detail) was the condition or state of international relations known as *cold war*, whose passing only recently was due to a shift in the 'correlation of forces' that favoured the socialist system. When coming thus under systemic pressure United States policies could no longer be sustained, and the United States was herself obliged to introduce some modification of her *policies of anti-communism* by adopting some of the principles subsumed by the Soviet policy of peaceful coexistence. But before elaborating on this point let us now take a closer look at the basic types of international relations.

Of these, quite clearly *proletarian internationalism* is the fundamental type. From it all other types – such as socialist internationalism and national liberation movement – derive, and other relations – above all peaceful coexistence – can be discussed only within the context of that basic type. In the cryptic phraseology and self-conscious symbolism of Marxism-Leninism, the adoption of an 'uncompromising attitude' by the progressive forces *vis-à-vis* the capitalist states[169] amounts to the employment of such 'just' means as they might choose. In this context wars of national liberation are construed as 'just', and into this category also there falls encouragement for any subversive action, industrial or otherwise, that undermines the capitalist system. The 'goodness' and morality of such actions are assessed, need it be said, in terms of the advancement of the world-wide communist cause – as interpreted by the Soviet Union.

Since the time of Marx and Engels, proletarian internationalism was constituted a quintessential part of the doctrine, conveying as it does in typically hieratic terms the rejection of the nation-state partition of the world in favour of division by class. A Soviet definition is perhaps less obscure: 'Proletarian internationalism expresses the community of interests and the solidarity of the working class and the working people of all lands, their concerted action in the struggle for the revolutionary transformation of society.'[170] It is then possible to decipher the interpretation further and give some tangible meaning to such expressions as, for example, 'solidarity', 'community of vital interests', etc.

On investigation, not only, as we have suggested, is the meaning of proletarian internationalism difficult to establish, but so too is the task of determining precisely to whom, or between which groups, it is to apply. Certainly a century of experience of the working-class movement would seem to throw some suspicion on Soviet assurances of its unshakeable nature. In a simplistic marxist interpretation (since it is directed against the common enemy (capitalism) and against the entire system of exploitation and social and national oppression) it is intended that the struggle be waged in each separate nation-state by contingents culled from across the spectrum of the working class so that it might thereby acquire the characteristics of a common revolutionary struggle. Hence the battle cry: 'Workers of All Lands Unite', that expresses the essence of proletarian internationalism, adopting the class (or vertical) approach to the international revolution. An approach, need we say, that is so characteristic of Marx and Engels. Thus, from the mid-nineteenth century until the victory of the Great October revolution, proletarian internationalism, in its 'nascent stage', meant 'mutual aid and support to various working class detachments in their struggle against capitalism'.[171] From the October revolution until the end of the Second World War proletarian internationalism entered its second stage, a stage in which there took place a considerable broadening of its base – along lines opened up by the leninist theory of imperialism. The October revolution was conceived to have given a powerful impetus to the national-liberation movement in the colonial and dependent countries, becoming a link between the working-class movement in the capitalist countries and the liberation struggle of imperialism's oppressed peoples who have joined the 'mainstream of the world revolution'. Therefore, Lenin could modify the original slogan to read 'Workers of All Lands, and Oppressed Nations, Unite!' In its practical consequences this has meant offering the same advantages to elements other than the proletariat. The beneficiaries of these advantages had, through the narrow definition of Marx and Engels, been so far fully guarded from establishing false links with other classes – such as the peasants – but now a broadening had been made possible. In this way, proletarian internationalism today has come to act as the base for a twin offensive launched by both the Soviet Union and the socialist system; it is targeted towards the proletariat and other working people of the capitalist countries, and towards the national-liberation movement in the dependent or newly liberated countries of the Third World.

It is at this point that we may summarise the purposes that are served by both concepts ('progressive forces' and 'proletarian internationalism'): they are an expression of the ubiquitous (vertical) class undercurrent. First, as regards the correlation of forces that refers to the over-all conflict of capitalism and socialism, in which the latter side receives an enormous boost by virtue of the fact that the Soviet Union can lay (spurious) claim to the active support of more than half of mankind (!) Second, once thus defined as 'progressive forces' and occupying a category *sui generis*, the way is open for action to be taken by the socialist states *vis-à-vis* the remaining fellow progressive forces that would normally be put down as outright subversion of the state and in breach of international law. 'Proletarian internationalism' or, more correctly, *'progressive forces internationalism'* legitimises the 'all-round support' and 'aid' for these groups as a major continuation of the ongoing struggle of capitalism and socialism. As examples of such 'all-round support', 'fraternal aid', etc., Brezhnev at the 25th CPSU Congress could refer to Soviet aid to Arab countries in the Arab-Israeli conflict, and to active Soviet support of the IRA (one such progressive force in a capitalist country) in Northern Ireland. In real terms, this principle ('proletarian internationalism') means that 'all-round support and aid' is forthcoming (always providing the Soviet Union deems it convenient) *irrespective* of any formal or informal types of relations at *governmental* level with those states in which the 'detachments of the revolutionary forces of our day' are located.

In sharp contrast to proletarian internationalism, *peaceful coexistence* is *not* a class principle, but an exclusively horizontal, inter-state principle addressed to member states of the capitalist world. The principle has no application to socialist states[172] and its correct designation is the 'peaceful coexistence of states [sic] of different socio-economic systems [sic]'. 'Inseparable from the principle of proletarian internationalism'[173] to which it is secondary, that principle followed proletarian internationalism in its origin and forever in its importance. Peaceful coexistence, we are told, *supplements* proletarian internationalism and will *vanish together with the capitalist system*. Because in its practical implications peaceful coexistence means that 'all controversial problems that arise between countries with different social systems must be solved by peaceful means', it acts as a *shield* for proletarian internationalism by preventing the world class contradictions from leading to a nuclear war, serves as a brake for the assumed aggressive nature of capitalism, while also creating favourable conditions for the people's struggle for national and social liberation. Thus it neither means a preservation of the *status quo* (because it actually creates the conditions for the successful continuation of world revolutionary processes) nor does it conjure up an idyll of reconciliation between capitalism and socialism. Peaceful coexistence is a specific *form of class struggle* which leads to the victory of socialism.[174] In other words the policy of peaceful coexistence does not modify the essence of capitalism or socialism,[175] both systems remain antagonists. It does not mean that 'the opposition between the two social systems – socialism and capitalism – has disappeared. Bourgeois states remain bourgeois, while socialist states remain socialist'.[176] Peaceful coexistence is never to be applied between 'oppressors and oppressed, colonialists and victims of colonial oppression'.[177]

Peaceful coexistence, it may be gathered from such Soviet pronouncements, does not signify moderation, but rather an intensification of competition and struggle in the economic, political, military-readiness, psychological, and ideological fields. According to the theory of class struggle, the class struggle manifests itself in three main spheres: economic, political, and ideological. In fact, peaceful coexistence applies only to the first two: in the economic sphere the 'struggle' transforms itself into competition to 'demonstrate the advantages of the socialist system'. Unacknowledged by the Soviets, as Shulman points out, peaceful coexistence in the economic sphere surrogates the costly internal reforms of a limping economy and boosts the scientific and technological revolution by providing an ideological permit to import Western technology and know-how without compromising the ideological terms of reference of the principle itself. In the political and military sphere it means the curbing of the capitalist countries by endeavouring via political agreements to restrict the 'aggressive forces'. In the third (ideological) area of class struggle, peaceful coexistence simply does not apply. There can be no ideological compromise, and Soviet authors feel obliged to state and restate this axiom, for it seems to them that it is to ideologies alone that the West would prefer to believe that peaceful coexistence applies.[178] Perhaps some of the confusion is due to the fact that whereas the ideology itself is sacrosanct the actual foreign policies designed to achieve ideological ends are subject to change, as circumstances dictate. Such change, we might add, is less acceptable in the area of strategies than in that of tactics.[179] On the subject of ideological compromise Lenin's warning is quoted to the effect that there is 'no middle ground'; there is no 'third ideology between bourgeois and socialist ideology'. 'Hence to belittle the socialist ideology, *in any way*, to turn aside from it in the slightest degree means to strengthen bourgeois ideology.'[180]

Here then, in the reciprocal interaction of peaceful coexistence and proletarian internationalism, we have a zero-sum equation and pre-ordained victor, with a vengeance. While peaceful coexistence means that the West is unilaterally restrained from 'exporting counter-revolution', i.e. from opposing and resisting revolutionary and national liberation movements in the capitalist countries and the Third World, proletarian internationalism (the prior principle of the two – and one which has never been renounced by the Soviets) is intensified, and means just that, to those socialist countries that adhere to it. Bound thus by the so-called principles of peaceful coexistence,[181] the West is *explicitly* told in the same breath that observance of these principles does not deny to oppressed peoples the right to use any methods, armed or peaceful, in their struggle, since their participation in proletarian internationalism confers upon them that right. In fact, the Soviets tell us, peaceful coexistence does not even necessarily mean the avoidance of war.[182] Peaceful coexistence relates only to war between the major powers and the Soviet Union. It does not preclude war by, or on behalf of, revolutionary and national liberation movements, nor does it preclude support by the USSR and the other socialist states given to such wars. Indeed, since 1971, the Soviet authorities have in fact increasingly represented support for the revolutionary forces in the world as one of the main functions of the Soviet Armed Forces. We must not 'ban' civil or national liberation wars. We must not ban 'uprisings', and by no means must we 'ban' revolutionary mass movements aimed at changing the political and social *status quo*.[183] As a matter of fact, peaceful coexistence does not aim at achieving a 'balance of power', neither is it intended to establish 'an equilibrium which rests on the atomic parity of the world powers', nor is it for the maintenance of any 'equilibrium of terror'. It could not be so, for, by its very ideology, the Soviet Union is committed to demolishing any situation of *status quo*.

The concept of 'correlation of forces' is not a desideratum but a loose term used merely to describe the state of the revolution any struggle at any given moment in time, and on the basis of which strategies and tactics can be worked out. A 'reading' of the correlation of world forces at any given moment is described by the Soviets as the actual *state*[184] or *condition* of international relations, particularly the strategy of peaceful coexistence aimed at the capitalist states.[185] The chart presented by Soviet sources maps the skirmishes and battles in the ideological campaign. In the great period of the socialist advance after the Second World War when the Soviet Union was joined by other socialist states, and the world socialist system was born, the co-operational aspect of peaceful coexistence with the allies of the war years carried over into (from the Soviet side) a fully fledged peace 'offensive'. The free and unfettered deployment of the peaceful coexistence principle met with such a response from the capitalist quarter where anti-communist feeling ran high that the cold war period of confrontation came into existence. During that period, to be sure, there were moments of incipient international *détente*, but these were always 'short lived, few and far between'. Only of very recent date, the Soviet historical account tells us, and particularly since Nixon's visit to the USSR in 1972, did the time become right for the emergence of the imago of *détente* from the chrysalis of peaceful coexistence – still carefully nurtured by the Soviet Union, even during the cold war. *Détente*, then, is that *stage* of the relationship between capitalism and socialism, when, as a result of an unfavourable 'correlation of forces', capitalism is obliged to yield to the pressures of the peaceful coexistence drive and, however reluctantly, is made to acknowledge all of the principles on which the concept rests. Inevitably, of course, increasingly disadvantaged by the irresistible pressures of an ever-tilting correlation of forces, the West must succumb to the peace offensive. Already the wording of the USSR-United States communiqué declares that their mutual relations are based on the principles of peaceful coexistence, tending to confirm the fact that the cold war is fading away and giving way to *détente* in the economic, political, and recently also in the military spheres.[186] The ideological struggle, be it noted in all of this, remains totally unaffected, it being set apart for special attention. Intensification and deepening of the ideological dimension is indeed a function of *détente* and it would not be going too far to say that widening of the ideological gap proceeds in inverse ratio to the advance of *détente*. And so, international relations still remain the major battlefield where the ideological struggle is fought and interacts with political, economic, and social factors. Since the 24th Congress of the CPSU the ideological struggle has been paid a great deal of attention, in particular the combating of various brands of revisionism and 'left and right opportunism'.

Neither the English nor Russian languages possesses a direct translation of the word '*détente*'. Because of the possible misunderstandings to which the word may give rise, Soviet authors, when possible, try to avoid the use of the term, and suggest that it be replaced in English by the more meaningful more widely understood term 'peaceful coexistence'. *Détente* (*Razrjadka*) is after all no more than the state of relations resulting from the capitalist acceptance of peaceful coexistence in terms such as we have outlined above. That Americans do not properly understand the term *détente* has sometimes been suggested, associating it as they may do subconsciously with the word '*entente*' or even '*entente cordiale*' which they have heard at school.[187] Yet other, and even informed, interpretations may be as perilously wide of the mark; for example, *détente* is sometimes interpreted as a state of international relations in which is maintained a *status quo* 'as petrified and lifeless as a lunar landscape, a world without cataclysms and storms, where imperialism could continue unhindered its tyranny in the areas remaining in its sphere of influence'.[188] And again, that the concept could mean a relaxation of the ideological struggle both internationally and internally, and be hailed in the West – the Soviets lament – as the harbinger of more 'human rights and liberties' within the Soviet bloc. Nothing could be further from the truth. One of the key principles of peaceful coexistence is in fact the non-interference in the internal affairs of others[189] – a fact of international life which capitalist states now begin to accept. In fact, a contributory source of tension is the simple failure on the part of some observers to reconcile or to understand from Soviet statements Soviet intentions.[190] While assuring us of a desire to co-operate with the West they apprise us, through their espousal of the ideology of proletarian internationalism, of their intention to destroy us. We may well stand appalled at the prospect of this one-way street. Peaceful coexistence, we are told, will last as long as capitalism because, as we have indicated, it is a strategy; a strategy to encompass the final destruction of the capitalist system, a Soviet strategy at the heart of the struggle for the establishment of world communism.

What, we may well ask, happens then? When the system has prevailed and the strategy is irrelevant? The answer given is that it would be replaced by socialist internationalism – or that ideological concept which is a 'form' of proletarian internationalism and which now already is the '*prototype* [our italics] of the international relations which will fully and undividedly prevail in the world when the revolutionary transition from capitalism to socialism is completed on a world scale'.[191]

After the Second World War when a new socialist system emerged, the process of broadening the basis of proletarian internationalism which we described above progressed beyond the loosening of the definition of 'class'. As the process continued a new name had to be devised to comprehend the changes that the original concept had undergone and the new term *socialist internationalism* was added to the nomenclature. Proletarian internationalism – hitherto a *class* principle only (albeit in its expanded version) – has become, according to Soviet authorities, 'a basis of inter-state relations among socialist countries'.[192] Evidence, we might say, of the continuing awareness of those two Marxist-Leninist axes of analysis that are here made explicit but are more often implied. In the Soviet authors' own words, the case we are witnessing is that of *a class principle becoming a principle of inter-state relations.* Thus, quite clearly, proletarian internationalism continues to function as a class principle among the world revolutionary forces and at the same time operates as the principle of inter-state relations of those 'detachments of the working class' that 'made' it and established themselves in state units. Defined as the 'basis for the solidarity of all working people, and all revolutionary forces of our day'[193] the functioning of the principle of proletarian internationalism is made possible by virtue of the fact that: 1 There is a similarity in the main and essential aspects of the position of the proletariat in all bourgeois societies within the system of capitalist production. 2 The conditions necessary for the emancipation of the working class are of a uniform nature. 3 There is a common enemy. 4 Members of the system all share the same historical aim, namely, the achievement of socialism and communism. 5 They share the Marxist-Leninist ideology.

As the Soviets argue, the change of name from proletarian to socialist internationalism was necessary. It recognises the change to a principle which rests on a base broad enough to embrace the people's democracies.[194] The fact that the socialist world system is still organised into states seems of course to be inconsistent. It can be explained within our terms of reference by seeing the Soviets joining the club of *states* as a necessary compromise. They are, after all, one of the basic realities of the present day to which the Soviet Union adapts, and in so doing might regard the fact of their existence as a useful bulwark against capitalist infiltration through the operation of the principles of non-interference, sovereignty, etc. so vehemently put forward as part and parcel of peaceful coexistence. And when the question arises as to the continuing need to acknowledge the institution of state *within* the socialist system it then becomes necessary to consider the perceived functions of the socialist state.[195] Having discussed the origins of the principle we come to the principles at the roots of socialist internationalism as they apply within that sector of the Soviet model. These are: 'Complete equality, respect for territorial integrity, state independence and sovereignty, non-interference in domestic affairs.'[196] Which all sounds once again rather like peaceful coexistence. However these turn out to be only part of socialist internationalism, that part which has been described as the general democratic minimum on which relations of any sovereign states should be based.[197] And so it follows that socialist internationalism is peaceful coexistence *plus* something else, the 'something else' having been defined, following the 1957 Communist Summit, as 'fraternal mutual assistance and mutual support'.[198] Since this is described as qualitatively higher than peaceful coexistence then the next question that poses itself concerns changes in the meaning of that other 'general democratic minimum' – peaceful coexistence.

The socialist states, because of their commitment to building communism, are assumed to be endowed with *communal morality*. It is assumed that the 'harmonic connection between international and national interests' is achieved not only because once in the socialist system the various national interests (by virtue of the class interpretation of national interests) begin to coincide, but because individual states can flourish only within the framework of the bloc. The occasional divergence is of a 'non-antagonistic nature'[199] or, in less stalinist terms, they are referred to as mere 'partial conflicts' and are supposed to be easily (by comradely discussion and persuasion) resolvable. The addition of 'fraternal and mutual aid' not only changes the meaning of these other principles that socialist internationalism shares with peaceful coexistence, but adds a moral (and also legal!) right, and duty, for these states to 'protect their unity and mutually assist one another in the struggle against capitalism', as well as to 'co-operate and mutually assist one another in building socialism and communism in a comradely manner'. This merger of moral and political is reflected also in the merger of the moral and legal aspects. The documents and declarations of communist parties (sic) and governments constitute international agreements *sui generis* and in fact are considered as a source of international law valid among the socialist states.[200] Thus, socialist internationalism places a moral duty upon all socialist states for the joint protection of socialist achievements,[201] or in practical terms, sanctifies and lends moral and legal weight to such as the 'Brezhnev doctrine'. In so far as it can be argued that socialist internationalism is arrived at by extension of the old classical principle of proletarian internationalism,[202] the Brezhnev doctrine is not so much Brezhnev's as Lenin's and Stalin's and is in its essence deeply embedded in Soviet Marxist-Leninist thought.

At this point and before going further with the outline of the Soviet model of international relations, we should draw attention to the most blatant inconsistency of the Soviet model so far, namely the attitude adopted towards, and the placement within the Soviet model, of the Chinese Republic.[203] The 25th CPSU Congress was the culmination of a gradually evolving attitude over a period of years and the crystallisation of that attitude in Brezhnev's address (cited below) must raise doubts as to the internal consistency of the Soviet theory. The issues raised, one presumes, will now become the subject of urgent debate. Although Brezhnev opened by saying that the attitude to China remains basically the same as that of the previous Congress, his subsequent proposal to 'normalise' relations with the Chinese People's Republic on the basis of *peaceful coexistence* implies a serious theoretical change:[204]

> If in Peking they will return to politics genuinely based on
> Marxism-Leninism, if they abandon the hostile course *vis-à-vis* the
> socialist countries, [if they] place themselves on the path of co-
> operation and solidarity with the socialist world, then an
> appropriate response will be forthcoming from our side and the
> possibility will present itself for the development of good relations
> between the USSR and PRC to correspond with the principles of
> socialist internationalism.

213

Let us inform ourselves on the more serious of the implications to which we refer.

In the first place the People's Republic of China has never in Soviet thinking been unequivocally excluded from the socialist world. Apart from references to the Chinese 'estrangement' from the socialist world[205] and the 'departure from the principles of Marxism-Leninism and proletarian internationalism[206] there are other statements quite clearly still including the PRC in the 'world revolutionary forces', directly or by implication.[207] There is too the frequently reiterated relative territorial and population division of the world with (in Soviet theory) its disadvantageous power implications for the capitalist bloc[208] if, and only if, the PRC is included in the socialist bloc. There have previously appeared warnings to China of excluding her from Soviet nuclear protection,[209] suggestions that perhaps China may have taken herself out of the socialist camp,[210] or occasional references to peaceful coexistence in the context of the relationship with the PRC but, even when these have been made by a political leader of Brezhnev's stature,[211] the occasion has been at a relatively low level. So well defined a standpoint had not until now been voiced in such august surroundings as a Congress, or Meeting (of International Communist Parties), nor had it appeared in documents issuing from such assemblies. The main previous indications would have favoured the continued inclusion of the PRC within the socialist bloc and in this regard where previously reference has been made to her standing it has always placed her among other socialist countries (albeit at the tail end of these). In brief, the attitude has been one in which the schism has been seen as an aberration resulting from the misguided actions of a 'military-bureaucratic' clique which led to the 'ousting of the working class from the real bodies of power' and the loss by its party and proletarian ideology of the 'leading role in society'.[212] In this interpretation the majority of the Chinese population was still thought of as being firmly committed to the building of communism[213] – with Moscow as mentor and guide. And until now it was even possible to find optimistic reference to the anticipated end of the aberration, and the reconciliation of theoretical deviations – whether from the Left or the Right (including China) – was conceived to herald the onset of the second (present) phase of our epoch described as the general crisis of capitalism.[214]

But now Brezhnev's invitation at a Party Congress to 'normalise'[215] relations with the rest of the socialist community on this basis is a step of potentially far-reaching (theoretical) consequence. The 25th Congress with its seemingly casual relegation of China to a peaceful coexistence relationship would appear to place the PRC in curious company. The principle of peaceful coexistence as we have shown above had been kept exclusively thus far to characterise relations with the capitalist world, or, more recently, with those countries within the Third World whose inclination is towards the capitalist bloc and who do not subscribe to the 'socialism-oriented' path of development.[216]

This diversification of attitude towards the countries of the Third World still made sense within the theoretical model (since the capitalist-oriented might be regarded after all as of a different socio-economic system and therefore 'deserving' of the accolade of peaceful coexistence). In the case of China, however, are we witnessing a similar diversification within the countries of the same (socialist) socio-economic system leading to their partaking variously of the principle of peaceful coexistence or of socialist internationalism? A dangerous precedent indeed. But if China does not 'come to her senses' might it alternatively lead to her final exclusion in theory from the socialist world? And, if so, into what theoretical limbo?

In fact the relocation of the PRC in either the capitalist or Third World would be highly improbable. Because of her possession of certain undeniably socialist characteristics[217] – among them economic foundations not so different from those of the Soviet Union herself. China's location within the capitalist camp would be more difficult for the Soviet Union to justify in theoretical terms than is her own traducement in identical terms at present by the Chinese.[218] No less incongruous for Soviet theory would be the placement of China in the Third World, of which she at present considers herself a leader.[219] What other theoretical alternatives can be conceived? In the event that her basic fulfilment of the requirements of membership of the socialist community continues to be acknowledged and her relations with it remain those characterised by the principle of peaceful coexistence then clearly the theory itself would have to be altered to accommodate the aberration (of two different types of international relations operative simultaneously within one group). In terms of theory the eventuality is not inconceivable – nor have its potential advantages gone unremarked by some socialist countries. Towards the privilege, for example, of immunity from interference in internal affairs that the type of peaceful coexistence relations affords (relative to that of socialist internationalism), both Romania and Czechoslovakia have striven in recent years, and Yugoslavia's progress is watched with interest tinged with not a little envy. If this privilege were now to be extended to the PRC it would mean that a crack had opened in the theoretical dike and that a polycentric character for the socialist bloc had become for the first time an acknowledged fact making the 'three world' division of the world difficult to sustain.

Two further alternative solutions suggest themselves. Either the emergence of a quadrilaterial[220] to replace the 'triangular' configuration – an eventuality that would however remove the dialectical justification for the triangular model (that consisted of tacit acknowledgment of the fact that the basic conflict was never conceived as other than taking place between the two blocs with the Third World as their arena),[221] or disintegration of the present model of international relations with its clearly differentiated types of relationship and mutually non-interchangeable rules. Instead of the present monolithicity of socialist internationalism there is seen the emergence of a theoretical hybrid, and acknowledgment of the polycentric character of the socialist bloc.[222] Neither 'solution' need detain us for long. The fact that such a diversification of types of international relations is already allowed both within the capitalist world where there is perceived to have emerged a triangularity existing in its own right,[223] and within the socialist world where already relations with the third vertex (Third World) are permitted to conform to the degree of the individual country's orientation,[224] would be small consolation in the light of the problems posed by the sort of disruption that the theoretical relocation of the Chinese People's Republic would bring to the all-important consideration of theoretical consistency. In these circumstances we can hardly help but feel that we may well be on the verge of a crisis of Soviet theory of international relations; a crisis that could well involve Soviet thinkers in the search for a totally different conceptual approach, and a threshold that Soviet theory may well have crossed before the West has even taken full cognisance of its existence. Certainly the solution when it is found must meet the stern requirements of Marxist-Leninist ideology with which the theory of international relations must remain fully consistent, a by no means easy task in the circumstances.

However, and with that said, no disquiet from an official source has yet been voiced and the Soviet model to which we now return stands as yet unaltered.

The over-all international situation to which we have already alluded is described in Soviet terminology variously as 'the correlation of forces', the 'balance of world forces', or 'the real alignment of forces in the world arena'. Where English language translations have too often translated these concepts into the Western term 'balance of power' the fact is that traditionally, since Lenin's time, the Soviet 'correlation of forces' has represented a considerably broader concept which, not afflicted by 'Western reductionism', embraces in addition to military, also political, economic, psychological, ideological as well as other factors 'all interlocked into a single whole'.[225] The comprehensiveness of the concept we may see as due not only to the marxist proclivity for identifying a broad spectrum of actors but as a function also of the propensity to place great emphasis on historical and moral considerations.

One of the parts of the interlocking 'correlation of forces' – and one that is similarly subject to Western misinterpretation – is the concept of *scientific-technological revolution*.[226] Since this factor has become greatly relied upon in contemporary Soviet thinking, and for the last two decades has exercised a powerful influence on their assessment of the world 'correlation of forces', we might digress briefly and attempt to clear up some aspects of the misunderstood term. The scientific-technological revolution, which is compared in importance to the Industrial Revolution, stands, according to Soviet authors, in 'dialectical interconnection and interaction' with world politics and international relations.[227] By ushering in a new wave of economic determinism the weight of revolutionary responsibility has been shifted from the shoulders of the 'progressive forces' with respect to the world communist revolutionary struggle, and, in connection with this shift, Marx's observation is cited: 'steam, electricity, and the self-acting mule were revolutionists of a rather more dangerous character than even citizens Barbès, Raspail and Blanqui'.[228] Brezhnev, in his description of the activity of the 'progressive forces' in the area of anti-colonialism as 'powerful accelerators of present-day history',[229] acknowledges the shift, with the implication that the revolutionary onus lies elsewhere, namely in the objectively determined processes and, as the most important of such processes, in the scientific revolution.

The scientific-technological revolution itself is seen as a process affecting the material-technological foundations[230] of both socialism and capitalism. Heralding the advent of 'qualitative changes in science and technology' the scientific-technological revolution

217

introduces the development of automated systems of control and electronic computerisation, the use of nuclear energy, the beginning of the conquest of space and 'penetration into the depths of the world oceans', a revolution in transport and communications.[231] With the role of science and technology thus drastically enhanced they for the first time become one of society's productive forces.[232] In terms of the work cycle, man is gradually freed from it – that is from those stages from which he was not yet removed by the Industrial Revoltuion. Beyond the first stage (preparatory) which, according to Soviet theory, remains forever man's preserve, the stage from which his removal is thus specifically assured is the third, or controlling, stage.[233] Although, as we have indicated, the processes of the scientific-technological revolution, irrespective of the division into systems, have already brought change in the world as a whole, it brings to each of the two systems diametrically opposite results: where in the capitalist system it is seen only further to sharpen the contradictions inherent in that system (that is, the contradiction between the increasingly 'socialised' nature of the forces of production and the still predominantly private nature of the relations of production), in the socialist world it promotes the socialist cause by generating such societal wealth that the communist stage of development, operating on the principle 'to each according to his needs', will become possible. Thus, irreversible in its operation, the scientific-technological revolution is a 'silent partner' of the socialist system, each fresh advance fuelling and itself fuelled by the main capitalist contradictions now thrown into high relief, until, with 'iron necessity', capitalism is led into a situation from which there is no escape.[234] It goes without saying that the difficulties of measuring and assessing such a factor when attempting an evaluation of the actual 'correlation of forces' are formidable, and yet, as Yermolenko points out, it is assumed to play in that equation a prominent part: 'the importance of any state and [any] world system in international affairs now largely depends on their scientific and technological potential, and the scale of their scientific and technological research and training of corresponding personnel'.[235] In this context the paradoxical nature of Premier Kosygin's comments to the 25th CPSU Congress[236] can be appreciated. Kosygin proudly drew the attention of the delegates to the accomplishment of a most difficult task on the part of the Soviet Union who had proved herself able 'to surpass the USA in the production of steel, oil, pig iron, coal, cement, tractors, cotton, wool, etc.

etc.' What Kosygin omitted to say was that the USSR had nevertheless failed to match her rival in technological and indeed scientific
know-how – a result (arguably) of the built-in resistance to
innovation in the Soviet system of economy.[237]

In regard to accurate over-all interpretation of Soviet theory we
would then heartily endorse the recommendation of Soviet theorists
as to the importance of understanding the model 'as a whole'.[238] It is
to be viewed and understood in its entirety and not one single aspect or
relation should be taken out of context. Take again the example of
proletarian internationalism, which, theorists never tire of repeating,
'requires' peaceful coexistence, while peaceful coexistence 'is possible
only on the basis of proletarian internationalism'. This is because 'all
principles of socialist foreign policy [are] organically connected, and
their interconnection follows from their class content'.[239]

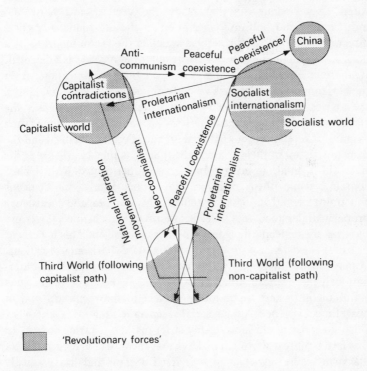

Figure 11 The Soviet categories of international relations

This 'organic interconnection' brings us to a central question, and one that before going further requires to be answered. This is the question as to where precisely Soviet theory would fit into that horizontal (state)/vertical (class) matrix which has been used throughout this book. To put it another way: while Marx's emphasis was, as we have indicated, on the vertical line of enquiry (that is the class conflict within the individual horizontal units),[240] and while Lenin subscribed to the notion of 'horizontalising' the class struggle (by perceiving it to shift on to the international level), where within these terms of reference would be placed the main emphasis in contemporary Soviet theory?

With this horizontal-vertical matrix clearly in view we would maintain that the Soviet position was determined as the process of establishing herself among other states proceeded, and in these circumstances there would be no specific moment of 'shift', but rather a gradual, almost imperceptible, relocation. Like vectors in physics when they operate simultaneously the vertical and horizontal influences would pull no longer in either the horizontal or vertical directions alone. With the vertical sweep of the vector modified by a horizontal pull (and vice versa) the result, as in physics, is a diagonal. If, therefore, we were to attempt to locate the Soviet position within the horizontal-vertical matrix as we did in the case of Marx and Lenin, the answer, we believe, would be that Soviet theory 'diagonalises' the class conflict.[241] Thus the categories we have already mentioned such as state, sovereignty, international organisation, nationalism and the rest, horizontal in their origin and adjuncts as they clearly are at the state (horizontal) level, are immediately permeated with a class content, while their reciprocating action brings simultaneous constraint upon that (class) content. In this way peaceful coexistence properly understood does indeed conform to Kapchenko's thesis and requires the concept of proletarian internationalism. This is because peaceful coexistence, a principle of inter-state (horizontal) relations, is perpetually modified by the (class) 'sweep' of proletarian internationalism – whose functioning can never be 'pure' since it is simultaneously and continuously subject to the reciprocal pull of peaceful coexistence. Among socialist *states* the situation is otherwise, since no *state* should indeed – by strict marxist doctrine – exist. In this latter context we might observe that the bearer and custodian of marxism – the Soviet state – is itself a state and has gradually adjusted to assume membership within the international community of states. Just as its membership of the community was by way of adjustment and along the compromise path of 'diagonalisation' in its approach to the class struggle, so a simultaneous adjustment to the marxian doctrine – so inappropriate to the requirements of the inter-state community – was called for. Two observations flow from the matrix – and the concept of 'diagonalisation' – as set forth above. In the first place it can be understood that the approach towards a proper understanding of all of the categories of international relations must be made through an appreciation of whether they are meant to adhere to the horizontal or to the vertical axis. There is also to be taken into account (as was the case in an assessment of the reciprocal inter-action between peaceful coexistence and proletarian inter-nationalism) some consideration of that category with which they may operate in conjunction. In the second place, Soviet theory, by definition, stops one step short of its Western counterpart and never reaches the Western theoretical level of abstraction. Owing to class considerations Soviet theory – and this cannot be sufficiently stressed – refuses point blank to take that further step and go *beyond* the dichotomised picture of the world. That is to say that the world simply cannot be seen as consisting of some one hundred and fifty basically equal and directly comparable states. According to Soviet theorists the capitalist-socialist distinction forms the theoretical barrier beyond which no theory can ever go – unless it is designed to lead to deliberate confusion: 'by reducing international relations to inter-state relations, they [bourgeois theories] identify the latter with the interaction of so-called "national state interests". Moreover, "national state interests" are emasculated of their class content and, even if the existence of class factors is admitted, their influence is ignored.'[242]

It is to these institutions traditionally associated with the horizontal (state) axis (and incidentally around which revolves the Western theory of international relations) that we now turn. It is not only the notion of national interest but also the very concepts of state, sovereignty, international organisations, war, intervention, inter-national law, and diplomacy which are, in the Soviet perception, removed from that traditional horizontal level of analysis and filled with a class (vertical) content. As we have said above, the end result is that they pertain neither to the horizontal level proper, nor yet to the vertical, but respond best in the analysis to the notion of 'diagonal' employed as the methodological tool. This 'diagonalising' influence is of course generated by the vertical 'class approach'. As a result of it the custodian or bearer of sovereignty is never a government, a person, or an international organisation, but a 'nation' possessed of certain class characteristics and may in certain circumstances be a state.[243] The circumstances referred to in which the 'nation' or state may be invested with the status of legal personality have, in Soviet eyes, to do with the convenience or interest of the Soviet Union – as when, for example, the Soviet Union perceives the interests of the nation/state to be compatible with its own and finds it convenient to describe that nation/state as a hitherto oppressed class. In the interests of separatism, revolution, irredentist activity, etc., the status of legal personality is extended very generously to *nations* and *peoples* in *capitalist states*. In socialist states, the national (popular) will and the will of the state are assumed to coincide. The construction that accords to these 'nations' and 'peoples' engaged in a struggle for national liberation the status of sovereign legal personality is based on a most convenient subjective criterion that is bound up with the manipulation of the institution of sovereignty – an approach that leads to a sharp conceptual split between the concept of national sovereignty (which should really read class-national sovereignty) and the concept of state. Since this divergence forms the basis of a number of otherwise illogical doctrines in Soviet international law, we might be forgiven for quoting two relevant passages from an authoritative Soviet source:[244]

> The question of the relationship between state and national sovereignty is of great theoretical importance. By national sovereignty we understand the right of each nation to self-determination and independent development. Each nation has this right, regardless of whether or not it has its own statehood. National sovereignty merges with state sovereignty if the nation has achieved independence and formed its own state. When the nation has not yet been able to form its own independent state, its sovereign right to self-determination constitutes the basis for its just struggle to establish such a state.

And in an even more explicit statement Selyaninov writes:[245]

> Under capitalism when the state is an instrument of bourgeois dictatorship, regardless of the external form it assumes, the

exploiting class is the vehicle of sovereignty and uses its role to dominate the working class and the broad masses of the working people.

By contrast, the sovereignty of socialist states is an expression of the supreme power of the working class . . . an expression of the supreme right of the people to set up a new social system . . . their readiness to come at once to the rescue whenever any people's sovereignty and consequently – and this is most important – their very socialist state is menaced. The rendering of such assistance does not in any way infringe the supreme right of the people, who continue to be the real masters of their country. This act is directed only against those who try to deprive the Communist Party of its leading role . . . thereby doing damage to the whole socialist community.

Such is the inter-connection between proletarian inter-nationalism and the sovereignty of socialist states. The former is the guarantee of the latter without restricting it in any way.

These statements bring us directly to a consideration of the question of the Soviet Union's attitude to the institution of state. Because of the different conceptual connotations of the concept of sovereignty in capitalist and socialist systems, there is in the Soviet theory no uniform approach to the institution of state. States, it was concluded by Soviet authors some time ago, exist and are a reality of the present world and therefore, in the true marxist tradition, their usefulness must be exploited and turned to account. This position, in which state units are regarded as the building blocks or a 'common currency or language' of otherwise inter-system relations, is suggested by Tunkin among others: 'modern international relations are characterised by the existence of sovereign states belonging to different socio-economic systems'.[246] Until the final victory of socialism they (the states) constitute a conceptual tabu which is well reflected in the Soviet attitude to international organisations, and particularly to attempts at transnational organisations. The thrust of the Soviet argument is that only those international organisations are acceptable which operate on the 'basis of the principles of peaceful coexistence and the sovereign equality of states'.[247] Thus, international organisations will receive support only in the event of their being either socialist in character (for example the Warsaw Treaty Organisation and the Council for Mutual Economic

223

Assistance), or if they lend themselves to manipulation so as to advantage socialist interests (most notably in this category the Organisation of African Unity and the League of Arab States), or if support (through membership) is a precondition of participation in the international life of nations – assuming that socialist interests are thereby served by such participation. To this latter category belong the United Nations and such international organisations as ILO, GATT, WHO, etc. But beyond those groupings and towards those which though purporting to be supra-national in character consist of capitalist members alone, a hostile face is turned. Such organisations can themselves only be hostile to the socialist world, and since they represent a contradiction of that principle of peaceful coexistence to which the socialist bloc is totally committed, the outright rejection of any global initiative on their part – such as a move towards world government – is inevitable and should come as no surprise. The rejection of such a (world government) initiative would for example be on two counts: on the legal count it would constitute an intolerable violation of the sacrosanct Soviet principle of the sovereignty of the state, and on a second (ideological) count there is the sheer impossibility of devising a government generally acceptable to both parties in a world split into two hostile, ideologically irreconcilable socio-political systems. The situation is summarised by Mikhailov: 'In the conditions of the existence of states of two systems, international organisations with broad supranational powers are not possible, and the creation of such organisations in the framework of the capitalist world leads to the policy of diktat and interference in the internal affairs of states.'[248]

Then again, the continuous process of integration of the capitalist states and of the socialist states respectively in exclusive capitalist or socialist organisations is interpreted variously, and, it is claimed, the integration processes are diametrically different. This, despite the fact that there are misleading surface appearances that would seem to indicate the comparability in depth of the resultant international organisations – as between the Common Market and Comecon, or between NATO and the Warsaw Pact. Here again we find in the Soviet conception that essence of the integration to be determined above all by the particular relations of production prevalent in the integrating groups of states.[249] Accordingly, while the tendency to integrate is inherent in the socialist system, and takes place as an objective process,[250] serving to 'integrate the necessary conditions for the growth of social production, increase its efficiency, and achieve improvement of the well-being of the peoples',[251] the substance of capitalist integration is to extend 'the sphere of application of capital and [to increase] the scope of the exploitation of wage labour to obtain maximum profit . . . leading to subordination of less developed countries to more developed ones'.[252] The Soviet authors argue, therefore, that there is no valid basis of comparison between the EEC and CMEA where the latter is described not as a 'supranational organisation' but rather as an 'arranging instrument' whose task it is to 'preserve national statehood with the simultaneous increase of economic cohesion'.[253] It further follows that world government along capitalist lines would, of necessity, be oriented towards the maintenance of a *status quo* – a totally unacceptable position for the ideological revolutionary tenets of Soviet theory. Of course a 'world state' made up of socialist states is another proposition altogether and we are told that 'on the way to classless, stateless, communist society many forms of state groupings of socialist states are possible. The creation of a world federation or another form of combination of free states and nations is thinkable only as a means of eliminating exploitation, class and national contradictions, and the creation of socialism and communism'.[254] It is worth recalling in this context the comments we made above on the principle of socialist internation-alism from which it may be deduced that the integration of the present socialist bloc into a single 'state' is indeed a confident expectation. We leave it to Tunkin to sum up (in typically vague terms) the Soviet Union's attitude to international organisation: 'The vitality of any such organisation, even though created by states, is determined in the first place by the extent to which its character, its fundamental principles correspond to the *laws of social development*.'[255]

The glib familiarity with 'the laws of social development' and the proprietory claim to rectitude is once again apparent in the Soviet lexicon. It turns out that the permissibility or otherwise – and indeed the legality or illegality – of intervention depends wholly upon the identity of the state involved. By definition, only capitalist states can 'intervene' in the internal affairs of other states. 'Intervention', according to the Soviet dictionary of political terms, is 'the armed invasion or interference of one or several capitalist states in the internal affairs of another state aimed at the suppression of a revolution, seizure of territory, acquisition of special privileges, establishing domination, etc.'[256] Socialist states, on the other hand, are by definition freed from all taint of 'intervention' and when such action as might be described as 'intervention' – if performed by capitalist states – is taken it is referred to as *fraternal assistance*. Intervention, then, is understood as a sin peculiar to capitalist states and nothing incongruous is seen in the fact that both the principle of proletarian internationalism and of socialist internationalism base and justify their very existence on 'intervention' in its inverted (socialist) form – mutual assistance. A Soviet theorist, Sanakoyev, supports this view: 'It is perfectly clear that defence of the socialist system and efforts to counteract attempts of bourgeois counter-revolutionary forces does not require any special, supplementary legal justification; it stems from the very nature of the class struggle and, far from contradicting, fully conforms to a genuinely democratic interpretation of the content of sovereignty.'[257] In regard to the Hungarian and Czechoslovak uprisings (perceived by the Soviet Union to be non-socialist in character) a Soviet view would claim that neither of them was sanctioned by the principle of self-determination, therefore their crushing by the Soviets could not be intervention – intervention's main criterion being the violation of the principle of self-determination. In other words, in the Soviet understanding, everything is classed as intervention with the exception of those actions that are compatible with Soviet policy and which lend themselves to characterisation in some other way. Interference or intervention – if one might be permitted to use these terms – in the affairs of socialist states is the cornerstone of socialist internationalism and is taken to be so by reference to the greater interest of the socialist commonwealth to which the 'national interests' of individual socialist states must be subordinated.[258] The principle of socialist internationalism is fully compatible with the principle of sovereignty. Where national sovereignty is taken to mean the right of states to an independent existence that right is best protected against the imperialist assailant by participation in the socialist system and by strict observance of the principles of socialist internationalism.

It will be remarked that the basis on which rests the Soviet right to intervene in the name of socialist internationalism derives directly once again from Soviet ethics. As we have previously suggested, Soviet foreign policy, since it is explicitly committed to the construction of world-wide communism, is, by definition, right and moral and is seen always to coincide with the requirements of socialist internationalism (as defined by the Soviet Union), and with the interests of the proletariat of all countries.[259] This coincidence of interests is well stated by Granov:[260] 'The Soviet state's internal interests, economic, above all, coincide with those of the over-whelming majority of mankind, i.e. its working masses, who are likewise striving to get rid of all forms of exploitation and oppression, poverty and the threat of war. . . . The vital interests of the victorious Russian proletariat in its own country coincide with the mature requirements of world historical development, for socialism and communism embody the future of the entire planet.' Thus a licence is established for significant restraints (in the Soviet interest) upon state actions of the socialist states, as well as a wide range of interventionism in the name of world historical process. If the sovereignty is defined in this way and if it is regarded as the key element of international law it becomes obvious that international law as well as diplomacy become useful instruments in Soviet hands for assisting the 'historical process'.[261]

As to the actual institution of state,[262] the treatment meted out to these organisations should by now have been made clear from the above. That state which becomes a repository of national (class) sovereignty – which means those of the socialist system and (some of) those of the Third World – is a morally good and worthy institution. In fact the state in such surroundings assumes a highly positive and laudable role since it surrogates the traditionally postulated dynamics derived from the class struggle (which in these states, of course, cease to exist). In addition to this positive 'internal' function of the socialist states, the state performs 'external' functions, the most important of which is to act as a protective bulwark against capitalist influence. In this perception, therefore, the concepts of state and of sovereignty are endowed with both a defensive capacity which, taken in conjunction with the important integrative role *vis-à-vis* the population, helps to explain the reasoning by which the moral code actually turns the love of one's country (state?) into a moral obligation. From this point in the chain of moral reasoning – and bearing in mind the double standard approach to all of these 'neutral' institutions – it is not difficult to determine the attitude towards patriotism and nationalism: positive within the socialist context and negative within the capitalist.

Patriotism, we are told, has an economic (social ownership of the means of production and the socialist system of management), political (the Soviet state system, Soviet democracy), and ideological-theoretical (the teaching of Marxism-Leninism) basis.[263] Thus

227

'patriotism is totally different from bourgeois cosmopolitanism, which always expresses the interest and the spirit of the ruling classes, and disguises the necessity of class conflict'.[264] In contrast to bourgeois cosmopolitanism, proletarian internationalism is 'that moral quality which expresses itself in the attempts to harmonize national and all-human interests, to consider all nations'.[265] With a class understanding of patriotism and proletarian internationalism it is of course possible to conclude that proletarian internationalism 'does not hinder national sovereignty',[266] a sovereignty which is similarly defined in class terms. It is to be noted, however, that the theories that underlie these assertions are often riddled with contradictions and inconsistencies. The process of 'coming together' (*Sblizhenie*), or 'merging' (*Slianie*) of nations is difficult to reconcile with the parallel tendency to flourishing (*Rastsvet*) on the part of individual nations in the USSR and in the socialist system at large, and we still have to hear an explanation that carries more conviction than that which holds that these processes are dialectical – and that the theory of nation does indeed lag behind the theory of state.

Over the years the theory of state has of course come in for refinement and greater elaboration – possibly in an attempt to destalinise and make more palatable the flavour of the dictatorship of the proletariat which Stalin had taken *ad absurdum*. To this end, Khrushchev had suggested interposing another stage in the development of the socialist state to replace that of the dictatorship of the proletariat – namely, a 'state of all the people'.[267] This khrushchevian stage, although temporarily suppressed in the period when an anti-Khrushchev mood prevailed, has come back into currency, is enshrined in the articles of the new Soviet Constitution and regarded as fully consistent with Brezhnev's 'developed socialism'. The implication of this concept is that now that there are no hostile classes remaining to be suppressed, the 'dictatorship of the proletariat' has become an anachronism: 'For the first time there has arisen in our country a state that is not a dictatorship of any class but the instrument of society as a whole, of all the people.'[268] The Programme of the CPSU[269] likewise embodies the idea: 'The dictatorship of the proletariat . . . underwent changes. The state began to grow over into a nationwide organisation of the working people of socialist society.' The Programme links the dictatorship of the proletariat only to the stage of building socialism[270] and introduces this new state as 'a state of the entire people, an organ expressing the interests and will of the people as a whole', as the state which will 'deliver' society and lead to the 'complete victory of communism'.[271] Another innovation from the Khrushchev era that is retained is the name given to the states of the Third World. These, inadequate as they are in class structure, in order to qualify as objects of the friendly socialist embrace are described as states of national democracy.[272] There is however one important notion the failure to alter which seems in our view to give rise to one of the glaring contradictions within Soviet theory as it relates to the role of the Communist Party. Whilst it is true that the denial of Stalin's assumption that the class struggle must necessarily intensify with the approach of socialism gave a new lease of life to postulates of democratisation of a socialist state on its way to becoming a communist public self-government, nevertheless no such denial has been issued nor qualification effected to the assumption that the leading role of the 'vanguard of the workers, agricultural workers and intelligentsia' (i.e. the Communist Party) will increase rather than diminish in the process. Even the spectrum of Stalin's expectations did not encompass an endlessly deepening role for the Party, for if his pronouncements on the subject[273] were to be taken literally, then clearly in the 'all people state' stage the Communist Party would be out of business.

And so, if we may in summary return to our original concern for the difficulties arising from conceptual and semantic comparison, we might go so far as to say that *such categories that are that one inadmissible ('trans-class') step further on the level of abstraction* (such as national interest, state, sovereignty, self-determination, nation, nationalism, war, international organisation, diplomacy, international law) are always 'pulled back' on to the dichotomised capitalist-socialist level, filled with an appropriate class content, and judged variously in the light of that content. Thus it may be concluded that the major obstacles in the path of a comparison between Soviet and Western theories of international relations is the fact that one is to be understood as associated with and couched in terms of the horizontal level of analysis *alone* while the other joins the premises of the vertical axis to the horizontal and states its theoretical case *permanently* in terms of both. It comes as no surprise then that although the same terms are used, there exist such differences in their use within the intellectual context of one side or the other that they are no longer easy to compare or relate.

Postscript

The problem is further compounded by the paradox of the two strongest communist states simultaneously accusing one another of having deviated fundamentally from Marxist-Leninist principles. While the Soviets display – at least on the theoretical level – some ambivalence in their approach to the PRC and uncertainty as to her precise location in their model of the world, China's position, even theoretically, is quite unequivocal.

Briefly stated, the Soviet model as depicted above is rejected in its entirety.[274] Particularly is the rejection absolute as regards all theoretical innovations introduced *after* Stalin (i.e. starting with Khrushchev) and is applied to all of those originating with the present leadership. Among the more serious accusations is that which sees in the USSR not only a 'revisionist' power but an outright class enemy who in that post-stalinist period restored capitalism. Hence the Soviet claim to be building communism is regarded as fraudulent, and the main aspects of Soviet domestic structures (principally that of the concept of the leading role of the CPSU but including also the change from the state of the dictatorship of the proletariat to the 'all people state') are seen to be capitalist. Instead, China offers the gloomy prospect of the continuing need for 'class struggle' into many successive generations beyond the socialist victory, so as to ensure that any similar danger of 'capitalist degeneration' is avoided. Not only is the USSR rejected on non-socialist grounds but so too is the 'socialist camp' with all its (socialist internationalist) trimmings which are conceived to run counter to that notion of equal rights and independence among communist parties which is the Chinese favoured alternative. Found to be similarly objectionable are all of the changes by the 20th CPSU Congress in 1956 upon which, as we have pointed out, current Soviet conceptualisations remain firmly based. Apart from the undesirability of the denunciation of Stalin at that time the Chinese did not share the expressed Soviet 'fear' of the atomic bomb. We might add, however, that in this latter regard they have tended away from the bravado of the 'paper tiger' description, as within their own weapons system a similar capability has developed. Nevertheless, the emphasis has continued to be placed on the exploration of more forward (and more effective) alternatives along maoist lines based mainly on the estimation of strength–weakness ratios along lines unfamiliar to the rest of the world. In this development hidden sources of strength are to be found in for example the omnipotence of people as opposed to technology, and, not without reason as it turns out, substantial reliance is placed on processes of insurgency and protracted war. It follows then that the Chinese reject the idea of non-inevitability of war and argue both the impossibility of a peaceful transition to socialism and that the Soviet concept of peaceful coexistence is no more than a thin disguise for close Soviet co-operation with the United States. Although in theory the Soviets still subordinate the concept of peaceful coexistence to that of proletarian internationalism (the resultant hybrid we described as 'diagonal'), any such arrangement is unacceptable to the Chinese who see in the principle of proletarian internationalism the only generally acceptable basis of foreign policy, whether as strategy or as tactic. An area of conflict is produced also in so far as both maoism and the Soviet leadership each lay claim to being the sole legatee of the Marxist-Leninist heritage today. Each proclaims the relevance of its experience to the world at large. The maoists, proceeding still along lines reminiscent of Lenin, perceive the national liberation movement as the main revolutionary force, and we have become used to the strategic blueprint for conquest which sees as 'cities of the world' North America and Western Europe (wherein for a variety of reasons the class struggle since the Second World War has died away) and, as 'rural areas of the world' (with China as leader), Asia, Africa and Latin America – the latter areas already preponderant. The Chinese differ finally in their model of the world in so far as it returns the 25th CPSU 'compliment' by placing the Soviet Union in the imperialist camp and sees as the basic contradiction not that between socialism and imperialism but rather as between 'two superpowers' and all other countries. In the 'three worlds' of the Chinese conceptualisation the first refers to the USA and USSR, the second to the developed countries of Western Europe, Japan, Australasia, and the third to the underdeveloped areas, with China, the most highly developed socialist country, as the Third World leader. An additional refinement completes this world-view whereby the second 'intermediate' zone is subdivided into two sub-zones, the first of which (industrialised capitalist countries) is, as a result of its latent anti-Americanism, capable of incorporation within the socialist world. The picture bears a closer resemblance than does the Soviet model to some Western and Third World structural dependence models (see Chapter 6).

Can we then say that while Western international relations theory clings to the horizontal (state) approach, and the Soviets, by directing their thinking along both horizontal and vertical axes, represent a 'compromise' approach, the Chinese, by way of contrast, compound the problem by stressing the vertical (class) approach?

CHAPTER 4

The East and Marx

> What is involved here can perhaps be suggested by looking at literature, where, for instance, we often find similar plots of the same story cast in different ways, e.g., the story of Orestes as depicted by Aeschylus, Sophocles, Euripides, O'Neill and Sartre. . . . It is a start on the road to answering the question of just which doctrines are marxist.
>
> Richard T. de George

We have expressed our intention in the foregoing chapter of attempting a comparison between contemporary Western and Eastern theories of international relations. Before we can do that we shall attempt to place in a comparative context those theories we have already reconstructed of Marx and Engels, of Lenin and Stalin, as well as of the contemporary Soviet leadership. In these chapters, we have already tested some of the comparative bases, but as a result, largely of our having presented a historically ordered survey, often where the continuity of the argument seemed to require it, areas of divergence have been submerged. It is towards redressing this situation that, by focusing upon areas of divergence, we will here direct our attention. Having alerted the reader to the deceptiveness that can lie behind the bland features of continuity, we would further remind him of that logical rule that may deny any resemblance whatsoever between A and C where each resembles B.

And so, retaining in this chapter the structure of the argument as it has evolved so far, we shall compare the attitudes of each of four theories towards international relations in general. We shall compare the nature of each of those theories, as well as their philosophical-epistemological foundations, finally offering some explanation as to why it happens that the 'C' or indeed the 'D' and 'E' of our equation contrasts so sharply with the 'A'.

In this context the first observation to be made is that the extraordinarily radical departure from the original 'A', that we perceive to have come about, has been due to the basic inappropriateness of (classical) marxism for application to international relations. By this we do not of course refer to the quantity of serious predictive errors made by Marx and his successors, nor to the fact that Marx's marxism never did and never could explain for us the problems of the twentieth century; we refer simply to the painful accommodation on the part of the Soviet Union to the existence of states to whose destruction the Soviet Union since its very inception was ideologically committed. Our second observation concerns the concurrent metamorphosis of classical marxism into the official ideology of a great state – indeed of one (organised) third of the world. In this context it will be recalled that one of the many (contemporary) nineteenth-century reformist social doctrines – that of Karl Marx and Friedrich Engels – claiming scientific knowledge,[1] and critical (as were many others) of bourgeois capitalist society of the nineteenth century was acknowledged by Russian intellectuals to be superior in its comprehensiveness to the thought of the indigenous Russian revolutionary tradition. It is understandable that in the course of its adaptation to the conditions of that other revolutionary environment, it should have undergone a series of modifications. Armed ideologically with classical marxism thus modified, a successful revolution took place whose architects claimed to have followed Marx's blueprint. Having served that first revolutionary purpose the selected writings were pressed into fulfilling a no less important justificatory role. Not only had the revolution to be explained to a bewildered people but in its aftermath, and despite the removal of the much execrated area of private property, the continuing existence of problems hardly less tractable required explanation. The involvement of the entire populace was a prerequisite to social reconstruction and to this end a set of guidelines to chart the path of that reconstruction and guide the advance of the new state into the future was established. In this process of political socialisation a certain justification and tentative drawing of the future were found in the immense trove of Marx's condemnation of capitalism, private property, and exploitation. The notion of communism and its aspirations, similarly taken from Marx, fulfilled the functions of a secular religion and supplied the framework for the transformation of marxist social doctrine into a fully fledged ideology. In the circumstances it was natural that the links with Marx should prove to be too tenuous, or that the ideological bones were too bare, and required to be fleshed out. For example, the concept of dictatorship of the proletariat that was to become central to the corpus of the Marxist-Leninist doctrine had never constituted a vital part of Marx's teaching and it fell to Lenin – the new leader, and self-appointed heir to marxism – to conduct the fleshing-out process.

There is no doubt whatsoever that classical marxism possessed a great many of the characteristics needed for it to grow into the ideological colossus that it now is. The dead Marx, as Wesson points out,[2] unlike the living Karl Marx, has arrived at unexampled success. The promise is nothing less than total victory and absolute fulfilment of mankind. He who embraces the doctrine claims moral superiority over capitalism, it is given to him to discover the key to the future through revealed 'laws' – the revelation being, moreover, of a 'scientific' nature and encompasses the inevitable demise of capitalism. Unerringly, and selectively, classical marxism catered to certain aspects of human need, the underdog was assured that no blame or responsibility attached to himself for his unenviable condition. Not only that, but (by whatever means) the situation was open to redress, since any 'top dog' (other than marxist) had already stood trial in the marxist court and been found guilty.

But is this vague common denominator, that is to say the moral goal of communism, condemnation of a major opponent and some common methodology (dialectics) enough proof of a pedigree? Is the entitlement to marxism so easy to prove? Should marxism be no more than dissatisfaction with one's present condition/location, a vision of the future that amounts in substance to little more than a mirage and the possession of a (dialectical) compass whose polarity is demonstrably unreliable? The vision neither gains in definition nor comes closer. And just as the mind's eye, resentful of any interruption of an observed line, will supply its own definition, so successive generations of marxists have been at pains to supply the supposed omissions so as to obtain the total picture, the 'real theory'. We have observed how both Lenin and Stalin found it necessary to subdivide the stages outlined by Marx and to add numerous substages. This process, which some writers have preferred to describe as derevolutionisation and deradicalisation, we would describe rather as a process of desperate adjustment of classical marxist theory to their (Lenin, Stalin) practice; an attempt to rescue classical marxism from obsolescence. As R. T. de George has pointed out, as a result of the ideological uses to which the theory of Marx has been put, Marxism-Leninism has become wedded to the leadership who cannot (and this is increasingly the case) repudiate Marx without repudiating their society[3] – a repudiation that could hardly fail to encompass themselves. And so, it is hardly surprising that in Lenin's, Stalin's and Marxist-Leninist theories that can be described as ideological (as opposed to Marx's doctrine) we can detect basic similarities:

1 They are all ideological and have become devoid of the ambiguities deriving from Marx's scholarly style. They become simpler to read and understand, not only because of a different type of authorship but also because of the different type of audience to whom they are addressed, whose comprehension is eagerly sought – not to say required. In these circumstances the ambiguities arising from theoretical complexity are replaced by ambiguities arising from the need to oversimplify. With the exception of Lenin, leaders are no longer scholars and theoreticians no longer political leaders.

2 The same marxist language is retained; the same ideological, symbolical and sententious idiom. Here, therefore, another contributory cause of misconception, since the meaning of some terms undergoes dramatic change.

3 Another consideration in tracing similarities and inter-connections between later generations of marxist thinkers is the fact that thinking, on international relations in particular, is cumulative: Lenin begins where Marx left off, Stalin from Lenin's conclusion, and the cumulative layers depend on a tenuous linkage often established on the basis of an over-emphasis placed on one concept – or, indeed, on only several lines from the preceding thinker's pen. In the case of Lenin the notion of the dictatorship of the proletariat comes to mind, or, in Stalin, of socialism in one country; each taken as the starting-point, or foundation on which new theories are erected. We need hardly say that, through such gross amplification of some concepts, others as important, or even more so, become either distorted or undergo a reversal of meaning.

Among such amplifications there stand out most prominently the concept of theory and practice (the requirement that theory should constantly adjust to the changing situation) – contained in Marx but occupying not nearly as central a place as Lenin would wish us to believe. The new emphasis enabled Lenin to formulate that 'law of uneven capitalist development' that made possible the incorporation within the main corpus of ideology of such new theories as that of imperialism and of socialism in one country. It is this same 'law' that still allows the contemporary Soviet leadership to conceive of the world revolution.

The common denominator of all of those theories so far looked at has been the adherence to the same philosophical/epistemological postulates – a claim indeed that their proponents never tire of reiterating. Officially, in terms of the continuum that we introduced in Chapter 1,[4] the Soviet Marxist-Leninists would maintain that they share with Marx, Engels, and Lenin, the same epistemological/ philosophical foundation – not claiming to share with Stalin of course who although he used virtually the same words to the same effect is now rejected. In brief, the Soviet Marxist-Leninists retain, with Marx and Lenin, the belief that the human mind is on the way to the total knowability of social reality: which is to say, only a certain privileged type of human mind – that of the working class, which, qualified further by Lenin, becomes also in the non-antagonist socialist society the essential 'rightness' of the Party's perception of reality. The world is believed to be ordered in accordance with essentially discoverable laws. Hence, the goal of social theory is certainly not restricted to that of supplying taxonomies but is elevated even beyond the function of explaining past and present events and of prediction – to controlling future developments on the basis of a capacity to explain the functioning of the social laws of development. The degree to which reliance is placed on the historical objective process as opposed to subjective revolutionary forces has, as we have shown, significantly changed from Engels's rather strict determinism, via a somewhat ambivalent Marx, to a very unambivalent Lenin (as far as the primary importance of the subjective factor is concerned) to an extremely mixed (almost schizophrenic) standpoint taken by the Soviets today. While on the one hand they maintain within their own bloc that communism will not come about by itself but must be built subsequent to the discovery of all of the laws, they retreat from this internal subjectivist position on the other hand and, in terms of the world revolutionary process, place an almost Engels-like reliance on the scientific and technological revolution – a situation in which the world revolutionary process is relegated to a poor second place. Given the context of shared theoretical characteristics of marxist generations there is the persistent claim to be able to predict and indeed control future developments, of which, incidentally, the Soviet passion for planning all aspects of their international development might reasonably be construed as a by-product. Still harking back to the tradition of Marx and that of Lenin, there is no aversion from a philosophical standpoint to the use of mathematics in carrying out social science research, and in this connection particular mention might be made of the recent deployment of cybernetics right across the spectrum of the social sciences – an application that gained wider popularity than in the West whence it came. The Marxist-Leninist philosophy underlines all theoretical efforts, hence, again unlike the situation in the West, it is proper to describe Marxist-Leninist theory (as well as classical marxist) as a general theory based on the grand sociology of social conflict.

All of the theories of those included in our present sample adhere to, and advocate, absolute ethical values, from which it follows that ideologies come in for a great deal of attention. As a matter of fact all theories about society are considered to be, by definition, ideological and the Soviet theory is explicitly claimed to be one such ideological theory. Or, perhaps we should hasten to add, not simply one such theory but, of them all, a very special theory in that it differs from the others in so far as it corresponds to social reality and is the only one capable of being 'scientific' in the sense of its escaping the charge of 'false consciousness' levelled at all other Western theories. It is to be noted that in Marxism-Leninism an important distinction is made between theory and method and some Western methods may be seen to be correct and, borrowed by the Soviets and transplanted into the new context of Soviet theory, can prove useful. The preoccupation with the philosophical foundations of all social theory, including international theory, is overwhelming – a situation which a mono-lithic philosophical structure alone makes possible. There is within the framework of historical materialism the overt commitment to historicism so that no concept can ever be understood if torn out of its historical context.

Within this general framework, however, the actual content of marxist philosophy has changed enormously. We have already shown for example in the appropriate chapters how difficult it will be to heal the split between dialectical and historical materialism; and there is a real possibility that the rift will prove impossible to close. Other such major departures were Lenin's theory of knowledge as well as the vulgarisation of dialectics which is presently being imposed artificially on reality rather than discovered within it.

But the most important difference of all goes deeper – to the philosophical premises themselves. It is this area of affirmation of fidelity to Marx's philosophical position that we regard as fallacious and that offers a good example of the discrepancy that exists between official and 'unofficial' ideology – or, perhaps more precisely, exoteric and esoteric aspects of it. The philosophical assumptions of the Marxist-Leninists are very different from those formulated by Marx and Lenin. In fact, contemporary theoreticians are forced into a position of assuming – and having to act on the assumption – that they have reached the absolute end of the continuum:[5] it is as though they have reached the state of total knowing, and of therefore neither requiring nor seeking fresh knowledge. There are axiomatically given theories that identify general laws and from them derivative laws, there is the axiomatic 'knowledge' of the ways in which the future will unravel. Thus the applied effort of the theoreticians is restricted to the elaboration and repetition of these axioms – an area which, albeit augmented in extent since the stalinist era, still offers very limited scope for theorising in the Western sense of the word. Oddly reminiscent of the turns on a dialectical spiral, a stage has now been reached when most vigorous encouragement is given to development in the realm of theory, but (as on the spiral) with substantial variation from earlier periods. Now it is theorising *within* the politically given parameters – to, in effect, substantiate these axioms to which we have referred and which still remain beyond criticism. The degree of excellence is now being judged by the way in which these axioms are expressed and the virtuosity with which support for them in the classics is found. One would search in vain for an article, even in the most scholarly of journals, that is not aimed at a wide lay audience, an article that doubts the validity of the concept of the class approach to international relations, that questions, for example, the validity of dialectics, or that invites comment on the desirability/attainability of communism. Nor is the situation basically changed when from time to time either the axiom or one of its aspects becomes officially *déclassé* and the ideological floor is thrown open to debate. In this connection may be recalled the avalanche response in the Soviet Union when Stalin opened up the debate on the role of superstructure and substructure and their mutual relations. It could be said that the relative freedom and permissibility of debate on certain subjects is in inverse proportion to the extent of the writing on these subjects in classical marxism or to that handed down by Lenin. The less Marx and Engels had to say about certain subjects, in other words (most notably on ethics but to an extent also on international relations), the less likely is the sin of heresy to be committed.

So much for the philosophical foundations on which, within Marxism-Leninism, all social sciences, by definition, have to build. But the field of international relations exhibits peculiarities of its own and it is towards an understanding of these that we now turn. We have already noted the paradox in that, contrary to Marx's expectations, international relations not only continued in existence but that the situation has come about that it is through such relations that the world revolution will proceed. We would like in this connection further to draw attention to Brzezinski's proposition that only in the field of world politics do there exist the 'grand dilemmas' that were so much a commonplace for generations of marxists.[6] We refer primarily to issues of world politics which continue to divide the international communist movement of which, most notably, the idea of peaceful coexistence (a Sino-Soviet 'dilemma') in the context of the nuclear war/peace debate is an example. Although the 'clerical issues'[7] and, particularly since Stalin's time, the marxist debates that focused on international Soviet affairs have paled in significance against the loom of global 'dilemmas', the debates too are attuned and relate to this other, wider dimension. A continuing controversy that has plagued, and continues to plague, the international working movement is only one example of division at this level and one that demands of the Soviet world view more precise formulation.

Given the fact of 'so many masks' that the Soviet Union has been obliged to wear it should occasion no surprise to discover, as Aspaturian points out, that the behavioural configuration of the Soviet Union constitutes an absolutely unique historical pheno-menon. A full adjustment was in fact required to bring it into correspondence with such an unlikely bedfellow as marxism. The unsuitability of the doctrine as a theory of international relations lies above all in its attitude towards the state – and indeed to the horizontal level of analysis in general. The attempt to substitute a (vertical) class analysis for the (horizontal) state approach was a hazardous exercise and the retention of the nation-state is an explicit recognition of the fact that the class solidarity upon which Marx placed so much reliance failed to submerge national distinctions: to that extent proletarian internationalism lacked conviction.[8] Whatever the strength of the concept of proletarian internationalism today it is a shadowy version of what might have been and should have been. We have already given some explanation of the compromise Marxist-Leninist solution that slowly evolved: neither the abandonment altogether of the horizontal level and its displacement by the (vertical) class element nor an abandonment of the 'class approach'. Instead of a repudiation of the 'class approach' the so-called 'class approach to international relations' represents a meeting and merger of the two planes of analysis in such a way that they can no longer be meaningfully separated. We have described the way in which originally horizontal institutions such as state sovereignty, etc. veer in response to the vertical class pull while vertical institutions are subjected to a corresponding horizontal influence and react similarly. While the very suggestion of a theory of international relations would have been anathema to Marx (a theory after all that could have dealt only with mere epiphenomena) the Soviet compromise is a *sociology of international relations*, that is, a theory of international relations with class content.

The process of adaptation of marxism to international relations was initiated immediately after the Great October revolution when a decision had to be reached as to whether the Soviet Union would preside over the basically vertical non-state communist movement, or whether it was to lead a communist state system. The latter alternative – namely the progressive transformation of the world communist movement into a communist inter-state system – prevailed. The predominant attitude of Marx, Engels – and also Lenin – towards international relations and the future of such relations was a negative one. It came from the conviction that the world revolution was at hand which would eliminate states – and consequently inter-state relations – and replace them with some new, unprecedented type of relations between administrative units into which the communist world would have to be organised. All three men saw in world revolution the end of international relations, a view that differed only in detail. In Marx's understanding the world revolution was to take place within the separate state units and more or less simultaneously all over the globe, placing reliance not on international war but on civil war (or revolutions) contained within the state's frontiers. The scope of

Lenin's theory of international relations was more extensive and consisted basically of the theory of international relations of imperialism leading to the initial outbreak of a communist revolution. Thereafter, over a somewhat lengthier period than Marx had envisaged, the states would 'wither away' and become replaced by a communist organisation, the characteristics of which Lenin rehearsed in his writings on the Soviet Federation.

The equation 'world revolution equals an end to international relations' was to prove oversimplified and failed to allow the accommodation of any alternatives. If, in other words, the revolution did not reach world-wide proportions then international relations would not only continue in existence but would assume an altogether different – and in the event prominent – character. Becoming aware of the implications, Lenin had already 'upgraded' in importance international relations by shifting the focus of his analysis from the exploitation of the proletariat to the exploitation of colonies in the age of imperialism. In referring to this shift we have described it as horizontalisation of a hitherto strictly vertical class conflict. In Lenin's theory it was not the workers but the colonies who were to inaugurate communism. And so, in this way Lenin changed Marx's somewhat unsympathetic attitude to colonies and in so doing initiated the present paradox of marxism which has now become a doctrine of underdevelopment and the battle cry of underdeveloped countries.[9] The shift also meant that the achievement of communism could no longer be held to be possible only on a world-wide scale, and only in the highly industrialised countries. Furthermore, this shift had the effect of placing a crucial importance on *war* through which – or as a result of which – further communist revolutions were expected to take place. Thus, the nation-state, despised by Marx and Engels, and destined to become an exhibit in the museum of antiquities, received a new lease of life having now become the protagonist of class conflict. The impending division of states into blocs or systems became, and has remained, an essential part of the Marxist-Leninist conceptualisation ever since – and constitutes a most significant reversal of Marx's (implied) rejection of any coexistence between communist and capitalist states. Indeed 'communist state' would represent a *contradictio ad adjecto*. A new dilemma had presented itself where the equation could neither read 'world revolution equals the end of international relations' nor 'world revolution equals the impossibility of (protracted) coexistence between communist and capitalist states'.

With the breakdown of the equation a new formula had to be found and the duly revised version read as follows: Soviet revolution equals coexistence with capitalist states. Thus the idea of coexistence was born and, in this respect, the Soviet claim that 'peaceful coexistence' came into existence as soon as the victory of the October revolution had been achieved may be understood and to some extent justified. But perhaps before admitting too readily the proprietory claim we should pause for a moment to consider the conceptual implications.

Even at the time the term 'coexistence' meant no more than a Soviet acknowledgment of the necessity to join the system of states and of postponing (*ad infinitum*) their destruction. We may thus describe Lenin's theory (and oblige the Soviets) as a *transitional (short-term) coexistence theory*. Coexistence out of weakness, 'peaceful' only in so far as we can believe that peace was the genuine desire of those who believed that they were on the weaker side of a precarious equilibrium, and in subscribing to which, sight was not lost of the long-range objective of destroying a system whose rules had temporarily to be adopted in the name of survival. Painfully preoccupied with survival, and from the besieged mentality of 'capitalist encirclement', Stalin narrowed the theoretical and practical horizons of Soviet world politics by restricting them to that of the developed European capitalist states; in the process neglecting not only the colonies but also the proletariat of the capitalist countries. [10] He was obliged to face the fact that the transitory period of coexistence was less transitory than had been anticipated and in these circumstances he gradually disentangled the Soviet Union from the amalgam of exploited countries into which Lenin's theory of imperialism had placed her. Allocating to the Soviet Union a status and theoretical position of its own Stalin placed it on one apex of a (triangular) perception of the world that is still extant. Thus, it is Stalin's theory of international relations, and not that of Lenin, which in our view constitutes the first enduring coexistence theory [11] and that becomes the first real theory of coexistence rather than a theory of (fatal) conflict. Soviet theories of international relations in other words might well be described as theories of coexistence if it is borne in mind that the type of coexistence undergoes change. There is the additional qualification that the prefix 'peaceful' assumes some meaning only from the 20th CPSU Congress. Then, for the first time, and as a result of a changed attitude in regard to the inevitability of wars in the nuclear age, it became a strategy for victory without the necessity (but with the continuing possibility) of wars between states. It is no longer merely a tactic subordinated to a larger strategy for victory in which inevitable wars between states would play a decisive role.[12]

Khrushchev went further. In an equally important theoretical supplement ex-colonies – now developing or Third World countries – were rescued from their inclusion in the same category as capitalist countries, and in contrast to Stalin's lumping the two together, Khrushchev separated the developing countries from the capitalist by a newly demarcated 'zone of peace'. In the absence of the threat to the Soviet Union of encirclement, they were placed together with the socialist system.[13] This reaffirmation of triangularity was of particular importance and thinking along these lines was influenced by the development of nuclear armaments that made reliance on war as a positive factor unacceptable to the working-class audience. In these circumstances another revolutionary perspective had to be drawn. Thus, we now have in front of us the slow transformation from Marx's *intra*-state class conflict via Lenin's notion of conflict between groups of states to the concept of triangularity that emerged after the inception of the first socialist state which was soon after reduced once again to the two camp doctrine that shifted the main emphasis from Lenin's theory of imperialism (of conflict between oppressed and oppressor states) to the notion of conflict between the Soviet Union and the advanced capitalist countries. And finally, to a contemporary situation in which the two camp doctrine has become modified by the addition of a zone of peace and establishment thereby of a fully fledged triangularity of capitalist, socialist, and Third World.[14]

The theoretical progression can of course only be understood when taken in conjunction with parallel shifts taking place in the Soviet Union's position in international affairs. The first period – 1917 to 1939 – is that of relative weakness when Soviet aspirations and ideological forays were far in excess of her objective capabilities, and when the process of effecting a balance between ideology and the survival of the infant Union posed a serious problem. After 1944 the situation begins to change with the transformation of the Soviet Union from a relatively weak power into a great power, subsequently a superpower and, finally, a global power. In this latter period some of the objectives whose contemplation had hitherto been a matter of ideological rhetoric, now for the first time became the real objectives of Soviet foreign policy.[15] Commensurate with her growing strength, the Soviet Union under Khrushchev became increasingly committed

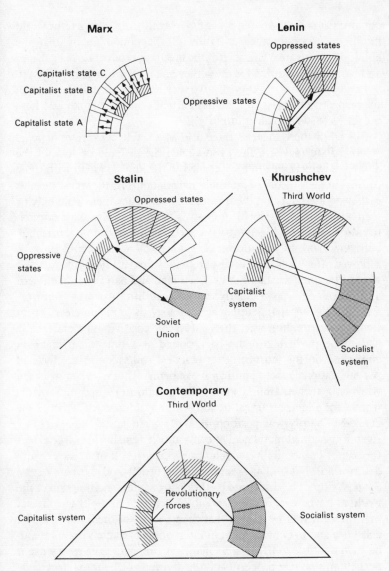

Figure 12 The models of the world compared

to competition with the United States on a global scale while, at the same time, she was called upon to respond to a brand-new set of problems that arose from the creation in Peking of a rival seat of communist power. Among other far-reaching implications, the world might well ponder the refutation of the notion finally that the abolition of private ownership of the means of production is a panacea and sufficient condition for the achievement of universal harmony.

Proceeding now to a comparative survey of the major differences in the respective theories, we will pay particular attention to those whose details have so far been omitted.

For all of these theories the world as a whole constitutes *a global system* (if we may use the expression): the differences arise in the degree of importance to be accorded to the global system within the context of their theory of international relations. As for Marx, we have earlier pointed out that the transcendance of alienation could only be seen against such a (global) framework. The underlying assumption for Marx (and his objective) was the possibility of potential harmony between man and the universe, a harmony which could only be achieved after all of the clutter of relationships that he in his alienated world identified as standing between man and nature had vanished. This message – particularly in his youthful works – notwithstanding the hegelian/kantian terminology, is loud and clear. From Lenin onwards, however, the concept of 'positive transcendence'[16] had to be pushed into the background at a time when marxism embarked on the journey of its practical realisation in the form of partial (national) socio-political movements. That is, when marxism was being turned from a global theory into organised movements which, for a long historical period – indeed 'for the whole era of the defence of hardly-won position – had to remain partial and limited'.[17] Even if the actual moral goal of communism remains to a large extent the same – a possibility which, partly as a result of Marx's scanty description of it and to a similar superficiality on the part of the Soviets, cannot be discounted – the changed view and function of the world as a whole is, in our view, absolutely crucial. So crucial in fact that it might well be argued that the very fact of the Soviet Union's existence and her engagement in international relations may at depth be incompatible with classical marxism. Indeed, since in a sense it perpetuates private property and the division of labour that fact alone could well be seen to characterise the Soviet Union as unmarxist and to place her (as well as the other socialist countries) firmly in the category of capitalist states.[18]

There are, too, other fundamental changes that affect the whole of Soviet thinking on international relations, among which is the concept of class. Both Western sociologists and sovietologists have provided an extensive literature on the subject but it will suffice for our purpose to draw attention to the fact that although the 'class approach' to international relations is maintained, the actual content of 'class' has changed. This is not to gainsay the possibility that such a change in definition of class was obligatory as, contrary to Marx's expectations, the proportion of proletariat to total population declined in the leading industrial nations and their wages failed entirely to sink to that subsistence level that Marx's theories – if they were to make any sense at all – required. Beginning with Lenin, who was obliged in a revolution that was more peasant than proletariat to modify considerably his requirements as to the identity of allies for the proletariat, the identity of the revolutionaries and their allies has become ever more comprehensive until today it embraces 'world revolutionary forces' whose definition would seem to hinge loosely on elements that may simply be described as anti-capitalist or anti-imperialist. And as to the usefulness/validity of a definition of class that can be formulated only in terms of a negation of its (similarly loosely defined) adversary we leave to the reader to judge. Though classes are still regarded as the primary analytic unit, we have travelled far from the unequivocal marxist emphasis on the working class, via Lenin's reliance on the Party, and have arrived at a party, independent of all classes, representative of none, seeking a base for the realisation of its own ambitions – in any case where it finds support. One could well agree with John Kautsky that 'The end of Marx's party – the class struggle – has been abandoned for the means: the party in quest of power.'[19]

Apart from the vagueness as to what precisely constitutes class, the progeny of class (the socio-economic political systems), by reason of the fact that they coexist and that revolution does not take place simultaneously across the world as a whole, must be seen to be a very far cry from that of the original marxism. Similarly, although Marx is once again conveniently ambiguous on the subject of nations, they are clearly ephemeral units and a nuisance, but other more important units such as states and classes display 'national' characteristics, as for example 'national class', 'national state'. The Soviets, however, reverse that attitude. Where clearly 'nation' is no longer merely an attribute of state or class we find evidence of the reversal in such statements as 'state is an attribute of a nation' (!) or to the effect that state is 'the most important socio-political condition [!] of its development'.[20] The reversal in respect of the institution of state is clear although when drawing attention to it we might add that in diagonalising its content, state is now perhaps a different institution to that which both Marx and contemporary Western international theorists have in mind. About the category of state in general there is very little to be said, since Soviet theory, in the same way as it approaches international organisations, deals rather with types of states and types of organisation and, depending upon whether they are capitalist or socialist, will depend also the favourable or unfavourable light in which they are viewed.

As the multiplicity of 'actors' in the international arena widened, the types of relationships among them also had to be refined, and instead of Marx's simple solidarity as opposed to antagonism, a whole range of types had to be added – basically still deriving from Marx. The important addition of non-antagonistic conflicts to the elaboration of proletarian and socialist internationalism helped to define and strengthen relations among the world revolutionary forces, while new varieties of relations consistent with basic antagonistic relations[21] had to be devised. Among these latter, peaceful coexistence was to be the most prominent.

It is no part of our purpose here to add to the already voluminous Western accounts concerning the irrelevance of Soviet ideology and marxism where understanding of world politics is concerned. We are committed rather to remaining on the theoretical level of comparison and consequently feel no great need to list either Marx's mistaken predictions/erroneous explanations, or those of his successors. Suffice it to say that Marx's works did not address themselves to the problems of the twentieth century and that viewed in that light the Soviet adaptations of the doctrine to our times have been relatively successful. Certain it is that the triangular model of the world has a much more convincing ring to it than has Marx's postulate of class conflict and, equally certain, that Lenin's theory of imperialism, though perhaps never 'marxist', relates with a certain congruency to reality – particularly to a reality in which the widening gap between rich and poor nations is more serious than is the capitalist-worker equation. But instead of such questions our main concern here is to trace the vagaries in theoretical thinking between Marx and the Marxist-Leninists: and we find ourselves wondering at the treatment that befell Marx's thought on its journey through time and space to become the contemporary ideology of a great power. A blanket denial of the doctrine's intellectual acceptability is not good enough and, in any case, could lead to the blanket assumption of a low IQ on the part of a large number of intellectuals in that part of the world. We seek then these areas of genuine continuity between Marx, Lenin, and the Marxist-Leninists that enabled a basic change *inter alia* in the theoretical perception of such important phenomena as international relations to take place. We suspect that there must have been a point when a 'qualitative' change took place between contemporary Marxism-Leninism and the thought of their illustrious ideological progenitor.

There is apparent in all these theories under examination shared features of system thinking. All three identify a 'set of interacting parts where change in any of the components, or in the interactions among them, produces changes throughout the system, or its break-down'.[22] Reynolds's two basic methods of system conceptualisation with their different starting-points as the criterion of differentiation is particularly helpful for our purposes. On the one hand, one begins by identifying and defining the significant units, and then attempts to identify the significant interactions that take place among these units (a process which has often led in the past to postulating state systems without considering that there could be other systems or even units other than states). On the other hand, one might begin from the interactions rather than from the units, when 'the system would then consist of all interactions of this kind among whatever units'.[23] And it is here, in our opinion, in this particular distinction that there is to be found (in addition to the above-mentioned philosophical/epistemological differences) the basic and perhaps unbridgeable methodological difference. With certain reservations in mind[24] it is possible to throw some light on the marxian interpretation as well as on subsequent variations. We begin with Marx.

In adult life Marx soon came to a total rejection of the society of which he was an observer – and with it most of contemporary general thinking about that society. He perceives the alienated man and quite clearly posits a goal for himself, the same man, after alienation has been transcended. The free, liberated man within a free society, free above all from those institutions whose alienated form apparently disturbed him so much and which he saw as constituting barriers between man and nature, and between man and man. This is the goal which all of society should have in mind; this is the goal to which he dedicated a lifetime of research. From the methodological point of view, save for a few concepts that he incorporates into his own new original framework, Marx rejects *in toto* previous ways of looking at society. Rejecting the clutter of units of which society as he knows it consists – and which bear upon it with degrading effect – Marx begins his analysis from the nucleus and, having observed the same basic interaction in its extensions as in the nucleus itself, moves outwards to the macrocosmic to discover the same effect throughout the whole of his society and in the world at large. To view the contribution of his political economy on the micro level alone is therefore to miss the point altogether.[25] Marx focuses on that basic antagonistic relation – the quintessence of which in his time being wage labour versus capital[26] – and proceeds to trace a projection of that same relation on different levels. He is led to the identification of specific entities and then, and only then, does he confront and analyse these in the light of the relation that brought them into existence, seeing them against the background of a multiplicity of relations with other entities – that leads to the forging of further links in the chain of identification. Hence the variety of his insight (wellnigh incredible for his time), an insight that led him beyond the established pattern of thinking that had hitherto concentrated so heavily on states. The pursuit of the same relation – as we have shown above – brings him to the state, and indeed to international relations, but since nothing less than the solution of the conflict in interactions will do he cannot tarry. He prophesies their end and hurries on. The system idea, involving interaction and not merely reaction, is no stranger to him and indeed is part of the natural flow of his thought. The notion that there is always not only interaction but also feedback is implied (without the modern *terminus technicus* of course) in his idea of the universal interdependence of things – an idea whose integrity remains unaffected either by the validation or the refutation of the concept of dialectics. In Engels's words, 'In society as in nature, nothing takes place in isolation. Everything affects and is affected by every other thing, and it is mostly because of this manifold motion and interaction that one is unable to see the simplest things.'[27]

The main relation that Marx pursues is that which 'has linked up the peoples of the earth . . . that each of them is dependent on what happens in other lands'. And what is more, the fact that the outward spread of the same interaction is so encompassing and far-reaching is to be seen from 'the social development of all civilised countries [and which] has become so similar'. Without much difficulty this interaction can be seen as the basis of a 'behavioural' system arrived at by the consistent analysis of the basic interaction. The system to comprise 'the whole material intercourse of individuals within a definite state and . . . insofar, transcends the state and nation'.[28] The entities that Marx overtakes and 'passes by' in his research have nothing of the inviolable about them and he has no particular reverence for any one of them. If the development of his relation (or behavioural system) had pointed to some other entity than that even of class he would unhesitatingly have followed that other direction. Indeed, there is no awe for either classes or states expressed in Marx's writings and although his name is often associated with the notion of class, in fact it is his opinion that the end of class is closer than the end of international relations. Just as much as he is concerned with the basic antagonist tension within his nucleus interaction he identifies a similar tension within the interactions that are – in his opinion – derived from the antagonism inside his basic interaction. This antagonism, however harmful in the short run, creates tensions that act in a progressive way ('no antagonism, no progress',[29] 'revolutions are the locomotives of history'[30]) to the point of communist revolution beyond which the identity of the motive force of the onward drive is not made clear. Traditional terms such as basis, superstructure, existence, although seemingly static, can be seen in the interpretation as a set of behavioural systems (economic, political, cultural, etc.) in mutual interaction. After all, the theory of the reflection of existence and consciousness, of ideology and basis, is only Lenin's innovation.

Lenin's interpretation facilitated such simplification as led to serious misunderstanding as to the way in which Marx perceived these pairs of entities (existence and consciousness, basis and ideology), but despite this it has to be admitted that Lenin retained to a degree Marx's way of thinking; perhaps to a larger degree than is generally accorded him in the West. Lenin too follows the concept of basic antagonistic interaction and as we have indicated his perception of the way in which it develops[31] leads him in other directions – and to conclusions which are at first sight at variance with those of Marx. In fact, if Lenin's ideas and those of Marx were to be juxtaposed within a system framework that is based on the identification of the entities, Lenin's hierarchy of 'actors' would differ so profoundly from that of Marx that the frequently expressed view that his is a distortion of Marx is understandable. Nevertheless, once beyond the differences stemming from his entities, and provided we accept the fact that Marx's methodological starting-point in his system building was interactions, then Lenin's continuity with Marx's teaching becomes apparent: we have already suggested how this fact caused such upset to Marx's system in terms of its entities – a source of confusion which theorists (theorising around the entities) have compounded.

The Marxist-Leninist theorists are the theorists of a party which has become the essential part of a system around which their theories revolve; and so it follows that their starting-point must be with the entities if interactions diverge from the system of entities. Thus if they juxtaposed the ideas of Marx and those of Lenin (or, more correctly, their way of system thinking) it would become obvious to them that this generation no longer shares with its predecessors the same methodological approach. How could they, since they selected with a heavy-handed dogmatism from Lenin – rather than from Marx – the entities of his system as he identified them, paying in the process scant regard to the interactions. Those interactions, in other words, that are at the very centre of Marx's theoretical system are ignored while the Marxist-Leninist theorists busy themselves with a system of entities (that Lenin established as a makeshift, temporary arrangement) and devote their energies to absolutising them. More than that, their concern for interactions is limited to those that threaten no disturbance of the set of entities of which the contemporary system is comprised.

Thus the Marxist-Leninist theorists arrive at a number of paradoxical conclusions; there is, for example, that of the increasing entrenchment of the principle that ascribes to the Communist Party a leading role as society approaches communism. How else is this notion to be explained if not by the absolutisation of the entity and its existence and by vested interest in such absolutisation? Far from resolving itself, the anomaly deepens as we ask ourselves on what theoretical grounds the leadership of a society whose interests and stratification (gradual disappearance of classes) are increasingly congruent should be confined to a self-perpetuating elite. Presumably also, such claims to leadership as might be presently valid will vanish as the elite diminishes in size proportionate to the whole of society, and as the advent of a classless society removes any claim to better class origin. After all, Lenin's concept of the Party is in its relevance over half a century old, and even then it was designed as an answer to a particular conjuncture of objective and subjective factors, at a particular moment in time. Nor even then did Lenin himself hesitate to change the concept of Party in his lifetime: now under the banner of 'Leninist Communist Party' the Marxist-Leninists go beyond theoretical distortion to the blatant abuse of the ideas of Lenin and Marx. Where the Marxist-Leninists do not find themselves confronted with class differences they go out of their way to create them.

Marx, Engels, and, with some reservations, Lenin, were scholars, and intellectually adventurous. Marx in particular, despising 'speculative, metaphysical thought' in his almost pansophical erudition did not hesitate to explore field after field, one theoretical school after another, in search of a formula which would embrace 'the best of them all' in a theoretical structure that was not only impressive in terms of the nineteenth century but also of the twentieth. In sharp contrast, Marxism-Leninism neither wants another 'Marx' or 'Lenin' nor can it afford them. And so we are brought to the conclusion that there may well be an unbridgeable theoretical gulf between East and West – the counterpart of which as we have seen lying between Marx and the East. Perhaps the fact that Marx's ideas, in all of their wide-ranging complexity, can be understood in system terms in the two senses suggested by Reynolds is an intrinsic reason why his ideas had to degenerate in their Marxist-Leninist context in the way that they did. It would seem that the ideologues in a movement employing Marx's ideas in their march to power must *inevitably* abandon the approach (starting from interaction), and however enlightened the ideologues of the new regime may be they must soon reorient their thinking along more static (entity) lines. If they were to pursue the approach that had swept the way to power clear of entities then in the changed post-revolutionary environment it would seem 'adventurous' or revisionist, reformist or otherwise deviationist and heretical when they themselves might by the same token be swept from power.

Lefebvre once asked how marxism could be surpassed when marxism itself is a system of thinking that contains the theory of surpassing and the internal law of the transformation of its own nature.[32] The anticipated answer clearly being that marxism cannot by definition be surpassed. The question undoubtedly shows a profound understanding of Marx, but not of Marxism-Leninism in the 'East' where the question becomes not at all rhetorical. The answer is that marxism can be surpassed quite easily – by the gradual removal from it of its surpassing elements together with the internal law governing its future. This can perhaps be better seen in the concept of international relations than in any other.

CHAPTER 5

International relations theory in the West and in the East

The main problem is not that the Soviets do not tell us what they are doing, but that we are reluctant to believe they mean what they say.

Foy D. Kohler

Bourgeois doctrines are *a sterile flower* undoubtedly, but a sterile flower that grows on the living tree.

A Soviet author quoting V. I. Lenin

In the preface we promised to conduct not only a 'debate' between Marx and his contemporary Soviet Marxist-Leninist heirs on the merits of their respective thoughts on international relations, but also to 'stage' one that is perhaps even more complex: between the Soviet Marxist-Leninist theorists on international relations and their contemporary Western counterparts. Such a dialogue has not as yet taken place despite frequent Soviet overtures. Moreover, the mass of criticism that is directed at the West is rarely read and even more rarely triggers a response from that quarter. That Soviet accusations to the effect that the West can, by definition, never come to grips with reality have been aggressively immoderate on occasion is beyond question, but the failure to differentiate between the deliberately provocative and the reasonable – and the tendency to dismiss both out of hand – is, we contend, as hazardous in the long term as it is intellectually timid at close range. Certainly it is true that the state of the 'debate' is highly unsatisfactory. A situation has come about where on the one hand we have an amalgam of Western neglect and incredulity as regards Marxist-Leninist theory and, on the other, the flood of unanswered criticism levelled by the Marxist-Leninists on the basis of their continuing close perusal of Western sources. That our attention should be drawn to the question of 'debate' between the two sides at this moment is timely. It is a moment when, associated with the spirit of *détente*, there is for the Soviets the inseparable notion of engagement in a newly intensified ideological 'battle of ideas'.

But quite apart from ideological considerations the problems of mounting such a debate are very real. Differences between the two schools of thought, in virtually every respect, could hardly be wider. In contrast, for example, to the philosophically pluralistic West with its plethora of theories, Soviet theory stands on a single firm philosophical base – interpreted variously as a pillar or a crutch according to the standpoint of the commentator. The range of theories in the East relative to that of the West is as a consequence considerably reduced and a set of strict rules governing methodology prescribes *a priori* the place a theory or method is to occupy as it is formulated or – more recently – 'borrowed' from the West. International relations theory in the East, though having its formalised beginnings later than its Western counterpart, already occupies within precisely enunciated disciplinary boundaries an equally precisely designated corner.

We have become accustomed to the punctuation of Western progress in international relations theory by such stirring pronouncements as: 'by and large, the great struggles over methodology of 1966–68 are over . . . [and] . . . we can now get to more interesting and more exciting matters like what are key variables'.[1] The statements are misleading and in fact (arguably due to the philosophical pluralism) Western methodology of the social sciences in general has never satisfactorily been taken care of. The East would go further and challenge the West's claim to having any methodology at all – or indeed the likelihood, in its present theoretically defocused state, of ever being able to develop one. As we have indicated, the basis for the challenge rests of course on the absence in the West of the underlying discipline provided by a 'unified' philosophy or methodology. In these circumstances, apart from any other consideration, the task of theory building must be so much harder in the West than in the East. In the Western context it means that every theorist has a dual function: that of theorising about international relations and at the same time 'philosophising' about the implications of his theories. It will be appreciated then that the theoretical/methodological schism is as fundamental as any that divides East from West – and will prove as enduring.

There follows yet another respect in which the Western theories differ from those of the Marxist-Leninist. Soviet academics must of necessity begin from the official ideological position and are circumscribed in their theorising by strict ideological parameters. Clearly in the circumstance of theories so derived the assessment of validity or otherwise cannot be made by comparison with the achievements of their Western *scholarly* counterparts. No matter how valuable these 'university-made' Western theoretical constructs may be, as often as not they are confined in their impact to a very small academic circle that only rarely includes the policy-makers. In contrast, Soviet theoreticians, though hampered by ideological constraints, can boast an incomparably wider audience and breadth of application for their writings. Thus, the Soviet theoretician has in fact not one counterpart in the West, but two: bearing in mind the absence in Western theory of that essential marxist principle of the unity of theory and practice we have in the West, not only the theorising of Western *academics* but also the theories (implicit or explicit, *ad hoc* or systematic) employed in practice by Western *statesmen*.

This is not to say that in the Soviet case the merger of theory and practice is always a happy one, or that Figure 13 represents the Soviet state of affairs *as it is*. As a matter of fact the unity principle whereby theory is the guide and is continuously validated (or invalidated) by practice[2] has become rather a case of the theorists being 'invalidated' if they do not meet the requirements of the politicians. In other words, from a pure marxian point of view, it is a situation where practice absolutised is artificially located prior to theory and where therefore the dialectical relationship between theory and practice has, in a most undialectical manner, been severed. What other (marxist) explanation could there be for the statement of a theory alone leading to the banishment of the theorist? The most probable marxian interpretation of the dialectical relationship between the two allows the recognition of theories of whatever kind or provenance until by failing to pass the remorseless, verificatory processes of practice they are 'proved wrong'. It would seem that the Party, the carrier of 'institutionalised truth', considers the risk of exposing all theories to the validation of practice to be too great. By the same token, however, there is no doubt in our minds that the philosophical position taken by the proponents of the principle of 'unity of theory and practice' represents at least potentially one of enormous advantage, though most Western philosophical schools, too worried by a perceived unbridgeable gap between theory and practice, deny there to be any such advantage.[3]

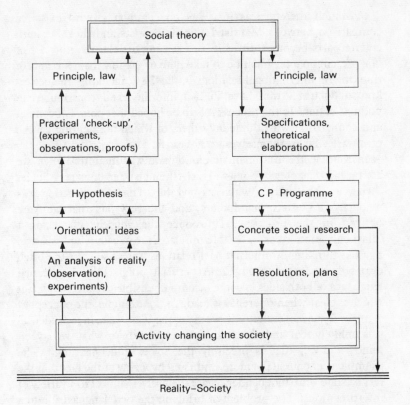

Figure 13 The intermediary system between theory and practice in a
socialist society, from I. T. Jakusevskij, *Leninizmus a
'sovietológia'*, Bratislava, Pravda, 1972, p. 143 (abbreviated
legend: *ibid*. 144).

The theoretical 'line' begins with the analysis of reality, on
the basis of which a hypothesis is arrived at, whereby the
border is crossed from the empirical to the theoretical
level; if the hypothesis is verified it becomes a new theory.
The practical 'line' begins with a certain theoretical idea,
law or principle which reflects the essence of certain
aspects of reality: however complex this theory might be, it
must be elaborated upon through the chain set out in
the figure and through the C.P. Programme in particular.

Inasmuch therefore as it seems no common ground exists, a comparison between Marxist-Leninist theorists and their Western counterparts becomes difficult, or even impossible: the purpose of our present chapter must be to take note of the few main streams of thinking on international relations in the West, including the better-known doctrines that have in fact informed and contributed to political action. In the process it is to be hoped that points of contact and comparison with the many others of which no mention can be made will suggest themselves to the reader.

In a sense the first part of our debate was mounted when we attempted (Chapter 3, Soviet Marxist-Leninists) to construct Soviet theory as coherently a whole as possible. The reconstruction was made from Western standpoints, and the very fact that we were obliged in the process to introduce the concept of a Soviet 'diagonalisation' so as to be able to relate it to Western and classical marxist thinking on international relations was to suggest the often opposed modes of thought. At crucial points, the intellectual languages of both sides become incomprehensible to the other, a fact which is clear when reference is made to, for example, the concept of state, or that of sovereignty. If we say in the West 'state independence' it is unlikely that 'independence from capitalism' is what we have in mind, and yet that is precisely the Soviet understanding.[4] The example is of course the more confusing by virtue of the fact that the terms 'state' and 'independence' are themselves subject to a variety of interpretations! The problem of bringing the two 'languages' into a sort of relationship is compounded by the fact that the Soviets often convey the impression that they do operate on the same intellectual wavelengths, a misleading impression that might in particular be gained from apparent similarities in the characteristics and style of their diplomatic instruments. Because of the fact that the concept of 'state' is defined in class terms the Soviets effectively transcend the Western ideological consensus. And because of the central place still allocated to that concept in the Soviet theory of international relations we see it as the hub around which the other concepts revolve and which, like the concept of state, also have to be 'translated' into Western terms.

The picture that we are trying to convey is of course only hypothetical, with arguments that have never been stated, in a debate that has not yet taken place. And in order that we can offer the major arguments in the Marxist-Leninist case *vis-à-vis* Western theory we will find it necessary to attempt first of all a summary of Western international relations theory and, following that exposition, will set forth the Western position *vis-à-vis* the Soviet Marxist-Leninist. Finally, we would like at that point to draw attention to those areas where, without the abandonment of any basic tenet in the opposed ideological framework, both sides might benefit from a closer scrutiny of the other.

Although the intellectual interchange between East and West has always represented a major problem, yet it seems, despite appearances, that on closer analysis intensive perceptual and emulative processes have taken place in the cultural sphere. At the very least there has derived from these processes the predisposition on both sides to take the other seriously, and a state of affairs has come about whereby a development of a certain kind on one side produces, sooner or later, a reaction on the other. It may be argued that Soviet concern for international theory, as yet only moderately established, has been boosted by Western activity in the field, and perhaps it would not be unduly speculative to predict that Soviet 'borrowing' from the Western social science field may, without overstepping the terms of the relationship, trigger in the West a corresponding desire to gain advantage from a closer attention to some of the cardinal points (such as the link between theory and practice) of Soviet theory.

Initially in the West, and at least until the mid-1950s, the amount of research into the situation obtaining in the East was minimal. One of the reasons for this was the dearth of information coupled with an absence of contact with the communist countries. The only authors able to study the political thought of the East were those with a facility in the relevant languages and who were prepared to carry out their own deductive research from the scant first-hand sources available in the West. The East, likewise, was initially debarred from pursuing Western studies because of considerations of 'ideological purity' that prohibited exposure to possible contamination by bourgeois methods regarded as irreconcilable with Marxism-Leninism. The West had been once and for all analysed and categorised, nothing could change it – and whoever expressed the wish to specialise in any aspect of that culture (including the languages) was regarded with suspicion. Beyond the traditional forecasts of inevitable doom so jubilantly accompanied by statistical evidence of high unemployment, working days lost through strike action, etc., nothing of the West could be received through official sources.

259

The next stage was the development out of isolated research projects in the West of a discipline of 'sovietology' that manifested a strong bias towards historical analysis and that was followed much later by a similar interest in the other communist countries.[5] After some considerable delay this development was followed by the advent of 'americanology' in the East, a field that was to go from strength to strength until at the present time of writing research into the United States of America has become something of a tradition.

Thus in the West, since the 1950s, we might distinguish two attitudes:

1 A group of theorists including a large number of sovietologists who espoused the belief that communist political and ideological matters might be studied only within their own terms of reference. In regard to this approach, E. H. Carr claimed that a certain methodological dichotomy had once and for all been effected:[6]

> A history of Soviet Russia written by an Englishman who has neither a Marxist nor a Russian background may seem a particularly hazardous enterprise. . . . No sensible person will be tempted to measure the Russia of Lenin, Trotsky, and Stalin by any yardstick borrowed from the Britain of MacDonald, Baldwin and Churchill or the America of Wilson, Hoover, and Franklin Roosevelt.

2 More typically, a second group whose views might be roughly summarised as follows: the claim of marxist political theory to be a global theoretical analysis of politics fell short. Not only could it be shown that it was not scientific (as the analysis claimed to be) but it was not even theoretical, and was too ideological to meet the requirements of objectivity. It had very small if any heuristic value, and provided no insights into an understanding of political phenomena. At best it might provide some (ideologically biased) taxonomies but certainly failed to supply explanations – let alone approach its vaunted facility to predict and control. A sorry indictment indeed when set against the theory's action-oriented nature. It was argued that the sole function of the theory was as an instrument for rationalising and *post facto* justification of policies which – ideology or no ideology – would have been

implemented by a superpower concerned more with the preservation of the (Russian) 'national interest' rather than with the advancement of the interests of world communism. Which is to say not only is its theoretical value seen to be small to non-existent, but the writings on international relations actually played no part in the inspiration or conduct of Soviet foreign relations. In this view the Soviet Union was seen as the true heir to the tsarist empire, its conduct informed by and directed towards the preservation of a national interest determined by geography, topography and natural resources. Far from moving to the dictates of a nonsensical communist ideology the Soviet Union's actions were seen to be in more consistent accord with such imperatives as derived from her position as the largest single continuous intercontinental empire in the world, and from the vulnerability to diplomatic pressures of her long and open borders.

Inasmuch as this second attitude might be said to have been the more prevalent and typified the Western standpoint, both East and West had been trying to see each other within the terms of reference of their own culture's analytical framework. Then in the last two decades – and perhaps as a result of a new emphasis on the importance of social science research in general for the actual advancement of ideological goals – the Soviet position began to change. Thus it was deemed necessary to follow carefully the convolutions of Western thinking in an era of peaceful coexistence where the field of combat is shifted to the clash of competing economies and to conflict between two systems of thought. An understanding of that other system, therefore, would doubly arm the Soviet protagonist in the peaceful coexistence battle – a tournament, it will be remembered, that does not even require the opponent to enter the lists. It is appreciated, furthermore, that certain areas of bourgeois thought might be co-opted to serve Soviet purposes, and in illustration of this awareness we cite the following.

Bourgeois political science is far from a monolithic and harmonic phenomenon. It is a disparate, socially and gnoseologically[7] conditioned conglomeration which is in a state of permanent flux. Although the same class nature is maintained [i.e. bourgeois] it is being modified and developed. It is subject to pressures of social

261

motion *inter alia* under the pressure from the theory and practice of
the socialist part of the world. . . . Therefore the criticism of
bourgeois political science is very complex and difficult. . . . A
further characteristic of bourgeois political science is its active role
vis-à-vis bourgeois political practice. It is not merely a
conglomeration of statements of ideology, mystification, false
imagination and apologetics, but it comprises a great number of
relatively correct [sic], relatively true pieces of knowledge and
theories. Note the investments of state institutions into
politological research: all American presidents since F. D.
Roosevelt including Nixon have been relying on their 'brain trusts'
[the English expression used in the Czech text] it is the primary task
of our [i.e. communist] political science to explore contemporary
bourgeois political science with regard to finding stimulation for
the development of Marxist sociology, politics in general, theory of
politics and numerous other disciplines.[8]

Elsewhere[9] the working questions for the analysis of 'contemporary
bourgeois political science' are outlined as follows: 'what kind of a role
does bourgeois political science play in capitalist society, what is its
place, its position in the contemporary ideological battle, what is the
essence of the contradiction between its philosophical grounds and
those of Marxism-Leninism, what are the objective facts on which
bourgeois political science can parasite' and, additionally, 'which
parts of bourgeois political science must be subjected to exceptionally
intensive scrutiny and why.'[10]

The jargon in which these two pronouncements are couched
smacks of the traditional variety, but the emphasis on the importance
of studies of 'bourgeois political science' is new. Such studies are seen
as possible ways of enriching marxist methodology quite apart from
their usefulness in offering insights into actual 'bourgeois policies' –
the latter a function which of course it might be expected to perform.

The Marxist-Leninist attitude towards Western international relations theory

Why, we might well ask, this sudden change of heart on the Soviet side? Why, of a sudden, permission given for an interest to be taken in what was previously seen as a danger area of potential ideological erosion. Or have changes taken place in 'bourgeois social science' that have brought it to a condition of acceptability – if not a state of grace – in Marxist-Leninist eyes? The answer of course is in the negative; all that it means is that Marxist-Leninist methodology, by classifying on a highly selective basis some theories and methods as ideologically neutral, anticipate that some of the by-products may be used to their advantage. A glance at Soviet (and Western) approaches to the whole question of methodology gives direct access to the essentials of the Soviet critique of Western theories and, consequently, to a reasonably correct assessment of which of the Western theories the East is likely to 'approve' – or even utilise.

It would seem that both sides define methodology in the same way. Both seem to be in agreement as to the criteria that govern the transformation of a field of study into an independent discipline. These are 1 the existence of a set of theoretical propositions and organising concepts, and 2 a distinct methodology.[11] Of course these criteria are so interconnected that in any discussion concerning the nature of theories certain methodological considerations are necessarily implied, and vice versa, although each of the two criteria represents one distinct dimension of the discipline in question. By methodology in general is understood in the West the analysis of scientific procedure,[12] more specifically:

1 'the study of the utility and validity of methods of investigation in the context of a particular scientific discipline or area under consideration . . .
2 the selection of methods, in advance of an investigation, that are considered likely to be appropriate and fruitful.'[13]

Thus in the field of international relations, methodology should then be *mutatis mutandis* concerned with the analysis of

1 various theories whatever their epistemological properties,
2 the methods and techniques that have been available for investigatory purposes, and their validity.

In other words, in international relations theory just as much as in other disciplines, methodology should act as the backbone to lend articulation and draw the individual theories into a coherent whole. And it is this unifying aspect that makes a concern for methodology an inevitable part of the study of international relations – a fact that may particularly be appreciated when it is recognised that attempts to unify the discipline by way of any one particular conceptual approach[14] have so far met with no success whatsoever. Marxist-Leninist influenced view or no, we would maintain that due to the enormously complex nature of the subject-matter and to the variety of possible approaches and methods (that might for other purposes be considered to represent an area of strength and of advantage to the field) methodology should play just such a unifying role. It might then be agreed that through the methodological prism, the various approaches, methods, etc. of which Western international relations theory produces a surfeit might be brought within the focus of an ordered relationship. In this connection it is necessary to offer at this juncture some details of the various strands of the Western theoretical tradition that have contributed to the present complex state of the field. The slight deviation from the main thrust of our argument will perhaps throw some light on the scope of the field as well as on the obstacles that have to be surmounted by Western international relations before the problems are resolved.

There is little that is novel in the actual *theorising* about international relations, except in so far perhaps as it attempts to delimit an intellectually more manageable area of human behaviour with the exclusion of as few as possible aspects of human behaviour relevant to it. This is perfectly in keeping with the general tendency observable throughout history whereby individual disciplines, one after the other, from the mathematics of the Greeks to the constitution of social sciences in the twentieth century, have each in their turn become disengaged from the philosophy which at one time comprehended all knowledge. In parallel with this growing tendency to specialisation and partition into separate sciences went increasingly a growing interchange between them and of this process, international theory – a young subject which has been interdisciplinary from its inception – is a good example.

Any attempt to divide the history of the subject into neat segments is bound to be arbitrary since 'the calendar is seldom so obliging'[15] as to make this possible. Indeed accounts dealing with the subject's past that are to be found in current international relations literature are not always congruent, often as a result of a different emphasis being placed by the various schools themselves. In these circumstances the notion of historical 'periods' becomes suspect and there is some merit and a greater accuracy in the alternative concept of 'waves'. This is the notion espoused by, for example, Karl Deutsch in his 'four wave' classification that suggests the highly dynamic character of the field as well as the pluralistic character of the trend.

Having said that theorising about international relations has an ancient lineage it would be wrong to leave out of the periodisation all forerunners (strictly speaking beginning from the Old Testament, if not before) of some of our modern concepts. Particularly is this only fair since we have claimed above that Marx, Engels and Lenin had their own theories of international relations. We therefore propose the following periodisation:

1 *The 'pre-theories' of international relations, prior to the twentieth century.* [16]
2 *Theory of international relations since the beginning of the twentieth century and the development of the social sciences.*
   2.1 *up to the First World War*
        characterised by the rise of interest in international law expressed in the Hague Conventions (1899, 1907) and in the many legal agreements and studies that followed,
   2.2 *the period between the two world wars*
        referred to as the 'idealist' period, characterised by
        2.2.1 the rise of diplomatic history following the opening of archives in the aftermath of the First World War,
        2.2.2 the simultaneous rise of interest in international organisations, and
        2.2.3 singular studies of current events.
   2.3 *since the beginning of the Second World War*
        a period characterised by its 'realist' orientation, stemming from an empirical orientation as sharp reaction to the optimism of idealism in the second period,
   2.4 *since circa 1950*
        the behavioural decade (although some authors [17] are of the opinion that this period begins as late as 1954).
        'Characterised by numerous importations of many relevant results and methods from younger social and behavioural sciences' [18] (such as anthropology, communications, economics, operational research, psychology, sociology,

mathematical techniques, probabilistic models, etc.). The scope of the field has been enlarged, thinking in terms of institutions or events has been replaced by thinking in terms of concepts. However, these importations have left the field in a state of 'conceptual disarray'.[19]

The central problem of integration of the new material within the confines of the field has not been successful.

2.5 *1965 onwards* (Deutsch's fourth wave)

while the main characteristics of the previous period continue 'a new wave has begun to reinforce it. This is the rise of analytic and quantitative methods and movements toward the comparative study of quantitative data and better use of some of the potentialities of electronic computations.' The attitude towards theory building has changed: the drive for an integrated theory has dissipated.[20]

Much of the discussion on international theory has centred upon dichotomised issues, and numerous volumes have been devoted to, and provide an exhaustive coverage of, these issues. Indeed the changeover from one period, or wave, to another has been described in terms of 'debates' since it has always involved a confrontation between the proponents of two basically different schools. First of all it was the 'Great Debate of Idealism versus Realism' that gave way in due course to the 'New Great Debate' and advent of the philosophical versus empirical controversy. Both debates swept through the field on altogether different levels, but regardless of 'victors' or vanquished, the debates brought to the field of international relations profound methodological consequences, and substantial benefit.

By now, probably every undergraduate student of international relations could recite the names of the main protagonists in the grand debates. What interests us here, however, is the place occupied by these debates within the framework of our assumptions. Also to be considered, however, is the fact that although enough has been said and written on the subject there still remains at the root of the debates enough of relevance for us to dwell briefly upon it. It will, for example, be recalled that some arguments suggest that the first debate was about the substance of international relations, whereas the second involved merely its mode of analysis.[21] Even allowing for some flexibility in the matter of what is meant by substance and mode of analysis the conclusion seems highly debatable. Although the first debate (idealism versus realism) was concerned with human nature and with the merits of national interest[22] among other seemingly profound questions, it can be said with certainty that it did not affect the field at any greater depth than did the so-called 'New Great Debate'. Let us consider the approaches of the two sides in that first debate.

Idealism	*Realism*
(Between the two wars) motivated by the shock of the disaster of the then biggest armed conflict that the world had ever seen.	Although the attitude that might be described as 'realistic' is virtually age-old, its main development came as the result of bitter disappointment that another world war was not avoided.
Based on *a priori* optimistic assumptions concerning human nature and harmony of interest (ascribing great importance to the value of peace); aimed at changing the world in the sense of avoiding further similar conflicts.	Cynical on the subject of human motivations, it was based on the allegedly axiomatic assumption that states seek to enhance power, a quest to which everything else is subordinated.
Basically a *normative* approach often containing very little more than hortatory descriptions of the world as those who described it would have liked it to be. Very few pretensions concerning such things as methods, theories, and concepts.	Basically a *non-normative* approach and exhibiting a profound concern (a new feature) for method, theory, and systematic accumulation of evidence. Realism brought a new awareness of thinking in terms of concepts rather than of institutions or events.

'Classical' (also called   versus   *'Scientific'* (H. Bull)
Traditional, or   *otherwise called*
Philosophical)   *behavioural*   } schools
                                               (Rosenau), or
                                               empirical (Platig)

267

(Aron, Carr, Hartz, Lippman, etc.)

(Almond, Apter, Deutsch, Easton, Snyder, etc.)

This school doubted that a universal theory is conceivable, researchable and attainable. Social activity is of such complexity that our knowledge is bound to be so restricted that it remains beyond measurement.

This school sought to identify regularities in human behaviour, which could, when discovered, be subjected to quantification, measurement and rigorous classification. Its critics point to its total failure to encompass human purpose expressed in terms of values and ideologies; insisting instead on precision and system in analysis.

Hence only techniques from philosophy, history, law, and reliance on judgment, can be utilised.

The theories evolved by both schools might well be found to have been descriptive in the main and to possess internal logical consistency as well as a correspondence with the factual data. The difference between them may be said to lie in the varying degrees of precision in which their propositions – and, it follows, the purposes of their theories – were formulated. In the case of the traditionalists – even allowing for the fact that their goals were not always uniform – they were certainly less ambitious and less explicit than the painstakingly explanatory and predictive objectives of the 'scientific' school. Developing side by side the two schools are often unrelated, if not antithetical.

Apart from the dichotomies to which we have referred and the divisions within the field consequent upon these, many criteria and bases of classification have been attempted in international theory literature, but on none of them so far has a consensus been reached. In this respect, therefore, the methodology of international relations still has a long and largely unexplored road to travel. This is not to say that the territory already pioneered has not proved interesting; indeed some of the criteria investigated have not only cast fresh light, but have from time to time proved diverting. There is not much more than entertainment value in, for example, Russett's[23] 'merit ladder' matrix formulated on the basis of a comparison of the degree of contribution to the field (or subsections of the field) made by various authors ('schools' and 'invisible colleges'). The data used for his comparison consisted of citations in particular texts and footnotes to international relations literature over a certain period and across a particular part of the world. Russett's notion was that the popularity of a concept – or popular aversion to it – that leads to its frequent – or infrequent – mention can give a picture of the state of the field.

One of the most widely used (and perhaps safest) ways of dealing with the problem is the well-known post-war 'two step' or 'two branch' solution[24] which, as the name suggests, offers two general categories into which (theory-wise) all concepts might be grouped (Table 1). One branch, the 'mini', would be virtually comprised of research having a foreign policy orientation, while the other would confine itself to the study of structures, relationships, interactions and processes between nations, to be generally known as the international system solution. In Forward's description the first of these examines the texture, whereas the latter concerns itself with the structure.[25]

Criticism of the 'two branch solution' has generally been along the following lines:

1 There is the suggestion in this sort of dichotomisation that one branch might exist without the other. Yet in any study of the fine structure of events and rational behaviour account must be taken of the operation and the long-range effect of underlying forces. There is, in other words, always the danger of failing to see the wood for the trees.
2 The solution involves the drawing of a conceptual demarcation line between domestic and foreign affairs, whereas, in reality, actions and interactions are related – a relationship, one might well conclude, that ought to be the starting-point. Rosenau has pointed out in this connection that boundaries were being projected where the real need was for the construction of bridges. And, in a general comment on the two branch organisation of the field, the same author was of the opinion that the argument had produced 'not a great debate but a reaction of indifference, boredom'.

Yet despite the criticism, the two branch solution has been seen by many as a useful, didactic method, that carries within it the possibility

Table 1 'Two step' organisation of the concepts of the dominant approaches

	Lerche	Snyder LINES OF ANALYTIC DEVELOPMENT	Sprout FOCI OF BASIC RESEARCH
1	ACTION THEORY dealing with state as it moves within the system – foreign policy analysis	SOCIETY as the acting unity – decision-making and policy	foreign policy analysis state techniques
	– ends-means analysis	– values, attitudes, opinions	state policy-making process
	– decision-making	– quantifiable indicators of society as unit characteristics	state capabilities
	– capability analysis		
2	INTERACTION THEORY relations of states to each other – international politics from systematic models of entire international system to very detailed examination of specific forms of interaction – balance – equilibrium – value – game – challenge response – image, expectation	INTER-UNIT AND INTER-ACTION FOCI – system and equilibrium analyses international system – experimental techniques inter-societal conflict intra-societal integration and political community	INTERNATIONAL SYSTEM ANALYSIS

at some later stage of the full integration of both branches.

In addition to the two branch or mini-maxi classification, the classification of theories has been attempted using as the basis of classification the several purposes towards the achievement of which the particular theory is directed (the advancement of knowledge, the achievement of securing the peace, advice to government and so on). Then again, varying conceptions of the nature of the over-all 'general law' conceived to operate in the background and to govern international relations have produced different approaches. In this connection chaos approaches assume the uncontrollability of events on the grounds of apparent inherent general disorder while order approaches conceive of international relations as developing in an 'orderly' manner from which observable trends might be inferred. In this way we have theories of progress: linear, spiral, dialectical, developmental, apocalyptical, or theories of doom: cyclical theories, equilibrium theories, etc. As a rule, however, most attempts so far at classification have been explicitly or implicitly restrictive or partial. Having a similar effect is the not infrequent inclusion of an explanatory note ('there are many others, not included') which in company with appropriate reasons for the omissions is found appended to a demonstrative list of theories. Needless to say such an appendix is the more confusing when the list aims at comprehensiveness.

Table 2 is not intended to illustrate the variety of theories but the variety of such lists of theories. The sample six lists is of course arbitrary, and beyond showing the diversity of perception of six authors within a short time span (1967–72), it can offer only an idea of which basic research orientations then existed in the field – or, more precisely, those deemed worthy of mention. It is of interest to note that the area of agreement reached by the six has been confined to an acknowledgment of the decision-making and system approach. Yet, even in these circumstances, and short of entering a detailed comparison of their notions as regards the decision-making or system approaches, it is difficult to assess the areas of shared agreement. Therefore, in the horizontal sense, no more can be derived from this table. (The difficulties of categorising are further compounded by the fact that a definition of the respective approaches is not in all cases to be found.) But by placing these lists alongside one another, and reading vertically, some interesting impressions are gained. Among these is the confusion that reigns in the mixture of methodological and substantive topics – as, for example, in the listing of decision-making and system analysis in the same context as research techniques (such as simulation). There are many such incongruous overlappings. Also made clear is the fact that none of these lists comes anywhere near a coverage of the entire field – though admittedly only Alger's list is intended to be comprehensive. Readers or monographs such as that by Dougherty and Pfaltzgraff Jr,[26] while coming as close to comprehensiveness as possible, tend to overwhelm by referring to a

271

Table 2   Selected lists of main approaches in Western international theory

	McClelland	Jordan	Ransom	Alger	Palmer	Tanter and Ullman
	1	2	3	4	5	6
Traditional commentary			×			
1 Decision-making theory	×	×	×	×	×	×
2 System theory (analysis)	×	×	×	×	×	×
3 Field theory	×					
4 Capability theory	×					
5 Deterrence theory	×					
6 Communication or cybernetics	×	×				
7 Conflict theory	×				×	
8 Game theory	×	×			×	
9 Integration theory	×	×				
10 Development theory	×					
11 Environmental theory	×					
12 Perceptual cognitive theory	×					
13 Power and influence			×			
14 Disarmament				×	×	
15 Simulation				×	×	
16 Peace research				×		
17 International organisations					×	
18 Elite studies					×	
19 Bureaucratic political model						
20 Ideological paradigms						×
21 Content analysis						×
22 Mathematical models						×
23 Content analysis						×
24 Psychological models						×
						Combination of 1 and 2

1 C. McClelland in James N. Rosenau, Vincent Davis, Maurice East (eds), *The Analysis of International Politics*, New York, Free Press, 1972.
2 David C. Jordan, *World Politics in Our Time*, Lexington, Mass., D. C. Heath, 1970.
3 Marian D. Irish (ed.), *Political Science*, Englewood Cliffs, N.J., Prentice-Hall, 1968.
4 Chadwick F. Alger, 'International Relations: The Field', in David L. Sills (ed.), *International Encyclopedia of the Social Sciences*, New York, Macmillan and Free Press, 1968, vol. 8.
5 Norman D. Palmer (ed.), *A Design for International Relations Research*, Philadelphia, American Academy of Political and Social Science, 1970.
6 R. Tanter, R. H. Ullman (eds), 'Theory and Policy in International Relations', Supplement to *World Politics*, vol. XXIV, 1972.

multitude of names of theories along with their proponents and by presenting these without adequate organisation.

A point to be made in regard to organisation and the reluctance of international theorists to disentangle phenomena and relationships, to allocate names and classify, is that this negative propensity may be said to argue a degree of responsibility. In a new field of study such as international relations which is virtually encyclopedic in its range, arrangement into a neat classification has not so far proved possible – a fact that becomes increasingly understandable the further one reads in the field. But if the sheer enormity of the task of classifying such a confused array of theories and approaches is sufficiently daunting to the Western expert, the task of initiating an uninformed Marxist-Leninist into the field might well be imagined.

The lack of an all-embracing methodology to give a clearer idea of what is comprehended by the field is explained by Soviet observers in philosophical terms. In this explanation, methodology – as in Golembiewski's definition – has a twofold meaning:

1 Theoretical problems concerning the determining and use of scientific methods *adequate* to the subject-matter under consideration.
2 These methods *in toto*.[27]

The gist of the Soviet argument lies in the differences between the Western and the Marxist-Leninist understanding of the 'adequacy' or 'validity' of theories and methods and it is therefore to these questions that we now turn.

'The main concerns of philosophy are the most general questions of the *Weltanschauung*,[28] above all the questions of relation between consciousness and reality. When applied to the practice of cognition and creation, the *Weltanschauung* becomes a methodology [!], i.e. the general method of both cognition [knowledge] and changing of the world.'[29] This statement from a recent Soviet textbook on philosophy provides us with a quite compact and comprehensive answer to the question as to what precisely methodology in the East entails: it implies a basic postulate that general marxist methodology in all branches of learning (Marxist-Leninist philosophy included) is materialist dialectic. It follows clearly enough from this that if a field such as international theory in the West has no uniform philosophical basis it has *ipso facto* no distinct methodology.

Marxism-Leninism, then, defines method as a certain mode or procedure of investigation; a definition that for some Western writers is quite acceptable.[30] But the Marxist-Leninist idea of a method turns out to be more specific: 'a system of regulatory principles on which transforming practical and cognitive theoretical activity is based'.[31] Remembering that 'transforming' or 'changing' in marxist literature are sometimes used co-terminously with 'controlling' it is clear from the statement that cognitive and controlling functions of a theory are automatically taken to be in conjunction. In other words, method is a certain mode or procedure of investigation, a system of regulatory principles serving theory in pursuit of its four functions (taxonomic, explanatory, predictive, and controlling), the attainability of all of which is assumed.

For our (East–West comparative) purpose it will suffice to take a closer look at two questions as they are posed by Marxist-Leninist gnoseology: 1 The concept of validity or adequacy of a theory. 2 Classification of methods.

We return first of all to the question as to what constitutes 'adequacy' and 'validity' in theories and methods. As we have already indicated[32] the Soviet definition of 'scientific' methods is based on their perception of the relationship between social existence and social consciousness. The method 'must correspond to the objective nature of the subject-matter under study; it must adequately express its content, and it must exactly and within the laws [i.e. the laws of its development] follow from it'.[33] In other words, unlike the situation in the West there is nothing accidental or arbitrary about the choice of a method in Marxism-Leninism. Hence, the 'only *intrinsically coherent* methodology' is predictably materialist dialectic, a fact which, however, does not exclude the utilisation of a variety of scientific methods – and indeed positively requires it.[34] Thus, according to Soviet Marxism-Leninism, every object under study (for example international relations) is possessed of its essence and of its phenomenon through which it enters into the consciousness of the subject of study (man). Even though in the working of the extremely complex relationship between the phenomenon and the essence, the essence is 'veiled' (distorted, or oversimplified by the phenomenon), by virtue of the fact that the essence is essentially knowable, it can never be placed beyond the reach of cognition. And this is of course the basic assumption of Soviet epistemology,[35] whereby 'science'[36] is regarded as a process of penetration from the phenomenon to its essence. The influence of the phenomenon itself upon the choice of methods is only of a marginal nature: the methods being objectively determined by the essence of the subject-matter.[37] It will have become clear to the reader that by claiming materialist dialectic to be the methodology there is implied that the methodology is tantamount to 'the class approach'. In these terms the criterion on which the description 'scientific' rests is the identification of the class nature and class function of the phenomena under observation. It follows, therefore, that all other approaches neglectful of this class analysis abandon any claim to being 'scientific'.

Seldom in Western definitions of 'scientific' would a special reference to 'adequacy' be made: the Marxist-Leninist stress laid upon that component – which seems to be assumed in Western definitions – is in the West laid instead upon concern for 'verifiability, validity, generality' and so on. In sharp contrast to the Marxist-Leninist interpretation verifiability is always a 'subjective question', or indeed – an intersubjective one.[38] In the Western approach a proposition is said to be verified when it has been checked or tested by a large number of specialists in the relevant field of knowledge and when, as a result of such testing, general expert opinion inclines to belief in the proposition.[39] The two concepts of 'science' could hardly contrast more – the one based on a 'correspondence' with objective reality via the class approach, and the other on 'correspondence' with the (ideological) consensus. It might of course be argued that in their practical implications these two divergent approaches do in fact virtually merge: the correspondence with objective reality will have to be established within a consensus, while, whether the West likes it or not, their consensus should clearly be arrived at by way of a 'correspondence to the reality'. Equally clearly the essence of the difference – and the unbridgeable component – is in the insistence on the 'class approach'.

In order to ensure that this 'class approach' remains sacrosanct, the Marxist-Leninists go to extreme and complicated lengths in their classification of methods. Of the range of writing on the subject we have space here to summarise only one sample author. In the classification that follows it will be seen that there are once again superficial resemblances to Western versions:

1 General methods of cognition and of bringing about world change.

2 Concrete methods used by individual disciplines.
3 Partial methods encompassing only a single aspect of the subject-matter investigated.

General methods are classifiable, and are classified in accordance with the philosophical framework within which they are placed and by which they are inescapably bound ('like philosophy, like its methodological role').[40] General methods are therefore divided into two groups, materialistic and idealistic, in accordance with the two 'main contradictory, mutually exclusive and incompatible' approaches to knowledge, to philosophy, and to the general *Weltanschauung*. This is not to say of course that the marxist-non-marxist distinction coincides with that of materialism and idealism respectively: there are also non-dialectical materialistic conceptions.[41] In these circumstances it is clear that in terms of approach also the iron curtain separates Soviet Marxism-Leninism from the others. And so Marxist-Leninist methodology is perceived as standing irreconcilably against a 'great number of methodological conceptions of a non-marxist nature, called as a rule according to the philosophical orientation within which they are placed (kantian, neo-kantian, positivist, phenomenological, sociological, behaviouralist, etc.)'.[42] As we have remarked,[43] because of the overwhelming plurality of philosophical schools in the West, nothing remains for the Marxist-Leninist but to lump them all together under the heading (Ideology/ *Weltanschauung*/Philosophy) of *anti-communism* – despite the fact that most of them can be regarded as idealistic.

Partial methods, in contrast, may be 'transferred' from one philosophical orientation to the other since they severally concentrate on one specific aspect of the subject. They, however, remain always subordinated to the philosophical framework – for example, the application of some logical procedures may be the same though their employment and the evaluation of their results will vary from a marxist to a non-marxist framework. This distinction is seen to be so important that a theoretical explanation of such mundane events as, for example, the Prague spring of 1968 would be construed as an attempt of revisionists and right-wing opportunists to bring about a switch in general and partial methods. In other words, we are told that the revisionists attempted to neglect the class approach, over-estimated some partial methods and placed them outside the Marxist-

276

Leninist framework. They 'overestimated empirical and sociological methods, abused in an amateurish manner the theory of modelling, attempted to substitute the socialist humanism with bourgeois philosophical social anthropology, used in a non-marxist way, mathematical and cybernetical methods, as well as system approach'.[44] In other words, as long as selected Western methods are strictly subordinated to the marxist class approach they are fully acceptable. Indeed, in so far as they channel Western ideas, they may be regarded as something of a labour-saving device!

In turning to the specific application of general methods to the field of international relations we find deployed not only the 'class approach' and the historical materialist method but, most importantly, the use in this field of the 'basic laws of dialectic, namely the law of contradiction, negation of the negation, transformation of quantitative changes into qualitative, and so on'.[45] The application of dialectic, we are told, helps to explain the revolutionary changes in the nature of state and nation, as well as in international relations, that have taken place down through the history of society. Besides the basic laws of the dialectic, other dialectical categories are applicable: to these belong, for example, categories of form and content, generality, particularity, and uniqueness, necessity and hazard, possibility and reality. A special place must be accorded also to dialectical logic which is, in contrast to Western formal logic, 'the method of discovering the truth and proving it with regard to the establishment of its formal correctness as a step towards the truth and its proving'.[46]

In order that partial methods qualify for recognition as scientific, they must also be 'adequate' to the subject-matter. And even when they meet this requirement, their role is confined to shedding light only upon a particular aspect of the object studied – hence no one of these is sufficient in itself to enable a full understanding. In these circumstances, therefore, they are deployed in any number of combinations – but such combinations remaining always within the general methodological framework of the materialistic dialectic. Kazimirchuk includes among partial methods the following: logical, comparative, concrete sociological research methods, modelling, mathematical methods, and so on, the meaning of which is sufficiently clear as to require no elaboration.

In the light of the foregoing it should come then as no surprise that irrespective of its schools, waves, etc., Western international relations theory is taken *en bloc* (!) by the Soviet theorists and, thus lumped together, is also rejected *en bloc* for reasons based upon the following 'errors': 'rejection of objective laws of history, disregard of the class basis of politics, attempts to study social phenomena using methods that are adequate only for natural science, substitution of analysis by description, objectivist attempts to go beyond classes and politics, refusal to acknowledge the unity of theory and practice'.[47] More specifically, after they have subdivided Western international relations theory into its various schools Soviet critics give their verdict: behaviouralism is rejected on the grounds of its psycho-sociological basis; apart from such approaches as decision-making they include in this group such authors as Aron and Boulding, and such theories as communication theory, images, and theory of power. Reasons adduced for their dismissal are: 'the sheer scientific impossibility of these theories is not only expressed by their absolutisation of psychological factors but by the perception of such factors along with subjective motives of human behaviour as a basic moving force of historical development. This theoretical orientation confuses objective laws that exist regardless of the will and wishes of individuals with subjective efforts and emotions. The cognitive processes are divorced from those deep-seated socio-economic relations that determine such processes. Ideologies in general, and progressive scientific ideologies (sic) in particular, are completely ignored as well as is the creative role of scientific social research. As a result, these schools of thought can never make predictions or reasonable deductions about international relations. This is acknowledged by some bourgeois scientists when they are brought face to face with Truth. It is then that they [i.e. the bourgeois theoreticians] are obliged to admit the error of their ways: "we have made false judgements in regard to Soviet development ever since the great October revolution".'[48]

The other mainstream of Western theory is especially system analysis,[49] with integration theories, derivative of structural-functionalism, also coming in for some favourable comment. However even these, as Professor Modrzhinskaya points out, 'cannot be scientific'. It is in these structural-functionalist derivatives that Modrzhinskaya herself finds that the West erroneously construes society as an organism, with its peculiar demands and institutions regarded as a means of maintaining itself. All causality is ignored and social functions are viewed from the standpoint of 'stability' and 'equilibrium'. She sees in this attitude one that is fully consistent with a bourgeois ideology of conservatism and 'social stagnation'. The fallacies are inherent in the main propositions of structural-functionalism in its application to international relations; that application, according to Professor Modrzhinskaya, being: 'society is a system of mutually linked parts. The system is maintained by the processes that take place in the society, the achievement of stability being the main object. The struggle of contradictions, which occurs in the social life and is the source of development, is regarded as a disease of society, a pathological feature.' Structural-functionalism, she concludes, on these grounds alone might be discounted as a guide to any understanding of the historical process.

From that Marxist-Leninist quarter, and in line with the typically dogmatic approach, criticism is levelled quite precisely at the absence in Western theories of features that are regarded by the Soviets as axiomatic. Thus elsewhere, Tunkin, with reference to Morgenthau, attacks balance of power theories on the grounds of their overstepping the Soviet analytical Rubicon (class approach) to identify 'neutral' categories, and the arrangement of states across a power spectrum. The theory of balance of power 'presents the regularities governing relations between capitalist states (the urge to supremacy, reliance on force, etc.) as universal regularities of international relations, ignoring the rise of the socialist system'.[50]

We may now leave the collating of Soviet arguments against general or specific aspects of Western international relations theories and, in the light of the criteria to which we have referred, take a closer look at the Western theory from the point of view of its 'compatibility' with Marxism-Leninism. We can then reach some conclusion as to which theories or methods exhibit total irreconcilability, and identify those which are sufficiently middle of the road to pass the Marxist-Leninist test of 'adequacy' and, by virtue of the fact that they contain a 'grain of truth', merit transplantation to the Marxist-Leninist system.

Bearing in mind the pronouncements of Professor Modrzhinskaya and other Marxist-Leninist writers on the subject, it is clear that explicitly ideological-oriented theories must be dismissed out of hand – while the insights of the behaviouralists may in some measure be found acceptably 'neutral'. Therefore in attempting here to supply a useful classification we shall omit from the categories those theories that are informed by 'traditional commentary' – since the inevitable Marxist-Leninist dismissal of them would make their inclusion pointless.

279

We have pointed out that the problem of classification of theories of international relations remains a peculiarly neglected area and we claim no originality for the categorisation set forth below to meet our own requirements. We base it on: 1 the points of criticism raised against the 'two step' classification 2 Van Dyke's distinction between theory and method[51] and 3 Knapp's distinction between general and partial methods. In the process we invite the reader to accept the proposition that, however marginal, the Marxist-Leninist classification of methods (and Knapp's distinction between general and partial methods in particular) is useful for our purposes.

In Figure 14 there are four circles. While each represents a group of theories the arrangement is not meant to suggest the relative proportions of the groups nor any sort of hierarchy attaching to them. Three of the circles are concentric, indicating the fact that they are

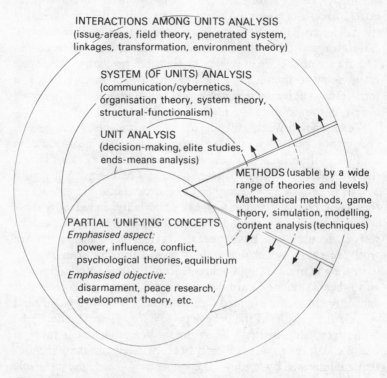

Figure 14 Classification of theories and methods in Western international relations

mutually exclusive, while the fourth (eccentric) circle does not share this condition. Below the rubrics within the 'eccentric' circle may appear theories from any of the concentric circles, and, as a matter of fact, the 'eccentric' circle could be assumed and omitted altogether – as has been done in the case of the two branch solution (Table 1). We retain the eccentric circle to indicate the existence, in however residual or 'dispersed' a state, of theories that have gone without trace from the other circles. The function of the sector is not to indicate a further theoretical group but rather to show methods that may be used by any of the theories within the concentric and eccentric circles (strictly speaking the arms of the sector could be extended from 0° to 360°).

Thus five groups can be distinguished:

1 *Integrative concepts* (the three concentric circles) that focus primarily on one particular feature of international relations, either by virtue of the fact that it is their departure point, or that it is for them of predominant concern. It may be of course that all three will concentrate upon the same feature, in which case each will see it in a different light.
(This same observation applies equally to group 2.)

1.1 *Unit analysis* – the building of theory around the analysis of units. Comprehends for instance decision-making, elite studies, bureaucratic political model.

1.2 *Analysis of units of a system*, to include some of the versions of system theory (those whose methodological starting-point is with the units of a system – others that set out from inter-actions would fall under the next heading). In addition to those versions, there could be included here communication and cybernetics, structural-functionalism and organisation theory.

1.3 *Analysis of interactions among units (of the system)*: Issue-areas, field theory, penetrated system, linkages, transformation, environment theory, etc. (apart from the 'behavioural' system in the sense used above).

2 *Partial (sometimes thought to be general) unifying concepts*. This comprises a rather heterogeneous group of theories which are arrived at either by

2.1 *Emphasising one aspect* (power, influence, conflict, psychological theories, equilibrium).

281

2.2 *Emphasising the objective* for which they are constructed
(disarmament, peace research, development theory, etc.).

In other words they (2.1 and 2.2) have a descriptive if not an
'onomatopoetic' name since they are designated either according to
their purpose or to the feature through which they look at the field or
try to organise it.

3 *Methods* such as simulation, mathematisation, gaming in
combination with a theory from either of the groups 1 or 2 unless
so combined cannot be operated; these are deployed mislead-
ingly under the name of the method used by a particular theory.
This distinction should be borne in mind. It will be appreciated
that, as the movable arms of the sector indicate, these methods
might be extended to cover the entire field.

It is by a process of elimination applied to the above categories that
we reach the following conclusions in regard to the Soviet attitude:

1 In the first place, because of adherence to the main principles of
historical materialism and its strictures concerning the role of the
individual, the principle of collective decision-making, etc., all
'bourgeois' analyses that place too much emphasis on the
individual, on psychological factors and so on are discounted,
and all theories of decision-making, psychological theories,
etc. are dismissed. There is, in other words, no possibility of
their compatibility with 'Marxist-Leninist decision-making
analysis'.
2 Similarly – and paradoxically enough – linkage theories, issue-
areas, penetrated systems, transformation and such theories,
notwithstanding their basic premise of non-separation of
domestic foreign politics (reminiscent of Marx) seem to be held
in even less regard than the first group. As we have pointed out,
Marxism-Leninism safeguards the sovereignty of the state and in
their failure to conform in this area would seem to lie the reasons
for the unacceptability of these concepts. It will be recalled from
our earlier comments on the subject that the Marxist-Leninist
notion of unity of foreign and domestic affairs has a somewhat
specialised meaning: states are classified in accordance with their
internal structure: hence, as a logical extension, whatever the

foreign policies of a capitalist state, however altruistically motivated, a hostile component within them is to be sought and found. By the same token, we have seen that the policies of the countries within the Marxist-Leninist bloc are, by definition, 'correct'.

3 Called into question too is the possibility of devising meaningful theories under the heading of peace research or disarmament, in connection with which, moreover, the notion of equilibrium runs counter to that idea of change that is the essence of the dialectical process. The only exception to this contradiction appears to be the relatively recent peaceful coexistence theory that assumes partial (if temporary) equilibrium.

4 Apart from the utilisation within their own Marxist-Leninist frameworks of virtually every method mentioned (most of them the subject of experimental deployment within other areas of social science), inspiration is found chiefly in the area of system analysis, and it has been pressed into use across a wide range of other Marxist-Leninist social sciences. An official explanation for this wide application is forthcoming: 'In the last century it was Marx who got further than anybody else in the system analysis of society.'[52] Král goes on to define the main characteristics of 'system thinking' and claims Marx's analysis of capitalist society to have been based not only 'on a wide use of empirical material but also it was at least a partial attempt to apply mathematical methods in this sphere'. Král continues: 'unfortunately this was rather forgotten by his [marxist] successors. . . . The aim of Marxist system analysis was above all to express the unevenness of Capitalism with all its consequences for macrosocial development, and in this respect even some non-marxists have regarded his attempt as a serious one. However, dialectic used by Marx in his analysis was not dressed up in the symbolic garb that cybernetics has donned and thus, despite the fact that it contained a great deal of insight into the goal-seeking processes, it did not have the influence upon thinking that it was believed to have had. Outside the field of philosophy it [the dialectic] was proclaimed but not in actuality methodically used. Generally it was only *a fortiori* observed that certain foremost scientists 'spontaneously' used the dialectic. The detailed analysis of goal-seeking processes elaborated by cybernetics and related disciplines offers to Marxist-Leninist

social science a new precise terminology through which, in terms of systems, a great deal of social reality can be explained. The more precise categories enable a deployment of mathematical methods.[53]

A fair enough assessment, supplemented by Král when he quotes H. A. Simon as saying that mathematised social science remains a social science and if it turns out to be a bad one, no mathematics will change it into a good one. Král implies that because Marx's system thinking was inherent in his analysis of capitalist society, modern system terminology can be grafted onto the dialectic with which in its basic nature it is in harmony. Moreover, the dialectic lacks the operationality which system thinking in general, and cybernetics in particular, has brought. The upshot is that there not only can be, but there is in existence, such a thing as marxist system thinking – a fact to which the fast growing library of marxist system literature in the social sciences in general offers testimony. However, although the bibliographies include long lists of 'Western system thinkers',[54] the transplant is accompanied sometimes by strange side-effects, and where, for example, Lamser's sociological theory of communication uses Western sources liberally it does so in so idiosyncratic a manner that they bear only a remote resemblance to their Western originals.

While interest in system theories appears to be general in the Marxist-Leninist world, not all Marxist-Leninists agree on the order of (Marxism-Leninism-system theory) priority. Král, for instance, postulates that the system approach is an advance on the dialectic, the latter 'not dressed up to the symbolic form that cybernetics has', whereas the Russians Lektorsky and Sadovsky suggest apropos of Bertalanffy's general system theory that 'as far as the development of methodological principles of system analysis is concerned, the works of Bertalanffy contain in a primitive form what had been formulated precisely and analysed in detail [sic] by the classical writers of dialectical materialism 50–75 years ago'.[55] Lektorsky and Sadovsky try to argue that the classical works of dialectical materialism have a profound significance for the investigation of methodological principles of systems: 'Written long before Bertalanffy's the works of K. Marx (*Capital, Critique of Political Economy*, and others) of F. Engels (*Anti-Dühring, Dialectics of Nature*) and of V. I. Lenin (*Materialism and Empiriocriticism, Philosophical Notebooks*) contain very rich material on the methodology of system research.'[56]

Admittedly Král refers to cybernetics, and Lektorsky and Sadovsky to Bertalanffy's general system theory but here as elsewhere the problem boils down to the question of interpretation. Does Marx's theory comprise a system theory more perfect than all those produced in the West so far, or did he merely anticipate (like so many other thinkers before him) some concepts that are now being re-emphasised?

We will bear these questions in mind in the next chapter and turn now to the second part of our 'debate'.

The Western dismissal of Soviet theories

While the Soviet Marxist-Leninists dismiss most of Western international relations on philosophical grounds, they are themselves on the receiving end of even more casual disregard by Western workers in the same theoretical field. Because of the serious implications in the 1970s of an offhand disregard more appropriate to, and even justifiable in, the stalinist era the situation warrants our attention.

Practice intervened and the disappointments and growing practical requirements which the body of marxism did not meet have succeeded where the armies of Western critics and revisionists totally failed.[57] Against a background of costly mistakes on the international scene and of stalinist terror and brutality that marked the internal advance, marxist ideology came to be increasingly seen as a social instrument for the achievement of both internal and external goals; and any construction that sees in the process of its continuous updating a process of ideological erosion would be a misreading of the situation. The time has gone when the Russian primary concern with social science had to do merely with enhancing their power and prestige. Now, very clearly, the quest is for information, and assistance of whatever provenance is sought to increase the effectiveness of their conduct. The dismissal of Soviet ideology – regrettably the predominant Western attitude – is quite clearly based on two grounds which though often confused should be viewed and dealt with separately. The first can be summed up briefly: that Soviet international relations writing does not constitute a 'theory', and second, the argument that (regardless of whether the non-'theory'

285

argument is tenable or not) maintains that Soviet thinking on the subject fails to inform in any appreciable way Soviet conduct of foreign affairs. Very clearly the implications of the second argument are the more far-reaching since they bring into question – and seek to repudiate – the usefulness of ideologies in general for the under-standing of world politics; a serious extension of the first position which implies no more than that Soviet writing, while failing to pass the (Western) 'theory' test, may still be capable of influencing foreign behaviour.

When we look more closely at the first (Western) argument the preliminary problem we encounter harks back to a difficulty we have already met[58] regarding the lack of a consensus in the West as to what in fact constitutes a theory. Therefore, the reasons for the dismissal of Soviet thinking on the grounds of 'non-theory' will themselves vary widely, depending on the standpoint of the critic concerned and in this case it is likely that they would rest their cases on definitions of theory other than that we have already offered: 'an integrated set of statements about phenomena under observation' – theory, in other words, as serving some or all of the following four purposes:[59]

1 Taxonomic: or the provision of taxonomies (that is, classifying data by their arrangement on the basis of some stipulated quality that they share so that data of a similar kind may likewise be arranged and compared).
2 Explanatory: to define (a) variables into which data may be organised (b) relationships between variables with some degree of precision.
3 Predictive: that is capable of anticipating with some degree of probability (relative, or absolute).
4 Controlling the occurrence of predicted events.

We will use Kenneth Waltz's seven-step procedure for testing theory as we have defined it, and that procedure may be referred to as a guide to the discussion that follows in the next pages. Without entering into too great detail the Waltz procedure is as follows:[60]

1 State the theory being tested.
2 Infer hypotheses from it.
3 Subject the hypotheses to experimental or observational tests.
4 In taking steps two and three, use the definition of terms as these

are found in the theory undergoing test.
5 Eliminate or control for perturbing variables not included in the theory.
6 Devise a number of distinct and rigorous tests.
7 If a test is not passed, ask whether the theory breaks down completely, needs repair and restatement, or requires a narrowing of the scope of its explanatory claims.

With Waltz's procedure in mind we believe we can say with some degree of assurance that, particularly in its reconstructed version, Soviet theory is relatively simply stated, it incorporates relatively few basic elements and through them claims to be able to explain the most important international political events. The theory offers explanations and, unlike most theories of the Western social sciences, claims a predictive capacity. Again unlike most Western theories where the propensity is for theoretical debate – without its translation into practice – the Soviets claim for theirs an actual controlling capability. The first problem in regard to testing the Soviet theory is whether the definition of terms and the relationships of variables are given with enough clarity and logic.

The first observation that comes to mind is the serious obstacle to testing offered first of all by unsatisfactory definitions of a large number of concepts (class above all) and by the unfortunate inclusion within the facts of mere values masquerading as fact. Of course this blurring of distinguishing features (which marxists themselves regard as a positive advantage) is the criticism levelled against marxism generally by non-marxists. The Western analysts credit themselves with having solved the problem by constructing such dichotomies as 'order versus justice', 'idealism versus realism', etc., a process that often indicates no more than their awareness of the need to distinguish, and a simple enough recognition that conveys a sense of 'objectivity' and freedom from the influence of values. We have already stressed the fact that the ill-defined concept of communism when stated as 'communism is the future of mankind' represents merely a value pronouncement. As such it is neither verifiable nor falsifiable, and yet just how important a concept communism is to the whole intellectual (and political) structure we have already tried to show. In the process, acting as devil's advocate, we tried to show also that to the believer, communism, as the future of mankind, can be distilled from the dialectical understanding of the objectively given march of history. The discovery in all previous societies of dialectical relationships between two classes and the progression from one to the other is taken to indicate (scientifically) the 'inevitability' of communism – an understanding that renders the entire intellectual system teleological. Thus the Soviets believe that Marx's *explanation* of past societies and the identification of the five basic successive modes of production gives them a licence to predict and, with help from the same dialectical laws, to proceed to the next step: communist society. According to some Western writers the serious error here lies in the admixture of elements of explanation and prediction – a criticism that we have already remarked apropos of the Soviet concept of communism. Always providing we accept that Soviet explanations *are* explanations then we see that the Soviet argument for communism is also based on just such an 'explanation' as it relates to human nature – a nature which is perceived as collectivist and only capable therefore of full realisation within a communist society. We repeat that at every step such 'explanations' offer grounds for serious criticism, and indeed this latter in regard to human nature is vigorously contested by many in the West.

One doesn't read far into Soviet theory without coming across frequent reference to 'dialectics', and in fact dialectics (which is also the Soviet methodology) is according to no less an expert than Lenin the very essence of marxist teaching. By dialectics marxism stands or falls. Exposition of a similar concept by *inter alia* Chinese philosophy predates Marx by a thousand years and the attractiveness to the human mind of the dialectical type of conceptualisation is beyond question. At the same time we should draw attention to the fact that in the Soviet version the concept of dialectics (and with it the so-called dialectical laws) leaves a great deal unsaid. In the first place there is no definition of 'contradictory', and as a consequence, virtually any three phenomena, providing only that they are dissimilar, may be classed as 'thesis', 'anti-thesis' and 'synthesis' and be presented as proof of virtually anything, including the dialectical march of history. The strength is obvious: shrouded in vagueness as the concept is, comprehending everything, excluding nothing, its conclusions are virtually irrefutable. To say that something is 'dialectically related' may therefore mean no more than that the writer is otherwise at a loss as to how to explain the relationship – or at best is indulging in tautology.

The direct application of dialectical analysis to world politics leads the Soviet theorist to the identification of two socio-economic systems, and to describing their relations as antagonistic, hostile. These systems are regarded as the offspring of the two major classes and through them (by way of the institution of nation-state) the major class conflict progresses towards its final unravelling. The emergence of the two systems is certainly a reality, but the question as to whether their class derivation is indeed an explanation of their nature goes unresolved.

With the exception of a lengthy definition of class by Lenin[61] marxism is traditionally vague on the notion and so the question of the influence of class on the origin of the systems is particularly apposite. No social scientist would doubt that class is an important agent in the historical process, but to argue that classes share common trans-national interests – however dimly aware of them they may be – is a very different matter. The argument seems to run counter to the available evidence, and particularly to that which has become available since the Second World War. In any case the proletariat in that argument is credited with only one such interest, and should it claim another or different interest then it is to be put down to false consciousness and to its inability to comprehend objective reality. So often does the argument refer to this mystical 'objective reality' that critics have speculated belief in the platonic world of shadows, beyond reality – beyond the range of empirical evidence. It may be appreciated that we find it difficult to accept the explanation of the existence of the two blocs in class terms alone where the very notion of systems derives from another Soviet axiom, namely the assumption of the unity of domestic and foreign policy. It is from this assumption that there comes the idea that the internal structure of the state determines its foreign policy, from which point it is only a short step to the theoretical apprehension of these informal socio-economic systems. In the further assumption of antagonistic relations between the systems the possibility of genuine co-operative relationships is discounted as something of an aberration, although it would seem to be one that throws doubt on the severity of the postulated antagonisms. It might also be noted that although the partially overlapping triangles of the Soviet theoretical model bear an undeniable resemblance to the contemporary environment, the model is not a description of the world but rather an attempt at an *explanation* of the origin, rationale, and basic relations between its constituent parts.

We need look no further than the socialist system itself to under-stand that the present reality diverges very sharply from the theor-etical ground plan. As a matter of fact, Soviet theorising in regard both to the condition of that system and to that of the Third World serves to draw attention to the inadequacies of the Marxist-Leninist scheme for the analysis of both areas. The strongest argument against Soviet notions of proletarian internationalism are provided by the Sino-Soviet split. Not only do these two giants standing against one another provide evidence in the clearest terms of their inability to override their respective 'national interests' but they also demonstrate the unsuitability of marxism for its deployment by 'state' units. Nor, contrary to marxist predictions then or now, is universal harmony and proletarian understanding necessarily consequent upon the absence of private property – a fact that became clear as soon as the Soviet Union ceased to be 'alone' and was joined in the socialist system after the Second World War by a group of 'people's democracies'. Then the principle of proletarian internationalism was pressed ruthlessly into service as an instrument for transforming what had been a subservience of parties into a system of state vassalage. It proved a formidable instrument in the hands of cynical and ruthless leaders, and notwithstanding Tito's expulsion (that only served to underline Stalin's intentions) the 'system' remained united as long as Stalin lived. As soon as the process of destalinisation was initiated the doctrine of 'separate roads' to socialism emerged whose hazards as well as its threshold position on the edge of an abyss were immediately recognised. Steps in this perceived retrograde sequence were: 1 'separate roads' that merged hazily into 2 'national deviations', to be followed by 3 modern revisionism, and 4 'bourgeois demo-cracy', culminating in 5 'the restoration of capitalism'. Yet the doctrine of 'separate roads' meant no more than the assertion of proletarian or communist nationalisms regardless of proletarian internationalism.[62]

At what point on that scale the Soviet Union would intervene was unpredictable, and varied in specific circumstances. Thus the situation was different in the cases of Rumania, Hungary, Poland, and Czechoslovakia, and only China and Albania contrived an effective and protracted disengagement. Ever since the death of Stalin, disagreements have multiplied which can be illustrated by the fact that there have been no further attempts at international communist organisation in the style of the first and second Internationals, of the

Comintern, or indeed even of regular international communist gatherings. The reason for the lack of encouragement to such organisation has been explained by the Soviet wish to disguise the condition of disunity (a condition evidenced by such developments as the Sino-Soviet rift, the Czechoslovak invasion, etc.). In other words, given free rein an international dialogue would damage rather than revitalise the communist cause. Nor could such international gatherings be expected to reach clear-cut judgments on specific issues by submitting these to the guidelines of marxist doctrine. The central ideological positions of the two major protagonists (China and the Soviet Union) in the long drawn-out conflict are *both* compatible with leninist thought. While China would be prepared to postpone her own (and Soviet) condition of developed affluence in favour of an international development, the Soviet Union still argues along stalinist lines that the communist cause is best served by strong example. The nationalism of both sides can hardly be dissimulated since they both present the argument that 'what is good for me is also good for the international workers' movement'. In like manner the conflicting positions of both sides on the notion of peaceful coexistence may be found compatible with the doctrine. Interesting enough in this context is that although China is against the idea of peaceful coexistence – which she alleges constitutes a revolutionary betrayal – she in fact exercises more restraint than the Soviet Union in the matter of initiating conflict situations. To make up for her power inadequacies China is most anxious to have the support of the Third World – but the Soviet Union is still *de facto* leader of the international workers' movement (and in this connection the Soviet theories do carry a certain conviction) and is tactically united with the Third World. Indeed if this were not so a Western preponderance could well be on the cards. At the same time it should be noted that Soviet 'leadership' of the Third World is at best tenuous, a state of affairs attributable to somewhat myopic marxist thinking in terms of two, and two only, ideologies – socialist and capitalist. As a consequence of this dichotomised approach, in order to number the Third World among her friends she has been obliged to perform some extraordinary ideological manoeuvres and in order to set to rest Third World ideological sensitivities has rung the changes on such concepts as 'national democracy', 'revolutionary democracy', etc., and, as we are frequently told, has brought herself to reaching accommodation with regimes engaged in diligent persecution of local communist parties. The Third

World, as Western sources have intimated, has been one of the most dismal 'testing grounds' for Soviet theory.

Similarly challenging to the Soviet theory has increasingly been the attitude of communist parties of Spain, Italy and France, mainly, referred to as Eurocommunism. Rejecting the Soviet model of development as a general model applicable also to themselves, explicitly rejecting the Soviet version of proletarian internationalism that implies an inherent Soviet hegemony, accepting pluralism of political and social forces and acknowledging Western democratic basic rights and political freedoms, and incorporating them into their own model, these parties (in addition to the PRC) make a mockery of the Soviet wishful thinking of 'world camp of socialism' and 'revolutionary forces'. Soviet theory, as in other instances, has so far been unable and unwilling to undertake a thorough and realistic appraisal of Eurocommunism. As in the case of the PRC, Eurocommunism has been regarded as a passing element and essentially a result of the swelling of these large parties with petty-bourgeois membership which necessarily brings petty-bourgeois elements – and nationalism above all. While incapable of making a break with Eurocommunism (the ideological consequences throughout the East European part of the 'world socialist system' and foreign policy considerations being far too serious to contemplate) the Soviet Union maintains a typical attitude: keeping all her options open for as long as possible and consistently evading decisions on matters of principle.[63]

We arrive now at our second argument concerning the actual influences on the Soviet thinking with regard to her foreign affairs. There is probably nothing in Soviet and East European international behaviour that could not be understood along power political lines alone but it has to be remembered that for Marxist-Leninists it is not a question of theory *or* power: for them that theory is most truly marxist which contributes most to the acquisition and maintenance of power and 'national interests'; ideology, in other words, is neither an apology nor a disguise for power politics. Marxism-Leninist ideology is all about power politics. It is here, as Brezhnev has observed, to assist the 'world socialist society to become stronger today than yesterday and tomorrow more than today' because the ultimate ideological goals are 'inseparable from the struggle against imperialism, for the winning of political power by the working class in alliance with all the other contingents of working people, for socialism'. It is of course true to say that wherever there is conflict between the ideology and a particular foreign policy direction it is the foreign policy orientation that prevails, and the ideology adjusted to correspond. But in such circumstances the major premises and goals of the ideology remain intact, and what starts out as an *a posteriori* justification may well become an *a priori* guideline. In these terms one can forget the need to redefine the state in Third World countries,[64] what remains unchanged is the fact that the Third World is regarded as one of the fields over which the terminal battle of capitalism and socialism is being fought. Thus while we would admit the probable truth of the contention that there is not one event that cannot be explained in terms of simple power politics, we would qualify the admission with the condition: in the short run, and in isolation.

Marxism-Leninism does not prescribe any particular course of action for any particular situation; indeed, as we have indicated, the Sino-Soviet split is illustrative of a situation in which the positions adopted and the actions taken, opposed and contradicting each other though they in themselves are, may well be compatible with Marxist-Leninist ideology. But since this is also the case with other ideologies and belief systems it is difficult to see why for this reason alone only the Soviet ideology should be rejected. The point is, however, that it is only by keeping Soviet ideological motivation in mind that their conduct of international affairs over a period of time can be understood. In other words, the ideology supplies the *end*, to the achievement of which all communist actions are explicitly directed. Here then is the first point we would like to make: briefly, that a careful study and understanding of Soviet ideology is a necessary precondition to an over-all understanding of their conduct of foreign affairs.

Our second point derives from the first even though its validity may be perhaps less readily apparent. Apart from setting the goal, the ideology, in the Soviet case, does provide a distinct set of methods, and produces quite discernible characteristics in Soviet behaviour that clearly derive from their acting in accord with an ideological image which they have very clearly in mind. Among such influences there is, first of all, that of dialectic. No matter how poorly defined or lacking in theoretical integrity the concept might be, a commitment to it leads quite clearly to a different, unmistakably distinct approach. It explains, for example, a Soviet preoccupation with change that places it beyond the simple terms of revolutionary versus *status quo* power only. For it seems that the Soviets want not only change for its own sake but, in the last analysis, international affairs appear to assume for them the characteristics of a struggle for survival. From this there results a frame of mind that is not conducive to the resolution of conflict and leads to a contemptuous disregard for that stability so cherished by their Western counterparts. Stability for marxism has always had a negative value.

It is in this light that Soviet international legal attitudes should be understood and with them their reluctance to be bound by political arrangements, since all international legal commitments are, so to speak, seen as staging posts 'along the way'. For the Westerner the conduct of international relations is something of a game and certainly not, as it is for the Soviets, a series of high intensity encounters terminable only by the *major internal transformation of one of the protagonists*. That terminal solution, and that one alone can be permanent – and satisfactory. A direct marxist influence (particularly in Lenin's version) on the outcome is to be found in the Soviet 'art' (as they themselves call it) of the utilisation of capitalist contradictions. These contradictions are their best allies, and by them they refer not only to those to be found at state or national level but to any set of group tensions providing their differences can be channelled to anti-capitalist action. The diligence with which they seek such contradictions, and the expertise accumulated in their exploitation, has particular relevance to the contemporary situation where under cover of the deployment of the peaceful coexistence strategy the other areas of smouldering animosity can be sought out and fanned. Another equally useful concern is the preoccupation with the domestic dynamics of societies which, associated with a full awareness of national economic processes as a source of internationally significant problems, is a potent deployment indeed. It is often more realistic a conflict source than that which purveys national interest and the like. Another awareness that flows from the dialectic is that of universal interconnections. Again a factor that sets them apart from Western theorists, it manifests itself in a readiness to relate events widely dispersed in time and space to other countries or to the world as a whole. Thus conflict situations, instead of being perceived in isolation, are seen as links in an orderly process moving to a fore-ordained conclusion. In contrast to the Western perceptual frame-work, the Marxist-Leninist ideological prism through which the Soviet policy-makers view the world reflects little of chance or accident, nor do the goals of Soviet politics that are brought sharply into focus bear any resemblance to Western *status quo* (or *status quo ante*, i.e. with elimination of communist power centres, etc.) objectives. If the areas of distinction we have tried to draw are still too vague we would refer for further argument to Aspaturian's contention (and endorsement of the above views) that in so far as the Marxist-Leninist intention is to forge a new universal consensus the struggle is not only one over power but exhibits features that are reminiscent of the wars of religion. For Soviet objectives transcend simple territorial expansion, self-defence, or the redistribution of power: they seek nothing less than the total annihilation of the capitalist-imperialist system and of the residual pro-capitalist order that depends upon it – all of it to be replaced by a new universal ideo-social system modelled on itself.[65] For evidence of these statements one need only consider the fundamental social and economic transformation that is taking place *wherever* the Soviet regime has come to power. If the premises we have sought to establish are denied then that fact makes no sense.

As a matter of fact it can already be argued that there no longer exists a simple diplomatic order because, whether recognised or not, there has already taken place a rupture in the diplomatic consensus. Aspaturian actually describes the new era of peaceful coexistence as a non-consensus diplomacy that is accepted more or less in the absence of any alternative, and it may already be too late to recharge the Soviet formula (peaceful coexistence) with content acceptable to the West.

A rejoinder

The reader will have noticed that we tested the Eastern and Western theories against those criteria that each finds wanting in the other. Accordingly, we looked at Western theories from the viewpoint of their alleged philosophical/methodological shortcomings and at Soviet theory from that of the question as to whether it constitutes a theory at all. Because of the explicitly ideological nature of the Soviet theory, we queried its actual role in the policy-making process. It may of course be argued that the criteria could be exchanged, with Western theories assessed from their degree of being 'theoretical' and 'ideological', and the actual role they play in the understanding/ conduct of world politics. But this would probably involve us in a second volume in which philosophical questions regarding the feasibility of theory making in the field would be bound to obtrude – an area which we prefer not to broach.

We may instead summarise the advantages that we perceive the West may derive from a continuation of that debate that was, hopefully, begun. In the first place we would recognise the over-all invigorating effect that derives from the simple exposure of one's values to a totally different intellectual value system. And if we take 'ideological' in the Mannheim sense – in which all ideas about political phenomena are by definition relative – then we believe such exposure to make for an increased awareness of the ideological nature of international theory in the West *en bloc*; a fact that has from time to time been so vehemently denied. If that is agreed then perhaps the word 'ideological' in its present Western sense could be dropped, and thus that Soviet theory could be treated on a par with that of the West. As Rapoport said, an ideology, like the axiomatic foundation of a deductive system, is visible only against the background of its negation.[66] That it is indeed most useful to question the axioms, nobody would deny – and by undertaking a comparison with Soviet Marxism-Leninism we hope to have brought some readers to the realisation that Western international relations theory does (however unwittingly) consist of a great many such axioms. It has, however, the 'ideological' advantage – unlike its Eastern counterparts – of being able to examine them and subject them to strict tests.

As to the actual attitude to be adopted towards Soviet Marxist-Leninist theories and the question as to whether they deserve to be read at all, we feel that it is imperative that they should. Particularly since he is regarded as a sovietologist and his position perhaps therefore not so familiar to the group of international relations theorists, we feel justified in quoting Professor Aspaturian in this connection:[67]

Soviet ideology is not simply a conglomeration of abstract norms, but an ideology cemented to state power, providing a framework for the execution of Soviet foreign policy. Consequently, whether it is, in fact, superior or inferior to the array of analytical devices contrived by Western professors is almost totally irrelevant, unless, of course, they eventually enjoy the same relationship to state power as does Marxism-Leninism. The pertinent question is not: 'is Marxism-Leninism a science?', which has diverted attention from the real issue, but: 'how effective is it in providing Soviet leaders with a map of international reality, enabling them to see their way through the complicated and bewildering maze of events to their objectives, as compared with the effectiveness of the maps of reality implicitly or explicitly employed by their Western counterparts?' Furthermore, in assessing the past forty years, have the expectations of the Soviet Union in world affairs, based upon the insights gained from their ideological prism, been more or less accurately fulfilled than those of their enemies?

And, again with Aspaturian, we can argue that in this context it does not matter at all whether dialectic is scientific or nonsensical: 'Historical inevitability and scientifically derived laws of social change may indeed be intellectual residues of the nineteenth century, little more than sophisticated and sophistic nonsense, but this misses the main point. Reality, in whatever dimension, is plastic, and while its transformations may not be predetermined, the implacable voluntarism of fanatics determined to realise what they say is inevitable, may render the difference between "objective inevitability" and the "self-fulfilling prophecy" irrelevant; for no matter how successfully they may be distinguished in the intellectual processes of the mind, the distinctions in terms of consequences in the world of reality are essentially nil. A purely intellectual critique of marxism inevitably wins the theoretical battle and loses the war on the plains of reality.'[68]

Soviet theory, however oversimplified and overweening, does provide some valuable insights into world politics; but of perhaps greater importance to us is the insight that it affords into Soviet *intentions* in regard to that same world. The need to contrive 'predictive theories' concerning someone's actions seems not to be so urgent when his intentions are actually laid bare before us. And particularly when the nation supplying the information is one of the pacesetters of world politics in our time is it difficult to justify inattention. As we have already indicated, these theories are in our opinion no more 'outlandish' or less relevant to a study of world politics than are their counterparts in the West.

CHAPTER 6

International relations theory in the West: Marx and Lenin

> Neither Marx, Lenin nor Stalin made any systematic contribution to international theory. . . .
>
> Martin Wight

By addressing ourselves now to the last question set forth in the preface we have, so to speak, come full circle. Why is it, we asked, that in international theory, unlike other branches of social science in the West, Marx has not become even 'a silent partner'? Or, in a paper entitled 'Why is there no International Theory', was such a towering figure in Western international relations theory as Martin Wight correct in saying of marxism that it 'is a theory of domestic society, a political theory . . . [which] has been tugged and cut about to cover a much wider range of political circumstances than it was designed for. . . . [and that] Neither Marx, Lenin nor Stalin made any systematic contribution to international theory; Lenin's Imperialism comes nearest to such a thing, and this has little to say about International Politics'.[1] Certainly with Wight's later observation regarding the conspicuous absence of a book on Marx's international theory and the difficulty one encounters when recommending reading from original source material on the subject, we find no fault. Indeed we have stressed the point ourselves,[2] and have drawn the reader's attention to the inherent difficulty of reconstructing Marx's theories. In the path of reconstruction where too many 'turning points' present themselves, the choice of one or the other can easily lead by way of divergent interpretations to conclusions that are sometimes sharply at variance. Of the 'paths' that have opened up to bemuse his successors there is, for example, that which is entered by taking into consideration only Marx's 'mature' works – while a no less enticing way has been found by placing the emphasis on the works of the younger

298

Marx. And then there is the route taken by those who treat Engels as Marx's equal and, far from drawing a clear line of demarcation between the two men, have gone so far as to allow Engels to speak for Marx. By way of these, among many other decisions, a more or less coherent – if perhaps unmarxian – picture is arrived at. But even with the turning point negotiated such questions as that of interpretation remained to torment generations of Marx's 'heirs'. There are ambiguities and vaguenesses that reach at times the point of evanescence to further plague the legatees – and yet at the same time have helped to explain the formidable staying power of marxism. In all of this we feel we should emphasise an awareness of the fact that our treatment of Marx would not necessarily be approved by all marxologists – let alone Marxist-Leninists – and yet it is our conviction that the treatment accorded in these pages to Marx and Engels has no more and no less 'legitimacy' than has any other; it might be agreed, that is to say, as long as we do not cross the theoretical Styx that lies between the political theory and the Marxist-Leninist theology of the twentieth century. Our objective has not been to show that Marxist-Leninist theory of international relations is or is not marxist, since in order to decide that particular issue, what Marx said may not really be a touchstone.

In setting that particular argument aside, together with our reiterated conclusion that the connection between Marx and marxism – and particularly between Marx and Soviet Marxism-Leninism – is merely inferential, we might also point out that there is, for that matter, no one 'marxism'. In this connection the distinction between marxologist, marxist, Marxist-Leninist and sovietologist is not always as clear as it should be, and we might be forgiven for troubling the reader once again at this point with a brief note as to the role played by each. Where the marxologist would wish to reconstruct the ideas of Marx (often without Engels) and seek to understand them in relation to Marx himself and his times, the marxist would end up with the ideas of Marx in relation to his own times, his own problems, and his own goals. The inclusion of the ideas of Engels and of Lenin (and dependent on his selection of which ideas) would make of our marxist either a Marxist-Leninist or a partisan of some other marxist denomination. As to the sovietologists, most would focus on the Marxist-Leninists alone and would study them against the background of their time and in relation to their problems and goals. The picture drawn by each of these groups brings with it obvious advantages and equally apparent limitations, and for that reason we have opted in these pages for an eclectic approach. The adoption of a kind of multifocality that has involved our frequent transference from one kind of approach to another has in fact introduced a self-imposed constraint in our writing. Such a structurally acrobatic exercise becomes of course manageable only when the anabasis of a particular concept such as that of international relations is followed, an exercise that has here involved the addition of yet one more focus. The focus – indeed the focal point of departure – has been Western international theory which, as the reader is aware, provided the parallel reference for our look at marxism (in its generic sense).

However divergent in all respects the perspectives of marxologists, marxists, and sovietologists might be they still shared some common interest in Marx and could be regarded as at least 'cousins', however distantly removed. The theory of international relations in the West, however, apart from a shared interest in international relations, is quite 'unrelated' to Marx. And this is precisely the point in our explorations that we have now reached. The conclusions we may reach through an investigation of Marx and the West in apposition we expect to be quite different from those of Chapters 3 and 4. There, it will be recalled, we attempted an investigation into the relationship between the contemporary Marxist-Leninist treatment of international relations and that of Marx, Engels and Lenin. Without attempting to make generalisations about other aspects of their works, the unavoidable conclusion reached in regard to international relations was that the ideas of Marx, Engels and Lenin have, in Marxism-Leninism, undergone such a transformation as to have become almost unrecognisable. This transformation, as we contended, was not a departure necessitated only by changes taking place in the world at large, but was of a basic epistemological and methodological nature. By way of contrast, we turn to the argument often put forward in the West[3] that the best of marxism has been assimilated into Western culture. This would mean in other words that the self-proclaimed marxists, and particularly those of the Soviet Marxist-Leninist persuasion who have abused the name and the bequest of Marx for political purposes, permitted the West to cull his major ideas and to benefit from the intellectual heritage more than they did themselves. In these circumstances we might well ask who, if anybody at all, can claim to be the real 'marxists'.

We have nothing to say to Lichtheim's 'to some extent we are all marxists now',[4] since without specifying the variety of 'marxism' such statements tend to have little meaning. Nor have we any desire to build another pedestal to Marx and his 'everlasting wisdom': there are many of those already and together they seriously obstruct one's vision. What we are driving at instead is to try to draw attention to the fact that knowledge is to a great extent cumulative and additive, and to remind ourselves (with C. W. Mills) that Marx is as much part of the Western mind as is for example Italian Renaissance architecture.[5] Indeed more so; Marx quite simply cannot be said to 'belong' to the East in any property-like sense. And as far as the East goes, all that can be said is that by erecting a monument to Marx, by building a political system in his name – and in the process amplifying some of his ideas to deafening pitch – they have succeeded in muting or silencing the remainder. This proprietorial attitude has at the same time turned many Western thinkers away from Marx fearful of the 'marxist' stigma. Aron's statement that the West has utilised the best of Marx so that there is nothing more left[6] may be true of sociology, economics, etc. where every last piece of his thinking has been carefully plotted but, as we pointed out at the beginning, it is not the case with international theory – at least not in terms of explicit acknowledgment or conscious adoption. We have already mentioned Martin Wight's interpretation as representative of an attitude that sees no international relations theory in Marx; and other Western writers have declared that marxism provides a firm basis for explaining international relations to only 'a very limited degree; for the original Marxian doctrine viewed international affairs from an exclusively national and economic angle. . . . Marx's theory of international relations was derivative and not original'.[7]

While nobody would disagree with the statement that Marx's doctrines were not original and were very often eclectic, this latter view would appear wrongly to absolutise the importance of nation-state as a prism through which international relations are to be viewed and studied. Given the acceptance of such emphasis it follows that Marx had indeed no theory of *international relations* (except of a very derivative nature) but, by the same token, the contention that he did not have a theory of *world politics* would be difficult to sustain. Indeed it would be true to say that part of the relatively recent Western debate hinged precisely on this point where, although the state was admitted to exhibit 'an impressive degree of staying power',[8] it has in terms of theoretical analysis become in the past something of a Procrustean

301

bed. Thus, in this respect, it is as if Western international relations theorists themselves spring to the defence of Marx's theory. They have defended as a most legitimate approach (and indeed one that has become rather fashionable) a disregard or contemptuous attitude towards the institution of state and inter-state relations with which students of Marx's theory will be familiar. To such an extent are the two approaches in sympathy that the difference between the Western and Soviet Marxist-Leninist attitude to *state* might be said to reflect the difference between the Western trend 'from international relations to world politics' and, as the propensity of the Soviet Marxist-Leninist East, 'from world politics to international relations'.

With regard to Marx and the field of international relations in the West the explanation for the re-emergence of Marx's ideas a hundred years after his time may be quite simply that through a quite ordinary grounding in, for example, sociology, and those branches of social science that have always regarded Marx as their progenitor, certain of the concepts that Marx used might also have been caused to 'surface' in international relations theory. It is also possible of course that new theories might have derived directly from the inspiration of some marxian concept – although in this connection Snyder's warning is pertinent; 'the danger lies in the illusion that by labelling something we have either said something significant about it or explained it'.[9] (As a matter of interest, Marx some time before Snyder had spoken of 'innate human casuistry to seek to change things by changing their names!')[10] Yet even in terms of such a 'rediscovery', it will be appreciated that a new theory even if built on old conceptual foundations may be helpful in providing fresh insights. And, finally – and not least important in considering reasons for Marx's 'surfacing' – it has to be recognised that human ingenuity did not end with Marx; a great many of the social phenomena that inspired certain of his theoretical propositions still persist, and the rediscovery of his concepts by thinkers of a later generation should occasion little surprise. However, one cannot help but wonder whether a familiarity with some of the fundamentals of marxism should not be a compulsory part of the education of every (including Western) political theorist.

It would be very difficult, and also pointless, to try to determine in cases of the 're-emergence' to which we refer the categories into which each newly surfaced idea should be placed. Similarly, to determine a precise location of each of Marx's own concepts continual reference would have to be made to Hegel, Kant, Feuerbach, Ricardo, Smith, Saint-Simon, Robert Owen – to mention only the more immediate sources of many of his ideas. After all, it is true that Marx's contribution to knowledge has consisted, not in the 'invention', but rather in the crossing of ideas of the most varied provenance. In the process, the connections made, and the constellations into which he placed other peoples' ideas, were novel. He made no secret of it; nor do the Marxist-Leninists.

It may be that in a reading of Chapter 2 some resemblance between Marx and present theories of international relations has already suggested itself. Our purpose here is to establish the nature of such 'resemblances': to determine what and who they involve. Of the many ways in which this might be established perhaps the most straight-forward, and certainly the shortest, would seem to be to dissect Marx's ideas, identify certain salient points of his 'theory of international relations' and try to relate these to Western international theories. Obviously the purpose of this exercise is not to establish any 'coefficient' of what makes or does not make a theory 'marxist' since, in our opinion, to arrive at that particular awareness only a con-sideration of all of these points in their totality – and indeed as Marx presented them – would suffice. (An exercise that would most prob-ably at the same time lead to the 'sifting' of many 'marxist' theories.) Before proceeding to a brief survey of Western theory in search of such ideas as are in some way reminiscent of Marx, we offer the proviso that none of the discoverable features alone would be 'sufficient' to warrant a theory's being designated as 'marxist' if its premises did not at the same time rest securely on his philosophical system (including the teleological belief in the advent of communist society). In our opinion the moral charge of his theories is an essential characteristic. And, should his philosophy itself be challenged, we would justify the following survey on grounds of the not infrequently advanced proposition that it is entirely possible that an apparently erroneous philosophy should furnish ideas from which may derive valid empirical theories.

Almost traditionally economic determinism or emphasis on economic factors is taken as synonymous with Marx's analysis, and although there are quite a number of 'economic theories of inter-national relations',[11] reductionism to this one factor, as we have said, would be a gross oversimplification. It would be more correct to say that marxian analysis in analysing past and contemporary societies stresses the importance of economic factors; or even that marxian analysis is that analysis which seeks to relate the attitudes of different social groups to socio-economic conditions. In other words, it is the framework in which Marx places the economic factors rather than the stress on these factors alone that can be regarded as his contribution. For emphasis on that one factor one might go to John Stuart Mill, Adam Smith, Richard Cobden and others before Marx.

Given this framework one can agree with the frequent assertion that Marx's analysis was a pioneer structural-functional analysis, and in fact Claude Lévi-Strauss admitted that he borrowed the notion of structure (among others) from Marx and Engels.[12] When defining his concept of 'structural' in his *Critique of Political Economy* (Notes on the method of political economy), Marx made it clear that he was aware of

1 The primacy of the totality over its constituent parts.
2 The primacy of the relations over the terms related to them.
3 The idea that the structure is not apparent but hidden behind the phenomenon.

It is a structural-functional model, but the obverse side of that model, for, as Bottomore remarks, the basic forces of both (that of Marx and of structural-functionalism 'proper') are exactly opposite: where functionalism emphasises harmony, Marx stresses social conflict, where functionalism directs attention to the stability and persistence of social form, Marx is radically historical in his outlook and emphasises the changing structure of society. Marx stresses the divergences of interests and values within each society, and the role of force in maintaining over a longer or shorter period of time a given social order. Marx stresses the conflict within society, the structural changes which result from such conflict, and its role in the underlying scheme of the progressive development of mankind.[13] As we have said above, Marx's law of civilisation expressly claims 'no antagonism, no progress'.[14]

Thus Marx's theory is a grand theory of conflict, and in this respect it converges with some Western conflict theories of international relations. An immediate point of divergence, however, with many such theories is the highly beneficial effect that Marx attributes to conflict. So beneficial in fact, and so central to his theories that, as we have remarked, the predicted disappearance of 'conflict' in communist society was described by many of Marx's critics as a basic inconsistency in his thinking. In fact, it has already been suggested (apropos of the present East European and Soviet regimes) that in view of the existence of a system of public ownership and state planning, society in those areas, far from being seen to have advanced to the superior stage of socialism, might strictly speaking be described in Marx's own terms as displaying characteristics of the 'Asiatic mode of production'.[15] In this context we should here point out that, in contrast to the attitude adopted in the East towards the idea of *progressive* development, it has been repeatedly rejected in the West on the grounds of its belonging to past centuries. It has also been pointed out that the conception of evolution as 'progress' is likewise ambivalent, not to say suspect, where all progress is defined in terms of goals (that is in teleological terms). We have discussed the implications in detail, in an earlier chapter, of marxism's erasure of the Divine Purpose and substitution of the 'laws of historical development' – laws which very often amount to no more than an extrapolation of selected historical trends in combination with an aspiration for a just social order. Or, as Rapoport argues, the 'inevitability' of the just order is based on the premise of the co-operative nature of modern production, implying that an organised society will survive as a matrix and that 'appropriation of the fruits of labour' is the only important form of exploitation.[16]

Marx and Engels themselves had problems with their approach to conflict. Engels suggested that the necessary contradiction[17] would be transferred on to the epistemological level – a shift that would, of course, blatantly contradict Marx's basic premise and emphasis on 'conflict' as an inherent characteristic of both matter and thought. Not of one without the other, for, as we have already shown above, Marx and Engels's concept of dialectic implied that it was a general science of connections and of development of *both* material and spiritual worlds.

In this universality of applicability of a concept there is a 'meeting point' (acknowledged by Bertalanffy[18]) between dialectical materialism and general systems approach (an influence that Easton for example acknowledges to have been brought to bear on his theories by the general systems of Bertalanffy). The general systems approach is based on observation of similarities in analytical schemes evolving from widely separate fields of knowledge, from biology to social science; a principle that is characteristic too of the dialectic. The basic difference between the two, that is between general systems approach and the dialectic, is that most general systems approaches would accord the concept of a system only an epistemological or analytical foundation, where, by way of contrast, Marx insisted that there are connections, contradictions, movement inherent in matter and in all the world (hence materialist dialectic). Consequently a marxist would disagree most violently with Singer's formulation that 'a system exists largely in the eye of the beholder'.[19] Curiously enough, Engels 'replies', as it were, to this attitude in his assertion 'without commiting blunders thought can only bring together into a unity those elements of consciousness in which or in whose real prototypes this unity already exists'. 'If I', continues Engels, 'include a shoe brush in the unity of mammals, this does not help it to get mammary glands.'[20] One might of course argue that there could be reasons for adding shoe brushes to mammals other than the wish to convert the brush into a mammal: this, however, is the marxist argument. And that is why marxists would find very objectionable 'eastonian' conceptualising that identifies the 'mechanism' on all levels and then fails to find it on the international level. The answer would invariably have to be – 'wrong conceptualisation'. The marxist 'mechanism' that is assumed to 'operate' everywhere and on all levels is the dialectic – in its most diverse and ambivalent meaning. Marxologues as a rule object to the dialectic's being broken down into separate 'laws' but Marx and Engels did talk about the transformation of quantity into quality (and the process in reverse), the law of the interpenetration of opposites, and the law of the negation of the negation – or development through contradiction. We have mentioned in an earlier chapter the built-in tendency to 'historicism', by which is meant the belief that there is a pattern in history which, once discovered, will enable an interpretation of the past and a prediction of the future. In what precise way the dialectic in a more meaningful twentieth-century garb is to be applied to the analysis of international relations we have not so far been informed by the Marxist-Leninists. However, in other social sciences the 'transplantation' of a kind of cybernetics on to the main dialectical notion has been done (arguably) without affecting radically the integrity of the dialectic core.

Elements of 'dialectical thinking' can be found in Western international theory. Johan Galtung's 'structural theory of aggression',[21] for example, is based on a particular characteristic in the structure of relationships among social entities (be it individuals, groups, or nations): Galtung calls this special relationship rank-disequilibrium, that is, the differential in status experienced in social intercourse. The theory sees a social system as a system of units in interaction and multi-dimensionally stratified according to a number of rank-dimensions. It tries to locate the maximum probability of aggression against other units; aggression ('the driving force in history and the motivational energy' [sic]) being defined as 'drives towards change, even against the will of others'. Disequilibrium, or the 'reservoir of aggression', is a result of stratification which is 'a universal phenomenon': '. . . those who have and those who have not, those who have more and those who have less, find, are given, or are forced into their positions'. Unlike the marxist, however, Galtung at this point calls a halt to the analysis of reasons why this should be the case, why this 'forcing into positions' has to take place. Compare this with, for example, Lenin's well-known definition of a class which describes the phenomenon in a similar way but then goes on to establish *why* it occurred:[22]

> Classes are large groups of people differing from each other by the place they occupy in a historically determined system of social production, by their relation (in most cases fixed and formulated in law) to the means of production, by their role in the social organisation of labour, and, consequently, by the dimensions of the share of social wealth of which they dispose and the mode of acquiring it. Classes are groups of people one of which can appropriate the labour of another owing to the different places they occupy in a definite system of social economy.

Galtung distinguishes between *top dog* and *underdog* positions, and in this respect, admittedly going further than Marx, identifies top dog and underdog positions mixed in the description of different 'groups, individuals or nations' (i.e. combinations TTTTT and UUUUU and all variations which this basic idea allows). Galtung, having assured us that he was inspired by Marx and de Tocqueville alike, goes on to correct both of them: he disagrees with Marx's idea of location of the source of the revolution low down in society, in the proletariat, and with his predictions of the occurrence of revolutions after a period of deteriorating conditions and exploitation. Regardless of the alternatives which Galtung elaborates in great detail, the underlying idea would seem to remain basically the same. Broadly stated, it is that the rank position of a national system will determine what the behaviour of that national system will be in the interaction flows of the international system. 'Economic development is a major issue of our time, for most people on earth probably the major issue', 'economic development *per se* will probably create more, not less rank-disequilibriums' (and hence more drives towards aggression?). These statements seem to devalue Galtung's insistence on classification as underdogs in some respects and top dogs in others. The element of interconnections is also very clearly pronounced: 'the rise of one is the fall of the other' and similar statements remind one of Engels: 'and so inequality is once more transformed into equality: not, however, into the former natural equality . . . but into the higher equality. The oppressors are oppressed. It is the negation of the negation.'[23] Galtung conceives his hierarchical theory to be the foundation upon which a number of other theoretical structures may be built – it is all undoubtedly very illuminating but it would be beyond the scope of this chapter to follow his further arguments. Suffice it to say that, the originality of some of his conclusions notwithstanding, the basic premises are not dissimilar from those of Marx and Engels. Prudently – since there may be no straightforward answers – Galtung, unlike Marx and Engels, does not attempt to go beyond the description of some observed phenomena, and the mechanisms of his 'forces' remain very much unclear – a mere description of appearances of certain dialectical processes, a marxist would say.

What is even more interesting is that McLelland comparing Galtung's 'structural theory of aggression' with Burton's conceptions (the two of them being 'in resonance') comes to the conclusion that Galtung's theory is the 'most fruitful of all the newer system formulations'; 'system components as social change processes' and 'this kind of system formulation has not been seen before in the field. . . . The preoccupation with change within and between social locations and the incompatibilities of society and state are unusual features' [!][24] and it is 'especially noteworthy if for no other reason than that it identifies system components without locking them tightly to state or governmental actors – as is still the most common practice'.[25]

The point of convergence with contemporary Western thinking and the developments presaged by Marx are too numerous and too significant to be ignored. One such, as we have tried to show, being in regard to the phenomenon of state. Marx himself could easily have advised that we 'must not concentrate too heavily on those social entities whose empirical references exist as central actors . . . such entities must not be ignored but they must not be permitted to overshadow those groupings which, at one stage or another in the systems evolution, played an equal or superior role . . . the national state is in the most theoretical formulations, assigned too prominent a role, and that competing entities must be more emphasised than has been customary'.[26] Hence one cannot agree with Singer's statement that the exclusive systemic effort via a focus on the national/international linkage is only very recent, even more recent than system thinking.[27] When, in criticism of linkage concepts and its efforts to bridge domestic and foreign policies, Hanrieder said that apples and pears make a good fruit salad but a bad theory,[28] the obvious rejoinder on behalf of Marx would be to point out that Marx did not think it necessary to see them as apples and pears, and indeed made no distinction between domestic and foreign at all. It might be argued of course that by virtue of the overpowering notion of class his 'system' could be seen as being very much 'sub-system-dominant' (Kaplan) but in any case how many 'linkage' theorists would agree that an *a priori* belittling or contemptuous attitude towards state and inter-state relations is the potentially right frame of mind in which to conduct a search for other 'alternative factors' that play an important role in world politics![29]

In addition to the fragmentary dialectic reminiscent of the writings of Marx and Engels, even the 'interpretation' of Lenin has found its way into the international theory of the West – Lenin, ostensibly so disregarded by Western political theory! Another of Galtung's articles on the subject of the 'structural theory of imperialism',[30] which he himself regards as a direct continuation of his 'structural theory of aggression', could easily have been written by Lenin in exile from the USSR, disappointed with the course of the revolution there and with the world in general. At this point we would draw attention once again to the fact that Lenin, following the practice of Marx and Engels, did not oblige us by spelling out all of his ideas on international relations in one coherent volume, and the fact that these references are strewn indiscriminately across the whole of his work makes the task of identification of his influence so much more difficult. The difficulties inherent in the task also make for a tendency in Western writers to pay less attention than they should, or to fail to make the effort.

A brief glance at Galtung's theory and the question of its relation to Marxism-Leninism will help us to understand the approach of at least one Western theorist to Marx's and Lenin's contribution to Western theory. In fact, Galtung brushes aside the possibility of an overlapping contribution with the remark that his approach is 'not reductionist in the traditional sense pursued in Marxist-Leninist theory, which conceives of imperialism as an economic relationship under private capitalism, motivated by the need for expanding markets and which bases the theory of dominance on a theory of imperialism'. In other words, Galtung sees Marxism-Leninism as reductionist on two counts: on the first count by its preoccupation with economic relations and on the second by the Marxist-Leninist assumption that imperialism and dominance will fall 'like dominoes when the capitalist conditions for economic imperialism no longer obtain'. In regard to the first count we would point out that Galtung himself builds his theory of imperialism on economic relationship. The other forms of imperialism, of which he identifies five, he admits can result as a 'spill over' from that economic imperialism which, judging by the attention he gives to it, would seem to be essential to an understanding of all of the other forms. On the second count, Galtung seems to have in mind the case of the contemporary Marxist-Leninists (who would certainly not describe themselves as imperialists) to whom his reservations would in some sense apply. Galtung is applying Lenin's framework some fifty years after Lenin and we would certainly not argue with the suggestion that there are good grounds for 'developing it' and attempting to make it operational. However, regardless as to what Lenin's thoughts might have been as to the fate of capitalism, the categories that Galtung covers with a new terminology bear a marked similarity to those of Lenin.

Galtung's point of departure is 'the tremendous inequality within and between nations in almost all aspects of human living' (cf. Lenin's unevenness of development) plus (and here we have a departure from Lenin) 'the resistance of this inequality to change'. He postulates the world divided into 'Center and Periphery nations' (cf. Lenin's exploited and exploiting nations), each nation having its own centre and periphery (cf. Lenin's exploited and exploiting classes within the state). The Centre is tantamount to government. (It is as much also in Lenin's framework since the exploiting class is assumed capable of establishing such a relationship to the government that it virtually merges with and becomes part of it.)

Galtung's concern is the 'mechanism underlying this discrepancy, i.e. the discrepancy between the center and the periphery, especially center in Center and periphery in Periphery'. (This is also Lenin's concern although he calls it a dialectical relationship of antagonism and, as developed in his work, it may assume various forms and degrees.) Galtung describes this phenomenon in terms of 'structural violence', inequality being one of its major forms (that is of course a new non-leninist term). Galtung then defines imperialism not in terms of collectivity dominating in the sense of exercising power but as a 'dominance relation between collectivities, particularly between nations; cutting across nations basing itself on a bridgehead which the center in the Center nation establishes in the center of the Periphery nation for the joint benefit of both' (which would be for Lenin a perfectly acceptable definition of the appearance of the same phenomenon). 'Conflict of interest' (Lenin's antagonism) between center and periphery is 'a situation where parties are pursuing incompatible goals'. The perception of the true interest, according to Galtung, takes two forms: 'living condition', or LC (*an sich* consciousness of Lenin) and what 'they explicitly say' before it may become 'false', or undergo distortion by reason of, for example, rationality (Lenin's *für sich* consciousness and/or concept of ideology, false consciousness, etc.). Galtung then proceeds to distinguish between 'conflict of disharmony of interest . . . when the living condition gap between them is increasing' (Lenin's antagonist relationship), and 'harmony of interest, no conflict . . . if the living condition is decreasing down to zero' (a very fair statement of non-antagonist relationship). Galtung, in an attempt to operationalise, introduces the terms 'decreasing' and 'increasing' to avoid 'simplistically' used terms of polar opposites (his classification nevertheless still retains the character of the two opposites), and refers to 'weak and strong harmony' (also conceptually akin to Lenin although called by another name). In his 'more detailed' definition of imperialism, Galtung acknowledges the borrowing from Lenin – an acknowledgment that is in fact the only reference to Lenin, and one that is so formulated as to suggest mainly reference to the Lenin/Engels's concept of workers' aristocracy. 'There is harmony of interest between center in the Center nation and the center in the Periphery nation, there is more disharmony of interest between the Periphery nation than within the Center nations, there is disharmony of interest between the periphery in the Center nation and periphery in the Periphery nation.' All of which brings Galtung to the conclusion that Lenin started out with, and one which Galtung calls a 'basic idea, namely, that there is more disharmony in the Periphery nation than in the Center nation (i.e. more inequality in the Periphery than in the Center').

And now there comes what Galtung describes as the 'essential trick of the game': 'within the Center the two parties may be opposed to each other. But in the total game, the periphery see themselves more as the partners of the periphery in the Periphery – and this is the essential trick of the game'. It has also been the essential trick of Lenin's version of marxism which brought him to the conclusion that the world in general, including international relations, had to be changed. Another 'new' conclusion (explicitly referred to as such) is to the effect that: 'If we presuppose that the center in the Periphery is a smaller proportion of that nation than the center in the Center we can also draw one more implication: there is disharmony of interest between the Center nation as a whole and the Periphery nation as a whole . . . which leads to the belief that Imperialism is merely an international relationship, not a combination of intra- and international relations.' Galtung goes so far as to suggest that international statistics should not be given for national aggregates since this conceals the true nature of relations in the world; it would be much more useful if statistics were to be given for the four groups as they are indicated above, a procedure with which no doubt Lenin himself would wholeheartedly agree. Thus Galtung comes to an 'important methodological conclusion' whereby we should try to study the precise nature of the interaction between the nations or groups of nations, and see whether the nations can be differentiated in terms of centres and peripheries that can relate to each other in the way indicated.

Galtung goes on to identify two mechanisms, five types, and three phases of imperialism – all of them consistent with Lenin's portrayal. The basis of the mechanism is 'vertical interaction as the major source of the inequality of this world' and 'no analysis can be valid without studying the problem of development in a context of vertical interaction'. The reader will recall that Lenin did just that and that Lenin's change to the classical marxian approach which we described as the 'horizontalisation of the class conflict' pre-empts Galtung's complaint. In turning next to the elaboration of the rules of the mechanisms and phases of imperialism, Galtung's discussion is very interesting and offers an unusual insight – which again, however, can be seen basically as a development of Lenin's scheme. Galtung's five types of imperialism, each corresponding to a type of exchange between Centre and Periphery nations are: economic, political, military, communication, and cultural. In this typology the economic is clearly the 'main' type since the others follow suit in many if not all respects. Again, Lenin's concept of social consciousness or ideological superstructure reflecting the 'main', i.e. economic, basis can be seen as encompassing all these types of imperialism since, as we have seen, Lenin accords a very independent existence to all superstructural phenomena so that what Galtung describes as 'spill overs and spin offs' easily fits in.

Galtung claims that his conceptualisation is valid, fully describes the contemporary world and, in the end, offers some strategies whose implementation should deimperialise the world by 'horizontalising' it. It is an interesting conclusion, and perhaps to that extent he is justified in asserting that his theory is not Marxist-Leninist. But for an admission that it is leninist in essence we look in vain.

Galtung's theory has sometimes been described as the 'most clear statement' of the growing, if rather disparate, group of theories of imperialism or structural dependence theories; their orientation neo-marxist, or neo-leninist, or simply radical. Some theorists also associated with dependence are: Baran and Sweezy, Magdoff, Samir Amin, Susan Boddenheimer, Frank Cardoso, Dos Santos, many of whom come from the Third World. Consideration of the orientation of these authors would be beyond the scope of our concern here, but they do in fact tend to be somewhat neglected, and in so far as they come under the heading of sociology of international relations or an explicitly ideological paradigm of international theory – and as such tend not to be included in Western international theories lists – share the fate of marxism in general. Inasmuch, therefore, as one takes Galtung's statement as representative of these groups the link with Lenin would apply – and most of them explicitly acknowledge the debt. We would, however, point out that the acknowledgment does not go so far as to encompass any of the philosophy of classical marxism; they neither share Marx's interest in dialectic as a method, nor do these authors subscribe to the belief in the inevitability of communism. In fact, their theories content themselves with a rather imprecise description of the divisions of the world, as viewed from a particular standpoint – the authors using in the process (in the true marxist tradition?) very vague concepts. Nor do the proponents of this branch of Western theory go out of their way to offer any solution

313

as to how to escape the undesirable pattern of structural dependence. Thus, beyond the centre-periphery dichotomisation reminiscent of Lenin, all that the theorists share with Marx is the conviction that there is a moral crisis in the world, to which, a century after Marx, they add the opinion that it is now global in extent. The inequities that Marx perceived to exist primarily within the domestic context have become global inequities and although such marxian predictions as the absolute immiseration of the proletariat have been disproved at a domestic level by historical development, no such development has given cause to suspect their validity in the global context. From a heuristic standpoint alone, they would contend, marxism is still best equipped to analyse such inequities, even as it is to comprehend the world as a whole.

However, just as much as the Soviet marxist claim to the legacy of Marx has been challenged, so the same claim advanced by this group of Western theorists has similarly come under attack. It has been argued, for example, that inequalities of states, and indeed of groups of states, is a different proposition from that of inequality of classes. And in fact, Lenin's own theory of imperialism has been deemed unmarxist on these grounds, since it turns away from Marx's theory of surplus value and changes the meaning of the concept of exploitation in Marx's sense into a concern for the exploitation of raw materials.[31]

A further criticism levelled at these neo-leninist writers has dealt with the fact that in order to salvage Lenin's thesis the definition of imperialism has had to be so broadened as to comprehend virtually any relation among unequals.[32] (In the context of broadening one cannot refrain from remarking that in order to permit an accommodation between Soviet marxism and the narrowness of Marx's too orthodox concepts, Soviet marxism also has been obliged to engage in a considerable 'liberalisation' of Marx's definitions.) And, finally, it has been argued that Arghiri Emmanuel's theory of unequal exchange – regarded by most structural dependence theorists as a central proposition – offers too tenuous a link to Marx's labour theory of value on which it claims to be based.

The reader will decide which of these 'marxist' elements outlined above is to be deemed attributable to Marx. What does seem to us to be beyond dispute is that Marx, with considerable assistance by Engels and Lenin, laid the solid foundations of a system of thinking which, despite its shortcomings, is still unique in the world today. It is the only system which provides a set of co-ordinates that enables one to locate and to define a thought in any sphere whatsoever. In this closely knit system of thought the singling out of one particular aspect (such as international relations) is practically impossible without repeated reference to the rest of the system: and this to our mind is another main characteristic of Marx's theory of international relations. In terms of structure it would be difficult to point to anything that is 'left out', and for every problem there is a 'marxist' answer – at least at first glance. Lenin's famous doctrine of the reflection of existence in consciousness, for example (a detailed answer from Marx on the subject is missing), says nothing as to how reality is reflected, and insistence on the conclusion that there are differences among perceptions and commitments according to class alignment, or, in Marxist-Leninist terms of reference, whether a theoretician operates from the so-called classless society or whether he is 'armed' with the knowledge of Marxism-Leninism is very difficult to verify, to say the least. The Marxist-Leninist would of course contend that apart from minor errors Marxism-Leninism is right in the long run – a fact which is increasingly confirmed as time goes on. The onset of each global economic depression, every single thrust towards polarisation – including those that take place behind the 'coexistence screen' drawn across the world by a technological (nuclear arms) factòr – makes that ideology the 'conscience of the century', a conscience quite impregnable to attempts to discover flaws on the part of a 'dying' antagonist.

Leaving Marxism-Leninism aside, Marx himself can only be admired for the theoretical structure which, despite numerous 'holes', inconsistencies, and ambivalences, has enabled the construction of Marxism-Leninism to be built upon it. Nor should the West be too reticent in its attitude. Surveying the Western international theory field one is drawn irresistibly to the conclusion that in a sense marxist theories comprehend the elements of the traditionalist-behaviouralist dichotomy; and his philosophy, for what it is worth, contrives to reconcile the two 'dichotomised' sides. Marx's theory of international relations would combine the postulates associated with (at least some) traditionalists – features which, following Golembiewski, we have described as 'conservative'. The human mind is on the way to total knowability is the gist of that philosophical message, and conjures up the possibility of discovering the laws, and general laws which, when discovered, will lead to prediction and the similar control of change in the world that is

315

called for by Marx in his *Theses on Feuerbach*.

These laws, however, do not exclude the possibility of quantification, and as Engels succinctly put it (confirmed by the statement of our previous chapters) 'knowledge of mathematics and natural science is essential'.[33] In this context of bridging there is an echo of Marx in the work of Quincy Wright, one of the great figures in the field of international relations, wherein too the possibility of reconciling the well-known dichotomy is optimistically viewed. And, in any case, when one turns to the behaviouralist position it is with a strong suspicion of their vaunted 'agnosticism' for, when all is said and done, the momentous research seems to betray their hope that a 'mathematical formula' is discoverable which will turn out to be 'the essential trick of the game'. We must ask the reader himself to judge Marx's position in all of this – bearing in mind Marx's belief that social science achieves a perfect state only in combination with mathematics. Was he in fact in important respects a more consistent behaviouralist than many of our contemporaries?

The failure to elaborate the rapport between theory and practice – an area that we have shown also to be sadly neglected in practice (although not in theory) by the Marxist-Leninists – may also be seen as an area of inconsistency on the part of the behaviouralists – and it may be from this very area that their disdain for ideologies stems. Strictly speaking, it is more consistent with the traditionalist attitude to accept the dichotomy and regard it as unbridgeable. Hoffman speaks for the majority of traditionalists when he points out: 'One should not expect an apple tree to produce cherries – one should judge it by the quality of its apples. A man without practical experience as a policy-maker or as an adviser to policy-makers is unlikely to contribute much by usurping a role for which he is unqualified; his best chance of being useful lies precisely in the realms of academic analysis.'[34] If theory is perceived to do no more than produce taxonomies, or at best offer some anaemic explanation of past events, then it is difficult to see much of a link between theory and practice. In line with this argument it might be said also that the outlook of a policy-maker before every decision he be required to make would be bleak indeed. It follows logically that the stronger one's belief in his ability to predict future developments and, further, believes it possible (and desirable) to change that predicted future, then the more he is likely to want his views heard and taken into consideration by the practitioner. The policy-maker who shares that

316

same belief would surely by the same token wish to have his decision guided by the theoretician. As the Eastern source quoted above does not fail to point out, the investment in international affairs research since the Roosevelt administration has been colossal and, coupled with the now established tradition of brains-trusts and think-tanks, is a strong indication that the self-declared and established dichotomy of practitioners and theoreticians in the West is, in the behavioural period in particular, not all that unbridgeable – and perhaps not quite sincere.

It is in this context that Quincy Wright said 'a general theory means a comprehensive, comprehensible, coherent and self-correcting body of knowledge, [capable of] the prediction, the evaluation, and the control [sic] of relations among states and of the condition of the world'.[35] How other than by the establishment of a definite link between theory and practice and by elaborating their relationship can it be hoped that a theory will help to control? The only hope for the West in this direction is in the anticipation that as soon as international relations in the East gains momentum (which, far from being ruled out, may within the Marxist-Leninist framework be reasonably expected) a closer co-ordination of theory and practice in the field of international relations will be given overt recognition. The proclaimed unity of theory and practice was inherited from Marx – and remains, albeit in emasculated form, the East's vantage point in the future.

We return now in conclusion to the continuum introduced in Chapter 1 of this work[36] and to the 'post-behavioural' period. The recognition indicators of the period are supposed to lie in a 'quest for greater relevance rather than for sophistication',[37] 'a better and less pendular balance' between the 'normative theory of the 1920s' and 'preoccupation with empirical-analytical theory of the 1960s' and a 'greater synthesis among those concerns that have been of principal importance in the stages through which the field has passed since its beginnings in the early years of this century'.[38] To take first the behaviouralist co-ordinates and then indicate in which direction a post-behavioural shift may be expected is, in our view, a useful starting-point.

Behavioural theories were more homogeneous in their philosophical epistemological assumptions than those of traditionalists. Where the traditionalists encompassed attitudes near both extremes of our continuum the behaviouralists tended to occupy a closely knit

317

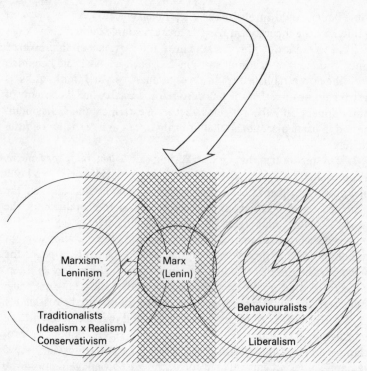

Figure 15 Diagrammatic representation of some of the main arguments of the book

middle of the continuum area with often only an implied (but none the less real) ambition of achieving predictability, if not controllability. That this is so was suggested by their attempts at mathematisation, that conveyed beyond any shadow of doubt their belief in a high level of regularity and repeatability of events.

Traditionalists – and a great deal of international relations may still be described as traditional – are much more difficult to sum up, and in seeking to identify them we find a variety of attitudes widely dispersed across the continuum. It is worthy indeed of careful note that the same basic attitudes may be found in both camps, with divergent theories resting upon them – some of which may be in closer harmony with the other camp than strike a sympathetic chord in their own.

The post-behavioural period is taken by us to mean a major shift of

318

the behavioural group to the centre so as to embrace, more explicitly, ideologies and values which in the immediate past attracted only their contempt. If Dougherty, Easton and others are right in their 'predictions' in regard to the post-behavioural decade, the shift of attitude would take place basically within the methodology – an area which will command greater attention than has so far been the case. In the quest for greater relevance, an exploration of past theories and establishment of links between them is likely to distinguish this from a behavioural period whose interpreters seemed so lost in the wonder of the behavioural 'revolution' that they tended to reject out of hand all that was traditional or old. Perhaps then, the post-behaviouralist era in international relations will mean an end to *ignoratio elenchi*. As Eugene Kamenka said in another context – the penalty imposed on the amateur is that he relives, unwittingly, the history of the subject and presents as his own discoveries, views that have already been held, elaborated, and discussed.[39] And who knows, perhaps it will be discovered, as we have argued here, that Marx has indeed a place in the history of international theory such as that which he already occupies in other branches of social science in the West.

Conclusion

So many different theories have been broached and comparisons attempted in the foregoing chapters that now it is difficult to discover in conclusion something that might apply to all of the sides of our multiple juxtaposition. We might begin with a little ground clearing and suggest that the time has come to draw aside the veil of quasi-religious mysticism through which in some aspect or other all of the sides have been viewed. Falling into the 'mystical' category for example are such pronouncements as: 'those who contracted marxism in their youth are apparently beyond cure' or, since both sides feel obliged to indulge in such wise saws: 'he, who has not his own firm Marxist-Leninist standpoint, cannot enter a critical dialogue with a non-marxist since he could not dialectically overcome it'. Into this aphoristic bracket also might fit such airy prognostications as that the communist movement (and its 'theories') will not survive the 'patient erosion of history', or its equally blithe counterpart that marxism (used as a generic term), in whatever garb, represents the unsurpassable truth of our time. There is in fact as little evidence of this 'patient erosion' of history as there is of the 'unsurpassable truthfulness' of marxism. And yet (let it be noted in this latter regard), there remains to be answered Wesson's question (in a sub-title to his book) – why the continuing success of a failed theory? In this irrational age, it would seem that things do take place without apparent 'reason' and de George may well be right in comparing the importance of Soviet marxism today with that of Christianity in the Middle Ages. With the mysticism removed, however, it becomes clear that what has in fact happened is that the split that divides the world politically and at depth is carried over into the world of the intellect as well. The two sides of the schism have conducted their respective 'monologues' for so long that their intellectual languages have grown apart.

320

The reader will appreciate the appropriateness of Lenin's words as a summary of the Soviet treatment of classical marxism – little though the writer himself could have suspected that these might one day apply also to himself: 'After their death [i.e. the death of great revolutionaries], attempts are made to convert them into harmless icons, to canonize them, so to say, and to hallow their *names* to a certain extent for the "consolation" of the oppressed classes and with the object of the duping of the latter, while at the same time robbing the revolutionary theory of its *substance*, blunting its revolutionary edge and vulgarizing it.'[1]

It will also be appreciated, however, that although it is true to say that the linkage between Marx and Soviet theories, though ideologically coterminous, has loosened[2] to the point where it very nearly becomes inferential, there are nevertheless more important less generally accepted conclusions to be derived from the comparisons we have attempted, the most important of all of these is the realisation that regardless of the marxian content and its questionable usages, and irrespective also of whether the end-product turns out to be more stalinist than marxist, the Soviets have developed a comprehensive, and, over a period of time, consistent picture of the world that embodies an image of the future – and on a particular interpretation of which they confidently base their actions. In this context the reader will have observed our avoidance of the term 'theory' – a term whose choice seems to us unnecessarily pretentious and exclusivist in describing what is after all 'the study of international relations'. Although perhaps lacking the intellectual merits of theories propounded by Western academics, Soviet theories, boosting as they do the reach of marxism – and supplying the basis for the only world-wide political movement of our time – are certainly as authoritative. In terms of sheer weight and importance, and irrespective of the remodelling that marxism has undergone across that global spectrum, about one-third of the world's population will be instructed at school in the Soviet theory, and its global projection, through the medium of this new intellectual language.

There is a further consideration. Conscious as we are of the fact that we are presently in an era of *détente*, we should, consistent with many Western interpretations of that word, be prepared to do all in our power to avoid a return to the spirit of cold war – an only too easy regression when we become aware that the Soviet definition of *détente* and peaceful coexistence is very nearly identical word for word with the earlier Western definition of cold war! But the stakes after all are considerable and even if it seems at this stage that only small benefit might accrue from a perusal of Soviet theory there are other compelling reasons for undertaking the task. To take peaceful coexistence as one example of a concept in whose interpretation there exist vast differences between West and East we observe that in the West peaceful coexistence and *détente*, taken literally, conjure up a highly desirable state of affairs. In the Soviet version, however (a version for which the Soviets claim already an increasing Western acceptance, commensurate with its retreat), the concept means that 'no holds are barred, at least on the Soviet side, other than that of attempts to shoot each other down'.[3] Peaceful coexistence thus defined becomes no longer a contest but a struggle with no limit placed either on the objectives or on the means by which they are to be achieved. Our quotation here is deliberately taken from the work of a Western sovietologist in the earnest belief that if sufficient attention were to be paid to the findings of such analysts international theory could only stand to gain. We would certainly be less inclined to treat the Soviet Union as though it were a carbon copy of the United States, and, in seeing her thus as merely another superpower, overlook her total ideological commitment. Is there then a lesson to be learnt in this respect from the Soviet approach? Might Western international theory in the process of taking into account other possible conceptual as well as semantic dimensions become less optimistic – and might it by the same token come closer to reality?

The determination with which the Soviet Union sets about rationalising marxism is testimony enough, it might be agreed, to the seriousness of their beliefs. Add to that the fact that in the process of developing a 'theory' they will go even to the 'enemy' for inspiration and are willing to incorporate – more even than from the marxian source itself – ready-made theories and methods, and we have some idea of the strength of their convictions. We have attempted to speculate in these pages as to the nature of the theoretical inspiration that is sought from the West – our hypothesis aided by the fact that in this area too, as in so many other branches of social science, concepts that have been virtually superseded in the West are subject to 'rediscovery' by the East. In fact their approach would seem to be a 'strict' systems or cybernetic one with a hallowed place reserved within it for the institution of state (!). These would appear to be the parameters that the Marxist-Leninist ideology, at least for the moment, allows. In addition to this eclecticism of approach we discern one further area from which the West might learn from its Eastern counterpart: whatever the constraints imposed by the ideology on the concept of the unity of theory and practice, we may be sure that as soon as international theory in the East has something to offer it will be translated into Soviet practice and utilised to capacity.

It has been a commonly held belief here in the West that East and West resemble each other more than either would want to admit. The reader will be aware that we do not agree and that as far as this notion is concerned the central argument of our thesis on international relations runs directly counter. In any case it is beyond the scope of this work (and probably beyond the scope of any work) to speculate as to whether the 'dialectic of hostility and imitation' continues until, as the Western argument has it, the two systems finally coincide (dialectically speaking, until the one negates the other) or whether indeed there will be no ultimate resolution but merely a situation of unending interaction. But whichever outcome eventuates, there remains in both camps a wide field for the exploration of the theory of international relations. To impose constraints upon it, whether these emanate from theory (as in the West) or from practice (as in the East) would indeed be a pity. As it stands now, so little resemblance is there in the conceptualisation of both sides to their shared global environment that, if the question were put to them, only the broadest of definitions of the field – such as we used in the Preface to this work – would be found acceptable in both. There we took the concern of international relations to be 'the study of the nature, conduct of, influences upon relations among individuals or groups operating in a particular arena . . . and the nature of, and the change factors affecting, the interactions among them'.[4] If either side were to begin to particularise any one of the terms contained therein the area of shared agreement would vanish into thin air.

As to Marx's thought and theory of international relations in the West, one can only express regret that this book could not have been written some twenty years ago: that, although in some respects it appears too soon, in other respects it comes too late. Assuming that one had then an insight as to the way in which Western theory of international relations was to develop, it could then have been argued that Marx 'has shown us the way'. Writing today, however, one can only point out that, contrary to what many international theorists may assume, Marx's ideas on international relations were not altogether sterile and, albeit in a very rudimentary way, many of the new 'discoveries' were advocated by Marx, Engels and Lenin long before international theory as a discipline was thought of. Indeed, even as the Marxist-Leninist increasingly accepts the concept of state and international relations, we may see in Western international theory an inclination towards the contemptuous 'marxian' disregard for the state. This tendency, already in evidence, may become more pronounced – until like Marx we may one day discard the words international relations and state! Despite the shortcomings and the imprecision of Marx's analysis there may yet prove to be a good deal yet for us to 'discover'. Apart from anything else, we would do well to consider the 'mind-seducing' comprehensiveness by which, without resorting to a preoccupation with one concept at the expense of the rest, that unusual breadth of perspective is achieved. Perhaps too we might bear in mind for possible emulation Marx's concern for penetrating surface appearances.

Theories of international relations, as we have suggested, are indeed like planes flying at different altitudes and in different directions[5] and in a way it cannot be otherwise. There is, in the first place, the vastness of the subject and its inherent difficulties from which they all, marxists and non-marxists alike, have suffered, and which have frustrated the assaults of both sides even at the level of explanation. There is indeed an endless multiplicity of directions to be followed, any one of which may lead on to the 'key variables' – of which equally a great number and variety can be perceived. The choice of 'altitude' brings with it also many extra-international theory considerations from which, symptomatic of the non-uniform human mind in an ideologically non-uniform world, a variety of attitudes may derive.

And so the attempt 'to connect those earth-bound theories with the sky-bound theories' called for by Stanley Hoffman (voicing the opinion and earnest wish of many other theorists) may not be all that imperative in any form other than on a methodological 'radar screen'. As long as the co-ordinates of all major theories are at least approximately established and their itinerary recorded, then, from the point of view of the over-all field, the launching of new ones will not only be that much more meaningful but also we may hope that wasteful duplications and even undesirable collisions can be avoided. That this procedure should be more difficult than the simple random launching of a theory in the dark and hoping for the best goes without saying, and international theory is still faced with a considerable way to travel in terms of such orientation.

One of the aims of this book has been to draw attention to the group of marxist theories whose omission from the record (or master 'flight plan') of international theory has left an undesirable and unnecessary gap – a gap that has been with us for too long.

Chronology of the main works of Marx and Engels

Marx alone	Marx and Engels	Engels alone
1818 (Birth of Marx)		1820 (Birth of Engels)
		1838–41 Articles for *Telegraph für Deutschland* and *Morgenblätter für gebildete Leser*
1841 Doctorate from Jena University ('Differenz der democritischen und epikureischen Natur-philosophie')		1841–2 *Rheinische Zeitung*
1843 *On the Jewish Question, Introduction to a Criticism of Hegel's Philosophy of Law*		
1844 edits the *Deutsch-Französische Jahrbücher*	1844 Marx and Engels	1844–5 *Condition of the Working Class in England*
1844 *Economic and Philoso-phic Manuscripts* (published 1932)	1844–5 *Holy Family* (Engels only minor part)	
1845 *Theses on Feuerbach*	1845–6 *The German Ideology* (published 1938)	

Marx alone	Marx and Engels	Engels alone
1847 *The Poverty of Philosophy*	1848 *Manifesto of the Communist Party* *Neue Rheinische Zeitung*	
1850 *The Class Struggles in France 1848–50*	1850 6 numbers of *Neue Rheinische Zeitung-Politisch-ökonomische Revue*	1851 until 1862 Under Marx's name articles for *New York Daily Tribune*, some appeared as a book *Revolution and Counter Revolution in Germany*
1852 *The Eighteenth Brumaire of Louis Bonaparte*		
1856 *Secret Diplomatic History of the 18th Century*		
1857–8 *Grundrisse der Kritik der politischen Ökonomie*		
		1857 Articles on military topics to the *New America Cyclopedia*
1859 *A Contribution to the Critique of Political Economy*		1859 Pamphlet *Po und Rhein*
1860 *Herr Vogt*		1860 Articles on military matters to the *Volunteer Journal for Lancashire and Cheshire*

Marx alone	Marx and Engels	Engels alone
1865 *Value, Price and Profit*		
1867 onwards *Das Kapital* (with Engels's co-operation)		1870–1 Articles to *Pall Mall Gazette* on the Franco- Prussian War
1871 *The Civil War in France*		
1875 *Critique of the Gotha Programme* (published in 1891)		1882 *Anti-Dühring* published
1833 (Death of Marx)		1884 *The Origin of the Family, Private Property and the State*
	1885 *Capital*, Volume II (ed. by Engels)	
		1888 *Ludwig Feuerbach and the end of Classical German Philosophy*
		1892 Three chapters from *Anti-Dühring* published as *Socialism, Utopian and Scientific*
	1894 *Capital*, Volume III (ed. by Engels)	
		1895 (Death of Engels)
		1925 Essays on natural philosophy and *Anti- Dühring* published under the title *Dialectics of Nature*

Karl Marx: *A Contribution to the Critique of Political Economy*, London, Lawrence & Wishart, 1971

[An extract from the Preface, pp. 20–3]

My inquiry led me to the conclusion that neither legal relations nor political forms could be comprehended whether by themselves or on the basis of a so-called general development of the human mind, but that on the contrary they originate in the material conditions of life, the totality of which Hegel, following the example of English and French thinkers of the eighteenth century, embraces within the term 'civil society'; that the anatomy of this civil society, however, has to be sought in political economy. The study of this, which I began in Paris, I continued in Brussels, where I moved owing to an expulsion order issued by M. Guizot. The general conclusion at which I arrived and which, once reached, became the guiding principle of my studies can be summarised as follows.

In the social production of their existence, men inevitably enter into definite relations, which are independent of their will, namely relations of production appropriate to a given stage in the development of their material forces of production. The totality of these relations of production constitutes the economic structure of society, the real foundation, on which arises a legal and political superstructure and to which correspond definite forms of social consciousness. The mode of production of material life conditions the general process of social, political and intellectual life. It is not the consciousness of men that determines their existence, but their social existence that determines their consciousness. At a certain stage of development, the material productive forces of society come into conflict with the existing relations of production or – this merely expresses the same thing in legal terms – with the property relations within the framework of which they have operated hitherto. From forms of development of the productive forces these relations turn into fetters. Then begins an era of social revolution. The changes in the economic foundation lead sooner or later to the transformation of the whole immense superstructure. In studying such transformations it is always necessary to distinguish between the material transformation of the economic conditions of production, which can be determined with the precision of natural science, and the legal, political, religious, artistic or philosophic – in short, ideological forms in which men become conscious of this conflict and fight it out. Just as one does not judge an individual by what he thinks about himself, so one cannot judge such a period of transformation by its consciousness, but, on the contrary, this consciousness must be explained from the contradictions of material life, from the conflict existing between the social forces of production and the relations of production. No social order is ever destroyed before all the productive forces for which it is sufficient have been developed, and new superior relations of production never replace older ones before the material conditions for their existence have matured within the framework of the old society. Mankind thus inevitably sets itself only such tasks as it is able to solve, since closer examination will always show that the problem itself arises only when the material conditions for its solution are already present or at least in the course of formation. In broad outline, the Asiatic, ancient, feudal and modern bourgeois modes of production may be designated as epochs marking progress in the economic development of society. The bourgeois mode of production is the last antagonistic form of the social process of production – antagonistic not in the sense of individual antagonism but of an antagonism that emanates from the individuals' social conditions of existence – but the productive forces developing within bourgeois society create also the material conditions for a solution of this antagonism. The prehistory of human society accordingly closes with this social information. . . .

Karl Marx
London, January 1859

Chronology of the main works of Lenin (1870–1924)

(Speeches, reports, theses, drafts of resolutions, etc., are not included)

1893
New economic developments in peasant life. On the so-called market question.

1894
What the 'friends of the people' are and how they fight the social democrats. The economic content of narodism and the criticism of it in Mr Struve's book.

1895
Explanation of the law of fines imposed on factory workers. What are our ministers thinking about? Friedrich Engels (Obituary).

1896
Draft and explanation of a programme for the social-democratic party.

1897
A characterisation of economic romanticism. The new factory law. The tasks of the Russian social-democrats. The handicraft census of 1894–5 in Perm Gubernia and general problems of handicraft industry. The heritage we renounce.

1898
On the question of our factory statistics. A note on the question of the market theory.

1899
The development of capitalism in Russia (written 1896–9). Capitalism in agriculture. A protest by Russian social democrats. A

draft programme of our Party. A retrograde trend in Russian social-democracy. On strikes.

1900

How the *Spark* was nearly extinguished. The urgent tasks of our movement.

1901

The workers' party and the peasantry. Where to begin. The persecutors of the Zemstvo and the Hannibals of liberalism. The agrarian question and the 'critics of Marx'. A talk with defenders of economism. Anarchism and socialism.

1902

What is to be done? The agrarian programme of Russian social democracy. Revolutionary adventurism. A letter to a comrade on our organisational tasks.

1903

To the rural poor. An era of reforms. The tasks of the revolutionary youth. The national question in our programme.

1905

The autocracy and the proletariat. Time to call a halt! The fall of Port Arthur. Working class and bourgeois democracy. The beginning of the revolution in Russia. Revolutionary days. A brief outline of the split in the R.S.D.L.P. European capital and the autocracy. Social-democracy and the provisional revolutionary government. The revolutionary-democratic dictatorship of the proletariat and peasantry. To the Jewish workers. Two tactics of social-democracy in the democratic revolution. Revolution teaches. While the proletariat is doing the fighting, the bourgeoisie is stealing towards power. The lessons of the Moscow events. The reorganisation of the Party. Our tasks and the Soviet of workers' deputies. Socialism and religion.

1906

The Russian Revolution and the tasks of the proletariat. Revisions of the agrarian programme of the workers' party. The victory of the Cadets and the tasks of the workers' party. The dissolution of the

Duma and the tasks of the proletariat. The political crisis and the
bankruptcy of opportunist tactics. Guerrilla warfare. The social-
democrats and electoral agreements. The crisis of Menshevism.

1907
The social-democrats and the Duma elections. The platform of the
revolutionary social democracy. The strength and weakness of the
Russian Revolution. Against boycott. The agrarian programme of
social-democracy in the first revolution, 1905–7. Preface to the
Russian translation of Marx's letter to Dr Kugelmann (on the
question of a nation-wide revolution). The International Socialist
Congress in Stuttgart.

1908
Materialism and Empiriocriticism. The agrarian question in Russia
towards the close of the nineteenth century. Leo Tolstoy as the mirror
of the Russian Revolution. Inflammable material in world politics.
Marxism and revisionism.

1909
The aim of the proletarian struggle in our revolution. Classes and
parties in their attitude to religion and the Church. The liquidation of
liquidationism. The fraction of supporters of Otzovism and God-
building.

1910
Notes of a publicist. The lessons of the revolution. The historical
meaning of the inter-Party struggle in Russia. The capitalist system of
modern agriculture.

1911
Leo Tolstoy and his epoch. In memory of the commune. The social
structure of state power. The new faction of conciliators, or the
virtuous. A Liberal Labour Party Manifesto.

1912
Liberalism and democracy. Revolutionary *élan*. Political parties in
Russia. The illegal party and legal work. The 'vexed questions' of our
Party.

1913
Critical remarks on the national question. The three sources and three component parts of marxism.

1914
The right of nations to self-determination. The bourgeois intelligentsia's methods of struggle against the worker. The tasks of revolutionary social-democracy in the European war. Karl Marx. On the national pride of the Great Russians. Philosophical notebooks (written 1914–16 and published in 1929–30).

1915
The collapse of the second International. Socialism and war. New data on the laws governing the development of capitalism in agriculture. Imperialism, the highest stage of capitalism.

1916
The caricature of marxism, i.e. 'economic imperialism'. The military programme of the proletarian revolution. The tasks of the Zimmerwald Left in the social-democratic party of Switzerland. The socialist revolution and the right of nations to self-determination. The discussion on self-determination summed-up.

1917
The bourgeois and socialist pacifism. A letter from afar. A letter about the tactics. The tasks of the proletariat in our revolution. Materials for the revision of the Party programme. Three crises. Constitutional illusions. Lessons of the revolution. On compromises. The impending catastrophe and how to combat it. The state and revolution. The tasks of the revolution. The crisis has matured. Revision of the Party programme.

1918
The revolutionary phase. The immediate tasks of the Soviet government. 'Left-wing' childishness and the petty-bourgeois mentality. The proletarian revolution and the renegade Kautsky.

1919
The third International and its place in history. The constituent assembly elections and the dictatorship of the proletariat.

1920
'Left-wing' communism – an infantile disorder. Our foreign and domestic position and the tasks of the Party.

1921
The Party crisis. Once again on the trade unions, the current situation and the mistakes of Trotsky and Bukharin. The tax in kind.

1922
A few words about N. Y. Fedoseyev.

1923
Pages from a diary. On co-operation. How we should reorganise the workers' and peasants' inspection. Better fewer, but better.

Constitution (Fundamental Law) of the Union of Soviet Socialist Republics

Adopted at the Seventh (Special) Session of the Supreme Soviet of the USSR, Ninth Convention, on 7 October 1977. Moscow, Novosti Press Agency Publishing House, 1977, pp. 31–3.

Chapter 4
Foreign Policy

Article 28   The USSR steadfastly pursues a Leninist policy of peace and stands for strengthening of the security of nations and broad international co-operation.

The foreign policy of the USSR is aimed at ensuring international conditions favourable for building communism in the USSR, safeguarding the state interests of the Soviet Union, consolidating the positions of world socialism, supporting the struggle of peoples for national liberation and social progress, preventing wars of aggression, achieving universal and complete disarmament, and consistently implementing the principle of the peaceful coexistence of states with different social systems.

In the USSR war propaganda is banned.

Article 29   The USSR's relations with other states are based on observance of the following principles: sovereign equality; mutual renunciation of the use or threat of force; inviolability of frontiers; territorial integrity of states; peaceful settlement of disputes; non-intervention in internal affairs; respect for human rights and fundamental freedoms; the equal rights of peoples and their right to decide their own destiny; co-operation among states; and fulfilment in good faith of obligations arising from the generally recognised principles and rules of international law, and from the international treaties signed by the USSR.

Article 30 The USSR, as part of the world system of socialism and of the socialist community, promotes and strengthens friendship, co-operation, and comradely mutual assistance with other socialist countries on the basis of the principle of socialist internationalism, and takes an active part in socialist economic integration and the socialist international division of labour.

Selective chronology

(Excluding works of Marx, Engels and Lenin, see Appendices 1 and 3)

1812–15	Napoleonic wars.
1818	Birth of Karl Marx.
1820	Birth of Friedrich Engels.
1830	Great Reform Bill.
1835	Marx at Bonn University, Zollverein in Germany.
1836	Marx at Berlin University.
1837	Queen Victoria begins her reign.
1838	Chartism.
1842	First meeting of Marx and Engels.
1848	Year of revolutions.
1852	Beginning of Second Empire in France.
1853–6	Crimean War.
1855	Darwin's *Origin of Species*; Mill's *On Liberty*.
1861	American Civil War begins; serfdom abolished in Russia.
1862	Bismarck becomes Minister-President in Germany.
1864	First International.
1866	Austro-Prussian War.
1869	Social Democratic Party founded in Germany.
1870	Lenin born; Franco-Prussian War.
1871	Paris Commune.
1872	Hague Congress of International.
1875	Gotha Congress.
1877	Russo–Turkish War.
1878	Anti-socialist laws in Germany.
1883	Death of Marx; foundation of Osvobozhdenie Truda (Liberation of Labour) in Geneva, predecessor of the Russian Social Democratic Labour Party.
1889	Engels takes part in founding of the second International.
1893	Engels honorary president of Zurich Congress of the International.
1895	Death of Engels.
1898	First Congress of All Russian Social Democratic Labour Party (Minsk).
1903	Second Congress of Russian Social Democratic Labour Party (London); split between Bolsheviks and Mensheviks.
1905	First Russian Revolution; Soviets formed.
1906	First Russian Constitution: transformation from absolutist auto-

cratic regime to constitutional system.

1914	Russia's entry into the First World War.
1917	Great October socialist revolution in Russia.
1918	Wilson's Fourteen Points; Soviets sign Treaty of Brest-Litovsk; Allied troop intervention in Russia; Civil War with White opposition.
1919	First Congress of the Communist International (Comintern) in Moscow; short-lived Hungarian and Bavarian Soviet Republics.
1920	Treaty of Versailles; Allies lift blockade of Russia; League of Nations established; Second Congress of the Comintern.
1921	Kronstadt Revolt; New Economic Policy; Anglo-Russian Trade Agreement; 10th Party Congress, Resolution on Party Unity – Intra-Party dissent outlawed; Third Congress of Comintern; failure of German communist attempt at revolution.
1922	Genoa Conference; Treaty of Rapallo (Germany and Russia); formal establishment of the USSR.
1923	Another German communist revolutionary failure.
1924	Lenin dies; Stalin, Zinoviev and Kamenev ally to isolate Trotsky; Mongolia becomes the second socialist state after the USSR; USSR recognised by the UK and other European countries.
1925	Diplomatic relations entered with Japan; Soviet-German trade agreement; possibility of the establishment of socialism in one country officially endorsed in the USSR.
1927	Germany admitted to the League of Nations; UK breaks off diplomatic relations with the USSR; Stalin eliminates residual opposition to his rule; Trotsky expelled from the CPSU.
1928	Kellogg-Briand Pact: Russia invited later by 'Litvinov Protocol' to join; Sixth Congress of Comintern adopts 'Left' tactics; collectivisation of agriculture in the USSR; first Five-Year Plan begins forced industrialisation of Russia.
1929	UK restores diplomatic relations with the USSR.
1930	Litvinov formally replaces Chicherin as Foreign Minister.
1932	USSR resumes diplomatic relations with China after conflict over Chinese-Eastern Railway (1929); USSR-France non-aggression pact.
1933	Hitler becomes German Chancellor; Japan leaves League of Nations; Germany leaves League of Nations; US and USSR establish diplomatic relations.
1934	USSR enters League of Nations.
1935	USSR signs treaties of mutual assistance, if attacked, with France and Czechoslovakia; Seventeenth Congress of the Comintern adopts 'Popular Front' tactics; Ethiopia invaded by Italy.
1936	Civil War in Spain; Soviet intervention; Germany and Japan sign 'Anti-Comintern Pact' which Italy joins a year later; USSR adopts new 'socialist' constitution.
1937	Chinese mainland invaded by Japan.

1937–8	Year of Stalin's great purges.
1938	German 'Anschluss' with Austria; Munich crisis.
1939	18th Congress of the CPSU; Molotov replaces Litvinov as Foreign Minister; German occupation of Bohemia and Moravia; end of Spanish Civil War; Nazi-Soviet Treaty of Non-Aggression; Germany invades Poland; UK and France declare war on Germany; Soviet troops invade Eastern Poland and Finland; USSR expelled from the League of Nations following invasion of Finland.
1940	Germany invades Denmark, Norway, Belgium, Luxembourg, the Netherlands and France; Lithuania, Estonia, Latvia become Soviet republics following Soviet military occupation; Molotov's meeting with Hitler in Berlin.
1941	Soviet-Japanese neutrality pact; German invasion of Russia; UK and USSR assistance pact; Battle of Moscow; Japanese attack on Pearl Harbor.
1942	Molotov signs twenty-year treaty of alliance with the US; in Washington, Molotov requests opening of second front.
1943	Russian victory at Stalingrad; Comintern dissolved; unconditional surrender of Italy; Moscow conference of Foreign Ministers of USSR, USA and UK; Teheran Conference between Roosevelt, Churchill and Stalin.
1944	Allies open second front in Europe; Churchill in Moscow: proposes 'spheres of influence'.
1945	Soviet Army liberates Warsaw; Yalta Conference between Roosevelt, Churchill and Stalin; death of Roosevelt, Truman succeeds; foundation of UNO in San Francisco; Soviets capture Berlin; unconditional surrender of Germany; first atomic bomb exploded; Truman, Stalin, Churchill (Attlee) meet at Potsdam; formal surrender of Japan.
1946	Churchill in Fulton, Missouri speech recognises the existence of an 'iron curtain'.
1947	Truman doctrine; Marshall Plan of reconstruction in Europe; Cominform founded.
1948	Communist revolution (*coup d'état*) in Czechoslovakia – last democratic regime in East Europe; Yugoslavian CP expelled from the Cominform; Soviets mount the first Berlin Blockade.
1949	Council of Economic Mutual Aid (Comecon or CMEA) founded; NATO established; Soviets lift Berlin blockade; USA announces first Soviet atomic bomb test; People's Republic of China (PRC) established; German Democratic Republic established.
1950	Chinese-Soviet thirty-year treaty of friendship, alliance and mutual assistance; North Korea attacks South Korea.
1952	19th Congress of the CPSU: Stalin's 'Economic Problems in the USSR'.
1953	Stalin dies, Malenkov Premier, Khrushchev Party Secretary; Malenkov announces Soviet development of hydrogen bomb.
1955	Malenkov resigns as Premier; West Germany joins NATO;

	USSR and East European states sign Warsaw Pact; Khrushchev's attempt to heal Yugoslav-Soviet breach; Khrushchev and Bulganin tour India, Burma and Afghanistan.
1956	20th CPSU Congress: condemnation of Stalin; proclamation of peaceful coexistence and zone of peace; Cominform disbanded; Polish October revolution; Soviets crush Hungarian revolt; Suez crisis.
1957	Moscow reports successful test of ICBM; Soviets launch the world's first satellite, *Sputnik*; twelve ruling communist parties meet in Moscow.
1958	Year of Chinese Great Leap Forward; new Berlin crisis.
1959	21st Congress of the CPSU; Chinese-Soviet nuclear agreement rescinded; Khrushchev's visit to the USA and China.
1960	Soviets shoot down U-2 plane inside USSR; break-up of summit conference in Paris; eighty-one communist parties meet in Moscow; Soviets recall experts from China; Congo crisis begins.
1961	Sino-Soviet rift becomes fully acknowledged.
1962	Bay of Pigs invasion by US-trained Cuban exiles; Khrushchev meets Kennedy in Vienna; construction of Berlin Wall; 22nd Congress of the CPSU: new Party Programme; Soviet attack on Albania; Sino-Indian War; Cuban missile crisis.
1963	Publication of letter by the CPSU on Sino-Soviet dispute; partial nuclear test ban between US and USSR.
1964	Khrushchev ousted: Kosygin Premier, Brezhnev Party Secretary; detonation of the first Chinese nuclear device.
1965	US bombing of North Vietnam; Kosygin visits Hanoi; nineteen communist parties attend consultative meeting in Moscow; suppression of abortive communist coup in Indonesia.
1966	Beginning of Chinese Cultural Revolution; 23rd Congress of the CPSU.
1967	Conference of European communist parties (not Albania, Yugoslavia or Romania) in Karlovy Vary; third Arab-Israeli War.
1968	US and USSR sign nuclear non-proliferation treaty; end of Chinese Revolution; invasion of Czechoslovakia.
1969	Year of Soviet-US numerical strategic nuclear parity; Sino-Soviet border clash; first withdrawal of US troops from Vietnam; meeting of Chinese and Soviet Prime Ministers in Peking; seventy-five communist parties meet in Moscow (absent: China, Albania, Yugoslavia, North Korea, North Vietnam); Soviet and US SALT delegations in Helsinki.
1970	Soviet military intervention in Egypt; ratification of Non-Proliferation Treaty by the US, UK and USSR; signing in Moscow of Soviet-German treaty; Egyptian-Israeli ceasefire.
1971	24th CPSU Congress adopts Programme of Peace; quadripartite agreement on Berlin signed; US, UK, USSR sign a treaty banning emplacement of nuclear weapons on the ocean floor; Nixon invited to Moscow; PRC takes seat in the UN; Indo-Pakistan war.

1972 Nixon's visit to China, USSR; signing of first US-USSR summit agreements; US troops withdrawn from Vietnam; treaty between the two Germanies signed; Egypt asks Soviet military advisors to leave.

1973 Extension of Common Market to Britain, Denmark, Ireland; Vietnam ceasefire agreement signed in Paris; Brezhnev visits Bonn, US: Agreement on Prevention of Nuclear War concluded; *coup d'état* in Chile; Geneva conference on co-operation and security; fourth Arab-Israeli war; contention over Portugal and Angola.

1974 Year of energy crisis; diplomatic relations between the US and East Germany; Indian explosion of nuclear device; third Soviet – US summit meeting; Nixon succeeded by Ford.

1975 US and USSR nullify their 1972 trade agreement: USSR cannot accept a trading relationship based on President Ford's 'Trade Act' linking free trade to Soviet emigration; President Ford announces the end of American involvement in the Vietnam War; South Vietnamese Government surrenders to the communists, thus ending the war in Vietnam; European summit conference in Helsinki on European Security and Co-operation (thirty-three European nations plus USA and Canada).

1976 25th CPSU Congress (boycotted by French CP); French CP Congress drops dictatorship of the proletariat as part of its ideology; US and USSR sign a five-year treaty limiting the size of underground nuclear explosions for peaceful purposes; twenty-nine European communist parties meet in East Berlin – all endorse policy of independent roads to socialism; North and South Vietnam become one country with Hanoi capital; Chairman Mao dies.

1977 Carter replaces President Ford; a new Soviet Constitution ('developed socialism'); Hua Kuo-feng replaces officially Mao Tse-tung.

1978 Rift develops between China and Vietnam over the passage and acceptance of refugees; Belgrade conference reviews Helsinki agreement: a direct reference to human rights expunged; World Federation of Trade Unions in Prague: French and Italian CPs criticise Moscow's authority; Spanish CP drops 'leninist' from its name; Brezhnev visits Germany; US National Security adviser Brzezinski visits China; Chairman Hua visits Iran, Rumania, Yugoslavia; suspected Cuban involvement in the crisis in the Shaba province (Katanga) of Zaïre; the summit meeting at Camp David (Carter, Begin, Sadat); 'Treaty of Peace and Friendship' between China and Japan.

Notes

Preface

1 'International relations theory' and 'international theory' will be used as synonyms in preference to 'world politics', 'global politics', international politics, etc., meaning 'study of the nature, conduct of, and influences upon, relations among individuals or groups operating in a particular arena . . . and with the nature of, and the change factors affecting, the interactions among them'. (P. A. Reynolds, *An Introduction to International Relations*, Longman, 1971, p. 10.)

2 The terms 'West' and 'East' are, of course, a rather objectionable shorthand. Taken literally they make some sense only inasmuch as the geographical borderline between them runs through Europe more or less from north to south (or rather south-east) which, quite logically, creates a West-East division within Europe only. These terms are here used for two reasons: brevity and 'neutrality' (except where 'West' and 'Western culture' implies superiority).

'West' and 'East' will be used instead of the traditional labels:

    1 (for East): 'Soviet bloc', 'communist bloc', Soviet Union and its satellites (as the West refers to the East); and the 'world system of socialism' or 'socialist countries' (as the East refers to itself);

    2 (for West): the USA and the West European countries, 'free world' (as they call themselves); and 'world capitalist system', or 'world imperialist system', 'bourgeois countries', or 'capitalist West', etc. (as they are referred to by the East).

By the East/West division we shall understand the post-Second World War situation that confirmed the tendency to division of systems on a world scale (suggested in the well-known speeches of Churchill and Byrnes in 1946 which intimated the replacement of the tripartite wartime alliance by a new two versus one pattern). The USA regarded Europe as an essential American sphere of influence and similarly all countries, or even parts of countries (Germany, Korea), that fell under Soviet influence were so regarded (Peter Calvocoressi, *World Politics since 1945*, Longman, 1971, pp. 20ff.) M. Djilas recorded Stalin as saying before the end of the war, 'In modern war the victor will impose his system, which was not the case in past wars.' (Milovan Djilas, *The New Class: an Analysis of the Communist System*, London, Allen & Unwin, 1966, p. 176.)

343

3 E.g. International theory 'seems to us to be principally contemporary international affairs with a semblance of a social-science analysis and a heavy ballast of incomprehensible jargon . . . too abstract, too uninformed about the historical dimensions of the subject to throw much light on the living realities'. (F. S. Northedge and M. J. Grieve, *A Hundred Years of International Relations*, Duckworth, 1971, preface.)

4 For the explanation of these terms see pp. 349–50, n.77.

5 Cf. Joseph Frankel, *International Politics: Conflict and Harmony*, London, Allen Lane, 1969, p. 98.

6 Z. Brzezinski, 'Communist Ideology and International Affairs', *Journal of Conflict Resolution*, vol. IV, no. 3, September 1960, p. 274.

7 Charles Lerche and Abdul A. Said, *Concepts of International Politics*, second ed., Prentice-Hall, 1969, p. 6.

8 Raymond E. Platig, *International Relations Research*, California, Clio Press, 1967, p. 15.

9 C. McClelland in J. N. Rosenau, V. Davis, and M. East, *The Analysis of International Politics*, New York, Free Press, 1972, p. 19.

10 *Ibid*.

11 Rosenau, Davis, and East, *op. cit.*, p. 29.

12 Lerche, *op. cit.*, p. 6.

13 Rosenau, Davis, and East, *op. cit.*, p. 35.

14 Platig, *op. cit.*, p. 18. According to Platig (p. 13) (the Catalogue of the Combined Book Exhibit, World Affairs, Book Centre for the Foreign Policy Association), in the 1964 World Affairs Book Fair, 'of 935 volumes, approximately one-third were judged to fall wholly or in large part within the core of international relations . . . of these 300–500 volumes, probably less than 10 per cent make significant use of one or more of the newer approaches'.

15 *Ibid*., p. 20.

16 Rosenau, Davis, and East, *op. cit.*, p. 22.

17 Platig, *op. cit.*, p. 5.

18 *The Programme of the Communist Party of Bulgaria*, 1971, quoted according to Zdenek Masopust, 'Ke kritice současné buržoazní vědy v USA', *Právník*, CXI, no. 8, 1972, pp. 622ff. (Wherever a bibliographical note is translated from a foreign language source the translation is our own.)

19 *Ibid*., Collegium of Czechoslovak Science, 1972.

20 V. I. Lenin, *Materialism and Empirio-criticism*, in *Collected Works*, Moscow, Progress Publishers, 1960, vol. 14, p. 317.

21 See below, the theories of Marx, Lenin, and Stalin, and of contemporary Marxist-Leninists.

22 C. G. Kernig, *Marxism, Communism and Western Society: A Comparative Encyclopedia*, vols 1–4, New York, Herder & Herder, 1972, introduction.

23 The few notable exceptions are, above all, the article by R. N. Berki, 'On Marxian Thought and the Problem of International Relations', *World Politics*, October 1971; R. Tanter and R. H. Ullman (eds), 'Theory and Policy in International Relations', *Supplement of World Politics*, vol.

XXIV, mentions 'explicitly ideological (such as marxist or maoist) paradigms' but only in terms of theoretical approaches which they do not investigate further (p. 4). Kernig's *Encyclopedia* (*op. cit.*) devotes a full article to international relations (vol. 4, pp. 370–8) but some of its conclusions are doubtful, e.g. marxism provides a sound basis for explaining international relations only 'to a very limited degree; for the original Marxian doctrine viewed international affairs from an exclusively national and economic angle . . . Marx's theory of international relations was derivative and not original'. W. B. Gallie (*Philosophers of Peace and War: Kant, Clausewitz, Marx, Engels and Tolstoy*, Cambridge University Press, 1978) explores mainly the contribution to theory of war.

24 *Marx and Contemporary Scientific Thought:* Papers from the symposium organised by UNESCO with the International Council for Philosophy and Humanistic Studies 1968, The Hague, Paris, Mouton, 1969, p. 20.

Chapter 1 Introductory: basic assumptions of theories of international relations

1 Cf. Anatol Rapoport, 'Various Meanings of "Theory" ', *American Political Science Review*, 1958, p. 972.
2 Greek 'theôria'.
3 Joseph Frankel, *Contemporary International Theory and the Behaviour of States*, London, Oxford University Press, 1973, pp. 22–3.
4 James E. Dougherty and Robert L. Pfaltzgraff, *Contending Theories of International Relations*, Philadelphia, New York, Toronto, Lippincott, 1971, p. 25.
5 Epistemology is taken to mean the theory of methods or grounds of knowledge.
6 Called by Piaget the 'internal epistemology' of each discipline. Jean Piaget, *Psychology and Epistemology: Towards a Theory of Knowledge*, Penguin, 1972, pp. 3 and 102.
7 J. D. Singer in Rosenau, Davis, and East, *The Analysis of International Politics*, New York, Free Press, 1972, p. 90.
8 C. F. D. Yermolenko, 'Sociology and International Relations', *International Affairs*, 1967/1, pp. 14ff.
9 Cf. P. A. Reynolds, *An Introduction to International Relations*, Longman, 1971, pp. 257ff.; J. David Singer, *The Scientific Study of Politics: An Approach to Foreign Policy Analysis*, Morristown, General Learning Press, 1972, pp. 5–6.
10 Oran Young in R. Tanter and R. H. Ullman (eds), 'Theory and Policy in International Relations', *Supplement of World Politics*, vol. XXIV, p. 183.
11 Stanley H. Hoffmann, 'International Relations: The Long Road to Theory', *World Politics*, vol. XI, no. 3, April 1959, pp. 357–8.
12 Carl J. Hempel and Paul Oppenheim in Herbert Feigl and May Brodbeck, *Readings in the Philosophy of Science*, New York, Appleton-Century-Crofts, 1953, pp. 322ff.
13 *Note:* This conclusion can be arrived at from two different starting-

points:
1 'Taxonomic and explanatory are all we can ever expect because of the nature of our subject matter and our capacity to understand it.'
2 'So far these are the only functions, but later we shall, with our improving knowledge, be able to go beyond them.'
14 Quincy Wright: 'The primary test of science is its capacity to predict and control' (Q. Wright, *The Study of International Relations*, New York, Appleton-Century Crofts, 1955, p. 112).
15 Q. Wright in H. V. Harrison (ed.), *The Role of Theory in International Relations*, Princeton, D. Van Nostrand Company, 1964, pp. 20–1; and Wright, *The Study of International Relations, op. cit.*, pp. 498ff.
16 G. K. Roberts, *A Dictionary of Political Analysis*, London, Longman, 1971, p. 213.
17 Raymond Aron in Norman D. Palmer (ed.), *A Design for International Relations Research: Scope, Theory, Methods and Relevance*, Philadelphia, The American Academy of Political and Social Science, 1970, p. 64.
18 Strauss in Herbert Storing (ed.), *Essays on the Scientific Study of Politics*, New York, Holt, Rinehart & Winston, 1962, p. 308.
19 Robert T. Golembiewski, William A. Welsh, and William J. Crotty, *A Methodological Primer for Political Scientists*, Chicago, Rand McNally & Co., 1969, p. 17.
20 John Plamenatz, *Ideology*, London, Pall Mall Press, 1970, p. 30.
21 Cf. Quincy Wright in Harrison, *op. cit.*, p. 22: 'our values are no more important than the values of others'.

Chapter 2   Marx and Engels on international relations

1 'To undertake a comprehensive criticism of Marx's theory of history would call for omniscience, since it touches on every phase of human knowledge. The critic would have to be familiar with the genesis and nature of such institutions as the state, law, family, religion, morality; he would have to feel at home in anthropology, biology, economics, history, sociology, psychology, philosophy, literature, and art (M. M. Bober, *Karl Marx's Interpretation of History*, Cambridge, Mass., Harvard University Press, 1962, p. 298).
2 E.g. the whole of *Das Kapital* is a series of criticisms of other men's doctrines; some knowledge of them is clearly essential. 'Try to imagine Rousseau, Voltaire, d'Holbach, Lessing, Heine, and Hegel combined in one person – I say *combined*, not thrown together – and you have Dr Marx', wrote Moses Hess in 1841 (having met Marx at the age of twenty-three). In G. Lichtheim, *The Origins of Socialism*, London, Weidenfeld & Nicolson, 1969, p. 178.
3 Not all English editions provide the translations of quotations from German, French, or Latin; the fact that the translations of Marx and Engels from the languages in which they wrote are frequently inadequate is well known. Where possible in this book, and especially in the case of quotations, English editions have been used. In some cases, where an

English edition has not been available, secondary sources on Marx have been consulted and their version of the relevant passages has been used. However, where the source is given in a foreign language the translation is our own.

4 *Marx and Contemporary Scientific Thought*: Papers from the symposium organised by UNESCO with the International Council for Philosophy and Humanistic Studies 1968, The Hague, Paris, Mouton, 1969, p. 20.

5 D. Senghaas, 'Horizonte einer Disziplin. Anmerkungen zur Theorie der Internationalen Politik', *Politische Vierteljahrsschrift*, 6, 1965, pp. 375–410, apropos of such concepts as balance of power and their incomparability with the modern notions.

6 R. N. Berki, 'On Marxian Thought and the Problem of International Relations', *World Politics*, October 1971, p. 81.

7 *Ibid.*

8 V. Pareto, *Systèmes socialistes*, II, Paris, 1902, p. 332.

9 *Ibid.*

10 Appendix 1 shows these problems in succinct form: the chronology of Marx's works side by side with that one of Engels with the phases of development marked.

11 We feel that some Soviet statements (cf. P. N. Demichev (ed.), *Marks i sovremennost* (Marx and the Present), Moscow, 1968, pp. 8 and 13, that deny vehemently the suggestion first that there is any justification for juxtaposing the young and old Marx and second that they themselves, explicitly or implicitly, emphasise the later works, do not alter the fact that Marxism–Leninism draws more on the older Marx.

12 'Granted that Marx's early works do not have to be taken into account (I know that this is to ask a concession which some people find difficult to accept . . .) and we subscribe to Marx's statement that *German Ideology* represented a decision to "settle accounts with his erstwhile philosophical consciousness".' (L. Althusser, *Lenin and Philosophy and Other Essays*, London, New Left Books, 1971, p. 39.)

13 Cf. Robert Payne, *Marx*, W. H. Allen, 1968.

14 However, Mészáros (*Marx's Theory of Alienation*, London, Merlin Press, 1970, pp. 93–5) calls this a 'legend' since '*all* of Lenin's important theoretical works . . . postdate his detailed *Conspectus of the Holy Family*, written in 1895'. In the *Conspectus* he quoted a number of important passages which originated in the *Economic and Philosophic Manuscripts of 1844*, since according to Mészáros, Lenin knew them from an enlarged Russian edition of the *Holy Family*. Besides, says Mészáros, 'he would have completely misread Marx if he did not deduce this notion from all Marx's work'.

15 Jean-Yves Calvez, *La Pensée de Karl Marx*, Paris, Seuil, 1956, p. 320.

16 'Exploitation' and 'oppression' are special cases (would be the rebuttal) of alienation – a concept that runs by implication throughout the rest of his works.

17 F. Engels, *The Condition of the Working Class in England in 1844*, London, 1950, p. x.

18 *Ibid.*, Preface (1892).

19 See D. McLellan, *Karl Marx: His Life and Thought*, London, Macmillan, 1973, pp. 295–6.
20 C. G. Kernig, *Marxism, Communism and Western Society: A Comparative Encyclopedia*, New York, Herder & Herder, 1972, vol. 3, p. 167.
21 Grace Carlton, *Friedrich Engels: The Shadow Prophet*, London, Pall Mall Press, 1965, introduction.
22 Cf. Bober, *op. cit.*
23 See above, pp. 2ff.
24 K. Marx and F. Engels, *Selected Works in One Volume*, London, Lawrence & Wishart, 1968, p. 30.
25 Engels, *Ludwig Feuerbach and the End of Classical German Philosophy*, in *Selected Works*, p. 609.
26 *Ibid.*
27 M. Curtis, *Marxism*, New York, Atherton Press, 1970, p. 3.
28 Engels, *Feuerbach, op. cit.*, pp. 609–10.
29 Cf. Marx's letter to Engels of 14 January 1858 expressing both his admiration for Hegel and also doubts about Hegel's theories. (K. Marx and F. Engels, *Correspondence 1846–1895*, London, Martin Lawrence, 1934, pp. 102ff.)
30 F. Engels, *Herr Eugen Dühring's Revolution in Science (Anti-Dühring)*, London, Lawrence & Wishart, 1943, p. 29.
31 K. Marx, *The Poverty of Philosophy*, New York, International Publishers, n.d., p. 127.
32 Engels, *Anti-Dühring, op. cit.*, p. 152.
33 Marx and Engels, *Correspondence 1846–1895, op. cit.*, pp. 102ff.
34 Sidney Hook (*Towards the Understanding of Karl Marx: a Revolutionary Interpretation*, London, Victor Gollancz, 1933, pp. 5ff) notes that Marx and Engels used the term dialectic in at least seven different meanings, not always compatible with each other.
35 Engels, *Feuerbach, op. cit.*, pp. 612–13.
36 Marx and Engels, *Holy Family*, Moscow, 1956.
37 Letter of Marx to Kugelmann, *Selected Works*, p. 671.
38 Engels, *Feuerbach, op. cit.*, pp. 612–13.
39 *Ibid.*, p. 614.
40 Bober, *op. cit.*, pp. 83ff.
41 Engels, *Anti-Dühring, op. cit.*, p. 347.
42 *Ibid.*, p. 25.
43 K. Marx, *Die Klassenkämpfe in Frankreich, 1848 bis 1850*, Berlin, 1911, p. 70
44 Marx and Engels, *Correspondence, op. cit.*, p. 518.
45 *Ibid.*
46 Marx and Engels, *German Ideology*, Lawrence & Wishart, 1965, p. 48.
47 Cf. the famous opening paragraph of the *Manifesto:* 'All the Powers of old Europe have entered into a holy alliance to exorcise this spectre [i.e. the spectre of communism]: Pope and Czar, Metternich and Guizot, French Radicals and German Police Spies.' (Karl Marx and F. Engels, *Manifesto of the Communist Party*, Moscow, Progress Publishers, 1969, p. 39.)

48 F. Engels, *The Origin of the Family, Private Property and the State*, in *Selected Works, op. cit.*, p. 464 (hereinafter referred to as *The Origin*).

49 K. Marx, *Capital, I*, Chicago, 1909, p. 198.

50 Marx and Engels, *German Ideology, op. cit.*, p. 22.

51 Engels, *Anti-Dühring*, New York, 1939, p. 221; also *Capital, I, passim*.

52 Marx, *Capital, III*, Chicago, Charles H. Kerr, 1933, p. 225.

53 Bottomore in Curtis, *op. cit.*, p. 99.

54 Engels, *Anti-Dühring*, London, *op. cit.*, p. 158.

55 Engels in *Feuerbach, op. cit.*, p. 160: 'The old method of investigation and thought which Hegel calls "metaphysical" which preferred to investigate things as given, as fixed and stable. . . . It was necessary first to examine things before it was possible to examine processes.'

56 See pp. 349–50, n.77.

57 Cf. John Plamenatz, *German Marxism and Russian Communism*, Longman, 1970, p. 17: 'the theory does not in fact rest on philosophy, which seems only to provide it with a vocabulary it would be better without'.

58 Engels, *Feuerbach, op. cit.*, p. 609.

59 Lichtheim in Curtis, *op. cit.*, p. 27; and pp. 36–7 of this book for Marx's own comment.

60 Lichtheim, *ibid.*; also see Appendix 2.

61 Kamenka in Curtis, *op. cit.*, pp. 118ff.

62 Lichtheim in Curtis, *op. cit.*, p. 27.

63 K. Marx, in *Selected Writings in Sociology and Social Philosophy*, T. S. Bottomore and M. Rubel (eds), Penguin, 1969, p. 40; and Bottomore in Curtis, *op. cit.*, p. 103.

64 Marx, *Selected Works*, p. 29.

65 *Strucný Filozofický Slovník* (Short Dictionary of Philosophy), Prague, Svoboda, 1966, pp. 449ff.

66 *Ibid*.

67 See the section on Lenin in Chapter 3.

68 J.-P. Sartre, *Critique de la raison dialectique*, Paris, 1960.

69 L. Dupré, *The Philosophical Foundations of Marxism*, New York, Harcourt, 1966, p. 217.

70 Marx is believed to have said in 1882 that he did not want to be a 'marxist'.

71 Marx, *Selected Writings, op. cit.*, p. 32.

72 It is interesting that Marx himself never used the term sociology, possibly because of his strong dislike for Comte.

73 See p. 304.

74 Curtis, *op. cit.*, p. 97.

75 V. I. Lenin, *The Three Sources and Three Component Parts of Marxism*, in *Selected Works in One Volume, op. cit.*, pp. 22ff.

76 Masaryk on Marx: an abridged edition of T. G. Masaryk, *The Social Question: Philosophical and Sociological Foundations of Marxism*, ed. and trans. by E. V. Kohak, Lewisburg, Bucknell University Press, 1972, p. 87.

77 Even these labels do not come from Marx but from Engels and Plekhanov respectively. Cf. the contemporary definitions of the separate sub-sections of marxist ideology, trans. from *Základy Vědeckého Komunizmu* (Foundations of Scientific Communism), Prague, NPL, 1965, pp. 117ff.

   Marxist philosophy defined as the science concerning the laws of development of objective reality, i.e. the development of nature, society and human knowledge (*poznání*), the most general theory of existence (ontology) and knowledge (gnoseology) and the general method of the process of social learning (*poznání*) and activity (*jednání*). It is at the same time the most general methodological basis of all natural and social sciences, i.e. the theoretical and methodological foundation of the other two parts of marxism.

   Historical materialism is defined as the general theory of society (dealing mainly with the relation between social existence and social conscious-ness, dialectic of social development, social conditioning of conscious-ness, the relation between objective and subjective in history, problems of the position of society in the whole of objective reality). The general conclusions of historical materialism will be the theoretical-methodo-logical starting point of other social sciences.

   Political economy deals with the development of the economic relations among people, the laws of social production and distribution, and is therefore the basic social science – 'the anatomy of human society'.

   Scientific communism then is a science about the social structure, organisation, and control of society at the point of transformation from class-antagonist society to communist society. Thus scientific communism is based on the theory of classes and class struggle and is a socio-political theory of the working class. In the words of Engels it is the culmination of the whole of marxist theory towards revolutionary practice. Thus it is the core of the developing marxist sociology.

78 Historical materialism is nowhere set out systematically and is usually reconstructed from the following works: *Economic and Philosophical Manuscripts* and *German Ideology* (in a rather embryonic form), *The Eighteenth Brumaire* (the first attempt at the application of the doctrine to a current political situation), Preface to *Contribution to the Critique of Political Economy* (very concise, but far too brief and schematic), and Engels's *The Origin of the Family, Private Property and the State*.

79 Marx, *Selected Writings, op. cit.*, p. 30.

80 Franz Mehring, *Karl Marx: The Story of his Life*, London, Bodley Head, 1936, p. 249.

81 The terms horizontal and vertical are used as explained above, since the bulk of recent literature on international theory (if it makes this distinc-tion at all) employs a similar classification. See for example, Berki, *op. cit.*, p. 81; W. Zimmerman, *Soviet Perspectives on International Relations 1956–1967*, Princeton, N.J., PUP, 1969; Johan Galtung, 'A Structural Theory of Imperialism', *Journal of Peace Research*, 1971/2, pp. 81ff.; Richard Rosecrance, *International Relations: Peace or War?*, New York, McGraw-Hill, 1973, p. 29.

82 K. Marx, *Early Texts*, D. McLellan (ed.), Oxford, 1971, pp. 115ff.
83 Lichtheim in Curtis, *op. cit.*, p. 27.
84 See Appendix 2.
85 Marx and Engels, *German Ideology*, *op. cit.*, pp. 38–9.
86 Masaryk, *op. cit.*, p. 198: another marxist division (not dissimilar to Old Testament perspectives):
   1 *Man subordinated to nature* – an original paradise: primitive communism, society organised along kinship lines, without state.
   2 *Goods take the place of nature* – civilisation (European), an ideological epoch, oppression, economic thralldom, state organisation of society, a half-way house in the development of mankind since it is followed by,
   3 *Man becomes the master* – the nascent epoch of freedom, of awareness (*Poverty of Philosophy*). The will and opinion of all is decisive. Society is again an association of free men, free from any state ties.
87 Engels, *The Origin*, *op. cit.*, pp. 466ff.
88 *The Origin* is consistent with Marx's *German Ideology*, at least on this same question.
89 Letter to Engels, 2 June 1853, *Correspondence*, *op. cit.*, pp. 64–5.
90 Letter to Kautsky, 12 October 1882, *ibid.*, p. 399.
91 Marx and Engels, *German Ideology*, *op. cit.*, p. 45.
92 *Ibid.*
93 Engels elaborates in great detail in *The Origin*.
94 *Ibid.*, p. 581.
95 *Ibid.*, p. 576.
96 Marx and Engels, *Correspondence*, *op. cit.*, p. 57. Letter from Marx to Weydermeyer of 5 March 1852.
97 See p. 307.
98 Calvez, *op. cit.*, pp. 196ff.
99 Engels, *The Origin*, *op. cit.*, p. 582.
100 Calvez (*op. cit.*, pp. 198–9) derives from one passage in the *Eighteenth Brumaire* the characteristics of class as follows:
   1 *'genre de vie'*;
   2 *'les intérêts'*;
   3 *'la culture'*; plus an awareness of having 1–3. Without this knowledge the class is not capable of taking by itself any political action.
101 Marx and Engels, *German Ideology*, *op. cit.*, pp. 92–3 and p. 45. ·
102 See Figure 3, p. 37.
103 Engels, *The Origin*, *op. cit.*, p. 528 and p. 575. An exposition of this concept comes mainly from Engels's Preface to Marx's *Civil War in France*, *Manifesto*, *The Origin*, and Engels's *Socialism: Utopian and Scientific*.
104 Engels, *The Origin*, *op. cit.*
105 *Ibid.*, p. 519.
106 Letter to A. Bebel, 18–28 March 1875, in *Selected Works*, *op. cit.*, p. 335.
107 K. Marx, *Critique of the Gotha Programme*, in *Selected Works*, *op. cit.*, p. 327.
108 Marx, *Poverty of Philosophy*, *op. cit.*, p. 197.

109 F. Engels, *Socialism: Utopian and Scientific*, London, Allen & Unwin, 1936, p. 75.
110 *Ibid.*, p. 77.
111 Marx and Engels, *Selected Works, op. cit.*, pp. 680–1.
112 *Ibid.*, p. 690.
113 Marx, *Critique of the Gotha Programme, op. cit.*, pp. 327–8, 320.
114 Marx and Engels, *Manifesto, op. cit.*, p. 76.
115 Engels, *Socialism: Utopian and Scientific, op. cit.*, p. 82.
116 *Ibid.*, pp. 71ff.
117 See pp. 67–9, 329–30.
118 Marx, *Critique of the Gotha Programme, op. cit.*, p. 327.
119 Engels, *The Origin, op. cit.*, pp. 564–5.
120 K. Marx, *Die Klassenkämpfe in Frankreich, 1848 bis 1850*, Berlin, 1911, p. 56.
121 It should be noted that many references to national questions come from the *New York Tribune*, where it is virtually impossible to distinguish which of the articles come from Engels's pen. Engels was known to have advocated more stringent attitudes in these matters than Marx. Marx himself took no one attitude consistently and his comments varied greatly according to the circumstances of each case. For detailed analysis of these questions see S. F. Bloom, *The World of Nations: a Study of the National Implications in the Work of Karl Marx*, New York, Columbia University Press, 1941.
122 See Bloom, *op. cit.*, pp. 58ff.
123 Marx and Engels, *Manifesto, op. cit.*, p. 58.
124 Marx and Engels, *Correspondence, op. cit.*, p. 517.
125 Marx and Engels, *Selected Works, op. cit.*, p. 265.
126 *Ibid.*
127 *Der Briefwechsel zwischen Friedrich Engels und Karl Marx, 1844 bis 1883*, A. Bebel and E. Bernstein (eds), 4 vols, Stuttgart, 1913, III, pp. 341–2.
128 Marx and Engels, *Manifesto, op. cit.*, p. 71.
129 Marx, *Critique of the Gotha Programme, op. cit.*, p. 323, with reference to the *Manifesto*, p. 59.
130 *New York Tribune*, 24 April 1852.
131 Marx, *Klassenkämpfe, op. cit.*, pp. 56ff.
132 Letter to Kugelmann, Bloom, *op. cit.*, pp. 39ff.
133 Marx, *Klassenkämpfe, op. cit.*, p. 61.
134 Marx and Engels, *German Ideology, op. cit.*, p. 32.
135 Marx to Annenkov, 28 December 1864, reprinted in *The Poverty of Philosophy*, Moscow, n.d., p. 151.
136 Marx and Engels, *Manifesto, op. cit.*, p. 43.
137 *Ibid.*, p. 46.
138 Marx and Engels, 8 October 1858, *Correspondence, op. cit.*, pp. 117–18.
139 Marx, *Capital, I, op. cit.*, p. 131.
140 Engels, *Principles of Communism*, in *The Communist Manifesto of K. Marx and F. Engels*, D. Ryazanoff (ed.), New York, Russell & Russell, 1963, p. 319.
141 Marx and Engels, *Manifesto, op. cit.*, pp. 47–8.

142 Marx, *The Civil War in France*, in *Selected Works*, p. 260.
143 Marx, *Critique of the Gotha Programme, op. cit.*, p. 323.
144 *Ibid.*, p. 306.
145 'Das Fest der Nationen in London', in Karl Marx and Friedrick Engels, *Historisch-Kritische Gesamtausgabe*, Frankfurt and Berlin, Marx-Engels Verlag, 1927–32, I, vol. 4, p. 460 (hereafter referred to as *Gesamtausgabe*).
146 Letter to Kugelman, 28 March 1870, NZ XX no. 2/478, p. 460.
147 Engels, *The Origin, op. cit.*, p. 581.
148 Marx and Engels, *Selected Works, op. cit.*, p. 306.
149 *Ibid.*, p. 678.
150 *Ibid.*
151 Marx, *The Civil War in France*, in *Selected Works, op. cit.*, p. 266.
152 Marx and Engels, *Manifesto, op. cit.*, pp. 56–7.
153 Marx, *Critique of the Gotha Programme, op. cit.*, p. 323.
154 Referred to by Marx as 'The Foreign Policy of the International'. Marx and Engels, *Selected Works in Two Volumes*, Moscow, 1962, vol. I, pp. 385ff.; and *Selected Works in One Volume*, p. 260.
155 Marx, *Critique of the Gotha Programme, op. cit.*, p. 323.
156 Marx, *The Civil War in France*, in *Selected Works, op. cit.*, p. 307.
157 *Ibid.*
158 Engels, *On the History of the Communist League*, in *Selected Works, op. cit.*, p. 447.
159 Marx and Engels, *Selected Works, op. cit.*, pp. 671–2.
160 *Ibid.*, p. 672.
161 Karl Marx, *The Paris Commune, 1871*, C. Hitchens (ed.), London, Sidgwick & Jackson, 1971, pp. 26ff.
162 Marx and Engels, *Selected Works, op. cit.*, p. 263.
163 *Ibid.*
164 Marx, *Selected Writings, op. cit.*, p. 40.
165 See below, Appendix 2.
166 Marx and Engels, *German Ideology, op. cit.*, p. 85.
167 *Ibid.*, pp. 85–6.
168 Marx and Engels, *Manifesto, op. cit.*, p. 59.
169 Marx, *Critique of the Gotha Programme, op. cit.*, p. 323.
170 Marx and Engels, *Manifesto, op. cit.*, p. 96.
171 Marx, *The Poverty of Philosophy*, Chicago, 1910, pp. 190–1.
172 Marx, *Capital, I, op. cit.*, p. 824.
173 Marx, *The Civil War in France*, in *Selected Works, op. cit.*, p. 287.
174 *Werke*, Berlin, 1956, vol. 17/652.
175 Congress of the International at the Hague in 1872, Marx, *Capital, I, op. cit.*, p. 32; Bober, *op. cit.*, pp. 264–5.
176 *The Marx-Engels Reader*, R. C. Tucker (ed.) New York, Norton & Co., 1972, p. 334.
177 Engels's Preface to *Capital, I, op. cit.*
178 Marx and Engels, *German Ideology, op. cit.*, p. 46.
179 Engels, *Principles of Communism, op. cit.*, pp. 332ff.
180 *Ibid.*

181 *Ibid.*
182 Marx and Engels, *Correspondence, op. cit.*, p. 118.
183 Marx, *Wage, Labour and Capital*, in *Selected Works, op. cit.*, p. 71.
184 *Marx and Contemporary Scientific Thought, op. cit.*, p. 35.
185 Berki, *op. cit.*, p. 86.
186 *Ibid.*, p. 86.
187 Marx, *Critique of the Gotha Programme, op. cit.*, p. 325.
188 Marx and Engels, *Selected Works, op. cit.*, pp. 335–6.
189 See p. 67.
190 See above, p. 25.
191 See above, pp. 47–8.
192 Marx and Engels, *Selected Works, op. cit.*, p. 260.
193 Cf. Engels: 'Administration of things in Communism', *Anti-Dühring, op. cit.*, p. 309.
194 Engels, *The Origin*, p. 520.
195 *Ibid.*, p. 562.
196 See above, p. 38.
197 See above, p. 50.
198 20 June 1866, *Correspondence, op. cit.*, p. 208.
199 K. Marx, *Economic and Philosophic Manuscripts of 1844*, London, Lawrence & Wishart, 1959.
200 *Ibid.*, p. 102.
201 *Ibid.*, p. 103.
202 *Ibid.*, p. 82.
203 *Ibid.*, p. 103.
204 *Ibid.*, p. 79.
205 *Ibid.*, p. 80.
206 Berki, *op. cit.*, p. 101.
207 Engels, *Ludwig Feuerbach*, in *Selected Works*, p. 590.
208 See above, p. 60.

Chapter 3   Theory of international relations in the East

1 See above, Preface, n.1.
2 'Theory', i.e. within the meaning of the term as defined on pp. 3–9.
3 In R. Aron, *Democracy and Totalitarianism*, London, Weidenfeld & Nicolson, 1970, p. 3.
4 A distinction suggested by Vernon Van Dyke, *Political Science: A Philosophical Analysis*, Stanford University Press, 1969, p. 109.
5 See above, p. 5.
6 John D. Bell, 'Ideology and Soviet Politics', in Richard Cornell (ed.), *The Soviet Political System*, Prentice-Hall, 1970, p. 101.
7 Gnosos = knowing; logos = word.
8 We might note that the area of the segments in Figure 4 bears no relation to the importance of their content. In the text the letters in brackets refer to the corresponding lettering on the chart.
9 The following summary is based on contemporary Soviet and Czech

textbooks of philosophy but in its essence it is basically that outlined in Lenin's *Materialism and Empirio-criticism*. See pp. 87–9 above.

10 The paired concepts 'social existence/social consciousness' and 'base/ superstructure', although they are at the very heart of Soviet thinking, still leave a great deal to be desired from the point of view of conceptual clarity and meaning. In the Soviet expositions their content and relationship have not as yet been satisfactorily clarified. For the debate on these categories, see for example A. E. Furman, 'O predmete istorich-eskogo materialisma' (Concerning the subject-matter of historical materialism), *Filozofskie nauki*, 1965–6, pp. 85–90; M. S. Dzhunusov, 'O vzaimosviazi osnovykh poniatii istroricheskogo materializma' (Concerning the relationship of basic notions of historical materialism), *Voprosy filozofii*, 1965/7, pp. 144–6; M. Kammari, 'Nekotorye voprosy teoria bazisa i nadstroiki' (Some questions of theory pertaining to base and superstructure), 1956/10, pp. 42–8; V. P. Tugarinov, 'O kategoriakh "obshchestvennoe bytie"; "obshchestvennoe soznanie" ' (Concerning the categories 'social existence' and 'social consciousness'), *Voprosy filozofii*, 1958/1, pp. 15ff. See also F. G. Fischer (ed.), *Science and Ideology in Soviet Society*, New York, Atherton Press, 1967, pp. 61–2.

11 *Relations of production* denotes one of the basic marxist categories. Crucial to an understanding not only of political economy but to the rest of Marxism-Leninism, it will suffice for our purposes to define the terms as the relations of people to the *means of production* (machinery and equipment); that is to say in a capitalist society, as capitalists or workers. In this context we should add the definition of cognate terms (in that they always go together): *forces of production* which denotes the appropriate level of technology of the machines that are in turn clearly associated and commensurate with the educational attainment of the particular society. *Forces of production* and *relations of production* combine in their specific historical circumstances to characterise a *mode of production* (another key term), which is to say a specific social system or an economic and social formation.

12 Giving similar rise to heated discussion is the question of placement of certain phenomena either in the category of social existence or of social consciousness. And then the problem arises as to whether certain other phenomena are to be exempted from inclusion altogether and to be conceived to exist 'outside' either social existence or social consciousness. The debate on these issues was introduced in 1950 with Stalin's *Marxism and Problems of Linguistics*, and has not so far been concluded.

13 This explains why in Figure 4 we have elected to draw the line of ideology straight across social consciousness.

14 A. L. Kroeber and Clyde Kluckhohn, *Culture: A Critical Review of Concepts and Definitions*, New York, 1963.

15 G. Almond, A. Powell Jr, and G. Bingham, *Comparative Politics: A Developmental Approach*, Boston, Little, Brown & Co., 1966, p. 23; and see Verba's 'Fundamental Beliefs about the Nature of Political System', in Lucian W. Pye and Sydney Verba, *Political Culture and Political*

Development, Princeton, New Jersey, Princeton University Press, 1965, p. 518.

16 H. Franz Schurmann, *Ideology and Organisation in Communist China*, revised ed., Berkeley, University of California Press, 1968.

17 John Plamenatz, *Ideology*, Macmillan, 1970, pp. 27ff. See also G. K. Roberts, *A Dictionary of Political Analysis*, London, Longman, 1971, pp. 96, 97, and *passim*.

18 Marx in his writings on capitalist society thus refers to the ideology of that society as a false consciousness – a reference that was to lend inadvertent encouragement to yet another source of controversy among his disciples.

19 Plamenatz quoting Mannheim, *op. cit.*, p. 63.

20 Beginning with Marx's VIth thesis on Feuerbach: 'but the human essence is no abstraction inherent in each single individual. In its reality it is the ensemble of the social relations.' Karl Marx, *Theses on Feuerbach*, in *Selected Works in One Volume*, London, Lawrence & Wishart, 1968, p. 29.

21 K. Marx and F. Engels, *The Communist Manifesto*, Penguin, 1967, p. 95.

22 The description of a regime in possession of an official chiliasm, i.e. a future-oriented ideology with a single mass party led by one man, a system of terrorist police control, a monopolistic control of communications and the armed forces, and a centrally controlled and directed economy, is to be found in Carl Friedrich and Zbigniew Brzezinski, *Totalitarian Dictatorship and Autocracy*, New York, Praeger, 1966, pp. 9–10.

23 F. C. Barghoorn, *Politics in the USSR*, Boston, Little, Brown, 1972.

24 Elite is 'a minority or a ruling few disposing of a share of access to authority and other values in a society far larger than their number entitles them' (Almond, Powell, and Bingham, *op. cit.*; and Barghoorn, *op. cit.*, p. 172).

25 *Ibid.*, p. 20.

26 Barghoorn, *op. cit.*, p. 23.

27 The 'process by which political cultures are maintained and changed' (Almond, Powell, and Bingham, *op. cit.*, p. 64).

28 G. A. Almond, *The Appeals of Communism*, Princeton, New Jersey, Princeton University Press, 1965, p. 15.

29 Barghoorn, *op. cit.*, p. 30.

30 *Ibid.*, p. 35.

31 XXIVth Sjezd KSSS, p. 87 (Ponomaryev's article).

32 F. J. B. Starr, *Ideology and Culture*, New York, Harper & Row, 1973, p. 19.

33 See Brzezinski, 'Communist Ideology and International Affairs', *Journal of Conflict Resolution*, vol. IV, no. 3, September 1960, p. 265: 'no doctrine however elaborated and sophisticated, can ever be comprehensive enough to provide answers and guidelines to fit all aspects of historical development'.

34 See pp. 83–4.

35 Jiří Cvekl, *Úvod do Dialektiky*, Prague, SPN, 1968, p. 34.

36 *Ibid.*

37 For the sake of completeness mention should here be made of one further Western approach: sovietology, or that study of all matters that help us to understand the meaning of current, politically significant Soviet communist behaviour and to forecast its future course (Authur E. Adams, in Cornell, *op. cit.*, p. 38).
38 Cf. the explanation given in Almond, Powell, and Bingham, *op. cit.*, p. 61: 'explicit, rigid and closed set of rules', 'inflexible image of political life', a system 'closed to conflicting information', 'specific explanation and code of political conduct for most situations'.
39 Cf. J. Frankel, *International Politics: Conflict and Harmony*, London, Allen Lane the Penguin Press, 1969, p. 98.
40 Zbigniew Brzezinski, *Soviet Bloc: Unity and Conflict*, Harvard University Press, 1967, pp. 388ff.
41 See pp. 171ff.

Lenin

1 Peter Wiles in *Marx and Contemporary Scientific Thought*: Papers from the symposium organised by UNESCO with the International Council for Philosophy and Humanistic Studies 1968, The Hague, Paris, Mouton, 1969, p. 39.
2 Specifically, *Economic and Philosophic Manuscripts of 1844*, London, Lawrence & Wishart, 1959; see also p. 347, n.14 above.
3 V. I. Lenin, *Selected Works in Three Volumes*, Moscow, Progress Publishers, 1971, 1/66. (Hereinafter referred to as Lenin, *Selected Works.*)
4 *Ibid.*
5 Perhaps the very interesting work by N. Harding, *Lenin's Political Thought*, Macmillan, 1977, will assist in changing this Western attitude.
6 Lenin, *Selected Works, op. cit.*, 1/422–443.
7 V. I. Lenin, *On the Foreign Policy of the Soviet State* (November 1915), Moscow, Progress Publishers, 1970, p. 123.
8 See Appendix 3.
9 V. I. Lenin, *Materialism and Empirio-criticism*, in *Collected Works*, Moscow, Foreign Languages Publishing House, 1962, 14/309. (Hereinafter referred to as Lenin, *Collected Works.*)
10 And the only one apart from the *Philosophical Notebooks*.
11 A very little read work in the West compared to the philosophical works of Engels.
12 David-Hillel Ruben (*Marxism and Materialism*, Brighton, Harvester Press, 1977, p. 2) argues that materialist ontology in fact demands a 'reflection' or 'correspondence' theory of knowledge and that therefore Lenin did not change the substance of marxist materialism.
13 Louis Althusser, *Lenin and Philosophy and other Essays*, London, New Left Books, 1971, p. 50.
14 Lenin, *Collected Works*, 14/130.
15 *Ibid.*, pp. 260–1.
16 Althusser, *op. cit.*, p. 50.
17 Lenin, *Collected Works, op. cit.*, 14/261.

18 *Ibid.*, p. 251.
19 *Ibid.*, p. 147.
20 *Ibid.*, p. 146.
21 Lenin, *Collected Works, op. cit.*, 14/159.
22 *Ibid.*, p. 262.
23 Althusser, *op. cit.*, p. 61.
24 Lenin, *Collected Works, op. cit.*, 14/355.
25 See pp. 31ff and 66ff.
26 R. T. de George, *Patterns of Soviet Thought*, University of Michigan Press, 1970, p. 149.
27 *Ibid.*, p. 151.
28 *Ibid.*, p. 189.
29 Lenin, *Collected Works, op. cit.*, 14/138.
30 *Ibid.*, p. 133.
31 *Ibid.*, p. 189.
32 Especially is this true of Engels's writings since it was he who mainly dealt with the subject.
33 Lenin, *Collected Works, op. cit.*, 5/384.
34 *Ibid.*
35 Lenin, *Collected Works, op. cit.*, 1/161.
36 In 1903 the Bolshevik–Menshevik split.
37 Outlined in *What Is to Be Done, Selected Works*, vol. 1, pp. 119ff.
38 'The degree of Russia's economic development (an objective condition), and the degree of class consciousness and organisation of the broad masses of the proletariat (a subjective condition, inseparably bound up with the objective condition).' Lenin, *Collected Works, op. cit.*, 9/28.
39 'The role of vanguard fighter can be fulfilled only by a party that is guided by the most advanced theory.' Lenin, *Collected Works, op. cit.*, 5/370.
40 Lenin, *Collected Works, op. cit.*, 1/446.
41 Lenin, *Collected Works, op. cit.*, 4/364.
42 *Ibid.*
43 Lenin, *Selected Works, op. cit.*, 1/675ff.
44 Lenin, *Selected Works, op. cit.*, 1/736.
45 *Ibid.*, p. 725.
46 Lenin, *Selected Works, op. cit.*, 1/727.
47 *Ibid.*, p. 736.
48 Engels wrote to Marx on 7 October 1858: 'The English proletariat is becoming more and more bourgeois so that this most bourgeois of all nations is apparently aiming ultimately at the possession of a bourgeois aristocracy and bourgeois proletariat *as well* as a bourgeoisie. For a nation which exploits the whole world this is of course to a certain extent justifiable.' K. Marx and F. Engels, *Correspondence 1846–1895: A Selection with Commentary and Notes*, London, Martin Lawrence Ltd, 1934, p. 115.
49 See Figure 5 (p. 94) and Figure 2 (p. 36).
50 Alfred G. Meyer, *Leninism*, New York, Praeger University Series, pp. 240ff.
51 Lenin, *Selected Works, op. cit.*, 1/741.

52 *Ibid.*, p. 743.
53 Cf. Meyer, *op. cit.*, pp. 252ff., who points out frequent inconsistencies in his classification of countries and predictions of the course the forthcoming revolution was to run.
54 Lenin, *Collected Works, op. cit.*, 9/236–237.
55 Brest-Litovsk Peace Treaty of 3 March 1918.
56 George Lukacs, *Lenin: A Study on the Unity of his Thought*, Cambridge, Mass., MIT Press, 1971, pp. 13 and 60.
57 See above, p. 42.
58 Lenin, *Selected Works, op. cit.*, 2/298ff.
59 Lenin, *Selected Works, op. cit.*, 25/411.
60 *The Proletarian Revolution and the Renegade Kautsky*, in Lenin, *Selected Works, op. cit.*, 3/85.
61 *Ibid.*, p. 72.
62 Lenin, *Selected Works, op. cit.*, 2/321.
63 *Ibid.*, p. 319.
64 V. I. Lenin, *Speeches at the Eighth Party Congress*, Moscow, Progress Publishers, 1971, p. 55.
65 Lenin, *Collected Works, op. cit.*, 4/177.
66 *Ibid.*, 6/229.
67 *Ibid.*, 6/454.
68 *Ibid.*, 6/455.
69 *Ibid.*, 8/267.
70 Lenin, *Selected Works, op. cit.*, 1/772.
71 *Ibid.*, 1/769.
72 *Ibid.*, 2/301.
73 Lenin, *Collected Works, op. cit.*, 8/267.
74 Lenin, *Selected Works, op. cit.*, 1/771.
75 *Ibid.*, 3/117.
76 *The Military Programme of the Proletarian Revolution*, in Lenin, *Selected Works*, vol. 1.
77 Lenin, *Collected Works, op. cit.*, 8/107.
78 Lenin, *Selected Works, op. cit.*, 2/118ff.
79 *Ibid.*
80 *Ibid.*, 2/301.
81 *Ibid.*, 1/772.
82 *Ibid.*
83 *Ibid.*, p. 777.
84 Franklyn Griffiths, 'Origins of Peaceful Coexistence: A Historical Note', in Walter Z. Laqueur and Leopold L. Labedz (eds), *The State of Soviet Studies*, Cambridge, Mass., MIT Press, 1965.
85 Lenin, *On the Foreign Policy of the Soviet State, op. cit.*, p. 70.
86 *Ibid.* (This belief that the revolution was imminent could be traced in the ideas of Russian leaders after Lenin's death until 1925–6. See p. 125 above.)
87 Lenin, *On the Foreign Policy of the Soviet State, op. cit.*, p. 124.
88 *Ibid.*, p. 294.
89 *Ibid.*, pp. 356–7.

90 *Ibid.*, p. 366.
91 *Ibid.*, *passim*; Lenin, *Selected Works, op. cit.*, 1/769ff.
92 Lenin, *On the Foreign Policy of the Soviet State, op. cit.*, pp. 211–12.
93 *Ibid.*, e.g., pp. 350, 362, and 264.

Stalin

1 Bruce Franklin (ed.), *The Essential Stalin: Major Theoretical Writings, 1905–1952*, New York, Doubleday, 1972, p. 3.
2 See above, p. 77.
3 If one subscribes to the marxist interpretation of these terms, every social theory would of course by definition be taken to be ideological (though ideology is not necessarily theoretical).
4 Isaac Deutscher, *Stalin: A Political Biography*, New York, Oxford University Press, 1949, p. 383.
5 The dates are those of the Second All-Union Congress of Marxist-Leninist Scientific Research Institutions (1929) at which all intellectuals were required to subordinate their views to the Marxist-Leninist interpretation and official line. Thereafter (and culminating in the year of the great purges of 1937–8) non-compliance was met with imprisonment or execution. The purges, show trials, and executions that followed eliminated dissident voices in other areas of social science, and that of international law in particular. The actions were already presaged in 1931 with the elimination of the Deborinists and with them debate in the realm of philosophy.
6 This work contained *Foundations of Leninism* (a series of lectures delivered in 1924 at Sverdlov University) and a lesser work, *Concerning the Questions of Leninism* (1926). *Problems of Leninism* was to reach as many as eleven editions.
7 In 1946 the CPSU called for the development of psychology and logic; in 1947 a Philosophical Conference was convened to discuss and criticise G. Aleksandrov's textbook *History of West European Philosophy*; in 1947 another philosophical journal (*Voprosy filozofii*) was founded (this journal, still extant, was designed to replace *Under the Banner of Marxism* which has been defunct since 1944).
8 Others focused, by order, on criticism of bourgeois theories. See G. Aleksandrov, 'O nekotorykh zadachakh obshchestvennykh nauk v sovremennykh usloviiakh', *Bolshevik*, no. 14, 1945, p. 23.
9 Implying the need to come up with new theories if the old did not work.
10 Stalin, 'The Foundations of Leninism', in Franklin, *The Essential Stalin, op. cit.*, p. 91.
11 *Ibid.*, p. 105.
12 *Ibid.*
13 *Ibid.*, p. 108.
14 See pp. 71ff. A position, we might observe, fully consistent with Lenin's stress on the subjective factor (above, pp. 90ff).
15 Stalin, 'Marxism and Linguistics', in Franklin, *The Essential Stalin, op. cit.*, p. 443.
16 *Ibid.*, p. 441.

17 In science and in art alike as in other areas (Zhdanovism). It is important
to add that towards the end of his life, Stalin (in the phase in which was
opened a modest path to discussion (n.7 above)) in some respects beats a
belated retreat from his earlier position: 'It is generally recognised that no
science can develop and flourish without a battle of opinions, without
freedom of criticism. But this generally recognised rule was ignored and
flouted in the most outrageous fashion.' 'Marxism and Linguistics', *op.
cit.*, pp. 427–8.
18 Party-mindedness: commitment to the Party, or rather to Stalin's line.
19 B. A. Grushin, 'Sotsiologiia i Sotsiologi' (Sociology and Sociologists),
Literaturnaia Gazeta, 25 September 1965, p. 1.
20 M. Bochenski, 'Philosophy Studies', *Soviet Survey*, no. 31,
January–March 1960, pp. 73–4.
21 See in this context R. T. de George, *Patterns of Soviet Thought*, Ann
Arbor, University of Michigan Press, 1970, p. 194.
22 *History of the CPSU: Short Course*, Moscow, Foreign Languages
Publishing House, 1951, pp. 7–25. (Hereinafter referred to as *Short
Course.*)
23 See p. 305.
24 *Short Course, op. cit.*, pp. 522–5.
25 'Marxism and Linguistics', *op. cit.*, p. 425.
26 *Short Course, op. cit.*, pp. 22–3.
27 Stalin, *Problems of Leninism*, Moscow, Foreign Languages Publishing
House, p. 778.
28 Apropos of language in 'Marxism and Linguistics', *op. cit.*, p. 431.
29 See pp. 349–50, n. 77.
30 Such as for example those attempted in Bavaria, Hungary, etc.
31 14 May 1918, Lenin, *Collected Works, op. cit.*, 27/372–373.
32 *Ibid.*, 28/189–90.
33 4 January 1923, *ibid.*, 33/468.
34 16 January 1923, *ibid.*, 33/478–79.
35 An instance of this 'flexibility' is to be seen at the Fifteenth Party
Congress (December 1927) when, despite his previous predictions in
regard to twenty peaceful years, Stalin put to the delegates the possibility
that this period had come to an end: 'Two years ago one could have talked
about the relative balance between the Soviets and capitalist countries
and about their "peaceful coexistence". Now we have every reason to say
that the period of "peaceful coexistence" recedes to the past, giving place
to a period of imperialist attacks and of preparation of intervention
against the USSR.'
36 *Kommunisticheskaia Partiia Sovetskogo Soiuza v Rezoliutsiakh i
Resheniakh, 1898–1953* (The CPSU in Resolutions and Decisions),
eleventh ed., Moscow, 1953, II, pp. 46–9.
37 Herbert Marcuse, *Soviet Marxism: a Critical Analysis*, Harmondsworth,
Penguin Books, 1971, p. 14.
38 See p. 42.
39 Stalin, *Sochinenia*, VIII, p. 263.
40 In a rare moment of clarification Stalin assures us ('On Capitalist

Encirclement', *Bolshevik*, August 1951) that it is to a political rather than a geographical notion that the term 'encirclement' refers.

41 See p. 41.

42 Whereby monolithic capitalist economies would be replaced by monolithic socialist ones.

43 A position, it will be recalled, that Marx himself adopted, see above, p. 55.

44 'Whether the dictatorship of proletariat in Russia leads to socialism or not, and at what rate and over what stages, will depend on the further fate of European and international capitalism.' (L. Trotsky, *The Permanent Revolution*, Calcutta, 1947, p. 61.)

45 L. Trotsky, *The Third International After Lenin*, New York, 1936, pp. 54–5.

46 See pp. 191, 201ff.

47 V. L. Verger, *Pravo i gosudarstvo perekhodnogo vremeni* (Law and State of the Transitional Period), Moscow, 1924, p. 200.

48 E. A. Korovin, *Mezhdunarodnoe pravo perekhodnogo vremeni* (International Law of the Transitional Period), Moscow, 1924, p. 94.

49 E. A. Korovin, *Sovremennoe mezhdunarodnoe publichnoe pravo* (Contemporary Public International Law), Moscow, 1926, p. 8.

50 Evgenii A. Korovin, 'Soviet Treaties and International Law', *American Journal of International Law*, 22, 1928, p. 753, quoted from R. J. Erickson, *International Law and the Revolutionary State*, New York, Oceana Pubs; Leiden, Sijthoff, 1972, p. 5.

51 Evgenii A. Pashukanis, *Ocherki po mezhdunarodnomu pravu*, Moscow, 1935, p. 16.

52 Fedor I. Kozhevnikov, 'Concerning the Most Backward Sector of Soviet Law', *Sovietskoe Gosudarstvo i Revolutsiya prava*, 1930, no. 3, pp. 147ff.

53 A. Ia. Vyshinskii, *The Law of the Soviet State*, New York, Macmillan, 1948, pp. 52–61.

54 See Figure 6.

55 See Stalin. 'Concerning the Question of Proletariat and Peasantry', in Franklin, *The Essential Stalin, op. cit.*, pp. 187ff.

56 Stalin, *Sochinenia*, VII, 298, 18 December 1925.

57 *Kommunisticheskii Internatsional v dokumentakh, 1919–1932* (The Communist International in Documents, 1919–1932) Bela Kun (ed.), Moscow, 1933, pp. 34–5. (Hereinafter referred to as *Kom Int.*)

58 Lenin, *Pravda*, 9–11 May 1918.

59 Lenin, *Sochinenia*, XXII, 482.

60 See p. 101.

61 Stalin, 'Marxism and Linguistics', in Franklin, *The Essential Stalin, op. cit.*, p. 440.

62 *Ibid.*, pp. 440–1.

63 Stalin, Report to the 18th CPSU (Bolshevik) on the Work of the Central Committee, 10 March 1939, in Franklin, *The Essential Stalin, op. cit.*, p. 384.

64 In contrast to the apparently similar capitalist treatment of societal

sections the repression in the socialist situation should be on behalf of the majority of society.

65 *The Essential Stalin*, pp. 386–7.
66 'Marxism and the National Question', in *ibid*.
67 For a near exhaustive account of great Russian pressure exerted over all other Soviet nationalities, see W. Kolarz, *Russia and her Colonies*, Hamden, Connecticut, Anchor Books, 1967; and also by the same author, *The People of the Soviet Far East*, New York, Praeger, 1954.
68 'Marxism and the National Question', in Franklin, *The Essential Stalin*, *op. cit.*, p. 60.
69 *Ibid.*, p. 61.
70 *Ibid.*, p. 69.
71 'Only the nation itself has the right to determine its destiny, that no one has the right *forcibly* to interfere in the life of the nation [sic], to *destroy* its schools and other institutions, to violate its habits and customs, to *repress* its language, or *curtail* its rights.' Stalin, 'Marxism and the National Question', in *ibid.*, p. 70.
72 *Ibid.*, p. 80.
73 Stalin in *Sochinenia*, X, 51, August 1927.
74 'The whole Stalinist conception actually leads to the liquidation of the Communist International. And indeed, what would be its historical significance if the fate of socialism is to be decided by the highest possible authority – the State Planning Commission of the USSR? In that case, the task of the Comintern . . . would be to protect the construction of socialism from intervention, that is, in essence, to play the role of frontier patrols.' Trotsky, *The Permanent Revolution* (introduction to the German edition), London, New Park Publications, 1962, p. 27.
75 Trotsky, 'Rech po italianskomu Voprosu na III Kongresse Kominterna', 1921, in *Piat' let Kominterna*, Moscow, 1924, p. 222.
76 These were in 1924, 1928, 1935, and with a gap of seven years between the last two – despite a statutory provision for convening congresses every two years.
77 1928, *Kom Int.*, pp. 13, and 35.
78 Robert H. MacNeal (ed.), *International Relations among Communists*, Prentice-Hall, 1967, p. 11.
79 Goodman traces the start of the decline of the Comintern to 1937 and Austen Chamberlain's overtures to Stalin in that year. Thereafter pressure was brought on Stalin at intervals to dissolve the Comintern. (E. R. Goodman, *The Soviet Design for a World State*, New York, Columbia University Press, 1960, p. 45.)
80 Discourse to the students of Sverdlov University on 9 June 1925, in Deutscher, *Stalin: a Political Biography, op. cit.*, p. 389.
81 *Ibid.*
82 Marcuse, *Soviet Marxism, op. cit.*, p. 52, and *passim*.
83 'The presence of a certain minimum of industrial development and culture in that country, a certain minimum of industrial proletariat, the revolutionary spirit of the proletariat, and a proletariat vanguard, and a serious ally of the proletariat (the peasantry for instance) capable of

following the proletariat in the decisive struggle against imperialism', these according to Stalin would be the characteristics of a country on the way to becoming the next weakest link in the chain. (Stalin, *Neobkhodimaia popravka*, in *Sochinenia*, XII, Moscow, 1946–51, pp. 138–9.)

84 'Concerning the Question of the Proletariat and the Peasants', in Franklin, *The Essential Stalin, op. cit.*, p. 88.

85 See above, p. 95.

86 See section on Marx.

87 Franklin, *The Essential Stalin, op. cit.*, pp. 188–9.

88 'Ob osnovakh Leninizma', 1924, in 'O Lenine i Leninizme', pp. 24–6; 'K itogam rabot XIV', in *Sochinenia*, VII, 96; 'Politicheskii otchet', *ibid.*, VI, pp. 263–81, 18 December 1925; 'Eschche raz o sotsial-demokraticheskom uklone v nashei partii', 1926, IX, 26; 'Politicheskii otchet', *ibid.*, 27 June 1930, XII, pp. 248–54.

89 In his political economy Marx fully supported this analysis.

90 Marxist observers who duly noted these periods of recovery were invariably confident of their short-lived temporary nature. This attitude was particularly true of observations made in this respect during the first decades following the formation of the Soviet Union.

91 E. H. Carr, *The Bolshevik Revolution*, 3 vols, London, Macmillan, 1953, vol. 3, p. 331.

92 Stalin to Chicherin, 10 March 1921, in *Sochinenia*, V, 42.

93 Stalin, 'Two Camps', in Franklin, *The Essential Stalin, op. cit.*, p. 85.

94 Litvinov's address to the League Assembly on the occasion of the entry of the USSR into the League of Nations, 18 September 1934 (in J. Degras (ed.), *Calendar of Soviet Documents on Foreign Policy*, London, Oxford University Press, 1953, III, pp. 92–3). Stalin himself developed tirelessly the notion that only after the Soviet Union has prevailed would there be genuine 'peaceful coexistence' and the fraternal collaboration of nations. See Stalin, 'Deklaraciia ob obrazovanii SSR', *Sochinenia*, V, 159.

95 See Figure 8.

96 The 'first experiment in peaceful coexistence with bourgeois states' is how the apostle of peaceful coexistence, Chicherin, described the peace treaty signed with Estonia on 20 February 1920 (Louis Fischer, *The Soviets in World Affairs, 1917–1929*, 2 vols, Princeton University Press, 1951, I, p. 254).

97 Lenin, *On the Foreign Policy, op. cit.*, pp. 242 and 354; Lenin, *Selected Works, op. cit.*, 1/675.

98 *Short Course, op. cit.*, pp. 259–60.

99 From the declaration of the founding Cominform conference, 'Deklaratsia', September 1947, in *Informatsionnoe Soveshchanie*, Moscow, 1948, pp. 6–7.

100 'Economic problems of Socialism in the USSR', in Franklin, *The Essential Stalin, op. cit.*, p. 471.

101 *Ibid.*, p. 472.

102 Capitalist responsibility for the Second World War was of course assumed.

103 Cf. Stalin: 'To eliminate the inevitability of war, it is necessary to abolish imperialism.' Franklin, *op. cit.*, p. 473.

104 Malenkov, *Otchetny Doklad XIX Sezdu*, Moscow, 5 October 1952, p. 6.

105 Goodman, *The Soviet Design for a World State, op. cit.*, p. 287.

106 'Of course, in the remote future, if the proletariat is victorious in the principal capitalist countries, and if the present capitalist encirclement is replaced by a socialist encirclement, a "peaceful" path of development is quite possible for certain capitalist countries, whose capitalists, in view of the "unfavourable" international situation will consider it expedient "voluntarily" to make substantial concessions to the proletariat. But this supposition applies only to a remote and possible future.' Stalin, 'The Foundations of Leninism', in Franklin, *The Essential Stalin, op. cit.*, pp. 128 and 129.

107 With this caveat in mind and for the reason only that 'Stalin', rather than 'stalinism' was chosen as the title of this section we bring it to a close with Stalin's death. It will be remarked that until 1956 and Khrushchev's denunciation of both Stalin and stalinism no major theoretical alteration to the theory was made.

108 That had previously comprised the Soviet Union and the Mongolian People's Republic.

109 Cf. the 12th Congress of the CPSU of the USSR in 1923. Also Richard Pipes, *The Formation of the Soviet Union*, Cambridge, Mass., 1954; and V. Aspaturian, *The Union Republics in Soviet Diplomacy*, Geneva, Droz, 1960.

110 That is to say, following the path preferred by the country concerned; free to conform or diverge according to its degree of sympathy with the direction taken by the Soviet Union.

111 Liu Shao-chi, cited in Goodman, *The Soviet Design for a World State, op. cit.*, p. 315.

112 The Popular (or Peoples') Democracy – a term paradoxically first used by Tito in 1945 – was to become a very important addition to the Marxist-Leninist theory of state. Because of the highly diversified internal political structures of the countries involved – that were certainly not identical with the Soviet system – there was formed, so to speak, a hybrid growth. If the first form of dictatorship of the proletariat was the Paris Commune, and the second the Soviet state, recognition had now to be extended to this third category.

113 Still beyond the perimeters of the expanding system in 1947 were Czechoslovakia (its allegedly 'peaceful' communist revolution to take place only in February 1948), Eastern Austria (which did not become a popular democracy), and Yugoslavia (which did assume the main features although owing them not entirely to the Soviet liberation).

114 Note the incidence of delegations whose entitlement is always preceded by 'Party and state'.

115 Cf. 'by being made an ambassador, he does not cease being a communist' (in a Soviet note to the Yugoslavs cited in MacNeal, *International Relations among Communists, op. cit.*, p. 21).

116 Known in the West as the Cominform, the organisation was founded in

1947 and comprised seven communist parties in power and two others. The first major split in the communist ranks – that with Tito in 1948–9 – was brought to the Cominform's attention only after it had happened. As the rift widened, and in contrast to the central role of bilateral inter-party discussion of the causes of the dispute, the Cominform made no contribution whatsoever.

117 See George W. Hoffman and Fred W. Neal, *Yugoslavia and the New Communism*, New York, Twentieth Century Fund, 1962, p. 14. Also Adam B. Ulam, *Titoism and the Cominform*, Cambridge, Mass., 1952; and 'Titoism', in M. Drachkovitch, *Marxism in the Modern World*.

118 Comecon, as it became known in the West, was the response to the Marshall Plan and comprised: Bulgaria, Czechoslovakia, Hungary, Poland, Romania, USSR, East Germany. (Yugoslavia's application for membership in 1949 was rejected.) The first intra-bloc political organisation (the Warsaw Pact) was created in 1954 in the year after Stalin's death.

Soviet Marxist–Leninists

1 See Appendix 5 for selective chronology.

2 Perceptiveness is implied in such titles as 'stalinism without Stalin', 'khrushchevism without Khrushchev', etc. See S. L. Sharp, 'The USSR and the West', in John W. Strong, *The Soviet Union under Brezhnev and Kosygin: The Transition Years*, New York, Van Nostrand Reinhold, 1971, p. 245.

3 Beyond, one might say, the three stages of Stalin's death: the physical passing away in 1953, the official exorcism of the spirit in 1956 when Khrushchev in his 'secret speech' to the 20th CPSU Congress denounced all that Stalin had stood for; and the immurement of 1959 when, following the final confirmation by the 21st CPSU Congress of the findings of the previous Congress, the body was removed to the Kremlin Wall.

4 It remains a fact that most Soviet and Western analysts of Soviet foreign policy have taken the year of Stalin's death as a turning point. In this connection, see W. Welch, *American Images of Soviet Foreign Policy*, New Haven, Yale University Press, 1970, pp. 22–4, for a periodisation arrived at by the author's assessment of a consensus which he perceived to exist in this respect in the field of sovietology. For one example of a similarly based Soviet periodisation see 'Chronicle of Grand Achievements: Fifty Years of Soviet Foreign Policy', *International Affairs*, nos 11 and 12, 1966; and nos 1–7, 1967.

5 N. S. Khrushchev, *Report of the Central Committee of the Communist Party of the Soviet Union to the 20th Party Congress*, 14 February 1956, Moscow, Foreign Languages Publishing House, 1956, p. 26.

6 Richard T. de George, *New Marxism*, New York, Pegasus, 1968, p. 29.

7 Khrushchev, *op. cit.*, p. 38.

8 In the well-established Marxist-Leninist tradition of subdividing stages of the transformation to communism (see Stalin, p. 126), Brezhnev, obviously in an effort to establish his political ascendancy and to make also a substantial theoretical contribution to the Marxist-Leninist

treasure trove, introduced in 1967 (more clearly in 1971 and particularly in the new Soviet Constitution of 1977) the concept of 'developed' or 'mature' socialism. However, it seems to be a substage defined primarily in domestic economic terms with no major consequence for the main line of our argument. See A. B. Evans Jr, 'Developed Socialism in Soviet Ideology', *Soviet Studies*, vol. XXIX, no. 3, July 1977, pp. 409–28.

9 We see this latter post-Stalin period as falling into two clearly discernible stages upon whose distinguishing features we shall comment in due course. Otherwise the distinctive characteristics of the period referred to above may be said to serve as a common denominator, and to predominate. As far as differences in the Soviet concept of peaceful coexistence are concerned, these are sometimes seen to be mainly of style. Our own preference is to agree with those writers who argue that the difference is more profound and that since Khrushchev there has been a 'steady and constantly strengthening trend towards more solid work and less boastful talk'. Cf. F. D. Kohler, in M. L. Harvey, Leon Gouré, Vladimir Prokofieff, *Science and Technology as an Instrument of Soviet Policy*, University of Miami, Center for Advanced International Studies, 1972, p. vii.

10 Khrushchev, *op. cit.*, p. 23.

11 A return to bipolarity is anticipated when the Third World becomes socialist.

12 Khrushchev, *op. cit.*, p. 42.

13 Brezhnev's speech to the 25th CPSU Congress, *Pravda*, 25 February 1976, p. 2.

14 *Ibid.*, p. 41.

15 *Ibid.*, p. 42.

16 W. Zimmerman, *Soviet Perspectives on International Relations 1956– 1967*, Princeton, N.J., Princeton University Press, 1969, p. 5, citing Khrushchev in *Pravda*.

17 *Pravda*, 6 January 1961.

18 Khrushchev, *op. cit.*, pp. 24–5.

19 *Ibid.*, p. 42.

20 For example, in a speech at the Leipzig All-German Conference of Trade Unions, *Tass*, 26 March 1959.

21 Clearly under Chinese pressure this attitude was subsequently relaxed. Cf. the text of the 1960 inter-party Moscow meeting and the Report to the 22nd CPSU Congress, both of which stated explicitly that the general line of peaceful coexistence could not be taken to exclude 'just wars of national liberation'. See also in support of this view, Foy D. Kohler, *Soviet Strategy for the Seventies; from Cold War to Peaceful Coexistence*, University of Miami, Center for Advanced International Studies, 1973, pp. 32–3.

22 They make the further distinction between those local wars that can be contained and those susceptible to escalation: the 'war-ban' in the case of the former being not nearly as stringent.

23 'Either peaceful coexistence or the most destructive war in history. There is no third way.' Khrushchev, *op. cit.*, p. 40.

24 For explanation of this term, see p. 209.

25 For explanation of the terms, see p. 203.

26 Kohler, *op. cit.*

27 Although Stalin took over Lenin's model of imperialism and added to it by removing permanently the Soviet Union from the orbit of the 'oppressed countries', he at the same time restricted himself in his conceptualisations to the elaboration only of intra-capitalist contradictions and to the relationship between capitalist countries and the Soviet Union. Colonies were relegated in this scheme to a very secondary and unimportant place (as one such intra-capitalist contradiction). We have already commented on his neglect also of the class elements within capitalist countries (see p. 143).

28 Page 96 and *passim* in Aspaturian, *Power and Process in Soviet Foreign Policy*, Boston, Little, Brown, 1971.

29 Section on Stalin above, pp. 125ff.

30 This would suggest the conclusion that as a vertical centre of revolution the Soviet Union should seek ideological followers: as a global power her search is (or should be) for client states of all political persuasions. See Aspaturian, *op. cit.*, p. 110.

31 See Aspaturian, *op. cit.*, pp. 97ff.

32 See Chapter 5.

33 Up to and including the leaders' present notion which could be described as encirclement of the capitalist world by the world revolutionary forces.

34 The reference applies in particular to Lenin, since Marx's experience as a political leader, despite Soviet claims to the contrary, was minimal.

35 Z. Brzezinski (ed.), *Dilemmas of Change in Soviet Politics*, New York, Columbia University Press, 1969, pp. 2ff.

36 Notwithstanding the obvious recent accumulation of powers, or rather, of top positions by such leaders as Brezhnev, Husák, and Ceausescu.

37 For details see W. Zimmerman, 'International Relations in the Soviet Union: The Emergence of a Discipline', *Journal of Politics*, vol. 31, 1969, pp. 52–70.

38 That is to say the nation-state system. Cf. C. G. Kernig (ed.), *Marxism, Communism and Western Society: A Comparative Encyclopedia*, New York, Herder & Herder, 1972, vol. 4, p. 370.

39 It was declared that with whatever 'inevitability' the advent of communism might still be regarded, if deprived of the knowledge and practical application of the 'laws of socialism' the 'inevitable' would not happen.

40 Zhukov, quoted by J. Keep (ed.), *Contemporary History in the Soviet Mirror*, London, Allen & Unwin, 1964, p. 16.

41 J. Frankel, *International Politics: Conflict and Harmony*, London, Allen Lane, 1969, p. 26.

42 If one excepts studies in diplomacy there was one journal devoted to the subject of international relations. See an article in the *Diplomatic Dictionary* (Diplomaticheskii Slovar) (I), A. Y. Vyshinskii and S. A. Lozovskii (eds), Moscow, 1948, and vol. II, A. Y. Vyshinskii (ed.), Moscow, 1950. Also the *History of Diplomacy* (Istoria Diplomatii), in 3 vols, V. P. Potemkin (ed.), Moscow, 1945.

43 Zimmerman in his *Soviet Perspectives on International Relations, 1956–1967*, sees 1962 as the turning point in the development of international relations as an autonomous discipline and cites Soviet statements at that time as well as of recent vintage that refer to the theory of international relations as a 'young science arising at the intersection of a number of sciences'. Zimmerman, *op. cit.*, pp. 54ff.

44 In *Izvestia, Bolshevik, Pravda*, etc.

45 Appearing since July 1957.

46 Institut mirovoi ekonomiki i mezhdunarodnykh otnoshenii founded in April 1956 as part of the Soviet Academy of Science.

47 At both earlier and later dates similar institutes were established in East European countries.

48 The theoretical and political organ of the Central Committee of the CPSU.

49 *Mezhdunarodnye otnoshenia: bibliograficheskii sparavochnik, 1945–1960*, Moscow, 1961.

50 Z. Masopust, 'Ke kritice současné burzoažní politické vědy v USA', *Právník*, 8, 1972, pp. 625ff.

51 See for example Alexandr Ort, 'International Relations and Political Science', *Czechoslovak Political Science*, IPSA Congress in Brussels, 18–23 September 1967, Prague, Svoboda, 1967, pp. 277ff.

52 *Ibid.*

53 *XXIV Sjezd KSSS a rozvoj marxisticko-leninské teorie* (24th Congress of CPSU and the development of Marxist-Leninist theory), cited from materials of the Scientific Conference of the Institute of Marxism-Leninism of the Academy of Social Sciences, the High Party School of the Central Committee of the Communist Party of Czechoslovakia and the Section for Social Sciences of the Academy of Sciences of the USSR, Prague, Svoboda, 1972, p. 150.

54 In F. V. Konstantinov (ed.) *Sociologicheskie problemy mezhdunarodnykh otnoshenii* (Sociological Problems of International Relations), Moscow, Izdatelstvo 'Nauka', 1970, pp. 5ff.

55 Any mention of departures from this outline contained in the works of other 'internationalists' (as they refer to themselves) is placed in brackets.

56 L. Pastusiak, 'A Marxist Approach to the Study of International Relations', *East European Quarterly*, vol. III, no. 3, pp. 285ff.

57 We refer to the split effected between dialectical and historical materialism. See above, p. 119.

58 *Fundamentals* was first published in 1958 (that is, as soon after the 20th CPSU Congress as was possible) by a team under the leadership of F. V. Konstantinov. *Scientific Communism*, Moscow, Progress Publishers, was published in 1967.

59 Of the many editions the one that appeared in 1962, and particularly the more popular *Fundamentals of Marxism-Leninism*, are noteworthy.

60 O. V. Kuusinen (ed.), *Fundamentals of Marxism-Leninism*, Moscow, Foreign Languages Publishing House, 1963, hereinafter referred to as *Fundamentals*.

61 de George, *Patterns of Soviet Thought*, *op. cit.*, pp. 207ff.
62 Cf. *Fundamentals*, p. 68: 'Materialist dialectics and philosophical materialism are inseparably connected. . . interwoven, being two aspects of the single philosophical system of marxism.'
63 *Ibid.*, p. 69.
64 *Ibid.*
65 *Fundamentals*, p. 77. For a comparison with Marx's definition, see above, p. 26.
66 *Ibid.*, p. 80.
67 *Ibid.*, p. 88.
68 *Ibid.*
69 *Ibid.*
70 *Ibid.*
71 *Ibid.*, p. 94.
72 *Ibid.*, p. 94.
73 *Ibid.*, p. 94.
74 *Ibid.*, p. 100.
75 *Ibid.*
76 *Ibid.*
77 *Ibid.*, pp. 94–5.
78 *Ibid.*
79 *Ibid.*, p. 95.
80 *Ibid.*, p. 9.
81 *Ibid.*, p. 97.
82 *Ibid.*, p. 98.
83 *Ibid.*, p. 99.
84 The first and second relating to development and contradiction respectively.
85 *Ibid.*, p. 101.
86 *Ibid.*, p. 101.
87 *Ibid.*, p. 102.
88 *Ibid.*
89 *Ibid.*
90 *Ibid.*, p. 104.
91 *Ibid.*, p. 104.
92 Our italics.
93 See above, p. 31.
94 *Ibid.*, p. 189.
95 *Ibid.*
96 *Ibid.*, p. 142.
97 *Ibid.*, p. 165.
98 See above, p. 23, Marx's comment 'History does nothing. . .'.
99 *Ibid.*, p. 166.
100 *Ibid.*, p. 216.
101 *Ibid.*, pp. 222–3.
102 *Ibid.*, p. 224.
103 *Ibid.*, p. 227.
104 *Ibid.*, p. 228.

105 An endorsement that glosses over the apparent lack of Party mechanisms to prevent it from happening at that time – a factor that did (and could now) facilitate the emergence of a personality cult.

106 *Fundamentals, op. cit.*, p. 605.

107 From primitive to slave, feudal, socialist and communist societies according to the mode of production.

108 *Programme of the CPSU*, Moscow, Foreign Languages Publishing House, 1961, p. 59.

109 In Marxism-Leninism 'moral' and 'good' have, since Lenin, been taken to mean that which advances the cause of the revolution; and after the revolution, the establishment of communism.

110 See above, p. 115.

111 Precisely how distant is not clear. The Programme declares that communism in the USSR should be achieved 'in the main' in the 1980s (*Programme of the CPSU, op. cit.*, p. 46) – the meaning of 'in the main' is not elaborated but the introduction in the 1970s of the new substage of 'developed socialism' and references to that substage as a 'long historical phase' indicate that Khrushchev was too optimistic – if not that the whole thing must be postponed; see also A. P. Butenko, 'O razvitom sotsialisticheskom obshchestve' (On the developed socialist society), *Kommunist*, no. 6, 1972, p. 51.

112 A position which Marxism-Leninism not only acknowledges but presents as a positive achievement.

113 Societies in the past are claimed to have operated in accordance with these laws.

114 See above, Chapter 1, pp. 6–7.

115 A. F. Shishkin, 'Chelovek kak vysshaia tsenost' (Man as the Highest Value), *Voprosy filozofii*, 1965, 1, pp. 3ff.

116 Cf. A. A. Guseinov, *Socialnaia priroda nravstvennosti* (Social nature of morality) Moscow, Izdatelstvo Moskovskogo Univerziteta, 1974, p. 10.

117 Marx and Engels, *Selected Works in One Volume*, London, Lawrence & Wishart, 1968, p. 29.

118 See Appendix 4.

119 See Chapter 5.

120 From which neither the policy-makers nor the 'theory-makers' are excluded.

121 The curricula content itself bears testimony to the degree of attention paid to Marxism-Leninism, irrespective of the student's major area of specialisation.

122 See above, p. 175.

123 See above, p. 175.

124 V. Israelyan, 'The Leninist Science of International Relations and Foreign Policy Reality', *International Affairs*, no. 6, 1967, p. 47.

125 *Ibid.*, p. 48.

126 *Ibid.*

127 *Ibid.*

128 *Ibid.*

129 See Kenneth Waltz, *Man, the State and War*, New York, Columbia University Press, 1959, p. 63.

130 See p. 221.

131 *The Road to Communism, Documents of the 22nd Congress of The Communist Party of The Soviet Union*, 17–31 October, Moscow, Foreign Languages Publishing House, 1961.

132 With notable (and unintentional) exceptions, such as the discrepancies noted above (p. 119) between dialectical and historical materialism.

133 *The Road to Communism, op. cit.*, pp. 566–7.

134 V. Gantman, 'Class Nature of Present-Day International Relations', *International Affairs*, 1969/9, p. 56.

135 V. Granov, 'The Struggle of Ideologies and Cooperation between States', *International Affairs*, 1975/1, p. 73.

136 See above, p. 162.

137 See pp. 209, 217.

138 Lenin's views on the subject continue to be quoted: 'Taking advantage of every, even the smallest "fissure" among the enemies, of every antagonism of interest among the bourgeoisie of the various countries, among the various groups or types of bourgeoisie in the various countries; by taking advantage of every, even the smallest opportunity of gaining a mass ally, even though this may be temporary, vacillating, unstable, unreliable and conditional.' V. I. Lenin, 'Left-Wing Communism, an Infantile Disorder', 1920, in *Selected Works*, New York, International Publishers, 1943, vol. X, p. 138.

139 D. Tomashevsky, 'The USSR and the Capitalist World', *International Affairs*, 1966/3, pp. 7ff.

140 *Ibid.*

141 The label describes an umbrella notion that covers the plurality of Western ideologies which would otherwise defy attempts at generalisation. Anti-communism is defined as that 'broad complex of political, economic, military and ideological actions directed against socialism, the revolutionary working class movement and all progressive forces'. Granov, *op. cit.*

142 S. Sanakoyev, 'The Leninist Methodology of Studying International Problems', *International Affairs*, 1969/9, p. 52.

143 Granov, *op. cit.*, p. 72.

144 *Ibid.*

145 For an example of statistics of the strike movements in the capitalist countries, see G. Nikolayev, 'Scientific and Technological Progress and the Class Struggle', *International Affairs*, 1974/5, pp. 86ff.

146 See p. 217.

147 Brezhnev's speech at the 25th CPSU Congress, *Pravda*, 25 February 1976, p. 2.

148 See above, p. 134.

149 See Figure 10, p. 200.

150 It is interesting to note that within these revolutionary forces norms not different from the biblical ten commandments apply – with the possible exception that work, which is regarded by some ethical systems as a

necessary evil, is 'promoted' to become a moral duty. Interestingly, the implication that the performance of this duty is a prerequisite for the building of communism (without which the vision would not materialise) conflicts with the notion of 'inevitability'. See in this context *The Road to Communism*, *op. cit.*, pp. 566ff.

151 CPSU Programme. See also K. Ivanov, 'National-Liberation Movement, and Non-Capitalist Path of Development', *International Affairs*, 1964/9, 1965/5, 1964/12.

152 Ivanov, *op. cit.*, 64/9, p. 35.

153 F. V. Konstantinov, 'Internationalism and the World Socialist System', *International Affairs*, 68/7, p. 3.

154 Yugoslavia, Albania, and China offer special problems.

155 Sanakoyev, *op. cit.*

156 *Ibid.*, p. 62.

157 Programme of the Communist Party of the Soviet Union, 22nd Congress, 31 October 1961, p. 134 (italics original).

158 Lenin, *Collected Works*, 30/239.

159 Except as a crucial part of the 'progressive forces'.

160 See Figure 10. In substantiation of this dependence Soviet writers endlessly reiterate Lenin's words: 'Economic interests and the economic position of the classes which rule our state lie at the root of both our home and foreign politics.' Lenin, *Collected Works*, 27/365, Moscow, 1965; and 'it is fundamentally wrong, non-Marxist and unscientific, to single out foreign policy from policy in general, let alone counterpose foreign policy to home policy'. Lenin, *Collected Works*, 23/43.

161 V. Kubálková, and A. A. Cruickshank, 'A Double Omission', *British Journal of International Studies*, vol. 3, no. 3, 1977, pp. 296ff.

162 F. V. Konstantinov (ed.), *Sociologicheskie problemy mezhdunarodnykh otnoshenii* (Sociological Problems of International Relations), Moscow, Izdatelstvo 'Nauka', 1970; cf. also D. Yermolenko, 'Sociology and International Relations', *International Affairs*, 1967/1, p. 14.

163 1 Among capitalist states 2 among socialist states 3 among countries of the Third World 4 between capitalist and socialist states 5 between the countries of the Third World and socialist states 6 between the countries of the Third World and capitalist states 7 between capitalist states and 'progressive forces' both in the Third World and within the capitalist states 8 between socialist states and 'progressive forces' in the capitalist states and in the Third World 9 among the 'progressive forces' themselves.

164 An example of such reordering is the People's Republic of China which once enjoyed the privilege of participation in that category of relations based on the principle of *socialist internationalism* and which since then has been downgraded to participation only in those characterised by *peaceful coexistence*.

165 For one of the clearest formulations of this leninist distinction see J. V. Stalin, *Foundations of Leninism*, New York, 1924.

166 The distinction is put succinctly in J. V. Stalin, *Foundations of Leninism*, International Publishers, 1939, p. 94:

Tactics are determination of the line of conduct of the proletariat in the comparatively short period of the flow and ebb of the movement, of the rise and decline of the revolution, the fight to carry out this line by means of replacing old forms of struggle and organisation by new ones, old slogans by new ones, by combining these forms, etc. While the object of strategy is to win the war against tsarism, let us say, or against the bourgeoisie, to carry the struggle against tsarism or against the bourgeoisie to its end, tactics concern themselves with less important objects, for they aim not at winning the war as a whole, but at winning a particular engagement, or a particular battle, at carrying through successfully a particular campaign or a particular action corresponding to the concrete circumstance in the given period of rise or decline of the revolution. Tactics are a part of strategy, subordinate to it and serving it.

167 We have noted above that the difference between the peaceful co-existence of the contemporary period and that of the stalinist era is in its changeover from being a mere tactic of the world revolution to become an actual strategy.

168 *Soviet World Outlook*, vol. 1, no. 1, 15 January 1976, pp. 2–3.

169 Proletarian internationalism describes also the type of relations in which the socialist 'sheep' are mutually involved as well as relations towards the capitalist 'goats'.

170 V. V. Zagladin (ed.), *The World Communist Movement: Outline of Strategy and Tactics*, Moscow, Progress Publishers, 1973, pp. 441–2.

171 Konstantinov, 'Internationalism and the World Socialist System', *op. cit.*, pp. 3ff.

172 See pp. 211, 215.

173 V. Trukhanovsky, 'Proletarian Internationalism and Peaceful Co-existence', *International Affairs*, 1968/11, p. 59.

174 V. Granov and O. Nakropin, 'Soviet Foreign Policy: Its Class Nature and Humanism', *International Affairs*, 1965/11, pp. 7–13.

175 S. Sanakoyev, 'Proletarian Internationalism: Theory and Practice', *International Affairs*, 1969/4, pp. 9–10.

176 Brezhnev, *Pravda*, 27 July 1973.

177 A. Kunina, 'The Ideological Strategy of Imperialism at the Present Stage', *International Affairs*, 1974/1, p. 85.

178 S. Morkovnikov, 'Soviet Foreign Policy: A Factor for Peace and Progress', *International Affairs*, 1974/11, p. 101.

179 See above, p. 203.

180 Lenin, *Collected Works, op. cit.*, 5/384.

181 Non-interference in internal affairs, equality, and self-determination of nations, strict respect for the independence, sovereignty and territorial integrity, the settlement of outstanding and disputed problems through negotiation and the renunciation of the threat or use of force; A. Stepanov, 'The Role of Public Forces in International Relations', *International Affairs*, 1974/12, pp. 37ff. Some such accounts also include co-operation of states in accordance with the UN Charter, and honest fulfilment of international obligations; cf. G. Zhukov, 'Peaceful Coexistence

in Contemporary International Relations', *International Affairs*, 1973/4, p. 11. More importantly it denotes a system of mutually advantageous economic, trade, scientific, technical and cultural ties; V. Medzhinsky, 'The Moscow Meeting on the Problem of Peaceful Coexistence', *International Affairs*, 1969/10, p. 45.

182 *Soviet World Outlook*, *op. cit.*
183 *Ibid.*
184 See above, p. 204.
185 Responded to by the capitalist policy of *anti-communism*, see p. 195.
186 Cf. SALT talks, Nuclear Test Ban Agreement.
187 *Soviet World Outlook*, *op. cit.*, p. 2.
188 *Ibid.*
189 Granov, *op. cit.*, p. 79.
190 *Ibid.*, p. 82.
191 V. Tsapanov, 'Proletarian Internationalism: The Basis of Relations Among the Fraternal Parties and Countries', *International Affairs*, 1972/9, p. 19.
192 *Ibid.*
193 P. Fedoseyev, 'Marxism and Internationalism', *International Affairs*, 1969/3, pp. 3–4.
194 States whose stage of (socialist) development at the time of their becoming members was so low that their inclusion on the basis of proletarian internationalism would be impossible if only proletarian states were allowed.
195 See p. 227.
196 B. Miroshchenko, 'Socialist Internationalism and Soviet Foreign Policy', *International Affairs*, 1966/3, p. 7.
197 Cf. S. Sanakoyev, 'Foreign Policy of Socialism: Unity of Theory and Practice', *International Affairs*, 1973/5, p. 75.
198 Quoted from R. H. MacNeal (ed.), *International Relations Amongst Communists*, Englewood Cliffs, N.J., Prentice-Hall, 1967, pp. 99–100.
199 Josef Mrázek, 'A Code of Socialist International Law', *Nová Mysl*, no. 2, February 1976, translated in RAD Background Report/63, 15 March 1976, p. 9.
200 *Ibid.*
201 See also *Documents Adopted by the International Conference of Communist and Workers' Parties*, Moscow, Novosti Press Agency Publishing House, 1969.
202 Konstantinov, *op. cit.*, p. 3.
203 See V. Kubálková and A. A. Cruickshank, 'The Soviet Concept of Peaceful Coexistence: Some Theoretical and Semantic Problems', *Australian Journal of Politics and History*, vol. XXIV, no. 2, August 1978, pp. 184–99.
204 Brezhnev's speech to the 25th CPSU Congress, *Pravda*, 25 February 1976, p. 2.
205 A. Nadezhdin, 'Peking Against the Socialist Community', *New Times*, no. 33, 1971, reprinted in *A Destructive Policy*, Moscow, Novosti Press Agency Publishing House, 1972, p. 320.

206 'Pseudo-Revolutionaries Unmasked', *Pravda* editorial, 18 May 1970, reprinted in *A Destructive Policy, op. cit.*, p. 33.

207 See references to the 'harm done to the interests of the revolutionary forces . . . operating in the ranks of these forces' (Nadezhdin, p. 330) or to Chinese 'sapping the unity of socialist community and weakening the world revolutionary movement' (Yu. Vladimirov, 'Concerning the Economic Relations Between the Soviet Union and China (1950–1966)', *Voprosy Istorii*, no. 6, 1969, reprinted in *A Destructive Policy, op. cit.*, p. 319). The same conclusion can be derived from articles urging the PRC to 'normalise [!] its relationship with the USA on the basis of peaceful coexistence of states of different socio-economic systems' (*Rudé Právo*, quoted in I. Alexandrov, 'Regarding Peking-Washington Contacts', *Pravda*, 25 July 1971, in *A Destructive Policy, op. cit.*, p. 235).

208 The population ratio as published in 1974 is as follows (territorial figures in brackets): the capitalist system 19.4 per cent (26.8); the socialist system 33.8 per cent (25.9); the Third World 46.8 per cent (47.8). Clearly included in the socialist 33 per cent is the Chinese People's Republic. V. Rymalov, 'Some Aspects of the General Crisis of Capitalism', *International Affairs*, 1974/7, p. 100.

209 Cf. A. Leontyev, 'Dogmatism at the Well', *Krasnaya zvezda*, 25 August 1963: 'China today is indebted to the power of Soviet nuclear weapons for the fact that it can calmly engage in solving its internal tasks of economic and state construction. The leaders of the Chinese People's Republic ought to recognise that they can permit themselves such luxuries . . . as their gross attacks on the Soviet Union and the CPSU only because the external security of China is guarded by the might of the Soviet Union and of the whole socialist commonwealth. . . . The great Chinese people have an ancient proverb: "When you drink water, remember who dug the well." It seems the Chinese leaders, judging by their statements, assume this wisdom can be disregarded.'

210 Cf. 'Combine National and International Interests', *Izvestia*, 4 June 1964: 'Casting doubts on the efficacy of the Soviet-Chinese treaty of friendship alliance, and mutual aid, C.P.R Minister of Foreign Affairs Chen Yi alleged in December 1963 that Soviet assurances are of no value. "Such promises are easy to make", he said cynically, "but they aren't worth anything. Soviet protection is worth nothing to us". Trying to justify the C.P.R. government's flirting with reactionary regimes, Marshal Chen Yi today declares that China is a "nonaligned" country. In political language, this means in fact that Chen Yi does not consider China a part of the world socialist camp. . . . True, the Chinese leaders assert occasionally that in a "complex situation" the U.S.S.R. and the C.P.R. would line up together against imperialism. A legitimate question arises: When are the Chinese leaders to be believed?'

211 Cf. L. Brezhnev reported in *Pravda*, 25 September 1973: 'We have already declared that we are prepared at this time to develop relations with the PRC on the basis of the principles of peaceful coexistence, if it is not considered possible in Peking to seek something more in relations with a socialist state. The Soviet Union not only declares this readiness,

but also translates it into the language of specific and constructive proposals – on the renunciation of force, on the settlement of border issues, on improving relations in various fields on a mutually advantageous basis. . . . Of course words about normalizing relations on the basis of the principles of peaceful co-existence are very good, but the decisive importance belongs to concrete deeds.'

212 O. Vladimirov, and V. Ryazanov, 'Concerning the 50th Anniversary of the Communist Party of China', *Kommunist*, no. 10, 1971, in *A Destructive Policy, op. cit.*, p. 56.

213 'Pseudo-Revolutionaries Unmasked', *op. cit.*, reprinted in *A Destructive Policy, op. cit.*, pp. 33–4.

214 E. D. Modrzhinskaya and C. A. Stepanian (eds), *Budushchee chelovecheskogo obshchestva* (The Future of the Human Community), Moscow, 'Mysl', 1971, p. 382.

215 The implication of Brezhnev's remark to the effect that 'good' relations can refer only to socialist internationalist ones would appear to be that peaceful coexistence relations are 'not so good'.

216 E.g. 'The Theory and Practice of the Non-Capitalist Way of Development', *International Affairs*, 1970/11.

217 'Despite the fact that these surviving socialist elements in the economy and social structure are neutralised by the military-bureaucratic dictatorship and deformed by the anti-socialist policy, so long as the economic basis of society has not undergone qualitative, radical changes, it can serve as the basis for China's development in a positive direction.' Vladimirov and Ryazanov, *op. cit.*, p. 60.

218 Yuri Lugovskoy, *A Dangerous Neighbour*, Moscow, Novosti Press Agency Publishing House, 1976, p. 15.

219 *Ibid.*

220 The length of the sides continuing to denote the relative importance of the relationship.

221 Theoretical justification based on the dialectic is thus found for those Third World states who lean too closely towards the capitalist bloc to be placed within that bloc, with its type of international relations (peaceful coexistence) adjusted accordingly. Those others who incline towards the socialist world and whose internal structure seems at least potentially to approximate to that of socialist bloc members might receive the accolade of socialist internationalism – with 'fraternal aid' up to and including military.

222 Nadezhdin, *op. cit.*, p. 330.

223 S. Madzojewski, 'The Arrangement of Forces in the Capitalist Camp', *International Affairs*, 1973/12, p. 11.

224 The inevitable diversification of attitude to the 'progressive forces' seems indicated by such recent developments as the rejection at the French Communist Party Congress of the dictatorship of the proletariat.

225 See Kohler, *op. cit.*, p. 41; and Mose L. Harvey, Leon Gouré, and Vladimir Prokofieff, *Science and Technology as an Instrument of Soviet Policy*, University of Miami, Center for Advanced International Studies, 1972, pp. 4–5.

226 The term originated with a marxist, J. D. Bernal, author of *The Social Function of Science*, London, Routledge, 1939, and *World Without War*, London, Routledge & Kegan Paul, 1958.

227 I. Shatalov, 'The Scientific and Technological Revolution and International Relations', *International Affairs*, 1971/8, p. 30.

228 Shatalov, *op. cit*, citing Marx, *Selected Works*, Moscow, 1958, p. 359.

229 A. Stepanov 'The Role of Public Forces in International Relations', *International Affairs*, 1974/12, p. 37, citing Brezhnev's speech of 6 October 1974.

230 Which is defined as that arsenal of forces of production and relations of production that are available to a society at a particular historical moment and which may consist of elements of different socio-economic formations, otherwise removed from each other temporally or in character (feudal, capitalist or socialist nature regardless). R. Richta, *Civilizace na Rozcestí* (Civilisation at the Crossroads), Prague, Svoboda, 1969, pp. 70ff.

231 D. Yermolenko, 'Scientific and Technological Revolution and Problems of Forecasting', *International Affairs*, 1970/10.

232 *Ibid*.

233 To complete the cycle: from the second (executive) stage the energies of men were replaced by the machines of the Industrial Revolution and it is in the work output associated with this stage that the automated technology of the scientific revolution will give an unprecedented and unimaginably powerful boost.

234 As Brezhnev observed at the last Party Congress, capitalism faced with this scientific-technological vision of the future has 'no future'.

235 Yermolenko, *op. cit*.

236 Daniel Yergin, 'Russia – No Risks and No Innovation', *Guardian*, 5 September 1976, p. 18.

237 Joseph S. Berliner, *The Innovation Decision in Soviet Industry*, MIT Press, 1976.

238 Even in a model of the world as intricately fashioned as is the Soviet model allowance must be made for numerous aberrations and exceptions. See p. 219. Figure 11 shows how, according to the Soviet model, the world would 'ideally' look.

239 N. Kapchenko, 'The Leninist Theory and Practice of Socialist Foreign Policy', *International Affairs*, 1968/9, p. 55.

240 Horizontal units being states as mere derivatives of classes.

241 Kubálková, and Cruickshank, 'A Double Omission', *op. cit*.

242 V. Gantman, 'After the Moscow Meeting of 1969', *International Affairs*, 1969/9, p. 55.

243 G. B. Zadorozhnyi, *Mirnoe Sosushchestvovanie i Mezhdunarodnoe Pravo* (Peaceful Coexistence and International Law), Moscow, Foreign Languages Publishing House, 1965, p. 461.

244 *International Law*, Moscow, Foreign Languages Publishing House, n.d., p. 98.

245 Trukhanovsky, *op. cit*.

246 G. Tunkin, 'The Principle of Non-Use of Force as a Law of International Life', *International Affairs*, 1973/4, p. 14.

247 G. I. Morozov, 'Poniatie i Klassifikatsiia Mezhdunarodnykh Organisatsii' (The Concept and Classification of International Organisations), *SGIP*, no. 6, 1966, pp. 67–76.

248 B. Mikhailov, 'Konferentsiia Iuristov Mezhdunarodnikov' (Conference of International Lawyers), *SGIP*, no. 10, 1963, pp. 147 and 149.

249 Dudinsky, 'Economic Integration – Law of Development of the Socialist Community', *International Affairs*, 1970/11, p. 3 (cf. Y. Belyayev, 'Two Types of Economic Integration', *International Affairs*, 1973/4).

250 Dudinsky, *op. cit.*, p. 3.

251 Belyayev, *op. cit.*

252 Belayeyev, *op. cit.*

253 Belayeyev, *op. cit.*

254 G. I. Tunkin, *Voprosy Teorii Mezhdunarodnovo Prava* (Problems of the Theory of International Law), Moscow, State Publishing House of Legal Literature, 1962, pp. 194–5.

255 (Authors' italics). G. I. Tunkin, 'Organizatsiia Obedinennykh Natsii, 1945–1965, Mezhdunarodopravovye Problemy' (The UN 1945–1965, International Legal Problems), *SGIP*, no. 10, 1965, pp. 58–68.

256 B. N. Ponomarev (ed.), *Politicheskii Slovar*, second ed., Moscow, State Publishing House of Political Literature, 1958, p. 211.

257 Sanakoyev, 'Proletarian Internationalism', *op. cit*, pp. 9–10.

258 'Basic national interests of individual countries can best be satisfied the more they correspond to the interests of the other socialist countries.' Bykov, 'CMEA: International Importance of its Experience', *International Affairs*, 1965/2, pp. 16ff.

259 Cf. Tunkin, *Voprosy Teorii, op. cit.*, p. 311.

260 Granov, *op. cit.*

261 Cf. V. K. Sobakin, *Kollektivnaia Bezopasnost – Garantiia Mirosnovo Sosushchestvovaniia* (Collective security – guarantee of peaceful coexistence), Moscow, Publishing House of the Institute of International Relations, 1962, p. 154: 'International relations of sovereign states constitute the basic premise of international law, and international law serves as one of the means of asserting sovereignty in international relations.'

262 The 1958 edition of the *Soviet Political Dictionary* defines states as 'the political organisation of society, the organ of dictatorship of the economically dominant class.' (Ponomarev (ed.), *Politicheskii Slovar*, second ed., *op. cit.*, p. 136.)

263 G. Bandzeladze, *Etika: opit izlozhenia systemy marksistkoi etiki* (Ethics, an Attempt to Systematise Marxist Ethics), second ed., Tbilisi, Izdatelstvo 'Sabchota Sakartvelo', 1970, p. 358.

264 *Ibid.*, p. 366.

265 *Ibid.*, p. 367.

266 *Ibid.*, p. 368.

267 Also translated into English as a 'popular state'. See George A. Brinkley,

'Khrushchev Remembered: On the History of Soviet Statehood', *Soviet Studies*, vol. 24, 1972–3, pp. 387ff., in which the author points out that the translation of the Russian '*vsenarodnoe*' or '*obshchenarodnoe*' into the English 'All People's State' or 'Whole People' misses the true meaning of the Russian term which properly translated must suggest the wholeness of the nation behind the state. Brinkley therefore proposes as an alternative translation a state of 'all of the people' denoting the state of all of the inhabitants of USSR regardless of social status, nationality, etc. It is this translation from the Russian that we prefer to use here.

268 22nd Congress of the CPSU, *Current Digest of the Soviet Press*, Ohio State University, vol. 13, no. 45, pp. 17ff.

269 1961 Programme, Moscow, pp. 91–2.

270 Socialism's first stage.

271 1961 Programme, Moscow.

272 'The 'national democratic state' was defined as 'a state that consistently defends political and economic independence and struggles against imperialism and imperialism's military blocs; opposes military bases on its territory; struggles against new forms of colonialism and penetration of imperialist capital; and rejects dictatorial and despotic methods of government; a state in which the people are assured of broad democratic freedoms', quoted from R. S. Ehlens (ed.), *Current Digest of the Soviet Press*, Ohio State University, vol. 12, no. 49, 4 January 1961. The concept of national democracy has undergone a few changes since its inception. According to more recent views such countries will be described as national or revolutionary democracies which irrespective of their class structure have a certain degree of internal democracy for progressive elements (not necessarily communists) and ties with socialist countries. No stress is being placed on the revolutionary mission of the proletariat. Cf. Y. Selezhnyova, 'Developing States and International Relations', *International Affairs*, no. 5, 1968, p. 72.

273 'When classes disappear and the dictatorship of the proletariat withers away, the Party will also wither away' (Stalin, *On The Foundations of Leninism*, in Franklin, *The Essential Stalin, op. cit.*, p. 180).

274 See W. Leonhard, *Three Faces of Marxism: The Political Concepts of Soviet Ideology, Maoism, and Humanist Marxism*, trans. by E. Osers, Holt, Rinehart & Winston, 1974, pp. 210–57.

Chapter 4   The East and Marx

1 By way of the discovery of the laws of social and historical development.

2 R. G. Wesson, *Why Marxism*, London, Temple Smith, 1976, p. 3.

3 R. T. de George, *New Marxism*, New York, Pegasus, 1968, p. 18.

4 See above, p. 3.

5 See Figure 1.

6 Of an internal nature such as the debate on permanent revolution and its virtues, socialism in one country, etc.

7 'A regime of clerks cannot help but clash over clerical issues.' Z. K.

Brzezinski, *Dilemmas of Change in Soviet Politics*, New York, Columbia
University Press, 1969, p. 15.

8 Cf. V. V. Aspaturian, *Process and Power in Soviet Foreign Policy*,
Boston, Little, Brown, 1971, p. 27.

9 Wesson, *op. cit.*, p. 100.

10 See Figure 7.

11 The theory of socialism in one country.

12 D. Kohler, *Soviet Strategy for the Seventies; from Cold War to Peaceful
Coexistence*, University of Miami, Center for Advanced International
Studies, 1973, p. 15.

13 The Soviet Union had moved from encirclement to become the leader of
an entire group of states and, conceptually, to the notion of the capitalist
bloc itself becoming encircled.

14 See Figure 12.

15 Compare the Soviets' own periodisation of the general crisis of capitalism
– itself paralleling, one might say, the gradual spread of world
revolution. With the periods as follows: 1917–45; 1945–60; 1960
onwards it will be observed that they do not admit of any initial
theoretical hesitation on the part of Lenin and Stalin.

16 I. Mészáros, *Marx's Theory of Alienation*, London, Merlin Press, 1970,
p. 21; and above, p. 61.

17 *Ibid.*

18 See above, p. 62.

19 J. H. Kautsky, *Communism and the Politics of Development*, New York,
John Wiley, 1968, p. 21.

20 V. M. Lesnoj, 'K otázce vzájemného vztahu státu a národa' (a
Russian article on the question of the relationship between state and
nation), *Právnik*, 8, 1972.

21 That is, the type of relations whose only hope of permanent or stable
solution lies through communist revolution.

22 P. A. Reynolds, *An Introduction to International Relations*, London,
Longman, 1971, p. 184.

23 *Ibid.*, p. 193.

24 One such reservation being that, in this approach as elsewhere, one might
argue that this is simply another way of looking at the same bats, and
arguing that some of them are birds and the others mice.

25 Cf. 'How can I accept a doctrine [Russian communist] which sets up as its
bible above and beyond criticism, an obsolete economic textbook [Marx's
Capital] which I know to be not only erroneous but without interest or
application for the modern world?' J. M. Keynes, *Laissez Faire and
Communism*, New York, 1926, p. 99.

26 Where (it is to be stressed) capital is a relation, not a static entity nor, for
that matter, anything of a material nature!

27 See above, p. 56 (Engels, *Selected Works*, p. 364).

28 Marx, *German Ideology*, in H. P. Adams, *Karl Marx in his Earlier
Writings*, Frank Cass & Co., 1965, pp. 153ff.

29 Marx, *The Poverty of Philosophy*, Chicago, 1910, pp. 65–6.

30 Marx, *Die Klassenkämpfe in Frankreich, 1848 bis 1850*, Berlin, 1911, p. 90.

31 See pp. 84–109.
32 'Comment dépasser une conception du monde qui inclut en elle-même une théorie du dépassement? et qui se veut expressement mouvante parce que théorise du mouvement? – et qui, si elle se transforme, se transformera selon la loi interne de son devenir?' (Henri Lefebvre, *Le Marxisme*, Paris, 1965, p. 125).

Chapter 5   International relations theory in the West and in the East

1 David Singer in Norman D. Palmer (ed.), *A Design for International Relations Research: Scope, Theory, Methods and Relevance*, Philadelphia, The American Academy of Political and Social Science, 1970, p. 287.
2 A. G. Spirkin, *Učebnice Marxistické filozofie* (Marxist philosophy textbook), Prague, 1971, p. 211.
3 With the exception of such few 'practice-oriented' schools as positivist, pragmatist, and existentialist.
4 'Hence independence and sovereignty of a socialist state means above all independence from capitalism'. E. Chernyak, 'Proletarian Internationalism', *Krasnaya Zvezda*, 1 December 1968 (apropos of the Warsaw Pact invasion of Czechoslovakia).
5 In the most recent authoritative (Soviet) anti-sovietological monograph, translated into many other East European languages, I. T. Jakusevskij, *Leninizmus a 'sovietológia'*, Bratislava, Pravda, 1972, pp. 17–21, names Joseph Bochenski, Gustaf Wetter, Alfred Meyer, Zbigniev Brzezinski, M. Fainsod, Adam Ulam, Bertram Wolff, I. Fetscher, Leonard Shapiro, Richard Löwenthal as the main sovietologists, to which he adds four groups of 'pseudo-sovietologists' who also attempt to write about the East: (a) Scholars, experts in separate disciplines with no education in the 'sovietological' field (b) Marxologists who know nothing about the twentieth century in general and communism in particular (c) Ex-communists (various renegades and opportunists without scientific education) (d) Politicians, journalists, clergy, etc., who do not possess even a minimal knowledge of the groups.
6 E. H. Carr, *History of Soviet Russia*, London, Macmillan, 1950, introduction to vol. 1, p. 5.
7 I.e. epistemologically
8 Z. Masopust, 'Ke kritice současné buržoazní politické vědy v USA', *Právník*, 8, 1972, pp. 622ff. See also papers of the Symposium on 'Combating present anti-communist ideology', Prague, 1972.
9 F. M. Burlackij, *Lenin, Gosudarstvo, Politika* (Lenin, State, Politics), Moscow, Izdatelstvo 'Nauka', 1970, p. 173.
10 Masopust, *op. cit.*, pp. 629ff.
11 R. T. Golembiewski, William A. Welsh, and William J. Crotty, *A Methodological Primer for Political Scientists*, Chicago, Rand McNally, 1969, p. 319.
12 Felix Kaufman, *Methodology of the Social Science*, New York, Oxford University Press, 1944, p. vii.

13 Geoffrey K. Roberts, *A Dictionary of Political Analysis*, London, Longman, 1971, p. 125.

14 See p. 266.

15 J. N. Rosenau, V. Davis, and M. East, *The Analysis of International Politics*, New York, Free Press, 1972, p. 1.

16 For example, see M. G. Forsyth *et al.*, *The Theory of International Relations: Selected Texts from Gentili to Treitschke*, London, Allen & Unwin, 1970; W. B. Gallie, *Philosophers of Peace and War: Kant, Clausewitz, Marx, Engels and Tolstoy*, Cambridge University Press, 1978.

17 For example, K. Thompson.

18 C. McClelland in Rosenau, Davis and East, *op. cit.*, pp. 22ff.

19 See Preface.

20 The beginning of a 'fifth wave' should perhaps be recognised, a wave whose ramifications it is as yet too early to assess. Although the name 'post-behaviouralism' has been conferred upon it and has met with wide acceptance the actual content of the 'new revolution . . . under way in American political science has still to become crystalised'. (Quotation from D. Easton, 'The New Revolution in Political Science', *American Journal of Political Science*, vol. LXIII, no. 4, December 1969, pp. 1051–61.)

21 Klaus Knorr and James N. Rosenau (eds), *Contending Approaches to International Politics*, Princeton, New Jersey, 1969, p. 12.

22 *Ibid.*

23 In Palmer, *op. cit.*, pp. 87–106.

24 See Table 1 for examples.

25 Nigel Forward, *The Field of Nations*, Macmillan, 1971, p. 8.

26 J. E. Dougherty and R. L. Pfaltzgraff, *Contending Theories of International Relations*, Philadelphia, New York, Toronto, Lippincott, 1971.

27 Viktor Knapp, 'Metodologické problémy vědy o státu a právu (podrobné téze)' (Methodological Problems of the Science of State and Law), *Právník*, 1972, p. 781.

28 It should be stressed that the English version is not really an adequate translation of the German term *'Weltanschauung'*. The French *'conception du monde'*, or the Russian *'Mirovozzrenie'*, as with the term 'ideology' often used in the same sense, have not only an *a priori* pejorative flavour but are much narrower in their connotations than any of the above terms. Therefore, when reading a marxist text, the triad (philosophy – ideology – *Weltanschauung*) should be kept well in mind since it cannot be assumed that they completely overlap one another. In the present text we use the well established German term *'Weltanschauung'*.

29 Spirkin, *op. cit.*, p. 17.

30 Cf. Vernon Van Dyke, *Political Science: A Philosophical Analysis*, Stanford University Press, 1969, p. 114. 'The operations or activities that occur in acquisition and treatment of data.'

31 Knapp, *op. cit.*, p. 781.

32 See above, pp. 67ff.

33 V. P. Kazimirchuk, *Pravo i metody evo izuchenia* (Law and Methods of Teaching it), Moscow, 1956, p. 44.

34 Knapp, *op. cit.*, p. 783.
35 Or gnoseology in Soviet terminology.
36 It should be remarked that 'scientific' means a correspondence with objective reality: which in turn means that marxism alone is scientific.
37 In this connection Soviet marxism presses the propositions as stated above to some rather grotesque lengths: social existence as it was discovered by Marxism-Leninism is not only a recognition of the existence of classes, but in particular the recognition of the existence of the proletariat and its revolutionary role in history. A further derivative is the leading role of the Communist Party and in this context Knapp draws the startling conclusion that the leading role of the Communist Party is therefore one of the basic categories of Marxist-Leninist methodology *vis-à-vis* all of the social sciences (sic!), Knapp, *op. cit.*
38 Cf. Van Dyke, *op. cit.*, pp. 191–3.
39 *Ibid.*
40 Spirkin, *op. cit.*, p. 17.
41 Knapp, *op. cit.*, p. 782.
42 *Ibid.*
43 See above, p. 195.
44 Knapp, *op. cit.*, p. 785.
45 *Ibid.*
46 Y. Nedbailo, *Metodologicheskie problemy Sovietskoj nauky* (Methodological Problems of Soviet Science), Kiev, 1965, pp. 29–30.
47 In F. V. Konstantinov (ed.), *Sociologicheskie problemy mezhdunarodnykh otnoshenii*, Moscow, 'Nauka', 1970, pp. 5ff.
48 Here Modrzhinskaya (*op. cit.*) quotes Fred Warner Neill (in Russian 'Nil'), former member of the US State Department, 1967.
49 *Ibid.*
50 G. I. Tunkin, 'International Law and Ideological Struggle', *International Affairs*, 1971/11, p. 25.
51 See above, p. 274, n. 30.
52 Miloslav Král, *Věda a civilizace* (Science and Civilisation), Prague, Svoboda, 1968, p. 75. An entire chapter on 'system thinking in social science' is included.
53 Král, *op. cit.*, p. 76.
54 K. Deutsch in particular, but also include works by Ashby, Charlesworth, Etzioni, Guetzkov, March, Simon, Parsons, Osgood, North, Rapoport, Young, etc. See in this regard Václav Lamser, *Komunikace a společnost* (Communications and Society), Prague, 1969, pp. 287ff.
55 V. A. Lektorsky and V. N. Sadovsky, 'On Principles of System Research', *General Systems*, vol. V, 1960, p. 176.
56 *Ibid.*
57 F. G. Fischer (ed.), *Science and Ideology in Soviet Society*, New York, Atherton Press, 1967, p. 78 (chapter by de George).
58 See above, p. 5.
59 It will be recalled from Chapter 1 our comment that where most

definitions of theory in the international relations field go no further than
aiming at the first and second of these purposes, a few, including all of the
marxist, embrace also three and four.

60 K. N. Waltz, 'Theory of International Relations', in *International
Politics*, F. I. Greenstein and N. W. Polsby (eds), *Handbook of Political
Science*, vol. 8, New York, Addison-Wesley, 1975, p. 12.

61 See p. 307.

62 In 1969 it was reaffirmed at the Meeting of the Communist Parties that
the defence of socialism was still the internationalist duty of all
communists.

63 Heinz Timmermann, 'Eurocommunism: Moscow's Reaction and the
Implications for Eastern Europe', *World Today*, October 1977,
pp. 376–80.

64 See above, p. 229.

65 V. V. Aspaturian, *Process and Power in Soviet Foreign Policy*, p. 191. Our
pp. 290–5 draw heavily on this book

66 A. Rapoport, in *Marx and Contemporary Scientific Thought*: Papers from
the symposium organised by UNESCO with the International Council
for Philosophy and Humanistic Studies 1968, The Hague, Paris,
Mouton, 1969, p. 112.

67 Aspaturian, *op. cit.*, p. 361.

68 *Ibid.*, pp. 361–2.

Chapter 6   International relations theory in the West: Marx and Lenin

1 Martin Wight, in H. Butterfield, and R. J. M. Wight (eds), *Diplomatic
Investigations*, London, Allen & Unwin, 1966, p. 25.

2 Above, Chapter 2.

3 See Raymond Aron in M. Drachkovitch (ed.), *Marxism in the Modern
World*, Stanford University Press, 1970, p. 9.

4 In M. Curtis, *Marxism*, New York, Atherton Press, 1970, p. 11.

5 C. Wright Mills, *The Marxists*, Pelican Books, 1969, p. 25.

6 Aron, in Drachkovitch, *op. cit.*, p. 9.

7 C. G. Kernig, *Marxism, Communism and Western Society: A Comparative
Encyclopedia*, New York, Herder & Herder, 1972, vol. 4, pp. 370–8.

8 Singer in J. Rosenau (ed.), *Linkage Politics*, New York, Free Press, 1969,
p. 27.

9 In R. Golembiewski *et al.*, *A Methodological Primer for Political Scientists*,
Chicago, Rand McNally, 1969, p. 330.

10 K. Marx and F. Engels, *Selected Works in One Volume*, London,
Lawrence & Wishart, 1968, p. 488.

11 Cf. Bruce M. Russett, *Economic Theories of International Politics*,
Chicago, Markham Publishing Co., 1968.

12 C. Lévi-Strauss, *Structural Anthropology*, Peregrine Books, 1977,
p. 343.

13 Curtis, *op. cit.*, p. 97.

14 See above, pp. 38, 251.

15 See above, p. 251.
16 A. Rapoport, in *Marx and Contemporary Scientific Thought*: Papers from the symposium organised by UNESCO with the International Council for Philosophy and Humanistic Studies 1968, The Hague, Paris, Mouton, 1969, pp. 112ff.
17 See above, p. 62.
18 See above, p. 284.
19 Rosenau, *op. cit.*, pp. 22ff.
20 F. Engels, *Anti-Dühring*, London, Lawrence & Wishart, 1943, p. 51.
21 Johan Galtung, 'A Structural Theory of Aggression', *Journal of Peace Research*, 1964/2, pp. 95–119.
22 V. I. Lenin, *Collected Works*, Moscow, Foreign Languages Publishing House, 1963, 29/421.
23 Engels, *Anti-Dühring, op. cit.*, p. 156.
24 J. N. Rosenau, V. Davis, and M. East, *The Analysis of International Politics*, New York, Free Press, 1972, p. 32.
25 *Ibid.*, p. 33.
26 Singer, in Rosenau, *Linkage Politics, op. cit.*, pp. 21ff.
27 Rosenau, *ibid.*
28 W. Hanrieder, 'Compatibility and Consensus: A Proposal for the Conceptual Linkage of External and Internal Dimensions of Foreign Policy', *American Political Science Review*, 1967, p. 975.
29 Singer, in Rosenau, *Linkage Politics, op. cit.*
30 Johan Galtung, ' A Structural Theory of Imperialism', *Journal of Peace Research*, 1971/2, pp. 8–117.
31 See R. Wesson, *Why Marxism*, London, Temple Smith, 1976, p. 126.
32 K. Waltz, *Man, the State and War*, New York, Columbia University Press, 1959, p. 29.
33 Engels, *Anti-Dühring, op. cit.*, p. 15.
34 Quoted according to J. Frankel, *Contemporary International Theory and the Behaviour of States*, London, Oxford University Press, 1973 (unnumbered).
35 Quincy Wright, *The Study of International Relations*, New York, Appleton-Century-Crofts, 1955, pp. 498ff.
36 Figure 15 repeats the symbolic arrow used in Figure 1 to suggest division into three sections within the co-ordinates that were explained in the introduction. The main groups of theories, Marx, and Marxism-Leninism, are depicted within these co-ordinates with the approximation that such a graphical representation imposes.
37 Easton, in J. E. Dougherty *et al.*, *Contending Theories of International Relations*, Philadelphia, Lippincot, 1971, p. 396.
38 *Ibid.*, p. 398.
39 E. Kamenka, *Marxism and Ethics*, Macmillan, 1970, p. 1.

Conclusion

1 V. I. Lenin, *Selected Works in Three Volumes*, 2, p. 289.

2 True in particular of the philosophical and methodological links.
3 F. Kohler, *Soviet Strategy for the Seventies; from Cold War to Peaceful Coexistence*, University of Miami, Center for Advanced International Studies, 1973, p. 3.
4 See above, p. 343, n. 1. P. A. Reynolds, *An Introduction to International Relations*, Longman, 1971, p. 10.
5 Stanley Hoffmann, *World Politics*, XI/3, p. 348.

Bibliography

1 Works of Karl Marx, Friedrich Engels and Vladimir I. Lenin

Karl Marx and Friedrich Engels
Selected Works in One Volume, London, Lawrence & Wishart, 1968 (referred to in the text and in this bibliography as *Selected Works*).
Selected Works in Two Volumes, Moscow, 1962.
The Marx-Engels Reader, R. C. Tucker (ed.), New York, Norton, 1972.
Aus dem literarischen Nachlass von Karl Marx, Friedrich Engels, Franz Mehring (ed.), Stuttgart, 1902.
Correspondence 1846–1895: A Selection with Commentary and Notes, London, Martin Lawrence Ltd, 1934 (referred to as *Correspondence*).
Der Briefwechsel zwischen Friedrich Engels und Karl Marx, 1844 bis 1883, A. Bebel and B. Bernstein (eds), 4 vols, Stuttgart, 1913 (*Briefwechsel*).
German Ideology, London, Lawrence & Wishart, 1965.
Holy Family, Moscow, 1956.
Letters, in *Selected Works*, passim.
Letters to Americans 1848–1895: a Selection, New York, International Publishers, 1969.
Manifesto of the Communist Party, Moscow, Progress Publishers, 1969.
The Communist Manifesto of K. Marx and F. Engels, D. Ryazanoff (ed.), New York, Russell & Russell, 1963.
The Civil War in the U.S., London, Lawrence & Wishart (n.d.).
On Colonialism, Moscow, Foreign Languages Publishing House (n.d.).
Historische, Kritische Gesamtausgabe, Frankfurt, Marx-Engels Verlag, 1927–32.

Karl Marx
Selected Writings in Sociology and Social Philosophy, T. B. Bottomore and M. Rubel (eds), Harmondsworth, Penguin, 1969 (referred to in the text as *Selected Writings*).
A Contribution to the Critique of Political Economy, London, Lawrence & Wishart, 1971.
Capital, I, A Critique of Political Economy, F. Engels (ed.), London, Allen & Unwin (n.d.); Chicago, 1909.
Capital, II, III, A Critique of Political Economy, F. Engels (ed.), Chicago, Charles H. Kerr & Co., 1933.

Contribution to the Critique of Hegel's Philosophy of Right, London, Watts, 1963.
Critique of the Gotha Programme, in *Selected Works*, pp. 311ff.
Die Klassenkämpfe in Frankreich, 1848 bis 1850, Berlin, 1911.
Economic and Philosophic Manuscripts of 1844, London, Lawrence & Wishart, 1959.
Economy, Class and Social Revolution, Z. A. Jordan (ed.), London, Michael Joseph, 1971.
Grundrisse: Foundations of the Critique of Political Economy (rough draft), trans. with a foreword by Martin Nicolaus, Harmondsworth, Penguin, 1973.
Inaugural Address of the Working Men's International Association, in *Selected Works in Two Volumes*, vol. I, pp. 377ff.
Letters to Dr Kugelmann, New York, International Publishers, 1934.
Letters to Dr Kugelmann, in *Die Neue Zeit, II* (1901–1902), no. 1, pp. 708–10; no. 2 pp. 222–3, 477–8.
On China (1853–1860), London, Lawrence & Wishart, 1968 (articles from the *New York Daily Tribune*, introd. by Dona Torr).
On the Jewish Question, London, Watts, 1963.
Pre-Capitalist Economic Formations, E. J. Hobsbawm (ed.), London, Lawrence & Wishart, 1964.
Preface to a Contribution to the Critique of Political Economy (1859), in *Selected Works*, pp. 180ff.
Secret Diplomatic History of the 18th Century and Story of the Life of Lord Palmerston, London, Lawrence & Wishart, 1969.
The Civil War in France, in *Selected Works*, pp. 271ff.
The Eighteenth Brumaire of Louis Bonaparte, in *Selected Works*, pp. 94ff.
The Poverty of Philosophy, London, Martin Lawrence Ltd (n.d.); New York, International Publishers (n.d.), p. 127.
The Poverty of Philosophy, Chicago, 1910.
The Paris Commune, 1871, C. Hitchens (ed.), London, Sidgwick & Jackson, 1971.
Theses on Feuerbach, in *Selected Works*, pp. 28–30.
Wage Labour and Capital, in *Selected Works*, pp. 64ff.
Wages, Price and Profit, in *Selected Works*, pp. 185.

Friedrich Engels
Apropos of Working-class Political Action, in *Selected Works*, pp. 314ff.
Dialectics of Nature, New York, 1940.
Herr Eugen Dühring's Revolution in Science (Anti-Dühring), London, Lawrence & Wishart, 1943.
Introduction to K. Marx's Work. The Class Struggles in France 1848–1850, in *Selected Works*, pp. 641ff.
Karl Marx, in *Selected Works*, pp. 365ff.
Ludwig Feuerbach and the End of the Classical German Philosophy, in *Selected Works*, pp. 586ff.
On Marx's Capital, Moscow, Foreign Languages Publishing House (n.d.).
On the History of the Communist League, in *Selected Works*, pp. 431ff.
Preface to the Peasant War in Germany (1850), in *Selected Works*, pp. 235ff.

Bibliography

Principles of Communism, in *The Communist Manifesto of K. Marx and F. Engels*, D. Ryazanoff (ed.), New York, Russell & Russell, 1963, pp. 319ff.

Socialism: Utopian and Scientific, in *Selected Works*, pp. 375ff.

Socialism: Utopian and Scientific, London, Allen & Unwin, 1936.

Speech at the Graveside of K. Marx, in *Selected Works*, pp. 429ff.

The Condition of the Working Class in England in 1844, London, Lawrence & Wishart, 1950.

The Origin of the Family, Private Property and the State, in *Selected Works*, pp. 449ff.

The Part Played by Labour in the Transition from Ape to Man, in *Selected Works*, pp. 354ff.

The Peasant Question in France and Germany, in *Selected Works*, pp. 623ff.

The Role of Force in History, a Study of Bismarck's Policy of Blood and Iron, London, Lawrence & Wishart, 1968.

Selected Writings, Henderson (ed.), Harmondsworth, Penguin, 1967.

Vladimir I. Lenin

Collected Works, Moscow, Foreign Languages Publishing House, 1963, 45 vols. Also London, Lawrence & Wishart 1960—.

Selected Works in Three Volumes, Moscow, Progress Publishers, 1971.

Against Imperialist War: Articles and Speeches, Moscow, Progress Publishers, 1966.

On Proletarian Internationalism, Moscow, Progress Publishers, 1967.

On Soviet Socialist Democracy, Moscow, Progress Publishers, 1970.

On the Foreign Policy of the Soviet State, Moscow, Progress Publishers, 1970.

On the International Working-Class and Communist Movement, Moscow, Foreign Languages Publishing House (n.d.).

On the Unity of the International Communist Movement, Moscow, Progress Publishers (n.d.).

The State and Revolution: the Marxist Theory of the State and the Tasks of the Proletariat in the Revolution, Moscow, Progress Publishers, 1968.

The Three Sources and Three Component Parts of Marxism, in *Selected Works*, pp. 23–7.

Speeches at the Eighth Party Congress, Moscow, Progress Publishers, 1971.

2 Books by other authors

Acton, M. B., *What Marx Really Said*, London, Macdonald, 1967.

Adams, H. P., *Karl Marx in His Earlier Writings*, London, Frank Cass & Co., 1965.

Afanasyev, V. C., *Základy vědeckého komunizmu*, Prague, Svoboda, 1972.

Airapetian, M. E., and Deborin, G. A., *Kommunizm i vneshniaia politika*, Moscow, Gospolizdat, 1962.

Allison, G. T., *Essence of Decision: Explaining the Cuban Missile Crisis*, Boston, Little, Brown, 1971.

Almond, G. A., *The Appeals of Communism*, New Jersey, Princeton University Press, 1965.

Almond, G. A., Powell, A., Jr and Bingham G., *Comparative Politics: a Developmental Approach*, Boston, Little, Brown, 1966.

Althusser, L., *Lenin and Philosophy and Other Essays*, London, New Left Books, 1971.

—— *Pour Marx*, Paris, François Maspero, 1966.

Aron, R., *Democracy and Totalitarianism*, London, Weidenfeld & Nicolson, 1970.

Aspaturian, V. V., *Power and Process in Soviet Foreign Policy*, Boston, Little, Brown, 1971.

—— *The Union Republics in Soviet Diplomacy*, Geneva, Droz, 1960.

Avineri, S., *Karl Marx on Colonialism and Modernisation: His Despatches and Other Writings on China, India, Mexico, the Middle East and North Africa*, New York, Doubleday, 1968.

—— *The Social and Political Thought of Karl Marx*, Cambridge University Press, 1970.

Ayer, A. J., *The Problem of Knowledge*, Harmondsworth, Penguin, 1971.

Bandzeladze, G., *Etika: opit izlozhenia systemy marksistskoi etiki* (Ethics: an Attempt to Systematise Marxist ethics), second ed., Tbilisi, Izdatelstvo 'Sabchota Sakartvelo', 1970.

Barghoorn, F. C., *Politics in the USSR*, Boston, Little, Brown, 1972.

Beard, C. A., *The Idea of the National Interest*, New York, Macmillan, 1934.

Bell, D., *The End of Ideology: On the Exhaustion of Political Ideas in the Fifties*, New York, Free Press, 1962.

Berlin, I., *Karl Marx*, second ed., London, Collins, 1965.

Berliner, J. S., *The Innovation Decision in Soviet Industry*, Cambridge, Mass., The MIT Press, 1976.

Bertalanffy, L. von, *General System Theory: Foundations, Developments, Applications*, New York, George Braziller, 1968.

Bloom, S. F., *The World of Nations: a Study of the National Implications in the Work of Karl Marx*, New York, Columbia University Press, 1941.

Bober, M. M., *Karl Marx's Interpretation of History*, Cambridge, Mass., Harvard University Press, 1962.

Boguzsak, J., *et al.*, *Teorie státu a práva I*, Prague, Orbis, 1967.

Bottomore, T. B., *Elites and Society*, Harmondsworth, Penguin, 1964.

Boudin, L. B., *The Theoretical System of Karl Marx*, New York, London, Monthly Review Press, 1967.

Boulding, K., *The Image*, Ann Arbor, Michigan University Press, 1956.

Brzezinski, Z. K., *Dilemmas of Change in Soviet Politics*, New York, Columbia University Press, 1969.

—— *Ideology and Power in Soviet Politics*, New York, Praeger, 1967.

—— *Totalitarian Dictatorship and Autocracy*, New York, Praeger, 1966.

—— *Soviet Bloc: Unity and Conflict*, Cambridge, Mass., Harvard University Press, 1967.

Burlackij, F. M., *Lenin, Gosudarstvo, Politika*, Moscow, Izdatelstvo 'Nauka', 1970.

Burton, J. W., *Systems, States, Diplomacy and Rules*, Cambridge University Press, 1968.

Butterfield, H., and Wight, R. J. M. (eds), *Diplomatic Investigations*, London, Allen & Unwin, 1966.

Calvez, J.-Y., *La Pensée de Karl Marx*, Paris, Editions du Seuil, 1956.

Calvocoressi, P., *World Politics Since 1945*, Longman, 1971.

Carlston, K. S., *Law and Organisation in World Society*, Illinois University Press, 1962.

Carlton, G., *Friedrich Engels: The Shadow Prophet*, London, Pall Mall Press, 1965.

Carr, E. H., *The Bolshevik Revolution*, 3 vols, London, Macmillan, 1950–1953.

—— *History of Soviet Russia*, London, Macmillan, 1950.

—— *Karl Marx, a Study in Fanaticism*, London, Dent, 1934.

—— *Twenty Years Crisis*, London, Macmillan, 1946.

Chang, S. H. M., *The Marxian Theory of the State*, New York, Russell & Russell, 1965.

Charlesworth, J. C. (ed.), *Contemporary Political Analysis*, New York, Free Press, 1967.

Cibulka, J., *Dialektika a ontologie*, Bratislava, SLAV, 1968.

Cízek, F., *Filozofie, metodologie, veda*, Prague, Svoboda, 1969.

Claude, I. L. Jr, *Power and International Relations*, New York, Random House, 1967.

Cole, J. P., *Geography of World Affairs*, Harmondsworth, Penguin, 1972.

Coplin, W. D., *Introduction to International Politics: A Theoretical Overview*, Chicago, Markham 1971.

Cornforth, M., *Communism and Human Values*, London, Lawrence & Wishart, 1972.

Cornu, A., *La Jeunesse de K. Marx*, Paris, PUF, 1934.

—— *The Origin of Marxian Thought*, Springfield, Thomas, 1957.

Curtis, M., *Marxism*, New York, Atherton Press, 1970.

Cvekl, J., *O materialistické dialektice*, Prague 1958.

—— *Úvod do Dialektiky*, Prague, SPN, 1968.

Czechoslovak Political Science on IPSA Congress in Brussels (n.n.), 18–23 September 1967, Prague, Svoboda, 1967.

Dahl, R. A., *Modern Political Analysis*, Englewood Cliffs, N. J., Prentice-Hall, 1963.

Davies, M. R., and Lewis Vaughan, A., *Models of Political Systems*, London, Macmillan, 1971.

de George, R. T., *New Marxism*, New York, Pegasus, 1968.

—— *Patterns of Soviet Thought*, Ann Arbor, University of Michigan Press, 1970.

Degras, J. (ed.), *Calendar of Soviet Documents on Foreign Policy, 1917–1941*, London, Royal Institute of International Affairs, 1948.

—— *The Communist International 1919–1943. Documents*, London, Oxford University Press, vol. 1, 1956, vol. 2, 1960.

—— *Soviet Documents on Foreign Policy, 1917–1941*, London, Oxford University Press, vols 1–3, 1951–3.

Demichev, P. N. (ed.), *Marks i sovremennost* (Marx and the Present), Moscow, 1968.

Deutsch, K. W., *The Analysis of International Relations*, Englewood Cliffs, N. J., Prentice-Hall, 1968.
—— *The Nerves of Government*, New York, Free Press, 1966.
Deutscher, I., *Marxism in Our Time*, Berkeley, Ramparts Press, 1971.
—— *Stalin: A Political Biography*, New York, Oxford University Press, 1949.
—— *Russia, China and the West 1953–1966*, Harmondsworth, Penguin, 1970.
Djilas, M., *The New Class: an Analysis of the Communist System*, London, Unwin, 1966.
Dmitriev, B., *Pentagon i vneshniaia politika SShA*, Moscow, Izdatelstvo IMO, 1961.
Documents Adopted by the International Conference of Communist and Workers' Parties, Moscow, Novosti Press Agency Publishing House, 1969.
Dougherty, J. E., and Pfaltzgraff, R. L. Jr, *Contending Theories of International Relations*, Philadelphia, New York, Toronto, Lippincott, 1971.
Drachkovitch, M. (ed), *Marxism in the Modern World*, Stanford University Press, 1970.
Dupré L., *The Philosophical Foundations of Marxism*, New York, Harcourt, 1966.
Easton, D., *Framework of Political Analysis*, Prentice-Hall, 1965.
—— *A System Analysis of Political Life*, New York, John Wiley, 1965.
Edmonds, R., *Soviet Foreign Policy, 1962–1973: The Paradox of Super Power*, London, Oxford University Press, 1975.
Emery, F. E., *System Thinking*, Harmondsworth, Penguin, 1971.
Erickson, R. J., *International Law and the Revolutionary State*, New York, Oceana; Leiden, Sijthoff, 1972.
Farrell, J. C., and Smith, A. P., *Theory and Reality in International Relations*, New York, Columbia University Press, 1967.
Favre, Pierre et Monique, *Les Marxismes après Marx*, Paris, Presses Universitaires de France, 1970.
Feigl, H., and Brodbeck, M., *Readings in the Philosophy of Science*, New York, Appleton-Century-Crofts, 1953.
Fischer, E., *Marx in His Own Words*, London, Allen Lane the Penguin Press, 1970.
Fischer, F. G. (ed.), *Science and Ideology in Soviet Society*, New York, Atherton Press, 1967.
Fischer, L., *The Soviets in World Affairs, 1917–1929*, 2 vols, Princeton, New Jersey, Princeton University Press, 1951.
Fisher, R. (ed.), *International Conflict and Behavioral Science*, New York, 1964.
Forsyth, M. G. *et al.*, *The Theory of International Relations: Selected Works from Gentili to Treitschke*, London, Allen & Unwin, 1970.
Forward, N., *The Field of Nations*, London, Macmillan, 1971.
Fox, T. R. (ed.), *Theoretical Aspects of International Relations*, Notre Dame, Ind., University of Notre Dame Press, 1959.
Frankel, J., *Contemporary International Theory and the Behaviour of States*, London, Oxford University Press, 1973.

393

—— *International Politics: Conflict and Harmony*, London, Allen Lane the Penguin Press, 1969.

—— *International Relations*, second ed., London, Oxford University Press, 1969.

Franklin, B. (ed.), *The Essential Stalin: Major Theoretical Writings, 1905–1952*, New York, Doubleday, 1972.

—— *National Interest*, London, Macmillan, 1970.

Friedrich, C., and Brzezinski, Z., *Totalitarian Dictatorship and Autocracy*, New York, Praeger, 1966.

Fundamentals of Marxism-Leninism, Kuusinen, O. V. (ed.), Moscow, Foreign Languages Publishing House, 1963.

Gallie, W. B., *Philosophers of Peace and War: Kant, Clausewitz, Marx, Engels and Tolstoy*, Cambridge University Press, 1978.

Garaudy, R., *Marxism in the 20th Century*, London, Collins, 1970.

Germino, D., *Beyond Ideology: The Revival of Political Theory*, New York, Harper & Row, 1967.

Golembiewski, R. T., Welsh, W. A., and Crotty W. J., *A Methodological Primer for Political Scientists*, Chicago, Rand McNally, 1969.

Goodman, E. R., *The Soviet Design for a World State*, New York, Columbia University Press, 1960.

Greenstein, F. I., and Polsby, N. W. (eds), *Handbook of Political Science*, vol. 8, New York, Addison-Wesley, 1975.

Gregor, A. J., *A Survey of Marxism: Problems in Philosophy and the Theory of History*, New York, Random House, 1965.

Griffith, W. E., *The Sino-Soviet Rift*, London, Allen & Unwin, 1964.

Guetzkow, H., *et al.*, *Simulation in International Relations: Developments for Research and Teaching*, Englewood Cliffs, N.J., Prentice-Hall, 1963.

Guseinov, A. A., *Socialnaia priroda nvaustvennosti* (Social nature of morality), Moscow, Izdatelstvo Moskovskogo Univerziteta, 1974.

Harding, N., *Lenin's Political Thought*, Macmillan, 1977.

Harrison, H. V. (ed.), *The Role of Theory in International Relations*, Princeton, D. Van Nostrand, 1964.

Harvey, M. L., Gouré, L., and Prokofieff, V., *Science and Technology as an Instrument of Soviet Policy*, University of Miami, Center for Advanced International Studies, 1972.

Herz, J. M., *International Politics in the Atomic Age*, New York, Columbia University Press, 1959.

History of the CPSU: Short Course, Moscow, Foreign Languages Publishing House, 1951.

Hoffman, George W., and Neal, F. W., *Yugoslavia and the New Communism*, New York, Twentieth Century Fund, 1962.

Hoffmann, Stanley, *Contemporary Theory in International Relations*, Englewood Cliffs, N.J., Prentice-Hall, 1960.

Holsti, K. J., *International Politics: A Framework for Analysis*, Englewood Cliffs, N.J., Prentice-Hall, 1967.

Hook, S., *Towards the Understanding of Karl Marx: a Revolutionary Interpretation*, London, Victor Gollancz, 1933.

—— *Marxism: Past and Present*, London, Geoffrey Bles, 1954.

Hunt, R. N. Carew, *The Theory and Practice of Communism*, Harmondsworth, Penguin, 1971.

Hyppolite, J., *Studies on Marx and Hegel*, London, Heinemann, 1969.

Hyvärinen, R., *Monistic and Pluralistic Interpretations in the Study of International Politics*, Helsinki, Soc. Sci. Fen, 1958.

Ionescu G., *Comparative Communist Politics*, London, Macmillan, 1972.

Irish, M. D., *Political Science: Advance of the Discipline*, Prentice-Hall, 1968.

Istoriia Vneshnei Politiki SSSR, Ponomarev, Gromyko, Khvostoi (eds), 2 vols, Moscow, 1971.

Jakusevskij, I. T., *Leninizmus a 'Sovietológie'*, Bratislava, Pravda, 1972.

Johnson, C. (ed.), *Change in Communist Systems*, Stanford University Press, 1970.

Jordan, D. C., *World Politics in Our Time*, Lexington, Heath, 1970.

Kamenka, E., *Marxism and Ethics*, London, Macmillan, 1970.

Kaplan, M. A., *System and Process in International Politics*, New York, John Wiley, 1967.

—— *Macropolitics: Selected Essays on the Philosophy and Science of Politics*, Chicago, Aldine, 1969.

Kaufman, F., *Methodology of the Social Science*, New York, Oxford University Press, 1944.

Kautsky, John H., *Communism and the Politics of Development*, New York, John Wiley, 1968.

Kazimirchuk, V. P., *Pravo i metody evo izuchenia*, Moscow, 1956.

Keep, J. (ed.), *Contemporary History in the Soviet Mirror*, London, Allen & Unwin, 1964.

Kelin, V. N., *Vneshnaia politika i ideologia*, Moscow, 1969.

Kernig, C. G., *Marxism, Communism and Western Society: A Comparative Encyclopedia*, vols 1–4, New York, Herder & Herder, 1972.

Khrushchev, N. S., *Nasushchniie voprosi razvitiia mirovoi socialisticheskoi sistemi*, Moscow, Gospolizdat, 1962.

—— *O mirnom sosushchestvovanii*, Moscow, Gospolizdat, 1959.

—— *Predotvratit' voinu, otstoiat' mir*, Moscow, Gospolizdat, 1963.

—— *Report of the Central Committee of the Communist Party of the Soviet Union to the 20th Party Congress*, 14 February 1956, Moscow, Foreign Languages Publishing House, 1956.

—— *Sovremennoe mezhdunarodnoye polozhenie i vneshniaia politika sovetsko o soyuza*, Moscow, Gospolizdat, 1962.

—— *Vsheobshcheie i polnoie razoruzhenie, garantiia mira i besopasnosti*, Moscow, Gospolizdat, 1962.

—— *Za mir, sa razoruzhenie, za isvobodu narodov*, Moscow, Gospolizdat, 1960.

Klofáč, J., *Materialistické pojetí dějin*, Prague, NPL, 1962.

Klokočka, V., *Volby v pluralitních demokraciích*, Prague, Svoboda, 1968.

—— *Ústavní právo kapitalistických zemí*, Prague, SPN, 1969.

Knapp, V., *Filozofické problémy socialistického práva*, Prague, 1967.

—— *O možnosti použití kybernetických metod v právu*, Prague, ČSAV, 1963.

Knorr, K. and Rosenau J. N. (eds), *Contending Approaches to International Politics*, Princeton, New Jersey, Princeton University Press, 1969.

Knorr, K. and Verba, S., *The International System: Theoretical Essays*,

Princeton, New Jersey, Princeton University Press, 1961.

Kohler, F. D., *Soviet Strategy for the Seventies; from Cold War to Peaceful Coexistence*, University of Miami Center for Advanced International Studies, 1973.

Kolakovski, L. *et al.*, *Spory o teorii odrazu*, Bratislava, Epocha, 1969.

Kolarz, W., *The People of the Soviet Far East*, New York, Praeger, 1954.

—— *Russia and her Colonies*, Hamden, Connecticut, Anchor Books, 1967.

Kommunisticheskii Internatsional v dokumentakh, 1919–1932 (The Communist International in Documents, 1919–1932), Bela Kun (ed.), Moscow, 1933.

Kommunisticheskaia Partiia Sovetskogo Soiuza v Rezoliutsiakh i Resheniakh, 1898–1953 (The CPSU in Resolutions and Decisions), eleventh ed., Moscow, 1953.

Konstantinov, F. V. (ed.), *Historický Materializmus*, Prague, SNPL, 1955.

—— *Sociologicheskie problemy mezhdunarodnykh otnoshenii* (Sociological Problems of International Relations), Moscow, Izdatelstvo 'Nauka', 1970.

Korovin, E. A., *Mezhdunarodnoe pravo perekhodnogo vremeni* (International Law of the Transitional Period), Moscow, 1924.

—— *Osnovnye problemy sovremennykh mezhdunarodnykh otnoshenii*, Moscow, 1959.

Kosík, K., *Dialektika konkrétního*, Prague, 1963.

Kouba, K. (ed.), *Politická ekonomie socializmu*, Prague, NPL, 1964.

Kovalev, S. M., *Základy marxisticko-leninské filozofie*, Prague, Svoboda, 1972.

Král, M., *Veda a civilizace*, Prague, Svoboda, 1968.

—— *Veda a rízení spolecnosti*, Prague, Svoboda, 1967.

Krupskaya, N., *Memories of Lenin*, London, Panther Books, 1970.

Kubes, M., *Clovek, svet a filozofie*, Prague, 1966.

Kulski, W. W., *Peaceful Coexistence, an Analysis of Soviet Foreign Policy*, Chicago, Regnery, 1959.

Lamser, V., *Komunikace a spolecnost (úvod do teorie spolecenske komunikace)*, Prague, Academia, 1969.

Lancelot, A., *Les Attitudes Politiques*, Paris, Presses Universitaires de France, 1969.

Laqueur, W. Z. and Labedz, L. L. (eds), *The State of Soviet Studies*, Cambridge, Mass., MIT Press, 1965.

Lefebvre, H., *Le Marxisme*, Paris, 1965.

—— *The Sociology of Marx*, Harmondsworth, Penguin, 1972.

Legg, K. R., and Morrison, J. F., *Politics and the International System: an Introduction*, New York, Harper & Row, 1971.

Leonhard, W., *Three Faces of Marxism: The Political Concepts of Soviet Ideology, Maoism, and Humanist Marxism*, trans. by Ewald Osers, New York, Holt, Rinehart & Winston, 1974.

Lerche, C. O., and Said, A., *Concepts of International Politics*, second ed., Englewood Cliffs, N.J., Prentice-Hall, 1969.

Lévi-Strauss, C., *Structural Anthropology*, Peregrine Books, 1977.

Levy, M. J., *The Structure of Society*, Princeton, N.J., Princeton University Press, 1952.

Lichtheim, G., *Marxism: a Historical and Critical Study*, London, Routledge & Kegan Paul, 1964.

—— *The Origins of Socialism*, London, Weidenfeld & Nicolson, 1969.

Liska, G., *International Equilibrium: A Theoretical Essay on the Politics and Organisation of Security*, Harvard University Press, 1957.

Low, A. D., *Lenin on the Question of Nationality*, New York, Bookman Associates, 1958.

Lukacs, G., *Lenin: A Study on the Unity of his Thought*, Cambridge, Mass., MIT Press, 1971.

Mackenzie, W. J. M., *Politics and Social Science*, Harmondsworth, Penguin, 1967.

McLellan, D., *Karl Marx: His Life and Thought*, London, Macmillan, 1973.

MacNeal, R. H. (ed.), *International Relations among Communists*, Englewood Cliffs, N.J., Prentice-Hall, 1967.

Marcuse, H., *Soviet Marxism: a Critical Analysis*, Harmondsworth, Penguin, 1971.

Masaryk on Marx: an abridged edition of T. G. Masaryk, *The Social Question: Philosophical and Sociological Foundations of Marxism*, ed. and trans. by E. V. Kohak, Lewisburg, Bucknell University Press, 1972.

Marx and Contemporary Scientific Thought: Papers from the symposium organised by UNESCO with the International Council for Philosophy and Humanistic Studies 1968, The Hague, Paris, Mouton, 1969.

Matheson, T., *Methodology in the Study of International Relations*, New York, Macmillan, 1959.

Meehan, E. J., *The Theory and Method of Political Analysis*, New York, Dorsey Press, 1965.

Mehring, F., *Karl Marx: the Story of his Life*, London, Bodley Head, 1936.

Mészáros, I., *Marx's Theory of Alienation*, London, Merlin Press, 1970.

Meyer, A. G., *Leninism*, second printing, New York, Praeger University Series, 1963.

Mezhdurnarodnye ekonomicheskie organizatsii (n.n.), Moscow, Izdatelstvo IMO, 1960.

Mezhdunarodnye otnoshenia: bibliograficheskii sparavochnik, 1945–1960, Moscow, 1961.

Mikulsky, K., *Lenin's Teaching on the World Economy and Its Relevance to our Times*, Moscow, Progress Publishers, 1975.

Mills, Wright, C., *The Marxists*, Harmondsworth, Penguin, 1969.

Modrzhinskaya, E. D., Stepanian, C. A. (eds), *Budushchee Chelovecheskogo obshchestva* (The Future of the Human Community), Moscow, 'Mysl', 1971.

Morgenthau, H. J., *Politics among Nations*, New York, Knopf, 1960.

Nedbailo, Y., *Methodologicheskie problemy Sovietskoj nauky* (Methodological Problems of Soviet Science), Kiev, 1965.

North, R., and Holsti, O. R. *et al.*, *Content Analysis*, Evanston, Northwestern University Press, 1963.

Northedge, F. S., and Grieve, M. J., *A Hundred Years of International Relations*, London, Duckworth, 1971.

Olson, W. C., and Sondermann, F. A., *The Theory and Practice of International Relations*, Englewood Cliffs, N.J., Prentice-Hall, 1966.

Outrata, V., *Mezinárodní právo verejné*, Prague, Univerzita Karlova, 1970.

Palmer, Norman D. (ed.), *A Design for International Relations Research: Scope, Theory, Methods, and Relevance*, Philadelphia, American Academy of Political and Social Science, 1970.

Pareto, V., *Systèmes Socialistes*, Paris, 1902.

Payne, R., *Marx*, London, W. H. Allen, 1968.

Petrovic, G., *Marx in the Mid-twentieth Century: A Yugoslav Philosopher Considers Karl Marx's Writings*, New York, Doubleday, 1967.

Piaget, J., *Psychology and Epistemology: Towards a Theory of Knowledge*, Harmondsworth, Penguin, 1972.

Plamenatz, J., *German Marxism and Russian Communism*, London, Longman, 1970.

—— *Ideology*, London, Macmillan, 1970.

Platig, E. R., *International Relations Research: Problems of Evaluation and Advancement*, California, Clio Press, 1967.

Ponomarev, B. N. (ed.), *Politicheskii Slovar*, second ed., Moscow, State Publishing House of Political Literature, 1958.

Potemkin, V. P., *Istoria Diplomatii* (History of Diplomacy), 3 vols, Moscow, 1945.

Potocný, M., *Mezinárodní organizace a orgány*, 2 vols, Prague, SPN, 1966.

Prelot, M., *La Science Politique*, Paris, Presses Universitaires de France, 1969.

Programme of the CPSU, Moscow, Foreign Languages Publishing House, 1961.

Pye, L. W., and Verba, S., *Political Culture and Political Development*, Princeton, New Jersey, Princeton University Press, 1965.

Ramundo, B. A., *Peaceful Coexistence: International Law in the Building of Communism*, Baltimore, Johns Hopkins, 1967.

Rapoport, A., *Fights, Games and Debates*, Michigan University Press, 1960.

Reynolds, P. A., *An Introduction to International Relations*, London, Longman, 1971.

Richta, R., *Civilizace na Rozcestí: spolecenské a lidské souvislosti vedeckotechnické revoluce*, Prague, Svoboda, 1969.

The Road to Communism. Documents of the 22nd Congress of the CPSU, 17–31 October 1961, Moscow, Foreign Languages Publishing House, 1961.

Roberts, G. K., *A Dictionary of Political Analysis*, London, Longman, 1971.

Rosecrance, R., *International Relations: Peace or War?*, New York, McGraw-Hill, 1973.

—— *Action and Reaction in World Politics*, Boston, Little, Brown, 1963.

Rosenau, J. N. (ed.), *International Politics and Foreign Policy*, The Free Press, 1969.

Rosenau, J. N. (ed.), *Linkage Politics*, New York, The Free Press, 1969.

Rosenau, J. N., Davis, V., and East, M. (eds), *The Analysis of International Politics*, New York, The Free Press, 1972.

Rosser, R. F., *An Introduction to Soviet Foreign Policy*, Prentice-Hall, 1969.

Ruben, D.-H., *Marxism and Materialism*, Brighton, The Harvester Press, 1977.

Russett, B. M., *Economic Theories of International Politics*, Chicago, Markham, 1968.

Sanders, B. L., and Durbin, A. C., *Contemporary International Politics:*

Introductory Readings, New York, John Wiley, 1971.
Sanderson, J. B., *An Interpretation of the Political Ideas of Marx and Engels*, London, Longman, 1969.
Sartre, J.-P., *Critique de la raison dialectique*, Paris, 1960.
—— *Marxisme et existentialisme*, Paris, Librairie Plon, 1962.
Schurmann, F. H., *Ideology and Organisation in Communist China*, revised ed., Berkeley, University of California Press, 1968.
Shub, D., *Lenin*, Harmondsworth, Penguin, 1969.
Singer, J. D., *The Scientific Study of Politics: An Approach to Foreign Policy Analysis*, Morristown, General Learning Press, 1972.
Snyder, R. C., Bruck, H. W., and Sapin, B. (ed), *Foreign Policy Decision Making: An Approach to the Study of International Politics*, New York, Free Press, 1962.
Sobakin, V. K., *Kollectivnaia Bezopasnost – Garantiia Mirovnovo Sosushchestvovaniia* (Collective security – guarantee of peaceful coexistence), Moscow, Publishing House of Institute of International Relations, 1962.
Soják, V., *Mezinárodni vztahy naší doby* (International Relations of our Time), Prague, Horizont, 1976.
Spanier, J., *Games Nations Play: Analyzing International Politics*, London, Nelson, 1972.
Spirkin, A. G., *Učebnice Marxistické filozofie*, Prague, 1971.
Sprout, H., and Sprout, M., *Toward a Politics of the Planet Earth*, New York, Van Nostrand Reinhold, 1971.
Stalin, J. V., *Sochinenia* (Works), 16 vols, Moscow, 1946–51.
Starr, F. J. B., *Ideology and Culture*, New York, Harper & Row, 1973.
Storing, H. (ed.), *Essays on the Scientific Study of Politics*, New York, Holt, Rinehart & Winston, 1962.
Strong, J. W., *The Soviet Union under Brezhnev and Kosygin: The Transition Years*, New York, Van Nostrand Reinhold, 1971.
Stručný Filozofický Slovník (n.n.), Prague, Svoboda, 1966.
Sweezy, M., and Magdoff, M. (eds), *Lenin Today*, 8 Essays on the 100th Anniversary of Lenin's Birth, London, New York, Monthly Review Press, 1970.
Tadevosian, E. B., *V. I. Lenin o gosudarstvennykh formakh reshenia nacionalnovo voprosa v SSSR*, Moscow, Izdatelstvo, Moskovskogo Universiteta, 1970.
Treadgold, D. W., *Soviet and Chinese Communism: Similarities and Differences*, Seattle, University of Washington Press, 1970.
Trotsky, L., *Europe and America*, Colombo, 1951.
—— *My Life*, New York, 1931.
—— *The Permanent Revolution*, Calcutta, 1947.
—— *Piat' let Kominterna* (Five Years of the Comintern), Moscow, 1924.
—— *The Real Situation in Russia*, New York, 1928.
—— *The Revolution Betrayed*, New York, 1945.
—— *Stalin*, New York, 1941.
—— *The Third International After Lenin*, New York, 1936.
Tucker, R. C., *The Marxian Revolutionary Idea*, London, Allen & Unwin, 1970.

Tunkin, G. I. *Voprosy Teorii Mezhdunarodnovo Prava* (Problems of the Theory of International Law), Moscow, State Publishing House of Legal Literature, 1962.

XXIV Sjezd KSSS a rozvoj marxisticko-leninské teorie (n.n.), Materiály Vědecké konference Ústavu Marxismu-Leninismu Akademie Společenských věd, Vysoké školy stranické při UV KSSS a Sekce společenských věd Akademie věd SSSR, Prague, Svoboda, 1972.

Ulam, A. B., *Titoism and the Cominform*, Cambridge, Mass., 1952.

Valentinov, N., *Encounters with Lenin*, London, Oxford University Press, 1968.

Van Dyke, V., *Political Science: A Philosophical Analysis*, Stanford University Press, 1969.

Verger, V. L., *Pravo i gosudarstvo perekhodnogo vremeni* (Law and State of the Transitional Period), Moscow, 1924.

Vigor, P. H., *A Guide to Marxism and its Effects on Soviet Development*, London, Faber & Faber, 1966.

—— *The Soviet view of War, Peace and Neutrality*, London, Routledge & Kegan Paul, 1975.

Vyshinskii, A. Ia., *The Law of the Soviet State*, New York, Macmillan, 1948.

Vyshinskii, A. Ia., and Lozovskii, S. A. (eds), *Diplomatic Dictionary*, 2 vols, Moscow, 1948–50.

Walter, G., *Lénine*, Paris, René Julliard, 1950.

Waltz, K., *Man, the State and War*, New York, Columbia University Press, 1959.

Wesson, R. G., *Why Marxism*, London, Temple Smith, 1976.

Wiles, P. J., *Communist International Economics*, Oxford, Basil Blackwell, 1968.

Winch, P., *The Idea of a Social Science and its Relation to Philosophy*, London, Routledge & Kegan Paul, 1970.

Wiseman, H. V., *Politics: The Master Science*, London, Routledge & Kegan Paul, 1972.

Wolfers, A., *Discord and Collaboration*, Baltimore, Johns Hopkins Press, 1962.

—— (ed.), *Changing East-West Relations and the Unity of the West*, Papers presented to the European-American Collegium, 1964.

Wright, Q., *The Study of International Relations*, New York, Appleton-Century-Crofts, 1955.

Zadorozhnyi, G. B., *Mirnoe Sosushchestvovanie i Mezhdunarodnoe Pravo* (Peaceful Coexistence and International Law), Moscow, Foreign Languages Publishing House, 1965.

Zagladin V. V. (ed.), *The World Communist Movement: Outline of Strategy and Tactics*, Moscow, Progress Publishers, 1973.

Zagoria, D. S., *The Sino-Soviet Conflict 1956–1961*, Princeton, New Jersey, Princeton University Press, 1962.

Základy Vědeckého Komunizmu (Foundations of Scientific Communism) (n.n.), Prague, NPL, 1965.

Zimmerman, W., *Soviet Perspectives on International Relations 1956–1967*,

Princeton, New Jersey, Princeton University Press, 1969.

3 Articles

Alexandrov, G., 'O nekotorykh zadachakh obshchestvennykh nauk v sovremennykh usloviiakh', *Bolshevik*, no. 14, 1945.

Belyaev, Y., 'Two Types of Economic Integration', *International Affairs*, Moscow, 1973/4.

Berki, R. N., 'On Marxian Thought and the Problem of International Relations', *World Politics*, October 1971.

Bochenski, M., 'Philosophy Studies', *Soviet Survey*, no. 31, January–March 1960.

Brezhnev, L., 'Speech to the 25th CPSU Congress', *Pravda*, 25 February 1976, p. 2.

Brinkley, G. A., 'Khrushchev Remembered: On the History of Soviet Statehood', *Soviet Studies*, vol. 24, 1972–3.

Brzezinski, Z., 'Communist Ideology and International Affairs', *Journal of Conflict Resolution*, vol. IV, no. 3., September 1960.

Butenko, A. P., 'O razvitom sotsialisticheskom obshchestve' (On the Developed Socialist Society), *Kommunist*, no. 6, 1972.

Easton, D., 'The New Revolution in Political Science', *American Journal of Political Science*, vol. LXIII, no. 4, December 1969.

Evans, A. B. Jr, 'Developed Socialism in Soviet Ideology', *Soviet Studies*, vol. XXIX, no. 3, July 1977, pp. 409–28.

Fedoseyev, P., 'Marxism and Internationalism', *International Affairs*, 1969/3, pp. 3–4.

Filkorn, V., 'Metodologia ako exatkna veda', *Filozofia*, 6, 1971.

Furman, A. E., 'O predmete istoricheskogo materializma', *Filozofskie nauki*, 1965–6.

Galkin, A., 'Some aspects of the problem of Peace and War', *International Affairs*, no. 11, Moscow, 1960.

Galtung, J., 'A Structural Theory of Aggression', *Journal of Peace Research*, 1964/2.

—— 'A Structural Theory of Imperialism', *Journal of Peace Research*, 1971/2.

Gantman, V., 'Class Nature of Present-Day International Relations', *International Affairs*, 1969/9.

Granov, V., 'Soviet Foreign Policy and the historical objective of the working-class movement', *International Affairs*, 1966/4.

—— 'The Struggle of Ideologies and Cooperation between States', *International Affairs*, 1975/1.

Grushin, B. A., 'Sotsiologiia i Sotsiologi' (Sociology and Sociologists), *Literaturnaia Gazeta*, 25 September 1965.

Hanrieder, W. F., 'Compatibility and Consensus: A Proposal for the Conceptual Linkage of External and Internal Dimensions of Foreign Policy', *American Political Science Review*, 1967.

—— 'International and Comparative Politics', *World Politics*, vol. XX.

Bibliography

Hoffmann, S. H., 'International Relations: The Long Road to Theory', *World Politics*, vol. XI, no. 3, April 1959.

Israelyan, V., 'The Leninist Science of International Relations and Foreign Policy Reality', *International Affairs*, 1967/6.

Ivanov, K., 'The National-Liberation Movement and Non-Capitalist Path of Development', *International Affairs*, 1964/9, 1965/5, 1964/12.

Kaplan, M. A., 'The New Great Debate: Traditionalism versus Science in International Relations', *World Politics*, vol. XIX.

Kindleberger, C., Scientific International Politics', *World Politics*, vol. XI.

Knapp, V., 'Methodologické problémy vedy o státu a právu (Podrobné téze)', *Právník*, 1972.

Konstantinov, F., 'Internationalism and the World Socialist System', *International Affairs*, 1968/7.

Kubálková, V., and Cruickshank, A. A., 'A Double Omission', *British Journal of International Studies*, vol. 3, no. 3, 1977.

—— and —— 'The Soviet Concept of Peaceful Coexistence: Some Theoretical and Semantic Problems', *Australian Journal of Politics and History*, August 1978.

Lektorsky, V. A., and Sadovsky, V. N., 'On Principles of System Research', trans. by A. Rapoport of 'O Printsipakh issledovania system', in *Voprosy Filozofii*, no. 8, 1960, *General Systems*, vol. V, 1960.

Lesnoj, V. M., 'K otázce vzájemného vztahu státu a národa', *Právník*, 8, 1972.

Liska, G., 'Continuity and Change in International System', *World Politics*, vol. XVI.

McClelland, C. A., 'Function of Theory in International Politics', *Journal of Conflict Resolution*, vol. IV.

Masopust, Z., 'Ke kritice soucasné burzoazní politické vedy v USA', *Právník*, CXI, no. 8, 1972.

Miroshchenko, B., 'Socialist Internationalism and Soviet Foreign Policy', *International Affairs*, 1966/3.

Modrzhinskaya, Y. D., Matous, M., *et al.*, 'Combating present anti-communist ideology' (Main papers from the symposium sponsored by the Institute of Marxism-Leninism of the Central Committee of the Communist Party and the High School of Politics of the Central Committee of the Communist Party of Czechoslovakia, Prague, 1972), *Nová Mysl*, 1972/7–8.

Mrázek, J., 'A Code of Socialist International Law', *Nová Mysl*, no. 2, February 1976.

Nicholson, M. B., and Reynolds, P. A., 'General Systems, the International System and the Eastonian Analysis', *Political Studies*, 1967.

Nikolayev, G., 'Scientific and Technological Progress and the Class Struggle', *International Affairs*, 1974/5.

Pastusiak, L., 'A Marxist Approach to the Study of International Relations', *East European Quarterly*, vol. III, no. 3.

Perry, S. E., 'Notes on the role of the Nation', *Journal of Conflict Resolution*, vol. I.

Prusák, J., 'Problémy Marx-leniniskej teorie poznania a skumania práva v právnej vede', *Právník*, no. 10, 1972.

Rapoport, A., 'Various Meanings of "Theory" ', *American Political Science Review*, 1958.

Rosenau, J. N., 'Compatibility Consensus and an Emerging Science of Adaptation', *American Political Science Review*, 1967.

Senghass, D., 'Horizonte einer Disziplin. Anmerkungen zur Theorie der Internationalen Politik', *Politische Vierteljahrsschrift*, 6, 1965.

Shatalov, I., 'The Scientific and Technological Revolution and International Relations', *International Affairs*, 1971/8.

Singer, J. D., 'Man and World Politics; The Psycho-Cultural Interface', *Journal of Social Issues*, vol. XXIV, no. 3, July 1968.

Sprout, H., and M., 'Environmental Factors in the Study of International Politics', *Journal of Conflict Resolution*, vol. I.

Tanter, R., and Ullman, R. H. (eds), 'Theory and Policy in International Relations', Supplement *World Politics*, vol. XXIV, 1972.

Tomashevsky, D., 'The USSR and the Capitalist World', *International Affairs*, 1966/3.

Tugarinov, V. P., 'O kategoriakh "obshchestvennoe bytie"; "obshchestvennoe soznanie" (concerning the categories 'social existence' and 'social consciousness'), *Voprosy filozofii*, 1958/1.

Ustinov, V. A., 'Primenenie elektronykh matematicheskikh mashin v istoricheskoi nauke', *Voprosy istorii*, no. 8, 1962.

Yermolenko, D., 'Sociology and International Relations', *International Affairs*, 1967/1.

Zhukov, G., 'Peaceful Coexistence in Contemporary International Relations', *International Affairs*, 1973/4.

Zimmerman, W., 'International Relations in the Soviet Union: The Emergence of a Discipline', *Journal of Politics*, vol. 31, 1969.

The following Soviet and East European publications have been consulted extensively:

1 *International Affairs*
2 *Journal of World Economic and International Relations*
3 *Kommunist*
4 *Kommunist Vooruzhennykh Sil*
5 *New Times*
6 *Pravda*
7 *Rudé Právo*
8 *Voprosy filozofii*
9 *Voprosy istorii*
10 *World Marxist Review*

Index

Index

Index

one country, 112, 122−6, 133, 154; in 'one zone', 158; Lenin on, 123−4; 'many roads' doctrine, 154−5, 159, 290; Marx and Engels on international, 46; metamorphosis of man under, 57−8; nationalism and, 138−9; scientific, 34, 349n.77; Stalin on, 126−7, 156; victory of, 127; *see also* building of communism; developed socialism

socialist commonwealth camp, *see* world socialist system

socialist internationalism, 202, 211−15

socialist revolution, 97, 107, 138

sociology of international relations, 241

sovereignty, *see* national sovereignty

Soviet leadership, 75, 170−8

Soviet patriotism, 228

Soviet−Yugoslav relations, *see* Titoism

sovietology, 141, 260, 356n.37

Stalin: on capitalist encirclement, 110, 116, 135, 151; on capitalist system, 143, 151; *Economic Problems of Socialism in the USSR*, 113; *Marxism and Linguistics*, 121, 355n.12; personality cult, 117, 170, 185; *Problems of Leninism*, 113; *Short Course*, 113, 115, 178; social theory, 112; socialist camp, 156; 'two camps', 133, 145, 146–7, 150, 151; *see also* dialectics; epistemology; historical materialism; party; revolution, from above; socialism in one country; state; 'withering away' of the state; world revolution

Stalinism, 121ff, 153, 158, 159

state, 242; Lenin on, 92−5, 100−2, 105, 106, 123, 128; Marx on, 39−43, 145; Soviet concept of, 223−5, 227−9; Stalin on, 116, 119−20, 128, 136−7; *see also* 'withering away'

'state of the entire people' ('state of all the people'), 228

strategy and tactics, 115, 166, 203, 210; *see also* peaceful coexistence

structural dependence, 309−14

structural functionalism, 278−9, 304

structural theory of aggression, 306−9

structural theory of imperialism, 309−13

struggle between two systems, 193

substructure, economic, 38−9, 67−9, 72, 97, 99, 112

superpowers, 167−70

superstructure, 58, 68−9, 97, 99ff, 120, 159

synthesis (dialectical), *see* dialectics

system: communism, 246; conceptualisation, 249−53; socio-economic, 192, 193, 289

system analysis, 278, 280−5, 305

Tactics, *see* strategy

theory: definition, 1, 3−9; functions, 4−8, 286; 'grand', 9; macro and micro, 269−70; natural and social science, 10−11; and practice, 31, 64, 89−90, 316, 356−7; predictability, 6; *see also* 'doctrine' and theory

thesis, dialectical, *see* dialectics

Third International, *see* Communist International (Comintern)

Third World, 163, 169, 193, 197−8, 202, 215, 244, 291; *see also* structural dependence

Titoism, 157−8

totalitarian ideology, 73−4

trade, foreign, *see* world market

traditional school, 318

transnational organisations, 223

Triangular model of the world, 132−3, 142, 154, 162−4, 200, 243, 248

Trotsky, Leon: Lenin and, 92, 106; on 'permanent revolution', 128; Stalin and, 124−5, 128; on the state, 135, 142

truth, absolute and relative, 31, 116

Tunkin, G., 271

'two-camp' theory, 133, 145, 146−7, 150, 151, 162; *see also* socialism, in one country

Union of Soviet Socialist Republics (USSR): Constitution (1936), 127; Constitution (1977), 161n.8, 226

United Nations, Soviet view of, 224

unity of theory and practice, *see* theory, and practice

utopianism in international relations, *see* idealism

values, and theories, 3, 10−11, 238

Varga, E. S., 144

vertical line of analysis, 35, 36, 57, 59−60, 90, 95, 147, 163, 168, 220−2, 240−1